CAMBRIDGE
EDUCATIONAL SERVICES

AMERICA'S PREMIERE TESTING READINESS PROGRAM

The Practice Book
Three Full-Length Practice Tests
and Eight Timed Quizzes for ACT® Test Practice

Our Mission: Progress Through Partnership
Cambridge Educational Services partners with educators who share the significant mission of educational advancement for all students. By partnering together, we can best achieve our common goals: to build skills, raise test scores, enhance curriculum, and support instruction. A leading innovator in education for twenty-six years, Cambridge is the nation's premier provider of school-based test preparation and supplemental curriculum services.

Cambridge Publishing, Inc.
www.CambridgeEd.com

TABLE OF CONTENTS

HOW TO USE THIS BOOK

USING THIS PRACTICE VOLUME

This book is designed to help you practice to take the ACT test. It will help you:

- Practice your pacing on each test section.
- Measure your mastery of tested concepts.
- Improve your confidence for test day.

To use this book effectively, you should work through the warm-up quizzes first, pacing yourself as you go. After you finish each quiz, use the answer key to check your work and review the questions you got wrong. As you review, read the explanation provided in Appendix A and also look at the category path at the beginning of the explanation to see what type of item you missed.

Once you have finished the quizzes, work through each practice test. Try to complete the tests in one sitting, following the pacing guidelines, to build your testing endurance. After you finish a test, check your answers using the answer key and read the explanations to figure out why you missed the questions you did.

CAMBRIDGE'S VICTORY PROGRAM

This book is most effectively used as part of Cambridge's *Victory* program. The categories used in the explanations and index of this volume match the categories in the *Victory* book, making it easy for you to review the concepts you miss in the quizzes and practice tests in this volume.

This book is designed to reinforce what your teacher covers in class in the *Victory* program. The program can be completed in six steps:

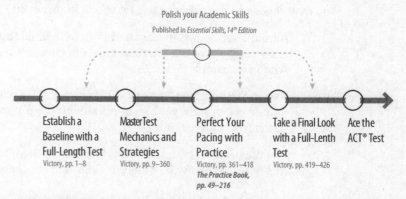

Polish your Academic Skills
Published in *Essential Skills, 14th Edition*

Establish a Baseline with a Full-Length Test	Master Test Mechanics and Strategies	Perfect Your Pacing with Practice	Take a Final Look with a Full-Lenth Test	Ace the ACT® Test
Victory, pp. 1–8	Victory, pp. 9–360	Victory, pp. 361–418 *The Practice Book, pp. 49–216*	Victory, pp. 419–426	

- **Establish a Baseline with a Full-Length Test.** You want to see your score improve, and to do that you need a baseline. The best way of determining your baseline is to take a full-length, retired ACT test under the same conditions that you'll experience on the big day. This is as close as you can get to taking the real ACT test without actually reporting to a testing center with your ID and several No. 2 pencils. Your teacher will send your answer sheet to Cambridge's Data Processing Center, and you'll receive score reports that will tell you your score and show you where you made mistakes. Then you and your teacher will develop a plan to reach your ACT goal.

- **Polish Your Academic Skills.** The ACT exam asks you to show what you know. *Essential Skills*, which is available both in print and online, serves as a refresher for the critical skills that you'll need on the ACT test. The beauty of *Essential Skills* is that the review is presented in multiple-choice format, just like the test. Plus, the skills are divided into three difficulty levels. So you will work at your present level and then move to higher levels.

- **Master Test Mechanics and Strategies.** Test Mechanics and Strategies are the "magic" of test preparation. You're going to learn how to manage the testing environment, what to do when you draw a blank, and how to answer algebra and geometry questions without using algebra or geometry. Mechanics and Strategies alone can raise your ACT score 4 or 5 points.

- **Perfect Your Pacing with Practice.** Pacing on the ACT Test is absolutely essential. You'll never get a top score unless you utilize every single second. So you're going to learn how long to spend on each item, when to skip items, when and how to guess, and how to get the most value from every minute. Of course, practice makes perfect. You have a full-length practice test in your *Victory* book and another three tests in *The Practice Book*.

- **Take a Final Look with a Full-Length Test.** After you've completed the steps above, you'll look back to see how far you have come and whether or not there is some clean-up work left to do. You will take a second full-length, retired ACT test. And again your answer sheet will be scored at our Data Processing Center, and you'll get your score and several reports to help with your self-evaluation. Self-evaluation is important because even though you may have prepared conscientiously, there may be some areas where you need to do a little more work.

- **Ace the ACT® Test.** On test day, other test-takers simply won't have the training that you've gotten. They won't have reviewed important skills, learned almost "magical" techniques for answering questions, and mastered the intricacies of the testing environment. Your training will give you an amazing advantage.

A NOTE FOR TEACHERS

You may choose to use this practice test book in three different ways:

- Administer the test in class, either in individual test sections or in an extended testing session. To make this exercise most effective, review the questions with your class when you complete the test.

- Assign the quizzes and tests as homework. This will be most effective if you collect the homework or have your students submit the progress reports available in the *Victory* Teacher Resource Center.

- Use the practice material in this book as an "item bank," using the index at the back of this book to certify the different skills and concepts that are tested.

You know your students best. Make sure to guide them as they practice to ensure that they get the most out of their preparation time.

ENGLISH
QUIZZES

This section contains two English quizzes. Complete each quiz under timed conditions. Answers are on page 218.

QUIZ I *(31 items; 20 minutes)*

> **DIRECTIONS:** In the passages below, certain parts of the sentences have been underlined and numbered. In the right-hand column, you will find different ways of writing each underlined part; the original version is indicated by the "NO CHANGE" option. For each item, select the choice that best expresses the intended idea, is most acceptable in standard written English, or is most consistent with the overall tone and style of the passage.
>
> There are also items that ask about a section of the passage or the passage as a whole. These items do not refer to an underlined portion of the passage; these items are preceded by statements that are enclosed in boxes.
>
> Read the passage through once before you begin to answer the accompanying items. Finding the answers to certain items may depend on looking at material that appears several sentences beyond the item. So, be sure that you have read far enough ahead before you select your answer choice.

Passage I

The Con Game Is No Game

Most people have a certain crime <u>that</u>
₁
<u>one believes</u> should be ranked as the worst of
₁

1. A. NO CHANGE
   B. that they believe
   C. which one believes
   D. that you believe

all crimes. For some, <u>its'</u> murder; for others,
₂
it may be selling drugs to children. I believe,

2. F. NO CHANGE
   G. they are
   H. it's
   J. its

<u>moreover,</u> that the worst of all crimes may be
₃
the confidence scheme.

3. A. NO CHANGE
   B. however
   C. further
   D. therefore

The confidence scheme may seem an <u>odd</u>
₄
choice for the worst crime since con games

4. F. NO CHANGE
G. obvious
H. irrelevant
J. apt

are usually <u>nonviolent. Although,</u> it is a crime
₅
that ranks in heartlessness. Con artists are

the most devious, the most harmful, and the

most disruptive members of society because

<u>they break</u> down <u>honesty, and trust, the</u> most
₆ ₇
important bonds of social order.

5. A. NO CHANGE
B. nonviolent, though
C. nonviolent, but
D. nonviolent, and

6. F. NO CHANGE
G. it breaks
H. of its breaking
J. of them breaking

7. A. NO CHANGE
B. honesty, and trust the
C. honesty and trust, the
D. honesty and trust the

The con games themselves are <u>simplistic</u>
₈
<u>almost infantile</u>. They work <u>on account of</u>
₈ ₉
<u>a con artist can</u> win complete confidence,
₉
talk fast enough to keep the victim slightly

8. F. NO CHANGE
G. simplistic; almost infantile
H. simplistic, almost infantile
J. simplistic, yet almost infantile

9. A. NO CHANGE
B. on account of a con artist's ability to
C. owing to a con artist's ability to
D. because a con artist can

confused, <u>and dangling</u> enough temptation
₁₀
to suppress any suspicion or skepticism. The

10. F. NO CHANGE
G. and dangles
H. and has dangled
J. and dangle

primary targets of these criminals <u>will be</u> the
₁₁

11. A. NO CHANGE
B. to be
C. are
D. is

elderly and <u>women. (And they prefer to work</u>
₁₂
<u>in large crowds.)</u>
₁₂

12. F. NO CHANGE
G. women, and the con artists prefer to work in large crowds.
H. women, preferring, of course, to work in large crowds.
J. women (who prefer to work in large crowds).

Ace the Pace

Remember that items like #13–15 that ask about the passage as a whole often require a little more time to answer than earlier items that just ask about grammar..

Items #13–15 ask about the preceding passage as a whole.

13. Which of the following is most probably the author's opinion rather than a fact?

   A. The most disruptive members of society are con artists.
   B. The majority of con games are nonviolent.
   C. The targets of con games are mostly the elderly and women.
   D. The con artists succeed when they win the complete confidence of their targets.

14. What would be the most logical continuation of the essay?

   F. A description of some confidence games
   G. An account of the elderly as crime victims in society
   H. An account of the author's experience with con artists
   J. An explanation of crowd psychology

15. What would strengthen the author's contention that con games rank first in heartlessness?

   A. Statistics to show the number of people who were taken in by the con artist
   B. A discussion of the way the police handle the problem
   C. An example that shows how the con artist breaks down honesty and trust
   D. An example to illustrate that con games are nonviolent and simple

Passage II

Elizabeth I's Intellect Ruled Supreme

Elizabeth I had a sensuous and indulgent nature that she inherited from her mother, Anne Boleyn (who was beheaded by

16
Henry VIII). Splendor and pleasure is the very

16   17
air she breathed. She loved gaiety, laughter,

16. F. NO CHANGE
G. (having been beheaded by Henry VIII)
H. beheaded by Henry VIII
J. OMIT the underlined portion.

17. A. NO CHANGE
B. is,
C. were
D. were,

and wit. Her vanity remained even, to old age.

18
The vanity of a coquette.

18

18. F. NO CHANGE
G. remains, even to old age, the
H. remains, even to old age the
J. remained, even to old age, the

The statesmen who she outwitted

19
believed, almost to the end, that Elizabeth I

was little more than a frivolous woman

who was very vain. However, the Elizabeth

20

19. A. NO CHANGE
B. that she outwitted
C. whom she outwitted
D. who she was outwitting

20. F. NO CHANGE
G. and she was also very vain
H. known for her great vanity
J. OMIT the underlined portion.

whom they saw was far from being all of

21
Elizabeth, the queen. The willfulness of her

father, Henry VIII, and the triviality of Anne

played over the surface of a nature so hard

22
like steel—a purely intellectual temperament.

22
Her vanity and caprice carried no weight

whatsoever in state affairs. The coquette of the

23

21. A. NO CHANGE
B. to be
C. having been
D. OMIT the underlined portion.

22. F. NO CHANGE
G. as hard as
H. so hard as
J. as hard like

23. A. NO CHANGE
B. no matter what
C. whatever, at all
D. whatever, despite everything

presence chamber <u>had became</u> the coolest and
                        24

hardest of politicians at the council board.

It was this part that gave her marked

<u>superiority over</u> the statesmen of her time.
     25

No <u>more nobler a group</u> of ministers ever
        26

gathered round the council board than those of

Elizabeth, but she was the instrument of none.

She listened and she weighed, but her policy,

as a whole, was her own. It was the policy of

good sense, <u>not genius, she</u> endeavored to
              27

keep her throne, to keep England out of war,

<u>and she wanted</u> to restore civil and religious
      28

order.

24. F. NO CHANGE
    G. became
    H. used to become
    J. becomes

25. A. NO CHANGE
    B. superiority in regard to
    C. superiority about
    D. superior quality to

26. F. NO CHANGE
    G. nobler a group,
    H. nobler a group
    J. more nobler of a group,

27. A. NO CHANGE
    B. not genius she
    C. not genius. She
    D. —not genius, she

28. F. NO CHANGE
    G. wanting
    H. and wanting
    J. and

Items #29–31 ask about the preceding passage as a whole.

---

29. What might logically have preceded this essay?

    A. Some biographical background on Elizabeth I
    B. A discussion of the wives of Henry VIII
    C. A discussion of the politics of Tudor England
    D. A discussion of the policies of Elizabeth's ministers

The Cambridge Edge

Were you circling key words as you read? They would probably help you answer item #30.

30. This essay is most probably taken from a:

   F. scholarly work on Renaissance England.

   G. biography of Elizabeth I.

   H. diary kept by one of Elizabeth's ministers.

   J. political science textbook.

31. Which of the following would most strengthen the essay?

   A. Knowing who the ministers were and what their policies were

   B. Examples of Elizabeth's dual nature

   C. A discussion of Henry VIII's policies

   D. A discussion of the role of the woman in Tudor England

QUIZ II BRAIN BUSTER *(20 items; 10 minutes)*

DIRECTIONS: The following sentences test correct, effective expression. Each sentence contains an underlined portion, or the entire sentence may be underlined. Following each sentence are four ways of phrasing the underlined portion. The first choice repeats the original; the other three choices are different. If you think the original is better than any of the other choices, choose "NO CHANGE," otherwise, choose one of the other choices.

In choosing answers, follow the conventions of standard written English. Make sure to consider issues of grammar, word choice, sentence construction, and punctuation. Your choice should produce the most effective sentence. It should be clear, precise, and free of ambiguity or awkwardness.

1. More than just a movie star, Audrey Hepburn was celebrated for her luminous beauty, for her acclaimed acting ability, <u>and everyone knew of her humanitarian work with organizations</u> such as UNICEF.

   A. NO CHANGE

   B. and everyone knew of her humanitarian organizations work

   C. and for her humanitarian work with organizations

   D. and her humanitarian work with organizations

2. Many geologists believe that the likelihood of a devastating earthquake of magnitude 8 or higher <u>is as great or greater in the eastern part of the United States than</u> in California.

   F. NO CHANGE

   G. may be at least as great or greater in the eastern part of the United States than

   H. is so great or greater in the eastern part of the United States than

   J. is at least as great in the eastern part of the United States as

3. The industry has seen a dramatic <u>increase in the churn of cell phone accounts caused by customer willingness to act on new promotional offers to switch</u> providers.

   A. NO CHANGE
   B. increase in the churn of cell phone accounts caused by willingness of customers to act on new promotional offers switching
   C. increasing churn of cell phone accounts caused by willingness of customers to act on new promotional offers by switching
   D. increase in the churn of cell phone accounts because of customer willingness to act on new promotional offers to switch

4. <u>The Bichon Frisé is a breed of non-sporting dog, descending from the water spaniel and originating</u> in ancient times in the Mediterranean area.

   F. NO CHANGE
   G. The Bichon Frisé, which is a breed of non-sporting dog descending from the water spaniel, originated
   H. The Bichon Frisé, a breed of non-sporting dog descended from the water spaniel, originated
   J. The Bichon Frisé, a breed of non-sporting dog, descended from the water spaniel which originated

5. Although the defense found the only lead that was likely to defeat the contract, the declarer <u>ruffed in, sloughed her losing club on dummy's ace of diamonds,</u> after drawing trumps, was able to score six spade tricks to make the grand slam.

   A. NO CHANGE
   B. ruffed in and sloughed her losing club on dummy's ace of diamonds
   C. ruffing in, sloughed her losing club on dummy's ace of diamonds
   D. ruffed in, sloughed her losing club on dummy's ace of diamonds, and

6. <u>Lincoln, discovering in young manhood the secret that the Yankee peddler has learned before him, knew</u> how to use a good story to generate good will.

   F. NO CHANGE
   G. Discovering in young manhood the secret that the Yankee peddler has learned before him, Lincoln knew
   H. Lincoln, discovering the secret that the Yankee peddler had learned in young manhood before him, knew
   J. In young manhood Lincoln discovered the secret that the Yankee peddler had learned before him:

7. The portfolio, which was apparently <u>left inadvertent on the bus, contained three completed watercolors, including several uncompleted sketches.</u>

   A. NO CHANGE
   B. left inadvertently on the bus, contained three completed watercolors, including several uncompleted sketches
   C. inadvertently left on the bus containing three completed watercolors, including several uncompleted sketches
   D. inadvertently left on the bus, contained three completed watercolors and several uncompleted sketches

8. Recent tests on a variety of herbal supplements designed to reduce cholesterol found that half did not contain the listed <u>ingredients, were so poorly manufactured that the active ingredients, when present,</u> could not be absorbed.

   F. NO CHANGE
   G. ingredients, which were so poorly manufactured that the active ingredients, when present,
   H. ingredients or were so poorly manufactured that the active ingredients, when present,
   J. ingredients were so poorly manufactured that the present active ingredients,

9. Both Samuel Beckett and Joseph Conrad were brought up speaking one language <u>and they wrote in another language when they wrote novels</u>.

   A. NO CHANGE
   B. having written novels in another language altogether
   C. but wrote their novels in another language
   D. yet when they wrote novels, they wrote them in another language

10. <u>The relationship of smoking and lung cancer have been firmly established, yet people continue to ignore warnings, jeopardizing their health and that of others.</u>

   F. NO CHANGE
   G. The relationship of smoking to lung cancer has been firmly established, yet people continue to ignore the warnings, jeopardizing their health and that of others.
   H. The relationship of smoking to lung cancer has been firmly established, yet people continually ignore the warnings that jeopardize their own health and that of others.
   J. The relationship between smoking and lung cancer has been firmly established, yet people continue to ignore warnings, jeopardizing their own health and that of others.

11. <u>Thrown onto the stage by adoring fans, the prima ballerina knelt gracefully and gathered up the bouquets of red roses.</u>

   A. NO CHANGE
   B. Throwing onto the stage by adoring fans, the prima ballerina knelt gracefully and gathered up the bouquets of red roses.
   C. Thrown onto the stage by adoring fans, the prima ballerina had knelt gracefully before gathering up the bouquets of red roses.
   D. The prima ballerina knelt gracefully and gathered up the bouquets of red roses that had been thrown onto the stage by adoring fans.

12. Although the Battle of Fort Ann is rarely mentioned in history texts, it <u>may have been the most significant engagement of the Revolutionary War because it led</u> ultimately to General Burgoyne's defeat at Saratoga.

   F. NO CHANGE
   G. could have been the most significant engagement of the Revolutionary War because it led
   H. could have been the most significant engagement of the Revolutionary War if it led
   J. might have been the most significant engagement of the Revolutionary War leading

13. The falling snow made the roadway slippery and reduced visibility to no more than a few feet, <u>and fortunately there were no</u> accidents despite the heavy volume of traffic.

   A. NO CHANGE
   B. but fortunately there were no
   C. and fortunately there were some
   D. while fortunately there were no

14. India's movie industry <u>may not be as well known as the United States, but it is much bigger because</u> film is the principal storytelling vehicle in a country where more than 40 percent of the population is illiterate and the cheapest ticket costs no more than a quarter.

   F. NO CHANGE
   G. may not be as well known as that of the United States, but it is much bigger because
   H. might not be as well known as that of the United States, but it is much bigger on account of
   J. could not be as well known as the United States, but they are much bigger because

15. <u>Although the American relay team did not qualify for the finals, the</u> anchor runner dropped the baton shortly after the hand-off.

   A. NO CHANGE
   B. When the American relay team did not qualify for the finals, the
   C. The American relay team did not qualify for the finals, and the
   D. The American relay team did not qualify for the finals because the

16. The <u>newly released worm is especially dangerous because</u> it directs infected computers to launch a distributed denial of service attack on the very web sites that offer instructions for combating the worm.

   F. NO CHANGE
   G. released new worm is especially dangerous because
   H. released new worm is dangerous especially because
   J. newly released worm is especially dangerous on account of

17. <u>To protest their being underpaid in comparison to other city agencies, a strike was called by the sanitation workers.</u>

   A. NO CHANGE
   B. To protest them being underpaid in comparison with other city agencies, the sanitation workers called a strike.
   C. To protest their being comparatively underpaid with other city agencies, a strike was called by the sanitation workers.
   D. To protest their being underpaid in comparison with workers of other city agencies, the sanitation workers called a strike.

18. Learning of the fall of Constantinople to the Turks in 1453, <u>the failure of the crusading movement became apparent to Christian Europe which had ignored earlier major defeats</u>.

   F. NO CHANGE
   G. Christian Europe realized that the crusading movement had failed, which had ignored earlier major defeats
   H. Christian Europe, which had ignored earlier major defeats, realized that the crusading movement had failed
   J. Christian Europe, ignoring earlier major defeats, realized that the crusading movement had failed

19. <u>Insofar as poultry is a good bargain and often less than a dollar a pound</u>, the per-person consumption of chicken and turkey has increased in the last ten years, while that of the more expensive meats such as beef and lamb has declined.

   A. NO CHANGE
   B. Because poultry is a good bargain and often less than a dollar a pound
   C. For the reason that poultry is a good bargain at less than a dollar a pound
   D. Because poultry is a good bargain at less than a dollar a pound

20. Because of the number of colleges and universities in and around the city, <u>the population of Boston has more percentage of students than any other</u> city in the United States of comparable size.

   F. NO CHANGE
   G. the population of Boston has more percentage of students than any
   H. Boston's population has a greater percentage of students as any other
   J. Boston has a higher percentage of students than any other

READING
QUIZZES

This section contains two Reading quizzes. Complete each quiz under timed conditions. Answers are on page 226.

QUIZ I *(18 items; 15 minutes)*

> **DIRECTIONS:** Each passage below is followed by a set of items. Read the passage and choose the best answer for each item. You may refer to the passage as often as necessary to answer the items.

Passage I

SOCIAL SCIENCE: The following passages are excerpts from two different sources that discuss particular approaches to history.

Passage A

As Carl Hempel demonstrates in his seminal essay "The Function of General Laws in History," a general law plays the same role in both history and the natural sciences.
5 According to Hempel's deductive-nomological model, proper scientific explanation—whether for history or the natural sciences—includes three sorts of statements:

(A) A set of statements about conditions
10 (that can be designated as C1, C2, and so on) that are true at a particular place and time.

(B) A set of universal hypotheses connecting events of type C with events of
15 type E.

(C) A statement asserting that E is logically deducible from the statements of A and B.

The "C" events are, of course, causes, while the "E" events are effects. Given a sufficiently
20 precise description of background conditions by Set A and an adequately articulated set of empirical laws in Set B, a conclusion such as "A popular uprising overthrew the government" can be logically deduced with as much
25 certainty as that of a syllogism.*

The notion that a historian cannot study past events in the same way that a chemist studies reactions or a physicist studies falling objects is due to a misunderstanding.
30 Historical explanations intentionally omit from Set A statements about human nature that are well-known to the sciences of psychology and sociology because they are too numerous to mention. Further, many of the general laws
35 used by historians do not seem susceptible to easy confirmation in the way that laboratory experiments are. It is difficult to find a sufficiently large number of revolutions to assess the validity of the assertion that a
40 drop of a certain magnitude in a population's standard of living will inevitably be followed by revolution.

Thus, we should more accurately speak not of scientific explanations of historical
45 events but of "sketches" of history. This terminology would call attention to the incompleteness and the imprecision in

historical explanation, while at the same time reminding us that the form of explanation is
50 the same as that of the natural sciences.

*A syllogism is a form of reasoning in which a conclusion is drawn from two statements:

> Major Premise: All ruminants are quadrupeds.
> Minor Premise: All cows are ruminants.
> Conclusion: Therefore, all cows are quadrupeds.

Passage B

The obvious distinction between history and the natural sciences is that history is concerned with human actions. The historian makes a distinction between what may
55 be called the outside and the inside of an event. The outside of the event is everything belonging to it that can be described in terms of bodies and their movements: the passage of Caesar across a river called the Rubicon on a
60 certain date or the spilling of Caesar's blood on the senate-house floor on another. The inside of the event can only be described in terms of thought: Caesar's defiance of Republican law or the clash of constitutional policy between
65 Caesar and Caesar's assassins. The historian is not investigating mere events (a mere event is one that has only an outside and no inside) but actions, and an action is the unity of the outside and inside of an event.

70 The task of the historian is thus distinguished from that of the natural scientist in two ways. On the one hand, the historian must undertake an additional investigation that is neither needed by nor available to the
75 natural scientist. The historian must inquire after the "why" of an event, that is, the thought behind it. On the other hand, the task of the historian is somewhat simpler than that of the natural scientist because once that question
80 has been answered there is no further question to be raised. There is no reason to look behind the thought associated with the event for a supervening general law.

Since the questions that the historian
85 asks are different from those posed by the natural scientist, the historian will employ a different method. The historian penetrates to the inner aspect of the event by the technique of *Verstehen*.* To be sure, the historian will
90 study whatever documents and other physical evidence are available, but these are important only insofar as they provide an access to the inside of the event.

A purely physical event can only be
95 understood as a particular occurrence governed by a universal or general law, but the inside of an event is a thought—unique, and as such, not subject to a law-like explanation. Nor is this reason for disappointment. It is not
100 the case that there are historical laws but the techniques just do not yet exist to find them. Rather, the laws just do not exist to be found. To expect to find causal explanation in history and to demand of history predictions about
105 the course of future events is an illegitimate expectation conceived and fostered by the false analogy of history to the natural sciences and the incorrect assumption that the natural sciences are the paradigm for all human
110 knowledge.

The positivist will object that this means that history is, in principle, less rigorous than natural science, but this objection ignores the point that there simply are no historical laws
115 to be discovered. In fact, because an historical event has both an inside and an outside, it is the events of natural science that are, in a sense, deficient. As R. G. Collingwood wrote so boldly in the concluding section of *The*
120 *Idea of History*, "Natural science...depends on historical thought for its existence." In history, there are no general scientific laws to be uncovered, and the search for them is the foolish pursuit of a will-o'-the-wisp that exists
125 only in the fables of positivist literature.

Verstehen is the German word for "understanding."

1. As used in line 5, the word "nomological" most nearly means:

   A. law-like.
   B. historical.
   C. accurate.
   D. logical.

2. In line 21, the phrase "adequately articulated" means:

   F. verbally presented.
   G. only preliminary.
   H. confidently denoted.
   J. sufficiently detailed.

3. In the second paragraph (lines 26–42) of Passage A, the author suggests that a series of historical events could serve the same scientific function as:

   A. eyewitness accounts.
   B. general laws.
   C. laboratory experiments.
   D. historical sketches.

4. According to the author of Passage A, it is difficult to formulate a general historical law about revolution because:

   F. revolutions, by definition, involve the overthrow of an existing government.
   G. too few revolutions are available for study to yield valid conclusions.
   H. details about a revolution are generally only known to a few key participants.
   J. historical events ordinarily involve a large number of unidentified actors.

5. The attitude of the author of Passage A toward psychology and sociology is one of:

   A. skepticism.
   B. indifference.
   C. confidence.
   D. outrage.

6. Passage A is primarily an argument AGAINST the position that:

   F. revolutions are caused by factors that can be identified.
   G. history is not a science like physics or chemistry.
   H. science is an undertaking requiring the use of logic.
   J. history is more important than the physical sciences.

7. Passage B explains that the technique of *Verstehen* is used to enable the historian to study:

   A. the outside of historical events.
   B. motives and intentions of historical actors.
   C. psychology and sociology.
   D. historical laws.

8. The author of Passage A and the author of Passage B would be most likely to agree with which of the following statements?

   F. Psychology and sociology use the same methodology as the natural sciences.
   G. Scientific historians should construct their explanations in the same way that the physicist does.
   H. The inability of historians to conduct laboratory testing shows that history is not a science.
   J. Events that have no element of thought are governed by law-like regularities.

Passage II

HUMANITIES: This passage explores the authorship of the poem commonly known as "The Night Before Christmas."

"A Visit from St. Nicholas," more commonly known as "The Night Before Christmas," is a poem first published anonymously in New York's *Troy Sentinel*
5 on December 23, 1823, and attributed to Clement Clarke Moore, a professor of Oriental and Greek Literature, in 1837. In that year, Moore claimed authorship and explained that the poem had originally been written
10 for his children and was later sent, without his knowledge, to the newspaper by a housekeeper. The poem was included in an anthology of Moore's work in 1844. It seems indisputable that the poem first appeared
15 on December 23, 1823, in the *Troy Sentinel*, that the manuscript originated in Moore's home, and that the person giving the poem to the newspaper, without Moore's knowledge, believed that it had been written by Moore.

20   In 1859, however, 26 years after the poem first appeared in print, the children of Major Henry Livingston, Jr., who was born in Poughkeepsie in 1748, claimed to have heard the poem recited by their father as early
25 as 1807—sixteen years before the poem's original publication and 37 years before Moore claimed authorship. The Livingston family also claimed to have found a copy of the poem with edits in Livingston's hand in their father's desk.
30 There is no evidence that Livingston himself ever claimed authorship of the poem. No print record has ever been found with Livingston's name attached to it. The manuscript claimed to have been found by Livingston's family was
35 allegedly destroyed in a house fire. Moore, however, personally made copies of the poem in his own hand as favors for family members and friends.

Like Moore, Livingston was an amateur
40 poet with several publishing credits to his name. Unlike Moore, who wrote only one other poem in anapestic form, the meter of "A Visit," Livingston frequently used the anapest. In fact, Livingston was apparently in the habit
45 of writing a holiday poem for his children each Christmas using anapest verse. Many of them borrowed language and form from Christopher Anstey, an English poet who died in 1805, and so resemble "A Visit." But, there
50 is also considerable evidence in the poem to support Moore's authorship: lighthearted, spontaneous-sounding mixed iambs and anapests, exclamation marks, the rare use of "all" as an adverb, syncopation, and familial
55 affection. In any case, Livingston might have been likelier to employ the anapestic style, but this does not mean that Moore never did so.

Setting aside direct testimony of authorship and the analysis of form, an
60 intriguing bit of evidence is names given in the poem, as originally published, to two of Saint Nicholas' reindeer: *Dunder* and *Blixem*. The names are Dutch for *thunder* and *lightning*. Moore did not speak Dutch; Livingston's
65 mother, however, was Dutch.

As intriguing as this point may be, it ignores the then-fashionable Knickerbocker movement which sought to find a Dutch beginning in everything associated with New
70 York. It would have been consistent with the prevailing style for the *Troy Sentinel* editor to change the German *Donder* and *Blitzen* to the Dutch equivalents. In fact, later emendations to the poem, in Moore's own hand, changed the
75 names back to the original *Donder* and *Blitzen*.

Moore's close friendship with the author Washington Irving, who was closely associated with the Knickerbocker trend, may also help to explain any other Dutch elements that are
80 found in "A Visit." But the Dutch influence proves much more. The Livingston family now claims that the poem was written by Henry Livingston around 1808. but the poem clearly reflects the later influence of Washington
85 Irving, the New York Historical Society, and the Knickerbocker Movement, which date the poem to 1822, consistent with all the other evidence that Moore penned the classic verse.

To be charitable to the Livingston
90 family, perhaps the most likely explanation for the seemingly conflicting evidence is the unreliability of human memory. Assuming that Livingston read to his children a special verse written in anapestic meter each year, it
95 would not be inconceivable that a quarter of a century later, the then-adult children would have a recollection of the meter and Christmas theme. Upon hearing "A Visit," the topical and stylistic similarities would make it easy to
100 conflate "A Visit" and the holiday poems by their father.

9. The author mentions Moore's friendship with Washington Irving in order to show that "A Visit" was probably written around:

   A. 1807
   B. 1822
   C. 1837
   D. 1859

10. The primary purpose of the passage is to:

    F. evaluate the poetic merit of "A Visit."
    G. examine the social setting of the first publication of "A Visit."
    H. assess the evidence for the authorship of "A Visit."
    J. compare the features of "A Visit" to other poems written by Livingston.

11. The fact that Moore's housekeeper submitted "A Visit" to the newspaper without Moore's knowledge helps to explain why:

    A. the poem was written in a meter seldom used by Moore.
    B. Moore did not make a claim of authorship at the time.
    C. "A Visit" has Dutch features even though Moore was not Dutch.
    D. the manuscript supposedly written by Livingston could not be found.

12. The author regards the evidence for Livingston's authorship presented in the third paragraph as:

    F. indisputable.
    G. inconclusive.
    H. irrelevant.
    J. complete.

13. It can be inferred that the author of the passage believes that Dunder and Blixem were names:

    A. used by Moore in his original manuscript.
    B. inserted by Moore into a later version.
    C. chosen by an editor at the *Troy Sentinel*.
    D. selected by Livingston, who knew Dutch.

14. The author's attitude toward the claim of the Livingston heirs to have once been in possession of a copy of "A Visit" handwritten by Livingston can best be described as:

    F. inquisitive.
    G. defensive.
    H. insightful.
    J. skeptical.

15. In context, "conflate" (line 100) means:

    A. confuse.
    B. plagiarize.
    C. approve.
    D. remember.

16. In the final paragraph, the author attempts to:

    F. reconcile the conflicting theories by proposing a third.
    G. show that Moore, rather than Livingston, wrote "A Visit."
    H. correct a longstanding misconception about "A Visit."
    J. excuse the Livingstons' claim as an honest mistake.

17. The use of the words "claimed" (line 33) and "allegedly" (line 35) to describe the loss of the Livingston manuscript suggests that the author is not:

    A. satisfied that Livingston's heir recalled the event accurately.
    B. convinced that the manuscript ever really existed.
    C. aware of any news reports to corroborate the report of the fire.
    D. likely to accept historical facts as proving a theory.

18. Which of the following is regarded by the author as the LEAST firmly established?

F. The poem was first printed in the newspaper on December 23, 1823.

G. Moore had a close friendship with the author Washington Irving.

H. The names Dunder and Blixem appear in the original version published in the newspaper.

J. A housekeeper in the Moore household was responsible for sending the poem to the newspaper.

QUIZ II BRAIN BUSTER (29 items; 30 minutes)

DIRECTIONS: Each passage below is followed by a set of items. Read the passage and choose the best answer for each item. You may refer to the passage as often as necessary to answer the items.

Passage I

SOCIAL SCIENCE: This passage discusses agricultural policy during Franklin D. Roosevelt's presidency.

President Roosevelt's administration suffered a devastating defeat when, on January 6, 1936, the Agricultural Adjustment Act of 1933 was declared unconstitutional. New Deal planners quickly pushed through Congress the Soil Conservation and Domestic Allotment Act of 1935, one purpose of which was conservation. It also aimed to control surpluses by retiring land from production. The law was intended as a stopgap measure until the administration could formulate a permanent farm program that would satisfy both the nation's farmers and the Supreme Court. Roosevelt's landslide victory over Landon in 1936 obscured the ambivalent nature of his support in the farm states. Despite extensive government propaganda, many farmers still refused to participate in the Agricultural Adjustment Administration's voluntary production control programs. The burdensome surpluses of 1933 were gone not as the result of the AAA, but as a consequence of great droughts.

In February of 1937, Secretary of Agriculture Wallace convened a meeting of farm leaders to promote the concept of the ever-normal granary. This policy would encourage farmers to store crop surpluses (rather than dump them on the market) until grain was needed in years of small harvests. The Commodity Credit Corporation would grant loans to be repaid when the grain was later sold for a reasonable profit. The conference chose the Committee of Eighteen, which drafted a bill. However, the major farm organizations were divided. Since ten of the eighteen members were also members of the American Farm Bureau Federation, the measure was quickly labeled a Farm Bureau bill, and there were protests from the small, but highly vocal, Farmer's Holiday Association. When debate on the bill began, Roosevelt himself was vague and elusive. He didn't move the proposed legislation into the "desirable" category until midsummer. In addition, there were demands that the New Deal's deficit spending be curtailed. Opponents of the bill charged that the AAA was wasteful and primarily benefited corporations and large-scale farmers.

The Soil Conservation and Domestic Allotment Act had failed to limit agricultural production as the administration had hoped. Farm prices and consumer demand were high, and many farmers, convinced that the drought had ended the need for crop controls, refused to participate in the AAA's soil conservation program. Without direct crop controls, agricultural production skyrocketed in 1937. By late summer there was panic in the farm belt that prices would again be driven down to disastrously low levels. Congressmen began to pressure Roosevelt to place a floor under farm prices by making loans through the CCC. However, Roosevelt made such loans contingent upon the willingness of Congress to support the administration's plan for a new system of crop controls. When the price of cotton began to drop, Roosevelt's adroit political maneuver finally forced congressional representatives from the South to agree to support a bill providing for crop controls and the ever-normal granary. The following year Congress passed the Agricultural Adjustment Act of 1938.

1. The primary purpose of the passage is to:

A. analyze the connection between changes in weather conditions and the movement of agricultural prices.

B. call attention to the economic hardship suffered by farmers during the 1930s.

C. pinpoint the weaknesses of the agricultural policies of Roosevelt's New Deal.

D. describe the events that led to the passage of the Agricultural Adjustment Act of 1938.

2. Which of the following is NOT a statement made by the author about the Soil Conservation and Domestic Allotment Act?

F. It was intended to be a temporary measure.

G. It aimed at reducing agricultural production.

H. It aimed at soil conservation.

J. It was drafted primarily by the Farm Bureau.

3. According to the passage, the Roosevelt administration wanted agricultural legislation with all of the following characteristics EXCEPT:

A. it would not be declared unconstitutional by the Supreme Court.

B. it would provide for direct control of agricultural production.

C. it would dismantle the Agricultural Adjustment Administration.

D. it would provide loans to help farmers store surplus grain.

4. According to the passage, all of the following were impediments to the passage of the Agricultural Adjustment Act of 1938 EXCEPT:

F. initial lack of clear Presidential support.

G. prosperity enjoyed by the nation's farmers.

H. opposition to the idea of a Farm Bureau bill.

J. doubts about the constitutionality of the bill.

5. The author implies which of the following conclusions?

A. Roosevelt's ability to gain passage of the Agricultural Adjustment Act of 1938 depended on the large harvests of 1937.

B. Secretary of Agriculture Wallace alienated members of the American Farm Bureau Federation by proposing an ever-normal granary.

C. The Agricultural Adjustment Act of 1933 was declared unconstitutional because it was written by the Farm Bureau.

D. The Commodity Credit Corporation was created to offer farmers incentives for taking land out of production.

6. It can be inferred from the passage that the Farmer's Holiday Association opposed the bill drafted by the Committee of Eighteen because:

F. the bill was not strongly supported by President Roosevelt.
G. the Farmer's Holiday Association opposed the American Farm Bureau Federation.
H. the Roosevelt administration had incurred excessive debt to finance its New Deal.
J. its membership consisted primarily of large-scale farmers.

7. It can be inferred that loans granted by the Commodity Credit Corporation would encourage farmers to store surplus grain by:

A. providing farmers a financial incentive to take arable land out of production.
B. implementing a comprehensive program of mandatory soil conservation practices.
C. conditioning financial assistance on a promise to participate in the Agricultural Adjustment Administration's program.
D. relieving farmers of the need to sell grain in order to obtain immediate cash.

8. The passage provides information that would help answer which of the following questions?

I. Who was Secretary of Agriculture during Roosevelt's second term?
II. Who was Roosevelt's major opponent in the 1936 Presidential election?
III. Who was President of the American Farm Bureau Federation in 1937?

F. I only
G. II only
H. I and II only
J. I and III only

9. Which of the following best describes the author's treatment of Roosevelt's farm policies?

A. Scholarly but appreciative
B. Objective but critical
C. Analytical but abrasive
D. Biased and condemnatory

Passage II

NATURAL SCIENCE: This passage discusses the development of medical views on alcoholism.

The present day view of alcoholism as a physical disease was not a scientific discovery; it is a medical thesis that has developed only slowly over the past 200 years and amidst
5 considerable controversy. Historically, the moral perspective of the Judeo-Christian tradition has been that excessive use of alcohol is a willful act, one that leads to intoxication and other sinful behavior; but in the early
10 nineteenth century, Benjamin Rush, a founder of American psychiatry, proposed that "The habit of drunkenness is a disease of the will." By the late nineteenth century, physicians generally viewed the habitual use of drugs
15 such as opiates, tobacco, and coffee as a generic disorder stemming from biological vulnerability, either inherited or acquired.

Prohibition represented a triumph of the older morality over a modern medical concept.
20 Where physicians who championed the disease concept of alcoholism emphasized the need for treatment, the Temperance Movement stressed that alcohol itself was the cause of drunkenness and advocated its control and
25 later its prohibition. Scientific interest in alcoholism, dampened by Prohibition, revived toward the middle of the twentieth century. This resurgence was not due to any new scientific findings but because of humanitarian
30 efforts to shift the focus from blame and punishment to treatment and concern.

The early 1960s witnessed a growing acceptance of the notion that, in certain "vulnerable" people, alcohol use leads to
35 physical addiction—a true disease. Central to this concept of alcoholism as a disease were the twin notions of substance tolerance and physical dependence. Both are physical phenomena. Substance tolerance occurs
40 when increased doses of a drug are required to produce effects previously attained at lower doses; physical dependence refers to the occurrence of withdrawal symptoms, such as seizures, following cessation of a
45 drinking bout. In 1972, the National Council on Alcoholism outlined criteria for diagnosing

alcoholism. These criteria emphasized alcohol tolerance and physical dependence. They treated alcoholism as an independent disorder,
50 not merely as part of a more general and underlying personality disorder.

In 1977, a World Health Organization report challenged this disease model by pointing out that not everyone who has
55 alcohol-related problems has true alcohol dependence. This distinction between dependence and other drug-related problems that do not involve dependence was not immediately accepted by the American
60 Psychiatric Association. The early drafts of the 1980 edition of its *Diagnostic and Statistical Manual of Mental Disorders* described a dependence syndrome for alcohol and other drugs in which tolerance and dependence
65 were important, but not essential, criteria for diagnosis. At the last moment, however, the inertia of history prevailed; tolerance and dependence were both included not as necessary to diagnose dependence but as
70 sufficient indicators in and of themselves.

It was not until 1993 that the American Psychiatric Association changed this position. In the fourth edition of the *Manual*, tolerance and withdrawal symptoms are the first two
75 of seven criteria listed for diagnosing alcohol and other drug dependence. However, the clinician is not required to find whether either is present or to what degree in order to make the diagnosis.

80 Despite the consensus among professionals, we should not forget that the moral perspective on alcoholism is still very much alive. It perhaps does not surprise us that the Reverend J.E. Todd wrote an essay
85 entitled "Drunkenness a Vice, Not a Disease" in 1882. But we should be concerned that the book *Heavy Drinking: The Myth of Alcoholism as a Disease* was published in 1988. Even as late as the mid-1970s, sociologists were
90 reporting that the term "alcoholic" was commonly used in the United States as a synonym for "drunkard," rather than as a name for someone with an illness or a disorder. Apparently, in the mind of the general public,
95 the contradictory notions of alcoholism as a disease and as a moral weakness can coexist quite comfortably.

10. The author's primary concern is to:

    F. refute the notion that drunkenness is a serious social problem.

    G. argue that alcoholism is less serious than it was 200 years ago.

    H. explain the evolution of the idea that alcoholism is a disease.

    J. give an example of the way that medical terminology changes over time.

11. According to the passage, members of the Temperance Movement:

    A. agreed with doctors that alcohol abuse was a serious problem.

    B. agreed with doctors that the solution to alcohol abuse was treatment.

    C. agreed with doctors that drunkenness should be treated as a disease.

    D. disagreed with doctors that alcoholism was a serious problem.

12. The author mentions Benjamin Rush in order to:

    F. mark the beginning of the concept of alcoholism as a disease.

    G. highlight the seriousness of habitual use of certain drugs.

    H. discredit a central tenet of the religious view of alcoholism.

    J. encourage physicians to treat alcoholism as a physical disease.

13. It can be inferred that the concepts of tolerance and dependence helped to establish the disease model of alcoholism because they:

    A. prove that alcoholism is not a manifestation of a fundamental personality disorder.

    B. are necessary but not sufficient findings to diagnose alcoholism.

    C. demonstrate that alcohol abuse is similar to abuse of opiates and other drugs.

    D. are evidence of physical addiction, which is an affliction of the body.

14. The author regards the essay "Drunkenness a Vice, Not a Disease" as:

    F. misguided and dangerous.

    G. incorrect and harmful.

    H. insightful and beneficial.

    J. outdated but harmless.

15. The author implies that all of the following are true EXCEPT:

    A. the long held view that alcoholism is a moral problem has finally been totally discredited.

    B. historically, alcoholism has been regarded as a weakness of the will rather than a disease.

    C. in modern times, the medical community has disagreed over the exact definition of alcoholism.

    D. the medical profession may make terminological distinctions that are not understood by the general population.

16. According to the fourth paragraph, the draft versions of the 1980 *Diagnostic and Statistical Manual of Mental Disorders* were similar to the final 1993 version in that they:

F. listed tolerance and dependence as both necessary and sufficient conditions for the diagnosis of alcoholism.

G. did not specify tolerance and dependence as essential elements of alcoholism.

H. suggested that alcoholism might be a generic, biological disorder.

J. argued that viewing alcoholism as a disease might actually encourage drunkenness.

17. With which of the following statements would the author most likely agree?

A. Shifting public opinion will force physicians to return to the view that alcoholism is a moral weakness.

B. A physician should not make a finding of alcoholism in a patient in the absence of either tolerance or dependence.

C. The decision to classify a problem as a disease depends in part on whether it is susceptible to medical treatment.

D. New scientific findings on the workings of tolerance and dependence warranted a shift to the disease model of alcoholism.

Passage III

HUMANITIES: This passage discusses the political thought of James Burnham.

Most thinkers have distinguished three political entities: the individual, society, and the state. It is normal to begin with the individual and then to consider society as the
5 embodiment of his nature as a social being. Thus, the individual is considered to be both logically and historically prior to society. Furthermore, society is considered both logically and historically prior to the state.
10 But in James Burnham's vision of the future state, the priority of the individual over the state is inverted. Burnham changed his mind on many points of detail between one book and the next, partly because he thought that
15 what was happening in world politics at any given moment was decisive. But his general sense of the form political power would take didn't move far from the version of it he gave in *The Managerial Revolution*. In that book he
20 predicted that the weaknesses of capitalism would eventually prove fatal. However, he thought the downfall of capitalism would not be the victory of the people followed by a Marxist paradise. Instead, capitalism
25 would be replaced by an autocracy even more extreme than that in Stalin's Russia. Under this autocracy, the instruments of production would be controlled by the state. The state, in turn, would be controlled by a ruling elite of
30 managers.

Burnham argued that managers would control the instruments of production in their own corporate favor. The economy of state ownership would provide the basis for
35 domination and exploitation by a ruling class to an extreme never before known. The masses would be curbed or constantly diverted so that they would, as we say, go along with the managerial order. Also in Burnham's future
40 state, history has come to an end. Existence has removed itself from historical process and become pure essence, its attributes those of official meaning. Perfection is defined as the state of being in complete accordance
45 with the terms prescribed for it by the state, much as a proposition in logic or a theorem in mathematics might be faultless.

In *We*, Yevgeny Zamyatin envisaged a one-world state. Burnham allowed for three states.
50 Three superstates would divide the world between them and would enter into shifting alliances with one another. In 1941, Burnham thought the three would be the United States, Europe, and Japan. The superpowers would
55 wage war over territory. Burnham said, "These wars will be directed from each base for the conquest of the other bases. But it does not seem possible for any one of these to conquer the others. Even two of them in coalition could
60 not win a lasting victory over the third."

By 1947, many of Burnham's predictions had already proved false, a result of his tendency to assume that present conditions would persist unchanged; but a more damning
65 indictment of his vision is the hypocrisy concealed behind the attack on power. Burnham was infatuated with the image of totalitarianism; he was fascinated by the power he attacked. He despised the democracy
70 he should have defended. Ultimately, Burnham voiced the secret desire of the English intelligentsia to destroy the old, egalitarian version of Socialism and usher in a new hierarchical society in which the intellectual
75 could at last get his hands on the whip.

18. The author's treatment of James Burnham's writing can best be described as:

F. analytical and condemnatory.
G. insightful and neutral.
H. speculative and jaded.
J. cynical and detached.

19. The statement that Burnham inverted the logical priority of the individual over the state means that Burnham believed that:

A. people are seen as aspects of the state and not as individuals.
B. history culminated in the existence of an all-powerful government.
C. individuals can reach perfection only as social beings.
D. the existence of individuals can be deduced from the existence of a state.

20. The author criticizes Burnham for:

    F. extrapolating from existing political and social conditions.

    G. failing to show how a totalitarian state could evolve from a democracy.

    H. thinking that democracy is a form of government superior to oligarchy.

    J. reversing the normal relationship between the individual and the state.

21. According to Burnham, in the completely autocratic state, history will have come to an end because:

    A. the state will define the social forms to which individuals must conform.

    B. the means of production will be controlled by a managerial elite.

    C. no one superpower will be able to wage war successfully against any other superpower.

    D. individuals will be diverted from a study of past events by the state.

22. The author's primary concern is to:

    F. present his own vision of the future.

    G. prove someone else's predictions were wrong.

    H. critique a political theory.

    J. criticize a literary style.

23. The passage supports which of the following conclusions about the writings of Yevgeny Zamyatin?

    I.   They are in large part derivative of the works of James Burnham.

    II.   They describe a future society in which the state is all-powerful.

    III. The descriptions they contain are based on conditions that existed at the time they were written.

    A. I only

    B. II only

    C. I and II only

    D. II and III only

Passage IV

NATURAL SCIENCE: This passage describes a meteorite that may have originated on Mars.

Meteorite ALH84001 is a member of a family of meteorites, half of which were found in Antarctica, that are believed to have originated on Mars. Oxygen isotopes,
5 as distinctive as fingerprints, link these meteorites and clearly differentiate them from any Earth rock or other kind of meteorite. Another family member, ETA79001, was discovered to contain gas trapped by the
10 impact that ejected it from Mars. Analysis of the trapped gas shows that it is identical to atmospheric gases analyzed by the spacecraft that landed on Mars in 1976.

The rock of ALH84001 was formed 4.5
15 billion years ago, but 3.6 billion years ago it was invaded by water containing mineral salts that precipitated out to form small carbonate globules with intricate chemical zoning. These carbonates are between 1 and 2 billion years
20 old. 16 million years ago, an object from space, possibly a small asteroid, impacted Mars and blasted off rocks. One of these rocks traveled in space until it was captured by the Earth's gravity and fell on Antarctica. Carbon-14
25 dating shows that this rock has been on Earth about 13,000 years.

The carbonate globules contain very small crystals of iron oxide (magnetite) and at least two kinds of iron sulfide (pyrrhotite
30 and another mineral, possibly greigite). Small crystals of these minerals are commonly formed on Earth by bacteria, although inorganic processes can also form them. In addition, manganese is concentrated in the
35 center of each carbonate globule, and most of the larger globules have rims of alternating iron-rich and magnesium-rich carbonates. The compositional variation of these carbonates is not what would be expected from high
40 temperature equilibrium crystallization; in fact, it is more similar to the variation that occurs during low temperature crystallization. Furthermore, it is consistent with formation by non-equilibrium precipitation induced by
45 microorganisms.

There are also unusually high concentrations of PAH-type hydrocarbons. These PAHs are unusually simple compared to most PAHs, including PAHs from the burning of
50 coal, oil, or gasoline or the decay of vegetation. Other meteorites contain PAHs, but the pattern and abundances are different. Of course, PAHs can be formed by strictly inorganic reactions, and abundant PAHs were produced in the
55 early solar system and are preserved on some asteroids and comets. Meteorites from these objects fall to Earth and enable us to analyze the PAHs contained within the parent bodies. While some of these are similar to the PAHs in
60 the Martian meteorite, all show some major differences. One reasonable interpretation of the PAHs is that they are decay products from bacteria.

Also present are unusual, very
65 small forms that could be the remains of microorganisms. These spherical, ovoid, and elongated objects closely resemble the morphology of known bacteria, but many of them are smaller than any known bacteria
70 on Earth. Furthermore, microfossil forms from very old Earth rocks are typically much larger than the forms that we see in the Mars meteorite. The microfossil-like forms may really be minerals and artifacts that
75 superficially resemble small bacteria. Or, perhaps lower gravity and more restricted pore space in rocks promoted the development of smaller forms of microorganisms. Or, maybe such forms exist on Earth in the fossil
80 record but have not yet been found. If the small objects are microfossils, are they from Mars or from Antarctica? So far, studies of the abundant microorganisms found in the rocks, soils, and lakes near the coast of Antarctica
85 do not show PAHs or microorganisms that closely resemble those found in the Martian meteorite.

There is considerable evidence in the Martian meteorite that must be explained by
90 other means if we are to definitely rule out evidence of past Martian life in this meteorite. So far, we have not seen a reasonable explanation by others that can explain all of the data.

24. The main purpose of the passage is to:

F. argue that the available data support the conclusion that life once existed on Mars.

G. examine various facts to determine what thesis about ALH84001 is most strongly supported.

H. answer objections to the contention that Martian meteorites contain evidence of primitive life.

J. pose challenges to scientists who hope to prove that ALH84001 proves that life exists on Mars.

25. According to the passage, what evidence most strongly establishes that meteorite ALH84001 originated on Mars?

A. Comparison of trapped gases and the Martian atmosphere

B. Presence of alternating iron and magnesium carbonates

C. Evidence of shapes that resemble known bacteria

D. Pattern of carbonate globules with unusual zoning

26. The passage mentions all of the following as tending to prove that ALH84001 may once have contained primitive life EXCEPT:

F. distinctive oxygen isotopes trapped in gases.

G. extraordinarily high concentrations of unusual PAHs.

H. presence of iron oxide and iron sulfide crystals.

J. unusual zonings of carbonate globules

27. According to the passage, the compositional variation of the carbonate deposits and the PAH–type hydrocarbons both:

A. result from chemical processes more likely to occur on Mars than on Earth.

B. might be the product of an organic reaction or the product of an inorganic process.

C. tend to occur at relatively cooler temperatures than other, similar reactions.

D. are evidence of chemical processes that occurred during the formation of the solar system.

28. The author mentions lower gravity and restricted pore space (lines 76–77) in order to explain why:

F. bacteria on Mars might be smaller than bacteria found on Earth.

G. no microfossil record of bacteria has yet been found in Antarctica.

H. the spherical, ovoid, and elongated shapes in ALH84001 cannot be bacteria.

J. restricted pore space in Martian rocks would hinder bacterial growth.

29. With which of the following conclusions about the possibility of life on Mars would the author most likely agree?

A. The available evidence strongly suggests that conditions on Mars make it impossible for life to have developed there.

B. The scientific evidence is ambiguous and supports no conclusion about the possibility of life on Mars.

C. Scientific evidence cannot, in principle, ever demonstrate that life existed on Mars.

D. Scientific data derived from ALH84001 is consistent with the proposition that life once existed on Mars.

WRITING
QUIZZES

This section contains one Writing quiz. Complete the quiz under timed conditions. Sample essay responses begin on page 235.

QUIZ *(1 Essay Prompt; 40 minutes)*

DIRECTIONS: You have 40 minutes to plan and write an essay. Read the prompt carefully and make sure you understand the instructions.

Freedom of Speech Online

Websites can offer open forums for debate and discussion, but sites can monitor users' comments and remove statements considered harmful or obscene. Some sites censor obscene language, such as racial slurs or hate speech. Others try to prevent "trolling," or the use of extreme statements for the purpose of offending readers rather than contributing to meaningful debate. If a person threatens someone online, his or her comments could have legal consequences. Limiting what is said online might restrict freedom of speech, but should site managers have the power to limit speech on their websites and/or impose legal consequences? With the rise of legal cases about freedom of speech online, it is important to examine what types of speech should be tolerated in certain online settings.

Perspective 1	Perspective 2	Perspective 3
Monitoring comments gives the website too much control over what is said. Although some issues, such as threats, should be monitored, eliminating all "offensive" speech could limit the range of viewpoints that are expressed on a website.	Allowing offensive speech could intimidate writers into silence, especially if they are covering a controversial topic. Some writers receive violent threats from people commenting on their articles. In a real-life setting, this type of speech would have legal consequences, and likewise, it should not be allowed online.	Site administrators argue that the anonymity of posting online can allow people to write offensive comments without ever facing the people they insult. If website users know that offensive speech can be censored, they will conduct themselves more civilly, as if they were talking to people face-to-face.

Essay Task

Write a unified, coherent essay in which you evaluate multiple perspectives on the impact of freedom of speech online. In your essay be sure to:

- Analyze and evaluate perspectives given
- State and develop your own perspective
- Explain the relationship between your perspective and those given

Your perspective may be in full agreement with any of the others, in partial agreement or wholly different. Whatever the case, support your ideas with logical reasoning and detailed, persuasive examples.

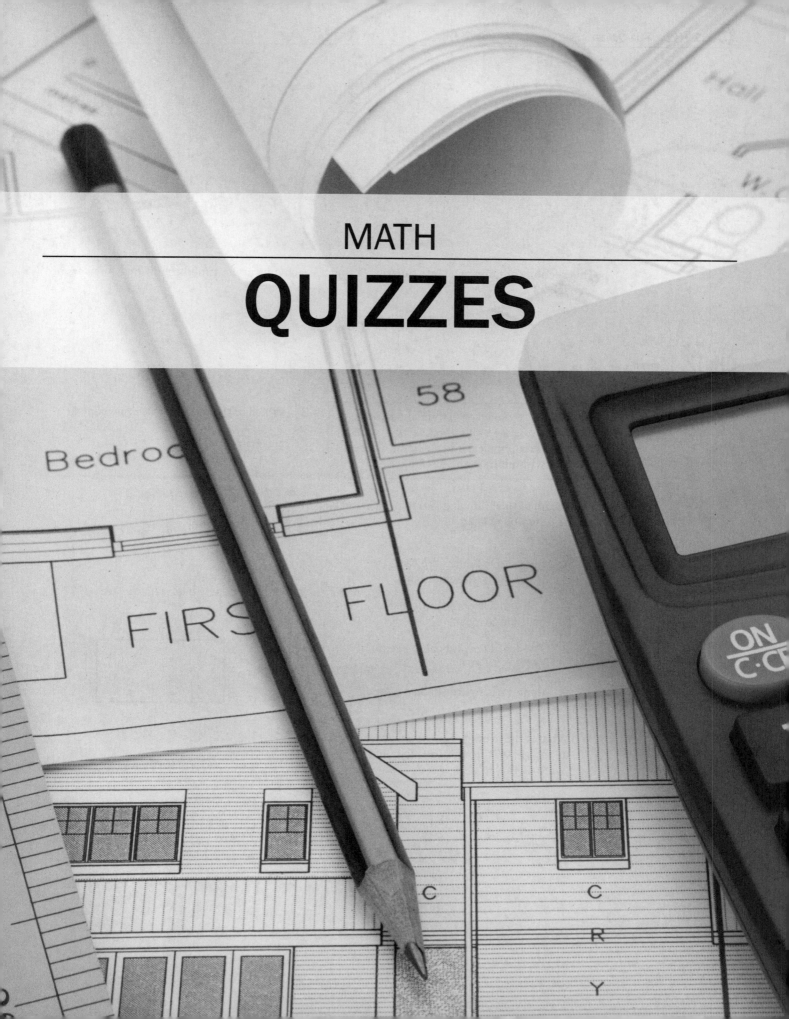

MATH
QUIZZES

This section contains two Math quizzes. Complete each quiz under timed conditions. Answers are on page 239.

QUIZ I *(20 items; 20 minutes)*

> **DIRECTIONS:** Solve each item and choose the correct answer choice. Calculator use is permitted; however, some items are best solved without the use of a calculator.

NOTES: All of the following should be assumed, unless otherwise stated.

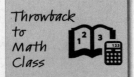

Throwback to Math Class

The area of a rectangle is equal to the length multiplied by the width: *lw*.

1. Illustrative figures are NOT necessarily drawn to scale.

2. The word *average* indicates arithmetic mean.

3. The word *line* indicates a straight line.

4. Geometric figures lie in a plane.

1. What is the average (arithmetic mean) of all integers 6 through 15 (including 6 and 15)?

   A.   6
   B.   9
   C.   10.5
   D.   11
   E.   21

2. Which of the following is equivalent to $\dfrac{3.2 \times 10^5}{8 \times 10^8}$?

   F. 4×10^{-4}
   G. 4×10^{-3}
   H. 4×10^{-2}
   J. 4×10^{3}
   K. 4×10^{13}

3. If the rectangle below has an area of 72, then $x = ?$

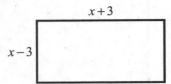

   A.   3
   B.   4
   C.   6
   D.   8
   E.   9

Throwback to Math Class

Here are the steps to find a missing element of an average:

Step 1: Multiply the average by the total number of quantities.

Step 2: Add together the known quantities.

Step 3: Subtract the result of Step 2 from the result of Step 1.

4. Machine X produces 15 units per minute, and Machine Y produces 12 units per minute. In one hour, Machine X will produce how many more units than Machine Y?

- F.   90
- G.   180
- H.   240
- J.   270
- K.   360

5. Which of the following pie charts represents the data shown below?

Team Expenses		
Transportation	$240	■
Lodging	$360	▨
Meals	$120	□

A.    D.

B.   E.

C.

6. On the first day after being given an assignment, a student read $\frac{1}{2}$ the number of pages assigned, and on the second day, the student read 3 more pages. If the student still has 6 additional pages to read, how many pages were assigned?

- F.   15
- G.   18
- H.   24
- J.   30
- K.   36

7. The average (arithmetic mean) of Pat's scores on three tests was 80. If the average of her scores on the first two tests was 78, what was her score on the third test?

- A.   82
- B.   84
- C.   86
- D.   88
- E.   90

8. In the figure below, $a + c - b$ is equal to which of the following?

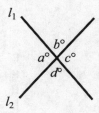

- F. $2a - d$
- G. $2a + d$
- H. $2d - a$
- J. $2a$
- K.   180

9. If $3a + 6b = 12$, then $a + 2b = ?$

- A.   1
- B.   2
- C.   3
- D.   4
- E.   6

10. Two circles with radii r and $r + 3$ have areas that differ by 15π. What is the radius of the <u>smaller</u> circle?

- F.   4
- G.   3
- H.   2
- J.   1
- K. $\frac{1}{2}$

11. If $x, y,$ and z are integers, $x > y > z > 1$, and $xyz = 144$, what is the <u>greatest</u> possible value of x?

    A.   8
    B.   12
    C.   16
    D.   24
    E.   36

12. For all integers, $x \, \Phi \, y = 2x + 3y$. Which of the following must be true?

    I. $3 \, \Phi \, 2 = 12$
    II. $x \, \Phi \, y = y \, \Phi \, x$
    III. $0 \, \Phi \, (1 \, \Phi \, 2) = (0 \, \Phi \, 1) \, \Phi \, 2$

    F.   I only
    G.   I and II only
    H.   I and III only
    J.   II and III only
    K.   I, II, and III

Throwback to Math Class

The slope of a line that runs between (x_1, y_1) and (x_2, y_2) on the coordinate plane is given by the following equation:

$$m = \frac{y_2 - y_1}{x_2 - x_1}$$
$$= \frac{\Delta y}{\Delta x}$$

13. In the figure below, what is the slope of line l?

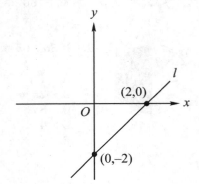

    A.   1
    B. $\frac{1}{2}$
    C.   0
    D. $-\frac{1}{2}$
    E. -1

14. If Yuriko is now twice as old as Lisa was 10 years ago, how old is Lisa today if Yuriko is now n years old?

    F. $\frac{n}{2} + 10$
    G. $\frac{n}{2} - 10$
    H. $n - 10$
    J. $2n + 10$
    K. $2n - 10$

15. In the figure below, $ABCD$ is a rectangle with sides $\overline{AB}$, $\overline{BC}$, and $\overline{CD}$ tangent to the circle with center O. If the radius of the circle is 2, what is the area of the shaded region?

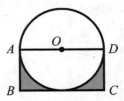

    A. $\frac{3\pi}{2}$
    B. $\frac{3\pi}{4}$
    C. $8 - 2\pi$
    D. $2 - \pi$
    E. $\pi - 1$

16. The sum of two positive consecutive integers is n. In terms of n, what is the value of the larger of the two integers?

    F. $\frac{n-1}{2}$
    G. $\frac{n+1}{2}$
    H. $\frac{n}{2} + 1$
    J. $\frac{n}{2} - 1$
    K. $\frac{n}{2}$

17. The table below shows a teacher how to convert scores for a test from the Old Scale to the New Scale. What is the Minimum Passing Score on the New Scale?

	OLD SCALE	NEW SCALE
Minimum Score	0	120
Minimum Passing Score	60	?
Maximum Score	100	180

A. 108
B. 136
C. 156
D. 164
E. 208

18. If a polygon with all equal sides is inscribed in a circle, then the measure in degrees of the minor arc created by adjacent vertices of the polygon could NOT be equal to which of the following?

F. 30
G. 25
H. 24
J. 20
K. 15

19. A jar contains 5 blue marbles, 25 green marbles, and x red marbles. If the probability of drawing a red marble at random from the jar is $\frac{1}{4}$, what is the value of x?

A. 25
B. 20
C. 15
D. 12
E. 10

20. In the figure below, the length of $\overline{AB}$ is 2 units. Which of the following is the best approximation for the number of units in the length of $\overline{BC}$? $\left(\cos 45° = \dfrac{\sqrt{2}}{2}\right)$

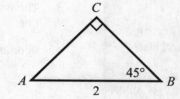

F. $\dfrac{\sqrt{2}}{2}$

G. $\dfrac{\sqrt{3}}{2}$

H. $\sqrt{2}$

J. $\sqrt{3}$

K. 2

QUIZ II BRAIN BUSTER (25 items; 20 minutes)

DIRECTIONS: Solve each item and choose the correct answer choice. Calculator use is permitted; however, some items are best solved without the use of a calculator.

NOTES: All of the following should be assumed, unless otherwise stated.

1. Illustrative figures are NOT necessarily drawn to scale.

2. The word *average* indicates arithmetic mean.

3. The word *line* indicates a straight line.

4. Geometric figures lie in a plane.

1. Maggie has to inventory her employer's collection of books. There are three categories of books. Historical novels account for one-fourth of the books. Classics comprise half of the remaining books and there are 30 travel books. How many books does she have to inventory?

   A. 50
   B. 70
   C. 80
   D. 100
   E. 120

2. The local university's enrollment figures for a six-year period are detailed in the table below. Between which two consecutive years did the university experience the greatest percent increase in student enrollment?

UNIVERSITY ENROLLMENT					
2006	2007	2008	2009	2010	2011
14,000	15,100	15,900	16,500	17,600	17,400

   F. 2006–2007
   G. 2007–2008
   H. 2008–2009
   J. 2009–2010
   K. 2010–2011

3. If $f(x) = \dfrac{x^2 + x}{x - 1}$ and $g(x) = 2x + 3$, then $g(f(-2)) = ?$

   A. $-\dfrac{4}{3}$
   B. $-\dfrac{2}{3}$
   C. 0
   D. $\dfrac{4}{3}$
   E. $\dfrac{5}{3}$

4. Set A contains all the positive factors of 24. Set B contains all the prime numbers less than 20. How many numbers are elements in both set A and set B?

   F. Zero
   G. One
   H. Two
   J. Three
   K. Four

5. The local modeling agency is looking for some new models for a specific job. The job requires that the model's height be within 2 inches of 70 inches. Which of the following absolute value inequalities describe this condition, where x is the model's height?

   A. $|x + 2| \le 70$
   B. $|x - 2| < 70$
   C. $|x + 70| < 2$
   D. $|x - 70| < 2$
   E. $|x + 70| \le 2$

Throwback to Math Class

The Big Angle/ Little Angle theorem comes in handy:

When two parallel lines are intersected by a third line, the following are true: (1) all of the big angles are equal; (2) all of the little angles are equal; and (3) any big angle plus any little angle equals 180°.

6. Tommy has blue, green, and red marbles. The number of blue marbles and green marbles combined total 25. The number of blue and red marbles combined total 30. There are twice as many red marbles as green marbles. How many green marbles does Tommy have?

   F. 5
   G. 10
   H. 15
   J. 20
   K. 25

7. At a wedding, three entrees are served: chicken, fish, and beef. The total number of people who ordered each entrée are shown in the matrix below:

$$\begin{array}{ccc} \text{chicken} & \text{fish} & \text{beef} \\ [85 & 58 & 68] \end{array}$$

   The percentage of each group who ordered potatoes as a side is shown in the matrix below:

$$\begin{array}{cc} \text{chicken} & [20\%] \\ \text{fish} & [50\%] \\ \text{beef} & [75\%] \end{array}$$

   Approximately how many servings of potatoes will need to be prepared for this wedding?

   A. 17
   B. 29
   C. 51
   D. 97
   E. 107

8. In the figure below, line *l* is parallel to line *m*. What is the value of *x*?

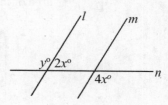

   F. 20
   G. 30
   H. 40
   J. 50
   K. Cannot be determined from the given information

9. If $x = a^2 - b^2$, $y = a^2 + 2ab + b^2$, and $a + b \neq 0$, then $\dfrac{x}{y} = ?$

   A. $2a^2 + 2ab$

   B. $\dfrac{a^2 - b^2}{a^2 + b^2}$

   C. $\dfrac{a+b}{a-b}$

   D. $\dfrac{-1}{2ab}$

   E. $\dfrac{a-b}{a+b}$

10. A 13-foot ladder is leaning against a building and the bottom of the ladder is 5 feet from the wall. The ladder begins to slide down the building. When the bottom of the ladder is 8 feet from the wall, about how far has the top of the ladder slipped down?

   F. less than 1 foot
   G. exactly 1 foot
   H. between 1 foot and 2 feet
   J. exactly 2 feet
   K. more than 2 feet

11. In rectangle $ABCD$ below, $\overline{AD} = \overline{DE}$, $\overline{AD} = 2$, and $\angle BAC = 30°$. What is the area of the shaded portion of the figure?

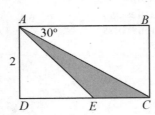

A. $2\sqrt{2} - 3$
B. $4 - 2\sqrt{3}$
C. $2\sqrt{3} - 2$
D. $2\sqrt{2}$
E. $2\sqrt{3}$

12. In the figure below, $\overset{\frown}{DE}$ is the arc of a circle with center C. If the length of $\overset{\frown}{DE}$ is 2π, what is the area of sector CDE?

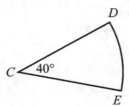

F. 4π
G. 9π
H. 12π
J. 18π
K. 24π

13. If a is the greatest prime factor of 24 and b is the greatest prime factor of 80, what is ab?

A. 4
B. 6
C. 10
D. 15
E. 16

14. If the average (arithmetic mean) of a, b, and c is z, which of the following is the average of a, b, c and d?

F. $\dfrac{z + d}{3}$

G. $\dfrac{z + d}{4}$

H. $\dfrac{3z + d}{3}$

J. $\dfrac{3z + d}{4}$

K. $\dfrac{3(z + d)}{4}$

15. When 21 is divided by a positive integer d, the remainder is 5. For how many different values of d is this true?

A. One
B. Two
C. Three
D. Four
E. Five

16. Let the operation ✪ be defined by x ✪ $y = xy + y$ for all numbers x and y. If 2 ✪ 3 $= z$ ✪ 1, what is the value of z?

F. 6
G. 7
H. 8
J. 9
K. 10

17. In a rectangular coordinate system, the center of a circle has coordinates $(3, -10)$. The circle touches the y-axis only once. What is the diameter of the circle?

A. 3
B. 6
C. 9
D. 10
E. 20

18. If $x^2 + 3x - 18 = 0$ and $2m = x$, which of the following could be a value of m?

F. -3
G. 1
H. 3
J. 6
K. 9

19. Which of the following coordinate points lie completely inside the circle whose equation is $x^2 + y^2 = 36$?

A. $(6, 0)$
B. $(0, -6)$
C. $(-4, 5)$
D. $(2, 7)$
E. $(4, 4)$

20. If $x - y = 7$ and $x^2 - y^2 = 35$, what is $x + y$?

F. 5
G. 7
H. 10
J. 28
K. 42

21. What is the product of the complex numbers $(2i - 1)$ and $(i + 3)$?

A. 1
B. 4
C. $-5 + 5i$
D. $5 - 5i$
E. $5 + 5i$

22. The expression $\cos^2 x - 7 + \sin^2 x$ is equivalent to:

F. -8
G. -7
H. -6
J. 6
K. 8

23. Which of the following values of x satisfies the equation $\log_x\left(\dfrac{1}{81}\right) = -4$?

A. 3
B. 4
C. 9
D. 18
E. 81

24. Assume an angle with radian measure θ exists such that $\cos\theta = -\dfrac{3}{5}$ and $\dfrac{\pi}{2} < \theta < \pi$. What is the value of $\sin\theta$?

F. $-\dfrac{5}{3}$
G. $-\dfrac{4}{5}$
H. $\dfrac{3}{5}$
J. $\dfrac{4}{5}$
K. $\dfrac{5}{4}$

25. If the polynomial $3x^3 + 12x^2 + 2x + 8 = 0$ has the root -4, which of the following are also roots of the polynomial?

A. $\pm\dfrac{\sqrt{6}}{3}$
B. $\pm\dfrac{\sqrt{6}}{6}$
C. $\pm\dfrac{i\sqrt{6}}{3}$
D. $\pm\dfrac{i\sqrt{6}}{6}$
E. $\pm\dfrac{i\sqrt{3}}{6}$

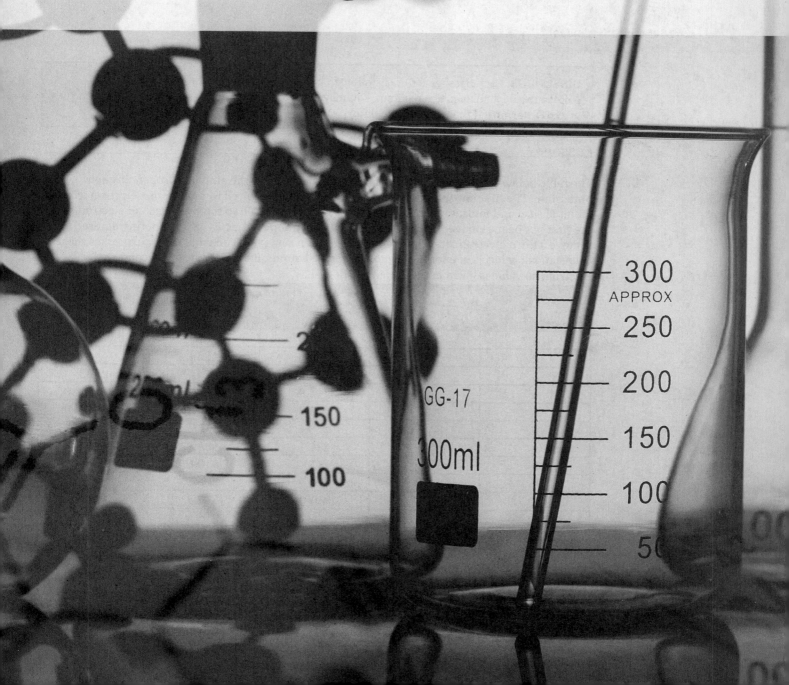

SCIENCE
QUIZ

This section contains one Science quiz. Complete the quiz under timed conditions. Answers are on page 248.

QUIZ (16 items; 15 minutes)

DIRECTIONS: Each passage below is followed by several items. After reading a passage, choose the best answer to each item. You may refer to the passages as often as necessary. You are NOT permitted the use of a calculator.

Passage I

The table below shows the first three ionization energies for the atoms hydrogen through potassium. The first ionization energy, E_1, is the energy required to remove one electron from an atom. The second ionization energy, E_2, is the energy required to remove a second electron once the first has been removed. Likewise, the third ionization energy, E_3, is the energy required to remove a third electron after the first two have been removed. The table below expresses these values in kilocalories of energy per mole of ionized atoms. If an atom lacks a second or third electron, no value is given in the table.

IONIZATION ENERGIES OF THE ELEMENTS (kcal/mole)				
Atomic No.	Element	E_1	E_2	E_3
1	H	313.6	-	-
2	He	566.8	1254	-
3	Li	124.3	1744	2823
4	Be	214.9	419.9	3548
5	B	191.3	580	874.5
6	C	259.6	562.2	1104
7	N	335.1	682.8	1094
8	O	314	810.6	1267
9	F	401.8	806.7	1445
10	Ne	497.2	947.2	1500
11	Na	118.5	1091	1652
12	Mg	176.3	346.6	1848
13	Al	138	434.1	655.9
14	Si	187.9	376.8	771.7
15	P	241.8	453.2	695.5
16	S	238.9	540	807
17	Cl	300	548.9	920.2
18	Ar	363.4	637	943.3
19	K	100.1	733.6	1100

1. For a given element, which of the following correctly orders the ionization energies from least to most?

   A. E_3, E_2, E_1
   B. E_2, E_1, E_3
   C. E_1, E_2, E_3
   D. Cannot be determined from the given information

2. A student suspects that there may be an atom for which the second ionization energy is roughly twice that of the first, and the third is roughly twice that of the second. Which of the following atoms best fits this relationship?

   F. Be
   G. C
   H. Ne
   J. Ar

3. Starting with He, as atomic number increases, the corresponding value of E_2:

   A. increases only.
   B. decreases only.
   C. increases for a few values, then decreases, followed by another increase, etc.
   D. decreases for a few values, then increases, followed by another decrease, etc.

4. In a mass spectrometer, an electron beam is used to remove an electron from an element that is being tested before it is deflected by a magnetic field. A particular mass spectrometer has an electron beam capable of ionizing atoms to a maximum intensity of 200 kcal/mol. How many different types of atoms could this device ionize?

   F. 7
   G. 8
   H. 11
   J. 12

Passage II

A physics student performed two sets of experiments designed to examine the factors that influence the motion of falling objects.

Experiment 1

A stone was dropped from a steep cliff while a camera, mounted on a tripod on the ground, took photographs at 0.1-second intervals. Back in the laboratory, the same procedure was repeated in the absence (nearly) of air inside a huge vacuum chamber.

Experiment 2

The experiments were repeated using a stone and a cork with identical masses dropped at the same time. At the cliff, the stone hit the ground first. In the vacuum chamber, both objects hit the ground together.

5. Assuming that air acts to resist the downward acceleration of the stone, how will the total time required to reach the ground in the vacuum chamber compare to the time required to reach the ground from the cliff?

   A. The time in air is greater than the time in the vacuum chamber.
   B. The time in air is less than the time in the vacuum chamber.
   C. The time is the same in each.
   D. Cannot be determined from the given information

6. If part of Experiment 1 were repeated on the moon, where the pull of gravity is one-sixth that on Earth, the stone's downward speed would increase as it falls (i.e., it would accelerate) but the rate of increase in speed would only be one-sixth as great as on Earth. When the photos taken at 0.1-second intervals on the moon are compared to the photos taken on Earth, the series of moon pictures of the stone will be:

   F. closer together.
   G. farther apart.
   H. identical.
   J. closer at some times and farther apart at others.

7. In Experiment 2, the observed results can be explained by the hypothesis that:

   A. heavier objects fall more rapidly than lighter ones.
   B. a cork of the same mass as a stone is smaller than the stone, and it encounters more air resistance.
   C. a cork of the same mass as a stone is larger than the stone, and it encounters more air resistance.
   D. the gravitational acceleration of objects toward the ground diminishes when air is not present.

8. In Experiment 1, gravity accelerates the stone as it falls from the cliff, causing it to pick up speed as it drops. Which of the following series of pictures most resembles how the stone appears as it drops?

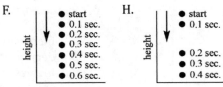

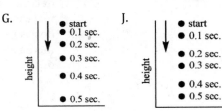

9. The experimenter devises a means of suspending Earth's gravity for short periods of time. Armed with this technique, he drops the stone (on Earth, in air, under conditions of normal gravity), and then suspends gravity 0.2 seconds after the stone has been falling and leaves it off for the next 10 seconds. Recalling that gravity causes the stone's downward speed to increase continually, choose the series of pictures that best illustrates, in 0.1-second intervals, this experiment.

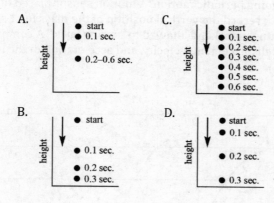

A.
● start
● 0.1 sec.
● 0.2–0.6 sec.

C.
● start
● 0.1 sec.
● 0.2 sec.
● 0.3 sec.
● 0.4 sec.
● 0.5 sec.
● 0.6 sec.

B.
● start
● 0.1 sec.
● 0.2 sec.
● 0.3 sec.

D.
● start
● 0.1 sec.
● 0.2 sec.
● 0.3 sec.

10. If Experiment 2 were repeated on the airless moon, which prediction would be correct?

F. The cork would fall more slowly than on Earth.
G. The cork would fall as rapidly as the stone.
H. Both (F) and (G) are correct.
J. Neither (F) nor (G) is correct.

Passage III

An object in periodic motion, such as a mass on a spring or a pendulum, vibrates about a fixed position in a regular and repeating fashion. There are two measurable quantities of periodic motion: amplitude and period. The amplitude is the maximum displacement of the object, in either direction, from its resting position. The period is the time it takes the object to complete one cycle of motion: from resting position through the maximum displacement on both sides of the resting position and then back to the resting position. Note that the period does not depend on how far the spring is initially stretched. This independence is a key feature of all systems that undergo periodic motion.

A student investigates the relationships between position, velocity, and acceleration of a vibrating mass-spring system undergoing periodic motion. A motion sensor placed directly below a mass hung from a spring is used to record the vertical position of the mass for 1 second after the spring is stretched (beyond its resting point) and allowed to "spring back." A computer program is used to analyze the data and plot displacement, velocity, and acceleration of the mass-spring system as a function of time (Figure 1).

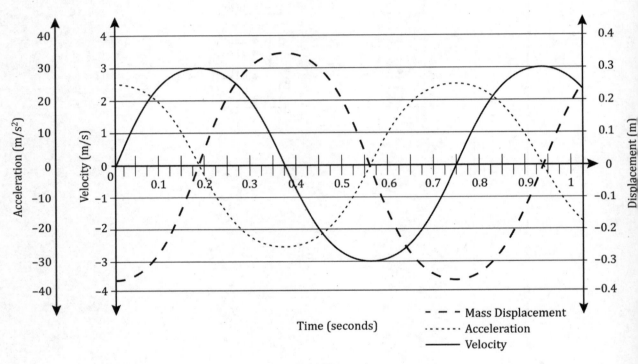

Figure 1

11. In Figure 1, a positive slope for acceleration data indicates that the mass-spring system is:

A. moving upward.
B. moving downward.
C. slowing down.
D. speeding up

12. The period of the mass-spring system is approximately:

F. 0.375 second.
G. 0.75 second.
H. 1 second.
J. Cannot be determined from the given information

13. Negative values of both displacement and velocity indicate that the mass-spring system is:

A. below the resting position and moving upward.
B. moving downward, but speeding up.
C. below the resting position and moving downward.
D. approaching the resting position and moving upward.

14. Which of the following statements about the relationship between displacement and velocity for a mass-spring system in periodic motion is best supported by the experimental results?

F. The velocity magnitude of a mass-spring system decreases as the system moves from maximum positive displacement to its resting position.
G. The velocity magnitude of a mass-spring system is least as the system passes through its resting position.
H. The velocity magnitude of a mass-spring system remains constant as the system moves from maximum negative displacement to its resting position.
J. The velocity magnitude of a mass-spring system is greatest as the system passes through its resting position.

15. Which of the following statements about the relationship between acceleration and displacement for a mass-spring system in periodic motion is best supported by the experimental results?

A. The acceleration of a mass-spring system increases as the system moves from maximum positive displacement to maximum negative displacement.
B. The acceleration of a mass-spring system is least (most negative) as the system passes through its resting position.
C. The acceleration of a mass-spring system remains constant as the system moves from maximum negative displacement to maximum positive displacement.
D. The acceleration of a mass-spring system decreases each time the system passes through its resting position.

16. The mass-spring system is released from 0.7 meters below its resting position and the experiment repeated. Which of the following results is most likely to occur?

F. The period of the mass-spring system remains unchanged.
G. The period of the mass-spring system doubles.
H. The amplitude of the mass-spring system remains unchanged.
J. The maximum velocity of the mass-spring system decreases by half.

PRACTICE TEST I

DIRECTIONS

Practice Test I includes five subject tests: English, Mathematics, Reading, Science, and Writing. Calculator use is permitted on the Mathematics Test only.

Cambridge offers several services for schools utilizing our practice tests. Ask your teacher whether your school has decided to send your answers to Cambridge for scoring or to score your answers at your school. If Cambridge is scoring your test, you will use a Scantron™ form provided by your teacher, or you will enter your answers online. If your school is scoring your test, you may use a Scantron™ form provided by your teacher, or you may write your answers on paper.

If you are entering your test answers on a Scantron™ form, please be sure to include the following information on the Scantron™:

Book and Edition	*Victory for the ACT Test, 14th Edition*
Practice Test Number	**Practice Test I**

If you are only completing a single section of this practice test, make sure to also include the following information:

Subject	English, Mathematics, Reading or Science
Section Number	**Section 1, 2, 3 or 4**

The items in each multiple-choice test are numbered and the answer choices are lettered. The Scantron™ form has numbered rows that correspond to the items on the test. Each row contains lettered ovals to match the answer choices for each item on the test. Each numbered row has a corresponding item on the test.

For each item, first decide on the best answer choice. Then, locate the row number that corresponds to the item. Next, find the oval in that row that matches the letter of the chosen answer. Then, use a soft lead pencil to fill in the oval. DO NOT use a ballpoint pen.

Mark only one answer for each item. If you change your mind about an answer choice, thoroughly erase your first mark before marking your new answer.

Note that only responses marked on your Scantron™ form or written on your paper will be scored. Your score on each test will be based only on the number of items that are correctly answered during the time allowed for that test. You will not be penalized for guessing. Therefore, it is in your best interest to answer every item on the test, even if you must guess.

On the Writing Test, write your response to the prompt using the essay response sheets or loose-leaf paper provided by your teacher. Your teacher might also direct you to enter your essay response online. (Note that the Writing Test is optional.)

You may work on each test only during the time allowed for that test. If you finish a test before time is called, use the time to review your answer choices or work on items about which you are uncertain. You may not return to a test on which time has already been called, and you may not preview another test. You must lay down your pencil immediately when time is called at the end of each test. You may not for any reason fill in or alter ovals for a test after time has expired for that test. Violation of these rules will result in immediate disqualification from the exam.

SECTION 1: ENGLISH TEST
45 Minutes—75 Items

DIRECTIONS: In the passages below, certain parts of the sentences have been underlined and numbered. In the right-hand column, you will find different ways of writing each underlined part; the original version is indicated by the "NO CHANGE" option. For each item, select the choice that best expresses the intended idea, is most acceptable in standard written English, or is most consistent with the overall tone and style of the passage.

There are also items that ask about a section of the passage or the passage as a whole. These items do not refer to an underlined portion of the passage; these items are preceded by statements that are enclosed in boxes.

Read the passage through once before you begin to answer the accompanying items. Finding the answers to certain items may depend on looking at material that appears several sentences beyond the item. So, be sure that you have read far enough ahead before you select your answer choice. Answers are on page 260.

PASSAGE I

Basic Principles of Nuclear Weapons

The challenge to start to begin to make timely
                              1
progress toward removing the threat of nuclear war

is the most important challenge in international

relations today. Three general principles guide our

defense and negotiation policies toward such a goal,

principles based on the technical realities of nuclear

war.

First, nuclear weapons are fundamentally
                                          2
different than non-nuclear weapons. These weapons
        2
of mass destruction that could do a lot of harm
                        3

1. A. NO CHANGE
   B. to begin making
   C. to begin the making of
   D. of beginning the making of

2. F. NO CHANGE
   G. different than fundamentally
   H. different from fundamentally
   J. fundamentally different from

3. A. NO CHANGE
   B. (and they could also do a great deal of harm)
   C. (owing to the fact that they could do a lot of harm)
   D. OMIT the underlined portion.

GO ON TO THE NEXT PAGE.

have a long and deadly radioactive <u>memory, the</u>
4
unknowns of nuclear conflict dwarf the predictable

consequences. The number of deaths resulting <u>from</u>
5
<u>injuries and the unavailability of medical care</u> and
5

the economic damage <u>as a result from</u> disruption and
6

disorganization <u>would be even more devastating than</u>
7

the direct loss of life and property. ⬜8

Second, <u>the sole purpose</u> of nuclear weapons
9

must be to deter nuclear <u>war, it is</u> neither a
10
substitute for maintaining adequate conventional

military forces to meet vital national security goals

<u>but</u> an effective defense against the almost total
11
mutual annihilation and devastation that results

4. F. NO CHANGE
    G. memory. The
    H. memory the
    J. memory and the

5. A. NO CHANGE
    B. from injuries and also from the
        unavailability of medical care
    C. from the unavailability of injuries and
        medical care
    D. both from injuries and also from the
        unavailability of medical care as well

6. F. NO CHANGE
    G. as a result to
    H. resulting from
    J. with a result of

7. A. NO CHANGE
    B. is even more devastating than
    C. are even more devastating as
    D. might be more devastating even as

8. Which of the following would be an appropriate
    final sentence for this paragraph?

    F. And so I believe nuclear weapons to be a
        challenge.
    G. Nuclear war could have no winners.
    H. Nuclear conflict is very dangerous.
    J. Nuclear conflict would be rather wasteful.

9. A. NO CHANGE
    B. solely, the purpose
    C. the solely purpose
    D. the purpose solely

10. F. NO CHANGE
    G. war. They are
    H. war they are
    J. war; it is

11. A. NO CHANGE
    B. and
    C. nor
    D. including

GO ON TO THE NEXT PAGE.

from a full-scale nuclear war. Third, arms control
12

is an essential part of our national security. Thus

far, we have had no effective controls on offensive

nuclear weaponry, and it is clear that each step

forward in the arms race toward more and improved

weapons has made less our security. Before
13

deploying additional weapons, they must develop a
14

coherent arms control strategy.

12. F. NO CHANGE
    G. Third
    H. (Begin a new paragraph) Third
    J. (Begin a new paragraph) Third,

13. A. NO CHANGE
    B. has lessened
    C. have lessened
    D. have made less of

14. F. NO CHANGE
    G. the development is necessary of
    H. it is necessary to develop
    J. it is necessarily to be developed,

Items #15–16 ask about the preceding passage
as a whole.

---

15. Which of the following best describes the overall
    structure of the essay?

    A. A three-part argument
    B. A two-part narrative
    C. A three-part comparison
    D. A four-part argument

16. Which of the following is the thesis of this essay?

    F. Nuclear weapons are fundamentally
        different from non-nuclear weapons.
    G. The sole purpose of nuclear weapons must
        be to deter nuclear war.
    H. There are three principles that guide our
        effort to remove the threat of nuclear war.
    J. Nuclear war is a frightening possibility.

PASSAGE II

Education for a New Republic

The founders of the Republic viewing their
17

17. A. NO CHANGE
    B. having viewed its
    C. viewed its
    D. viewed their

GO ON TO THE NEXT PAGE.

revolution primarily in political terms <u>rather as</u>
                                          18

in economic terms. <u>Therefore,</u> they viewed the
                     19

kind of education needed for the new Republic

largely in political terms instead of <u>as a means to</u>
                                        20

academic excellence or individual self-fulfillment.

<u>Talking about</u> education as a bulwark for liberty,
     21

equality, popular consent, and devotion to the public

<u>good goals</u> that <u>took precedence over</u> the uses of
   22   **23**

knowledge for self-improvement or occupational

preparation. Over and over again, the Revolutionary

generation, both liberal and conservative in

<u>outlook—assert their</u> faith that the welfare of the
        24

Republic rested upon an educated citizenry.

    All agreed that the principal ingredients of

a civic education <u>was</u> literacy and inculcation of
                    25

patriotic and moral <u>virtues some</u> others added the
                        26

study of history and the study of the principles of the

republican government itself. The founders, as was

---

18. F. NO CHANGE
    G. rather than
    H. but
    J. OMIT the underlined portion.

19. A. NO CHANGE
    B. Since
    C. However,
    D. On the contrary,

20. F. NO CHANGE
    G. as a means or a way to
    H. to
    J. as

21. A. NO CHANGE
    B. Talking
    C. They talked about
    D. With the talking about

22. F. NO CHANGE
    G. good. Goals
    H. good, goals
    J. good; goals

23. A. NO CHANGE
    B. precede
    C. precede over
    D. took precedence on

24. F. NO CHANGE
    G. outlook, asserted its
    H. outlook; asserted its
    J. outlook asserts their

25. A. NO CHANGE
    B. being
    C. were
    D. were like

26. F. NO CHANGE
    G. virtues—some
    H. virtues, some
    J. virtues; some

GO ON TO THE NEXT PAGE.

the case of almost all their successors, were long on

exhortation and rhetoric regarding the value of civic

education; since they left it to the textbook writers to
    27

distill the essence of those values for school children.

Texts in American history and government appeared

as early as the 1790s. The textbook writers turned
                                                  28

out being very largely of conservative persuasion,
28

more likely Federalist in outlook than Jeffersonian,

and universally almost agreed that political virtue
    29

must rest upon moral and religious precepts. Since

most textbook writers were New Englanders, this

meant that the texts had a decidedly Federalist slant.

In the first half of the Republic, civic education

in the schools emphasized the inculcation of civic

values, put less emphasis on political knowledge,

and no attempt to develop political skills. The
       30

development of political skills was left to the local

parties, town meetings, churches, coffeehouses, and

ale houses where men gathered to talk. 31

27. A. NO CHANGE
    B. education. And
    C. education. Since
    D. education, but

28. F. NO CHANGE
    G. turned out to be
    H. turning out to be
    J. having turned out to be

29. A. NO CHANGE
    B. almost, agreed universally
    C. almost universally agreed
    D. almost universally, agreed

30. F. NO CHANGE
    G. made no attempt to develop
    H. none at all on the development of
    J. none was put at all on developing

31. Which of the following correctly describes how
    the last paragraph of the essay functions?

    A. It contradicts much of what was said before.
    B. It continues the logical development of the
        essay.
    C. It reiterates what was said in the first para-
        graph.
    D. It is a transitional paragraph to introduce a
        new topic.

Item #32 asks about the preceding passage
as a whole.

32. This essay would most likely be published in a:

    F. history textbook.
    G. political science journal.
    H. journal for educators.
    J. biography of Jefferson.

GO ON TO THE NEXT PAGE.

PASSAGE III

Women and World War I

[1]

The contribution of women on the home front
33
during World War I was varied. It included a large

range of activities—from knitting and the operation
34
of drill presses—and engaged a cross section of the
34
female population, from housewives to society girls.

World War I marked the first time in the history of
35
the United States that a systematic effort was made,

through organizations like the League for Women's

Service, to utilize the capabilities of women in all
36
regions of the country.

[2]

While much of this volunteer work falls within
37
the established bounds of women's club work, many

women entered areas of industrial work previously
38
reserved by the male population. Women put on the
38
uniforms of elevator operators, streetcar conductors,

postmen, and industrial workers. However, they
39
were employed in aircraft and munitions plants as
39
well as in shipbuilding yards and steel mills.

[3]

Much of the work fell into the traditional

realm of volunteer activity knitting garments for
40
the boys overseas, canning for Uncle Sam, planting

33. A. NO CHANGE
B. Women, their contribution
C. The contribution of woman
D. Woman's contribution

34. F. NO CHANGE
G. from knitting with the operation of
H. from knitting and operating
J. from knitting to operating

35. A. NO CHANGE
B. has marked the first time
C. is the first time it is marked
D. was marked, the first time

36. F. NO CHANGE
G. being able to utilize
H. utilizing
J. and utilize

37. A. NO CHANGE
B. fell within
C. having fallen within
D. fell in

38. F. NO CHANGE
G. having previously been reserved
H. previously reserved for
J. reserved previous to then

39. A. NO CHANGE
B. workers. They were employed
C. workers, but they were employed
D. workers. Since they were employed

40. F. NO CHANGE
G. activity; knitting
H. activity: knitting
J. activity, knitting

GO ON TO THE NEXT PAGE.

victory gardens, etc. Through these activities, every

homemaker could <u>demonstrate their</u> patriotism
                        41

while still fulfilling her role as homemaker. Women

with more time volunteered to hostess at <u>canteens:</u>
                                              42

<u>make</u> bandages, and organize food and clothing
 42

drives. The Women's Land Army, dressed in bloomer

uniforms and armed with such slogans as "The

Woman with the Hoe Must Defend the Man with

the <u>Musket," was dispatched</u> to assist farmers in
         43

processing crops.

[4]

Women performed ably during the war and <u>laid</u>
                                            44

<u>the foundation</u> for more specialized jobs, increased
 44

wages, better working conditions, and a more

competitive job status in the labor market.

41. A. NO CHANGE
    B. be demonstrating
    C. have demonstrated their
    D. demonstrate her

42. F. NO CHANGE
    G. canteens make
    H. canteens, make
    J. canteens; make

43. A. NO CHANGE
    B. Musket," which was then dispatched
    C. Musket," and it was dispatched
    D. Musket," and it got dispatched

44. F. NO CHANGE
    G. the foundation was laid
    H. the foundation was lain
    J. laying the foundation

Items #45–46 ask about the preceding passage as a whole.

45. Which of the following represents the most logical order for the paragraphs?

    A. 1, 4, 3, 2
    B. 1, 3, 4, 2
    C. 1, 3, 2, 4
    D. 2, 4, 3, 1

46. Is the use of the sample slogan appropriate to the essay?

    F. Yes, because it helps the reader to understand one of the points being made.
    G. Yes, because all general statements should be illustrated with an example.
    H. No, because it does not help the reader to understand the point being made.
    J. No, because it is needlessly distracting.

GO ON TO THE NEXT PAGE.

Democracy in Japan

Following the end of World War II, substantial

changes <u>undertaken</u> in Japan to liberate the
    47

individual from authoritarian restraints. The new

democratic value system was <u>acceptable by</u> many
       48

teachers, students, intellectuals, and old <u>liberals,</u>
            49

<u>and</u> it was not immediately embraced by the society
49

as a whole. <u>Japanese traditions were dominated by</u>
        50

<u>group values</u>, and notions of personal freedom and
 50

individual rights <u>being</u> unfamiliar.
      51

    <u>Today, the triumph of</u> democratic processes
      52

<u>is clear</u> evident in the widespread participation of
53

the Japanese in social and political life. <u>Furthermore,</u>
            54

there is no universally accepted and stable

47. A. NO CHANGE
 B. will be undertaken
 C. have been undertaken
 D. were undertaken

48. F. NO CHANGE
 G. excepted to
 H. excepted by
 J. accepted by

49. A. NO CHANGE
 B. liberals, since
 C. liberals, but
 D. liberals; consequently

50. F. NO CHANGE
 G. Dominated by group values were the
   Japanese traditions
 H. Group values were always dominating the
   Japanese traditions
 J. Dominating Japanese traditions were group
   values

51. A. NO CHANGE
 B. were
 C. was
 D. are

52. F. NO CHANGE
 G. (Do NOT begin a new paragraph) Today the
   triumph, of
 H. Today, the triumph, of
 J. (Do NOT begin a new paragraph) Today,
   owing to the fact that

53. A. NO CHANGE
 B. is
 C. is clear and also
 D. are clearly

54. F. NO CHANGE
 G. Therefore,
 H. So,
 J. Yet,

GO ON TO THE NEXT PAGE.

value _system, values being_ constantly modified
55

by strong infusions of Western ideas. School

textbooks expound democratic _principles, and so_
56

emphasizing equality over hierarchy and rationalism
56

over tradition, but in practice, these values _are_
57

often sometimes misinterpreted and distorted,
57

particularly by the youth _that translated_ the
58

individualistic and humanistic goals of democracy

into egoistic and materialistic ones.

55. A. NO CHANGE
    B. system with that values are
    C. system since that values are
    D. system since values are

56. F. NO CHANGE
    G. principles, emphasizing
    H. principles and the emphasis of
    J. principles with the emphasis that

57. A. NO CHANGE
    B. had been misinterpreted and distorted often
    C. often misinterpreted and distorted
    D. are often misinterpreted and distorted

58. F. NO CHANGE
    G. that translate
    H. who translate
    J. translate

59. What type of discussion might logically follow this last paragraph?

    A. A discussion of goals of Japanese youth
    B. A discussion of democratic principles
    C. A discussion of Western education
    D. A discussion of World War II

PASSAGE V

Zoological Nature

From the beginning, humankind _always has_
60

shared some sort of link with the animal world. The
60

earliest and most primitive was surely that of hunter

and prey—with humans possibly playing the fatal

role of victim. Later, of course, humans reversed the

roles as they became more skillful _and intelligenter._
61

The later domestication of certain _animals and also_
62

the discovery of agriculture, made for a more settled

and stable existence and was an essential step in the

60. F. NO CHANGE
    G. have always shared
    H. is always sharing
    J. has always shared

61. A. NO CHANGE
    B. so intelligent
    C. and more intelligent
    D. but intelligent

62. F. NO CHANGE
    G. animals, also
    H. animals, along with
    J. animals; along with

GO ON TO THE NEXT PAGE.

not-so-orderly <u>and very chaotic</u> process of becoming
63
civilized. However, the intellectual distance between

regarding an animal as the source of dinner or of

material comfort and <u>to consider them</u> a worthy
64
subject for study is considerable.

Not until Aristotle did the animal world

become a subject for serious scientific study.

Although <u>he seemingly writes on</u> every <u>subject,</u>
65   66
<u>Aristotle's work</u> in zoology—studying animals
66
as animals—is considered his most successful.

He seemed to have had a natural affinity for and

curiosity about all the living creatures of the world,

<u>and</u> he took special interest in marine life.
67

Aristotle's zoological writings reveal him to be

a remarkably astute observer of the natural world,

<u>wedding his</u> observations to what might be called
68
speculative reason. He was therefore a theorist as

well. His overall theory was <u>simple. In</u> the works
69
of Nature," he said, "purpose and not accident is

predominant." A thing is known then when we know

what it is for. He linked <u>and combined</u> theory and
70
practice by saying that interpretation of an observed

63. A. NO CHANGE
B. (and very chaotic)
C. yet very chaotic
D. OMIT the underlined portion.

64. F. NO CHANGE
G. considering it
H. considering them
J. then to consider them

65. A. NO CHANGE
B. he wrote (seemingly) on
C. writing seemingly on
D. he wrote on seemingly

66. F. NO CHANGE
G. subject; Aristotles work
H. subject Aristotles' work
J. subject: Aristotle's work

67. A. NO CHANGE
B. so
C. but
D. because

68. F. NO CHANGE
G. who was wedded to
H. in that he wedded
J. with the wedding of

69. A. NO CHANGE
B. simple—in
C. simple. "In
D. simply. "In

70. F. NO CHANGE
G. combining
H. to combine
J. OMIT the underlined portion.

GO ON TO THE NEXT PAGE.

phenomenon must always be made <u>in light of its</u>
71

<u>purpose</u>. His zoological theory was thus a reflection
71

of the essentially teleological nature of his overall

philosophy. 72

71. A. NO CHANGE
B. always keeping its purpose in mind
C. without ever forgetting what its purpose is
D. given an understanding of what its purpose is

72. Is the quote from Aristotle in the last paragraph appropriate?

F. Yes, because it is important to quote the works of people you are talking about.
G. Yes, because it is a succinct statement of Aristotle's theory.
H. No, because the quote is irrelevant to what the author is talking about in that paragraph.
J. No, because it is wrong to quote when you can express the idea in your own words.

Items #73–75 ask about the preceding passage as a whole.

73. The author probably had which of the following audiences in mind for this essay?

A. Zoologists
B. Students who are studying Aristotle
C. The average person interested in science
D. Teachers of marine biology

74. What is the actual thesis of this essay?

F. People have always liked animals.
G. Animals and people reversed roles.
H. Aristotle was interested in the natural world.
J. The animal world became a source of serious study because of Aristotle.

75. How does the first paragraph of this essay function?

A. It poses questions to be answered.
B. It provides general background for the rest of the passage.
C. It introduces an argument.
D. It provides an anecdote related to the rest of the passage.

END OF TEST 1
STOP! DO NOT TURN THE PAGE UNTIL TOLD TO DO SO.

2 2 2 2 2 2 2 2 2 2 2 2

SECTION 2: MATHEMATICS TEST
60 Minutes—60 Items

DIRECTIONS: Solve each item and choose the correct answer choice. Then, fill in the corresponding oval on the bubble sheet.

Allocate time wisely. Try to solve as many items as possible, returning to skipped items if time permits.

Calculator use is permitted on this test; however, some items are best solved without the use of a calculator.

NOTE: All of the following should be assumed, unless otherwise stated.

1. Illustrative figures are NOT necessarily drawn to scale.
2. The word *average* indicates arithmetic mean.
3. The word *line* indicates a straight line.
4. Geometric figures lie in a plane.

Answers are on page 260.

1. If $\dfrac{1}{x} + \dfrac{1}{x} = 8$, then $x = ?$

    A. $\dfrac{1}{4}$
    B. $\dfrac{1}{2}$
    C. 1
    D. 2
    E. 4

2. If $x = 2$ and $y = -1$, then $3x - 4y = ?$

    F. -5
    G. -1
    H. 0
    J. 2
    K. 10

3. In a certain school, there are 600 boys and 400 girls. If 20% of the boys and 30% of the girls are on the honor roll, how many of the students are on the honor roll?

    A. 120
    B. 175
    C. 240
    D. 250
    E. 280

DO YOUR FIGURING HERE.

GO ON TO THE NEXT PAGE.

4. If p, q, r, s, and t are whole numbers, the expression $t[r(p+q)+s]$ must be an even number when which of the five numbers is even?

F. p
G. q
H. r
J. s
K. t

DO YOUR FIGURING HERE.

5. A student conducting a lab experiment finds that the population of flies in a bottle increases by the same multiple from week to week. If the pattern shown in the table continues, how many flies can the student expect to find in the bottle in Week 5?

Results of Biology Project Conducted by Student X					
Week	1	2	3	4	5
Number of Flies in Bottle	3	12	48	192	?

A.   195
B.   240
C.   384
D.   564
E.   768

6. At a school assembly, 3 students are each scheduled to give a short speech. In how many different orders can the speeches be scheduled?

F.   12
G.   9
H.   6
J.   4
K.   3

GO ON TO THE NEXT PAGE.

DO YOUR FIGURING HERE.

7. If points P and Q lie in the xy-plane and have the coordinates shown below, what is the midpoint of $\overline{PQ}$?

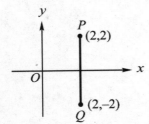

A. $(-2, 0)$
B. $(-2, 2)$
C. $(0, 2)$
D. $(2, 0)$
E. $(2, 2)$

8. If $xy = |xy|$ and $xy \neq 0$, which of the following CANNOT be true?

F. $x > y > 0$
G. $y > x > 0$
H. $x > 0 > y$
J. $0 > x > y$
K. $0 > y > x$

9. In the scale drawing of the floor of a rectangular room shown below, the scale used was $1\text{ cm} = 4\text{ m}$. What is the actual area, in square meters, of the floor of the room?

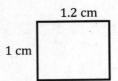

A. 9.6
B. 13.6
C. 15
D. 19.2
E. 38.4

10. If $30{,}000 \times 20 = 6 \times 10^n$, then $n = ?$

F. 4
G. 5
H. 6
J. 7
K. 8

GO ON TO THE NEXT PAGE.

11. Karen purchased 4 pounds of candy, which was a mix of chocolates and caramels. If chocolates cost $3 per pound and caramels cost $2 per pound, and if Karen spent a total of $10, how many pounds of chocolates did she buy?

   A. 1
   B. 2
   C. 2.5
   D. 3
   E. 3.5

12. The average of Al's scores on 3 tests was 80. If the average of his scores on the first 2 tests was 77, what was his score on the third test?

   F. 86
   G. 83
   H. 80
   J. 77
   K. 74

13. A book contains 10 photographs, some in color and some in black-and-white. Which of the following CANNOT be the ratio of color to black-and-white photographs?

   A. 9:1
   B. 4:1
   C. 5:2
   D. 3:2
   E. 1:1

14. If $\frac{4}{5} = \frac{x}{4}$, then $x = ?$

   F. 5
   G. $\frac{16}{5}$
   H. $\frac{5}{4}$
   J. $\frac{4}{5}$
   K. $\frac{5}{16}$

DO YOUR FIGURING HERE.

GO ON TO THE NEXT PAGE.

DO YOUR FIGURING HERE.

15. In the figure below, three equilateral triangles have a common vertex. What is the degree measure of $x + y + z$?

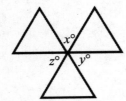

   A. 60°
   B. 90°
   C. 120°
   D. 180°
   E. 240°

16. Peter spent $\frac{1}{4}$ of his allowance on Monday and $\frac{1}{3}$ of the remainder on Tuesday. What part of the allowance does Peter still have?

   F. $\frac{1}{12}$
   G. $\frac{1}{4}$
   H. $\frac{1}{2}$
   J. $\frac{3}{4}$
   K. $\frac{11}{12}$

17. If 100 identical bricks weigh p pounds, then how many pounds do 20 of the identical bricks weigh in terms of p?

   A. $\frac{p}{20}$
   B. $\frac{p}{5}$
   C. $20p$
   D. $\frac{5}{p}$
   E. $\frac{20}{p}$

GO ON TO THE NEXT PAGE.

18. If the distances between points P, Q, and R are equal, which of the following *could* be true?

   I. P, Q, and R are points on a circle with center O.
   II. P and Q are points on a circle with center R.
   III. P, Q, and R are vertices of an equilateral triangle.

   F. I only
   G. I and II only
   H. I and III only
   J. II and III only
   K. I, II, and III

DO YOUR FIGURING HERE.

19. In the table below, the percentage increase in the price of the item was greatest during which of the following periods?

Year	1980	1985	1990	1995	2000	2005
Price	$2	$4	$7	$12	$20	$50

   A. 1980–1985
   B. 1985–1990
   C. 1990–1995
   D. 1995–2000
   E. 2000–2005

20. Which of the following is a factorization of $x^2 + 4x - 12$?

   F. $(x-2)(x+6)$
   G. $(x-4)(x+3)$
   H. $(x-6)(x+2)$
   J. $(x+2)(x+6)$
   K. $(x+3)(x+4)$

21. Two cartons weigh $3x-2$ and $2x-3$ pounds, respectively. If the average weight of the cartons is 10 pounds, the heavier carton weighs how many more pounds than the lighter carton weighs?

   A. 2
   B. 4
   C. 5
   D. 6
   E. 10

GO ON TO THE NEXT PAGE.

22. A group of 15 students took a test that was scored from 0 to 100. If 10 students scored 75 or more on the test, what is the lowest possible value for the average score of all 15 students?

    F.   25
    G. 50
    H. 70
    J.   75
    K. 90

23. For all real numbers x, 16^x is equal to which of the following expressions?

    A. x^{16}
    B. 2^{3x}
    C. 4^{2x}
    D. 8^{2x}
    E. 8^{4x}

24. What is the perimeter of the square in the figure below?

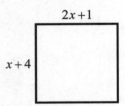

$2x+1$

$x+4$

    F. 28
    G. 16
    H.   9
    J.   3
    K.   2

25. If a certain rectangle has a length that is twice its width, what is the ratio of the area of the rectangle to the area of an isosceles right triangle with a hypotenuse equal to the width of the rectangle?

    A. $\dfrac{1}{8}$

    B. $\dfrac{1}{4}$

    C. $\dfrac{1}{2}$

    D. $\dfrac{4}{1}$

    E. $\dfrac{8}{1}$

DO YOUR FIGURING HERE.

GO ON TO THE NEXT PAGE.

26. In the coordinate plane, what is the shortest distance between the point with (x, y) coordinates $(1, 3)$ and the line with the equation $x = -2$?

F. 1
G. 3
H. 4
J. 6
K. 9

27. If 5 pounds of coffee cost $12, how many pounds of coffee can be purchased for $30?

A. 7.2
B. 10
C. 12.5
D. 15
E. 18

28. If the two triangles below are equilateral, what is the ratio of the perimeter of the smaller triangle to that of the larger triangle?

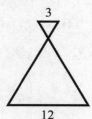

F. $\dfrac{1}{36}$

G. $\dfrac{1}{15}$

H. $\dfrac{1}{9}$

J. $\dfrac{1}{4}$

K. $\dfrac{1}{3}$

DO YOUR FIGURING HERE.

GO ON TO THE NEXT PAGE.

29. If $f(x) = -3x^3 + 3x^2 - 4x + 8$, then $f(-2) = ?$

    A. 16
    B. 22
    C. 28
    D. 36
    E. 52

DO YOUR FIGURING HERE.

30. A merchant pays $60 wholesale for a dress and then sets the retail price at a 40% markup on the wholesale cost. Two months later, the dress is put on sale at 30% off the retail price. What is the sale price of the dress?

    F. $70.00
    G. $64.70
    H. $58.80
    J. $56.30
    K. $42.00

31. If $\frac{1}{3}$ of a number is 2 more than $\frac{1}{5}$ of the number, then which of the following equations can be used to find the number x?

    A. $\frac{1}{3}x - \frac{1}{5}x = 2$

    B. $\frac{1}{3}x - \frac{1}{5}x = -2$

    C. $\frac{1}{3}x - 2 = -\frac{1}{5}x$

    D. $\frac{1}{3}x + 2 = -\frac{1}{5}x$

    E. $5\left(\frac{1}{3}x + 2\right) = 0$

32. In the figure below, the triangle is equilateral and has a perimeter of 12 centimeters. What is the perimeter, in centimeters, of the square?

    F. 9
    G. 12
    H. 16
    J. 20
    K. 24

GO ON TO THE NEXT PAGE.

33. If one solution of the equation $12x^2 + kx = 6$ is $\frac{2}{3}$, then $k = ?$

A. 1
B. $\frac{3}{2}$
C. 2
D. 5
E. 9

34. If a 6-sided polygon has 2 sides of length $x - 2y$ each and 4 sides of length $2x + y$ each, what is its perimeter?

F. $6x - 6y$
G. $6x - y$
H. $5x$
J. $6x$
K. $10x$

35. At the first stop on her route, a driver unloaded $\frac{2}{5}$ of the packages in her van. After she unloaded another 3 packages at her next stop, $\frac{1}{2}$ of the original number of packages in the van remained. How many packages were in the van before the first delivery?

A. 10
B. 20
C. 25
D. 30
E. 50

36. For all x and y, $12x^3y^2 - 8x^2y^3 = ?$

F. $2x^2y^2(4x - y)$
G. $4x^2y^2(2xy)$
H. $4x^2y^2(3xy)$
J. $4x^2y^2(3x - 2y)$
K. $x^3y^3(12xy - 8xy)$

DO YOUR FIGURING HERE.

DO YOUR FIGURING HERE.

37. When $\dfrac{1}{1+\dfrac{1}{x}}$ is defined, it is equivalent to which of the following expressions?

   A. $x+1$

   B. $\dfrac{1}{x+1}$

   C. $\dfrac{x}{x+1}$

   D. $\dfrac{x+1}{x}$

   E. x^2+x

38. If S is 150% of T, what percentage of $S+T$ is T?

   F. $33\dfrac{1}{3}\%$

   G. 40%

   H. 50%

   J. 75%

   K. 80%

39. In $\triangle PQR$, the lengths of $\overline{PQ}$ and $\overline{QR}$ are equal, and the measure of $\angle Q$ is 3 times that of $\angle P$. What is the degree measure of $\angle R$?

   A. $24°$

   B. $30°$

   C. $36°$

   D. $45°$

   E. $60°$

40. If the cost of b books is d dollars, which of the following equations can be used to find the cost, C, in dollars, of x books at the same rate?

   F. $C = xd$

   G. $C = \dfrac{dx}{b}$

   H. $C = \dfrac{bd}{x}$

   J. $C = bx$

   K. $C = \dfrac{bx}{d}$

41. An article is on sale for 25% off its regular price of $64. If the merchant must also collect a 5% sales tax on this reduced price, what is the total cost of the article including sales tax?

    A. $42.10
    B. $44.20
    C. $49.60
    D. $50.40
    E. $56.70

42. If $\dfrac{x}{z} = k$ and $\dfrac{y}{z} = k - 1$, then $x = $?

    F. $\dfrac{y}{z}$
    G. $z - y$
    H. $y - 1$
    J. $y + 1$
    K. $y + z$

43. If x is 25% of y, then y is what percentage of x?

    A. 400%
    B. 300%
    C. 250%
    D. 125%
    E.   75%

44. If x is an integer that is a multiple of both 9 and 5, which of the following *must* be true?

    I. x is equal to 45.
    II. x is a multiple of 15.
    III. x is odd.

    F. I only
    G. II only
    H. III only
    J. II and III only
    K. I, II, and III

DO YOUR FIGURING HERE.

GO ON TO THE NEXT PAGE.

45. If each edge of a cube is 2 units long, what is the distance from any vertex (corner of the cube) to the cube's center?

A. $\dfrac{\sqrt{2}}{2}$

B. $\dfrac{3}{2}$

C. $\sqrt{3}$

D. $2\sqrt{2}$

E. $2\sqrt{3}$

46. The figure below shows two circular cylinders, C and C'. If $r = kr'$ and $h = kh'$, what is the ratio of the volume of C' to the volume of C?

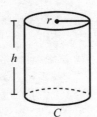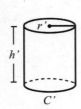

F. $1:\pi$

G. $\pi:1$

H. $k\pi:1$

J. $1:k^3$

K. $k^3:1$

47. In the figure below, if the triangle has an area of 1 square unit, what is the area of the circle, in square units?

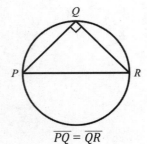

$$\overline{PQ} = \overline{QR}$$

A. π

B. 2π

C. $2\sqrt{3}\,\pi$

D. 4π

E. $4\sqrt{3}\,\pi$

48. In the figure below, P and Q are the centers of their respective circles and the radius of each circle is 1 inch. What is the perimeter, in inches, of the shaded part of the figure?

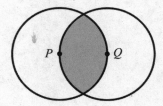

F. $\dfrac{4\pi}{3}$

G. π

H. $\dfrac{2\pi}{3}$

J. $\dfrac{\pi}{3}$

K. $\dfrac{\pi}{6}$

49. A student's final grade in a certain course is the average of his scores on 10 tests graded on a scale of 0 to 100, inclusive. For the first 6 tests, the student's scores averaged 83. If x is the student's final grade for the course, then which of the following must be true?

A. $8.3 \le x \le 83.0$

B. $49.8 \le x \le 83.0$

C. $49.8 \le x \le 89.8$

D. $54.7 \le x \le 89.8$

E. $83.0 \le x \le 89.8$

50. What is the multiplicative inverse of the complex number $2 - i$? ($\sqrt{i} = -1$)

F. $2 + i$

G. $i - 2$

H. $\dfrac{2 + i}{3}$

J. $\dfrac{2 - i}{3}$

K. $\dfrac{2 + i}{5}$

GO ON TO THE NEXT PAGE.

51. $\log_3 \sqrt{3} = ?$

DO YOUR FIGURING HERE.

    A. -1

    B. $\dfrac{1}{3}$

    C. $\dfrac{1}{2}$

    D. $\dfrac{2}{3}$

    E. 2

52. If $f(x) = (x-1)^2 + 2$, then what value for x creates the minimum value for $f(x)$?

    F. -3
    G. -2
    H. 0
    J. 1
    K. 2

53. If $2^n + 2^n + 2^n + 2^n = x(2^{n+1})$, then $x = ?$

    A. 2
    B. 4
    C. 2^n
    D. 2^{2n}
    E. 2^{n+1}

54. If $f(k) = k^2 + 2k + 1$, then what is the set of all k for which $f(k) = f(-k)$?

    F. $\{0\}$
    G. $\{1\}$
    H. $\{2\}$
    J. $\{1, 2\}$
    K. All real numbers

55. The limit of a function, $\lim\limits_{x \to a} f(x)$, denotes the value $f(x)$ approaches for values of x approaching a. What is $\lim\limits_{x \to 1} \dfrac{x^2 - 1}{x - 1}$?

    A. -1
    B. 0
    C. 1
    D. 2
    E. The limit does not exist.

GO ON TO THE NEXT PAGE.

56. If $0 \le x \le \pi$ and $\cos x = -1$, then $\cos\dfrac{x}{2} = ?$

DO YOUR FIGURING HERE.

    F. $-\dfrac{\sqrt{3}}{2}$

    G. $-\dfrac{1}{2}$

    H. 0

    J. $\dfrac{1}{2}$

    K. $\dfrac{\sqrt{3}}{2}$

57. Which of the following defines the range of the function $f(x) = \dfrac{1-x}{x}$?

    A. All real numbers
    B. All real numbers except -1
    C. All real numbers except 0
    D. All real numbers except 1
    E. All real numbers greater than -1

58. Which of the following graphs represents the equations $x = 3\,(\sin\theta)$ and $y = 2\,(\cos\theta)$?

    F.

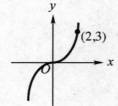

    J.

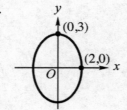

    G.

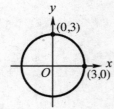

    K.

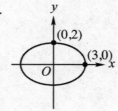

    H.

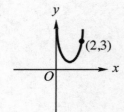

GO ON TO THE NEXT PAGE.

59. For all θ such that $0° < \theta < 90°$, which of the following is equal to $(\sin \theta)(\csc \theta)$?

A. 1
B. $\sqrt{2}$
C. $\tan \theta$
D. $\cot \theta$
E. $\sec \theta$

DO YOUR FIGURING HERE.

60. In the figure below, how many units long is $\overline{BC}$?

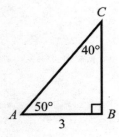

F. 4
G. 5
H. $\sin 10°$
J. $3(\tan 50°)$
K. $3(\tan 40°)$

NO TEST MATERIAL ON THIS PAGE

SECTION 3: READING TEST
35 Minutes—40 Items

DIRECTIONS: Each passage below is followed by a set of items. Read each passage and choose the best answer for each item. Fill in the corresponding oval on your bubble sheet. You may refer to the passage as often as necessary to answer the items. Answers are on page 271.

PASSAGE I

PROSE FICTION: In this passage, a young country man, alone in town for the first time, tries to find a relative, Major Molineux.

It was near nine o'clock of a moonlit evening, when a boat crossed the ferry with a single passenger, who had obtained his conveyance at that unusual hour by the promise of extra fare. When
5 he stood on the landing place, searching in either pocket for the means of fulfilling his agreement, the ferryman lifted a lantern, by the aid of which, and the newly risen moon, he took a very accurate survey of the stranger's figure. He was a youth of
10 barely eighteen years, evidently country-bred, and now upon his first visit to town. He was clad in a coarse gray coat, well worn, but in excellent repair; his under garments were durably constructed of leather, and fitted tight to a pair of serviceable and
15 well-shaped limbs; his stockings of blue yarn were undoubtedly the work of a mother or a sister; and on his head was a three-cornered hat, which in its better days had perhaps sheltered the graver brow of the lad's father. Under his left arm was a heavy
20 cudgel formed of an oak sapling, and retaining a part of the hardened root; and his equipment was completed by a wallet, not so abundantly stocked as to inconvenience the vigorous shoulders on which it hung. Brown, curly hair, well-shaped features, and
25 bright, cheerful eyes were nature's gifts, and worth all that art could have done for his adornment.

The youth, one of whose names was Robin, finally drew from his pocket a little province bill of five shillings, which, in depreciation in that sort
30 of currency, satisfied the ferryman's demand with the addition of a hexagonal piece of parchment, valued at three pence. He then walked forward into the town with as light a step as if his day's journey had not already exceeded thirty miles and with as

35 eager an eye as if he were entering London city, instead of the little metropolis of a New England colony. However, before Robin had proceeded far, it occurred to him that he knew not whither to direct his steps; so he paused and looked up and down
40 the narrow street, scrutinizing the small and mean wooden buildings that were scattered on either side.

"This low hovel cannot be my kinsman's dwelling," thought he, "nor yonder old house, where the moonlight enters at the broken casement; and
45 truly I see none hereabouts that might be worthy of him. It would have been wise to inquire my way of the ferryman, and doubtless, he would have gone with me and earned a shilling from the Major for his pains. But the next man I meet will do as well."

50 He resumed his walk and was glad to perceive that the street now became wide, and the houses were more respectable in their appearance. He soon discerned a figure moving on moderately in advance, and he hastened his steps to overtake it. Robin laid
55 hold of the skirt of the man's old coat, just when the light from the open door and windows of a barber's shop fell upon both their figures.

"Good evening to you, honored sir," said he, making a low bow and still retaining hold of the
60 skirt. "I pray you tell me whereabouts is the dwelling of my kinsman, Major Molineux."

The citizen answered him in a tone of excessive anger and annoyance. "Let go my garment, fellow! I tell you, I know not the man you speak of. What! I
65 have the authority, I have—hem, hem—authority; and if this be the respect you show for your betters, your feet shall be brought acquainted with the stocks by daylight, tomorrow morning!"

Robin released the old man's skirt and
70 hastened away, pursued by an ill-mannered roar

GO ON TO THE NEXT PAGE.

of laughter from the barber's shop. He was at first considerably surprised by the result of his question, but, being a shrewd youth, he soon thought himself able to account for the mystery.

75   "This is some country representative," was his conclusion, "who has never seen the inside of my kinsman's door and lacks the breeding to answer a stranger civilly. The man is old—I might be tempted to turn back and smite him on the nose. Ah, Robin,
80   Robin! Even the barber's boys laugh at you for choosing such a guide! You will be wiser in time, friend Robin."

1. In the final paragraph, the young man is talking to:

   A.   the Major.
   B.   the man in the coat.
   C.   the barbers.
   D.   himself.

2. The total cost of the young man's passage on the ferryboat was:

   F.   five shillings.
   G.   three pence.
   H.   five shillings less three pence.
   J.   five shillings plus three pence.

3. The young man believes that his relative is a:

   A.   barber.
   B.   wealthy person.
   C.   constable.
   D.   builder.

4. The incidents described in the passage take place:

   F.   in the late morning.
   G.   in the early afternoon.
   H.   in the late afternoon.
   J.   at night.

5. The passage suggests that thirty miles is:

   A.   a long distance to travel in one day.
   B.   easily traveled in a single day.
   C.   easily traveled in an hour.
   D.   a long ferryboat ride.

6. The young man believes that the barbers laughed at him because:

   F.   his clothes clearly show that he is from the country.
   G.   he asked a question of a stranger who obviously would not know the answer.
   H.   he badly needs a haircut and a shave.
   J.   the stranger he questioned is actually the man he is looking for.

7. The scenes in the passage are most likely set in which of the following time periods?

   A.   Eighteenth century
   B.   Nineteenth century
   C.   Early twentieth century
   D.   Present time

8. The young man approaches the stranger in the coat:

   F.   respectfully.
   G.   rudely.
   H.   coyly.
   J.   stealthily.

9. The young man is the only passenger on the ferryboat because:

   A.   he paid the ferryman extra for a private charter.
   B.   no one else was traveling at that hour.
   C.   the Major had sent the boat especially for him.
   D.   the ferryman was a good friend of the young man.

10. Just after he gets off the ferry, the young man finds himself in a:

   F.   poorer neighborhood.
   G.   wealthy neighborhood.
   H.   forest.
   J.   large city.

GO ON TO THE NEXT PAGE.

PASSAGE II

SOCIAL SCIENCE: These passages discuss Frederick Turner's hypothesis of the American frontier.

Passage A

In 1893, Frederick Jackson Turner presented a paper to a group of historians convening in Chicago during the Columbian Exposition. Entitled "The Significance of the Frontier in American History,"
5 Turner's paper drew little immediate reaction. Yet, no theory of history has had a greater influence on the direction and methodology of inquiry and the issues of debate in American history. Later historians took issue with some of Turner's interpretations;
10 even some of his own students were among those whose research proved some of his views to be wrong. However, these debates merely serve to illustrate the importance of Turner's hypothesis.

Turner's argument was a grand hypothesis
15 about how the settlement of the frontier had shaped the American experience and character. As with all general hypotheses in any field of study, it gave a coherent interpretation to many facts that had been largely ignored by historians up to that time.

20 Turner used statistical evidence from the 1880 census as the basis for a startling conclusion: Prior to 1880 there had been a frontier to be settled. By 1890, Turner pointed out, there was no longer any area of wilderness completely untouched by
25 settlements. The frontier had disappeared. The passing of the frontier, Turner concluded, was a historic moment.

Turner further claimed that the frontier experience had produced a distinctively American
30 character, which was not explainable simply as the predictable behavioral traits molded by English political institutions. Frontier settlers developed inquisitiveness, inventiveness, energy, and a great passion for freedom. These attributes defined a new
35 American character—one evidenced in nationalism, independence, and democracy. This new sense of national identity derived from the fact that people from every section of the country mixed at the Western frontier. Economic independence could
40 be traced to the fact that the settlers no longer depended on England for goods but had become self-sufficient. In addition, the frontier settlers, whose basic social unit was the family, enjoyed freedom from direct governmental interference.
45 Frontier life thus reinforced the fundamental ideals of populist democracy.

In addition, Turner argued that the frontier fostered democracy in the cities of the East. The availability of free land at the frontier provided a
50 "safety-valve" against possible social unrest: those discontented with social inequities and economic injustice could strike out and settle the free land that was available in frontier territories.

Turner's thesis was thus original in both what
55 it said and in the methodology that Turner used in formulating it. Up to the time of Turner's essay, history had been essentially the history of politics. A Midwesterner, Turner challenged this traditional approach of Eastern historians by incorporating
60 techniques of the social sciences, showing how factors of geography, economics, climate, and society influenced the development of the American West. Although now common among historians, at the time this interdisciplinary approach was novel.

Passage B

65 Three years before Turner put forth the frontier thesis, the U.S. Census Bureau had announced the disappearance of a contiguous frontier line. For Turner, the significance of the frontier was its effect on the American character.
70 According to Turner, uniquely American traits were developed by the frontier culture, including a can-do problem-solving attitude, a nervous energy, and rugged individualism.

Turner's essay reached triumphant heights
75 in his belief that the promotion of individualistic democracy was the most important consequence of the frontier. Individuals, forced to rely on their own wits and strength, were necessarily skeptical of hierarchies and fearful of centralized authority.

80 Turner's thesis that the frontier is the key to American history as a whole has rightfully been abandoned. There is too much evidence for the critical influence of factors like slavery and the Civil War, immigration, and the development of industrial
85 capitalism. But even as an account of the West and frontier, Turner's thesis was lacking.

Turner's formulation of "free land" ignored the presence of the numerous Indian peoples whose subjugation was required by the nation's
90 westward march. The many Indian wars started by American expansion belie Turner's argument that the American frontier, in sharp contrast to European borders between nation-states, was "free land."

GO ON TO THE NEXT PAGE.

More fundamentally, the very concept of a
95   frontier is dubious, because it applies to too many
disparate places and times to be useful. How much
do Puritan New England and the California of the
transcontinental railroad really have in common?
Many such critics have sought to replace the idea
100 of a moving frontier with the idea of the West as a
distinctive region, much like the American South.

Additionally, cooperation and communities
of various sorts, not isolated individuals, made
possible the absorption of the West into the United
105 States. Most migrant wagon trains, for example,
were composed of extended kinship networks.
Moreover, the role of the federal government and
large corporations grew increasingly important.
Corporate investors built the railroads; government
110 troops defeated Indian nations; even cowboys,
enshrined in popular myth as rugged loners, were
generally low-level employees of cattle corporations.

Questions #11–14 ask about Passage A.

---

11. According to Passage A, Turner's methodology
was original in its:

A.   reliance on the history of politics to explain
the American experience.
B.   use of an interdisciplinary approach to
study a historical question.
C.   reliance on a presentation at a professional
conference to announce a theory.
D.   suggestion that key terms like "frontier"
have to be more clearly defined.

12. The phrase "even some of his own students"
(line 10) implies that students are:

F.   not necessarily familiar with the most
recent scholarly work.
G.   ordinarily sympathetic to the views of one
of their professors.
H.   not likely to accept a theory until it has been
studied for some time.
J.   disposed to propose new theories that have
little merit.

13. The attitude of the author of Passage A toward
Turner's work can best be described as:

A.   suspicious.
B.   condescending.
C.   undecided.
D.   approving.

14. In this context, "grand" (line 14) means:

F.   incorrect.
G.   comprehensive.
H.   lavish.
J.   tentative.

Questions #15–18 ask about Passage B.

---

15. The author of Passage B lists the "factors" in
lines 83–85 in order to show that:

A.   Turner's thesis did not adequately explain
the history of the frontier.
B.   historians prior to Turner had tended to
focus on only a single explanatory factor.
C.   the frontier was only one of many important
factors in American history.
D.   different regions of America had different
experiences of the frontier.

16. The author of Passage B mentions wagon trains
(line 105) in order to show that:

F.   frontier land had previously been inhabited
by indigenous peoples.
G.   groups were as important in the westward
expansion as individuals.
H.   government army troops were needed to
secure the safety of settlers.
J.   groups from different regions came into
contact at the frontier.

17. It can be inferred that the author of Passage B
believes that:

A.   Turner's thesis is still generally valid.
B.   Turner's thesis had very limited usefulness.
C.   Turner was intellectually dishonest.
D.   Turner intentionally ignored evidence.

GO ON TO THE NEXT PAGE.

18. In context, "belie" (line 91) means:

    F.   tell an untruth about.
    G. conceal a flaw in.
    H. prove to be false.
    J.   retract a point.

Questions #19–20 ask about both passages.

---

19. Both passages mention all of the following as elements of Turner's view regarding the American character EXCEPT:

    A. practical inventiveness.
    B. pro-democracy attitude.
    C. skepticism toward authority.
    D. nationalistic feelings.

20. The evidence in Passage B that frontier land was not free (lines 87–93) most undermines what aspect of Turner's thesis as explained in Passage A?

    F.   Safety-valve theory
    G. Census data of 1880
    H. Claim of self-sufficiency
    J.   Mixing at the frontier

GO ON TO THE NEXT PAGE.

PASSAGE III

HUMANITIES: In this passage, the author expresses his opinion regarding the role of philosophy.

The service of philosophy, of speculative culture, towards the human spirit is to rouse, to startle it into a life of constant and eager observation. Every moment, some form grows
5 perfect in hand or face; some tone on the hills or the sea is choicer than the rest; some mood of passion or insight or intellectual excitement is irresistibly real and attractive to us—and for that moment only. Not the fruit of experience, but experience itself is
10 the end. Only a counted number of pulses are given to us of a variegated, dramatic life. How may we see in them all that is to be seen in them by the finest senses? How shall we pass most quickly from point to point and be present always at the focus where
15 the greatest number of vital forces unite in their purest energy?

To burn always with this hard, gemlike flame, to maintain this ecstasy, is success in life. In a sense it might even be said that our failure is to form
20 habits: for, after all, habit is relative to a stereotyped world, and in the meantime, it is only the roughness of the eye that makes any two persons, things, or situations seem alike. While all melts under our feet, we may well catch at any exquisite passion, or
25 any knowledge that seems by a lifted horizon to set the spirit free for a moment, or any stirring of the senses, strange dyes, strange colors, curious odors, or work of the artist's hands or the faces of one's friends. Not to discriminate every moment some
30 passionate attitude in those about us, and in the brilliancy of their gifts some tragic dividing of forces of their ways is, on this short day of the frost and sun, to sleep before evening. With this sense of the splendor of our experience and of its awful brevity,
35 gathering all we are into one desperate effort to see and touch, we shall hardly have time to make theories about the things we see and touch.

What we have to do is to be forever curiously testing new opinions and courting new
40 impressions, never acquiescing in a facile orthodoxy. Philosophical theories or ideas, as points of view, instruments of criticism, may help us to gather what might otherwise pass unregarded by us. "Philosophy is the microscope of thought." The theory or idea or
45 system which requires of us the sacrifice of any part of this experience, in consideration of some interest into which we cannot enter, or some abstract theory we have not identified with ourselves, or of what is only conventional, has no real claim upon us.

50 In one of his most beautiful passages, Rousseau describes the awakening in him of the literary sense. An undefinable taint of death had clung always about him, and now in early manhood he believed himself smitten by mortal disease. He asked himself
55 how he might make as much as possible of the interval that remained; and he was not biased by anything in his previous life when he decided that it must be by intellectual excitement.

We are all under sentence of death but with
60 a sort of indefinite reprieve; we have an interval and then our place knows us no more. Some spend this interval in listlessness, others in high passions, the wisest—at least among the "children of this world"—in art and song. Our one chance
65 lies in expanding this interval—in getting as many pulsations as possible into the given time. Great passions may give us this quickened sense of life, ecstasy and sorrow of love, the various forms of enthusiastic activity, disinterested or otherwise,
70 which comes naturally to many of us. Only be sure it is passion—that it does yield you this fruit of a quickened, multiplied consciousness. Of this wisdom, the poetic passion, the desire of beauty, the love of art for art's sake has most; for art comes
75 to you professing frankly to give nothing but the highest quality to your moments as they pass, and simply for the sake of those moments.

21. Which of the following best describes the overall structure of the passage?

   A. The author raises a question and then provides an answer.
   B. The author presents a theory, which he then proves.
   C. The author studies a widely held belief and then rejects it.
   D. The author defines a term and then provides examples.

22. In the passage, the author uses the word *pulsations* (line 66) to mean:

   F. children.
   G. lives.
   H. death.
   J. experiences.

GO ON TO THE NEXT PAGE.

23. According to the author, the function of art is to:

    A. depict reality accurately.
    B. stimulate strong emotions.
    C. encourage social reform.
    D. express the artist's feelings.

24. With which of the following statements would the author most likely agree?

    F. A person's lifetime is merely preparation for what comes after death.
    G. Only an artist can truly enjoy life.
    H. The original experience is more important than the memory of it.
    J. A perceptive person understands that all experience is repetitious.

25. The tone of the passage can best be described as:

    A. impassioned.
    B. scholarly.
    C. informative.
    D. speculative.

26. In the context of this passage, the phrase "short day of the frost and sun" (lines 32–33) refers to:

    F. the transient effect of poetry.
    G. a brief moment of passion.
    H. the life of a person.
    J. stimulation of the senses.

27. The phrase "awful brevity" (line 34) means that:

    A. philosophy is not really useful.
    B. art may not satisfy everyone.
    C. life is short.
    D. passion is the greatest virtue.

28. The "children of this world" (line 63–64) are NOT:

    F. passionate.
    G. wise.
    H. lovers of art and song.
    J. listless.

29. According to the author, the greatest passion is the love of:

    A. beauty.
    B. one's spouse.
    C. wealth.
    D. security.

30. The phrase "then our place knows us no more" (lines 61) means that we:

    F. move to another town.
    G. have children.
    H. die.
    J. divorce.

GO ON TO THE NEXT PAGE.

NATURAL SCIENCE: This passage explains how energy becomes usable through photosynthesis.

Every living cell must acquire energy in a usable form. According to the First Law of Thermodynamics, energy, which is the capacity for doing work, can be converted from one form into
5 another without any net gain or loss. An organism must have an outside source of usable energy. The Second Law of Thermodynamics states that every energy transformation reduces the free (usable) energy of the system. Living cells primarily use
10 chemical energy derived from complex organic compounds.

Photosynthesis is the process by which green plants transform sunlight into a usable energy source. Green plants utilize the energy of light to
15 combine carbon dioxide with water to form organic material (sugar) and oxygen.

$$6CO_2 + 12H_2O + light \overset{chlorophyll}{\Rightarrow} 6O_2 + C_6H_{12}O_6 + 6H_2O$$

Photosynthesis is a reduction reaction. Reduction is the addition of one or more electrons
20 to an atom or molecule. Oxidation is the removal of electrons from an atom or molecule. Reduction stores energy, while oxidation releases it. Biological systems rely on the addition or removal of an electron from hydrogen. Photosynthesis is based
25 on two key processes. Light energy is trapped and stored, and hydrogen atoms are transformed from water to carbon dioxide to form carbohydrate.

Photosynthesis takes place within the chloroplasts. The pigments within the chloroplasts
30 are precisely arranged within the membranes of flattened sacs called thylakoids. Thylakoids often lie close together in sacks called grana. The light reactions of photosynthesis take place within the thylakoid membranes, while the dark reactions take
35 place in the colorless matrix (stroma) surrounding the thylakoids.

Different wavelengths of light, especially red and blue light, are trapped by various pigment molecules contained within chloroplasts. When a
40 photon of light strikes a pigment molecule and is absorbed, the energy is transferred to an electron, which is raised to a high-energy state. A specialized form of chlorophyll passes the energized electron to an acceptor molecule, X, which has a high affinity
45 for electrons. X passes the electron to a series of acceptor molecules, each at a slightly lower energy

level. After being passed from molecule to molecule, the electron may return to the chlorophyll from which it started. Some of the energy released as
50 the electron is passed down the energy gradient is used to synthesize the compound ATP from ADP and inorganic phosphate.

ATP is a universal energy packet used by cells to do work. ATP is synthesized from
55 ADP and inorganic phosphate in a process called phosphorylation. Phosphorylation is a very high energy-demanding process. Cyclic photophosphorylation occurs when the energy used for ATP synthesis comes from light-energized
60 electrons as they are returned to the chlorophyll molecules from which they originated.

Another process that occurs in green plants is noncyclic photophosphorylation. In this reaction, some electrons are passed from the chlorophyll to a
65 different type of acceptor molecule called $NAPD_{ox}$, which retains the electron and is therefore reduced to become $NAPD_{re}$.

The ATP and $NAPD_{re}$ produced in the light reaction are used to reduce carbon dioxide to
70 carbohydrate in a series of reactions called the Calvin cycle (dark reaction). Basically, a five-carbon sugar, ribulose diphosphate (RuDP), is combined with CO_2. This process is called carboxylation. The products are then phosphorylated by ATP and
75 reduced by $NAPD_{re}$ to form PGAL, a three-carbon sugar.

Under certain conditions, the very same enzyme that under more agreeable conditions would facilitate its carboxylation oxidizes RuDP.
80 This process, called photorespiration, is seemingly a wasteful process since no ATP is created. Photorespiration predominates over photosynthesis when CO_2 levels are low and O_2 levels are high.

Some tropical angiosperm plants have a
85 unique leaf structure known as Kranz anatomy (C_4 plants). In Kranz plants, the bundle-sheath cells have numerous chloroplasts (other plants usually do not), and the mesophyll cells are clustered in a ring-like arrangement around the bundle sheath. These plants
90 can carry out photosynthesis under conditions of high temperature and concentrated light, when loss of water induces closure of the stomata. When the stomata close, the concentration of CO_2 in the air spaces inside the leaf falls, and the concentration of
95 O_2 rises. Under these conditions most plants (C_3) would experience a net loss of CO_2 because of photorespiration. Kranz plants (C_4) do not because

GO ON TO THE NEXT PAGE.

of their specialized way of initially fixing CO_2. They combine CO_2 with a three-carbon compound in the
100 mesophyll cells to form a four-carbon compound that passes into the bundle-sheath cells, where the CO_2 is regenerated. Therefore, Kranz plants can maintain a CO_2 level in the bundle-sheath cells that allows carboxylation of RuDP in the Calvin cycle to
105 predominate over its oxidation in photorespiration.

31. According to this passage, "the capacity for doing work" (lines 3–4) is the definition of:

    A. photosynthesis.
    B. energy.
    C. oxidation.
    D. thermodynamics.

32. In the equation in line 17, $C_6H_{12}O_6$ apparently names:

    F. oxygen.
    G. carbon dioxide.
    H. a sugar.
    J. photosynthesis.

33. Which of these could be considered the reverse of reduction?

    A. Oxidation
    B. Photosynthesis
    C. Transformation
    D. Phosphorylation

34. Which of the following conclusions is (are) suggested by the third paragraph?

    I.   Photosynthesis involves the addition of electrons.
    II. Photosynthesis involves action on hydrogen.
    III. Photosynthesis is a form of energy release.

    F. I only
    G. II only
    H. III only
    J. I and II only

35. The fifth paragraph deals mainly with:

    A. defining terms related to plant growth.
    B. comparing one reduction reaction to another.
    C. explaining the process of photosynthesis.
    D. expressing the author's opinion.

36. Which of the following statements is NOT true about ATP?

    F. It mixes with phosphate to make ADP.
    G. It is created through phosphorylation.
    H. It serves a purpose in the Calvin cycle.
    J. It is used by cells to do work.

37. The Calvin cycle involves:

    A. the combination of carbon dioxide and a five-carbon sugar, with a three-carbon sugar as the result.
    B. the combination of oxygen and a three-carbon sugar, with a five-carbon sugar as the result.
    C. a mix of ATP and sugar to create carbon dioxide.
    D. a reduction of carbohydrate to form carbon dioxide.

38. By "more agreeable conditions" (line 78), the author probably means:

    F. conditions that produce higher levels of oxygen.
    G. conditions that produce higher levels of CO_2.
    H. conditions with higher temperatures.
    J. conditions with longer growing periods.

39. Which of the following statements names a difference between photorespiration and photosynthesis?

    I.   Photorespiration involves RuDP.
    II. In photosynthesis, ATP is synthesized.
    III. Photorespiration is a reduction reaction.

    A. I only
    B. I and II only
    C. II and III only
    D. I, II, and III

GO ON TO THE NEXT PAGE.

40. Unlike the preceding paragraphs, the final paragraph discusses:

    F.   plants that do not photosynthesize.
    G. living matter other than plants.
    H. plants with an unusual structure.
    J.   plants that transform carbon dioxide into carbohydrate.

PRACTICE TEST I

4 4 4 4 4 4 4 4 4 4 4 4 4

SECTION 4: SCIENCE TEST
35 Minutes—40 Items

DIRECTIONS: Each passage below is followed by several items. After reading a passage, choose the best answer for each item. Fill in the corresponding oval on your bubble sheet. You may refer to the passage as often as necessary. You are NOT permitted the use of a calculator on this test. Answers are on page 276.

PASSAGE I

Alkanes are open-chain organic compounds that have the general chemical formula C_nH_{2n+2}. For example, propane has the following structural formula:

$$CH_3 — CH_2 — CH_3$$

For propane, $n = 3$ (the number of carbon atoms), and $2(3) + 2 = 8$ (the number of hydrogen atoms). The series of linked carbon atoms is called the carbon backbone of the compound, and the number of carbon atoms in the backbone gives the compounds their different names. Alkanes that differ by one carbon atom differ in molecular mass by 14u (one carbon atom of mass 12u and two hydrogen atoms of mass 1u each).

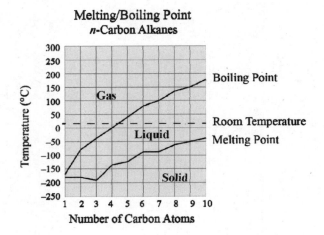

Melting/Boiling Point
n-Carbon Alkanes

Physical Properties of Straight-Chain Alkanes					
Name	# of Carbons	Boiling Point (°C)	Melting Point (°C)	Molecular Mass (atomic mass unit, u)	Flash Point (°C)	Density (g/cm³ at 290°C)
methane	1	−162	−183	16	–	0.466
ethane	2	−89	−183	30	–	0.572
propane	3	−42	−188	44	–	0.585
butane	4	0	−138	58	–	0.601
pentane	5	36	−130	72	−49	0.626
hexane	6	69	−95	86	−22	0.660
heptane	7	98	−91	100	−4	0.684
octane	8	126	−57	114	13	0.703
nonane	9	151	−54	128	31	0.718
decane	10	174	−30	142	46	0.730

GO ON TO THE NEXT PAGE.

1. According to the table, as the number of carbon atoms in the backbone of the alkane molecule increases, the:

    A. molecular mass decreases.
    B. boiling point increases.
    C. melting point decreases.
    D. density at 290°C decreases.

2. Which of the following is the structural formula for butane?

    F. $CH_3—CH_3—CH_3—CH_3$
    G. $CH_2—CH_3—CH_3—CH_2$
    H. $CH_3—CH_2—CH_2—CH_3$
    J. $CH_{12}—CH_{10}—CH_{10}—CH_{12}$

3. Considering the alkanes listed, if alkane X has a higher boiling point than alkane Y, then alkane X also has:

    A. a lower flash point.
    B. a lower molecular mass.
    C. more carbon atoms.
    D. fewer hydrogen atoms.

4. The alkane undecane has a backbone of 11 carbon atoms. What is the approximate molecular mass of the compound expressed in atomic mass units?

    F. 154
    G. 155
    H. 156
    J. 157

5. The alkane dodecane has a backbone of 12 carbon atoms. The compound has how many hydrogen atoms?

    A. 14
    B. 24
    C. 26
    D. 28

6. Which of the following is not a gas at room temperature?

    F. Methane
    G. Ethane
    H. Butane
    J. Hexane

7. Which of the following graphs most accurately depicts the density of the first ten alkanes as a function of the number of atoms in the carbon backbone in the alkanes?

A.

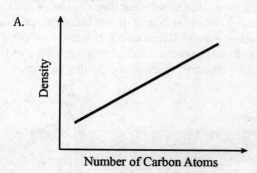

B.

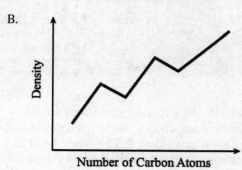

C.

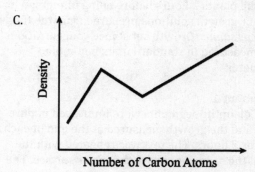

D.

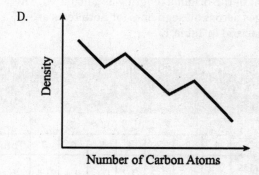

GO ON TO THE NEXT PAGE.

PASSAGE II

The protective sheath that covers the emerging shoot tip of monocotyledons, such as grasses, is called the coleoptile. Coleoptiles consist of specialized cells that do not divide but increase in size as they accumulate water. When the coleoptile pushes above the soil surface, it stops growing as the flag leaves emerge from it and continue to grow.

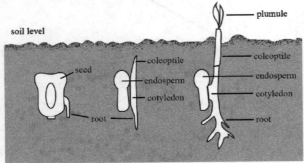

Figure 1

To study the impact of conditions on the growth rate of coleoptiles, *Avena* (oat) plants were grown in sand in the dark at 25°C and 85–90% relative humidity and harvested when 4 days old. Shoot tips 3 to 5 millimeters long were removed from the plants 2 hours before being immersed in water or growth solutions prepared from the fungus *Rhizopus suinus*. Growth substance concentrations were measured in standard units per cubic centimeter.

Experiment 1

Coleoptile segments were immersed in pure water and the growth measured at the end of each hour for 7 hours. The test was repeated with the tops of the segments above the water surface. The growth of each coleoptile segment per hour as a percent of the original length was calculated. The averages across all segments for both tests are summarized in Table 1.

Table 1: Growth of Coleoptile Segments in Water								
Average Growth per Hour as a Percentage of Original Length								
Test	End of Hour n							
	1	2	3	4	5	6	7	Total
1 (tops in water)	1.8	1.5	1.2	0.7	0.6	0.4	0.4	6.6
2 (tops in air)	2.5	2.5	4.0	4.3	4.7	3.3	–	21.3

The growth of the coleoptiles entirely immersed in water is attributable to a residuum of growth substance that remained after their removal from the plants. Those whose tops extended into the air produced additional growth substance.

Experiment 2

Coleoptile segments were submerged in growth substance solutions of varying concentrations and the growth was measured after 2, 4, and 24 hours. The cumulative growth of each coleoptile segment as a percentage of the original length was calculated after 2, 4, and 24 hours. The results are summarized in Table 2.

Table 2: Growth of Coleoptile Segments in Growth Substance Solutions			
Cumulative Growth			
Growth Substance Concentration (standard units per cm³)	End of Hour n		
	2	4	24
80	3.3	2.1	0.4
40	4.3	8.0	7.2
20	7.4	10.8	15.4
10	11.7	19.9	31.0
1	8.4	15.7	27.0
0.1	6.5	12.1	17.5
0.01	4.5	7.0	15.5
0	3.3	5.6	11.9

Coleoptiles in solutions of high concentrations of growth substance showed a shrinkage after 4 hours and, at the end of 24 hours, lost their turgidity due to a toxic effect of the high concentration of growth substance.

Experiment 3

The researchers theorized that either the action of the growth substance is a simple physical change of the cell wall or it depends on processes of a metabolic nature. If the action of the growth substance were a simple physical change, then it would not be affected by the presence of cyanide. If, however, it depends on metabolic processes, cyanide should inhibit the action of the growth substance. A series of tests were conducted to determine the impact of potassium cyanide (KCN) on the growth of coleoptile segments. Table 3 summarizes the results.

Table 3: Inhibition of Growth of Coleoptile Segments by KCN	
Solution	Total Percent Growth
Growth substance alone	23
Growth substance + 2×10^{-4} M KCN	5
Growth substance + 1×10^{-3} M KCN	2
Growth substance + 2×10^{-3} M KCN	-4
Growth substance + 2×10^{-2} M KCN	-3
Water + 2×10^{-2} M KCN	-4

8. The "flag leaves" referred to in the introductory paragraph of the passage correspond to which of the features shown in Figure 1?

    F. Plumule
    G. Endosperm
    H. Coyledon
    J. Root

9. According to the information provided, the greater growth rate recorded in Test 2 in Experiment 1 is explained by the:

    A. addition of growth substance to the water used to immerse the coleoptiles.
    B. production by the coleoptiles of additional growth substance following clipping.
    C. retention by the coleoptiles of growth substance already present in the plants.
    D. metabolism by the coleoptiles of a growth substance present in the air.

10. Which of the three experiments used water and no growth solution?

    F. Experiment 1 only
    G. Experiment 2 only
    H. Experiments 1 and 2 only
    J. Experiments 2 and 3 only

11. Which of the following graphs most accurately represents the average growth of the coleoptile segments as a percentage of original length for Test 1 in Experiment 1?

A.
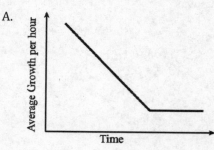

B.
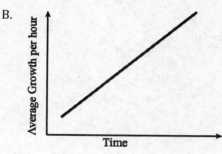

C.
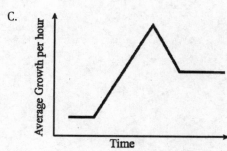

D.
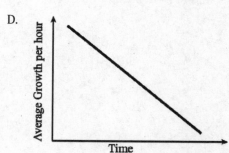

12. According to the data provided, the greatest growth of the coleoptile segments after 24 hours was for which concentration of growth substance in solution (in standard units per cubic centimeter)?

    F. 0
    G. 1
    H. 10
    J. 80

GO ON TO THE NEXT PAGE.

13. According to the data provided, the lowest concentration of growth substance in solution (in standard units per cubic centimeter) that showed any period of shrinkage of coleoptile segments was:

A   0
B.   1
C.   40
D.   80

14. The hypothesis that the action of the growth substance depends on metabolic processes is:

F.   disproved by the data in Table 3.
G.   weakened slightly by the data in Table 3.
H.   weakly supported by the data in Table 3.
J.   strongly supported by the data in Table 3.

GO ON TO THE NEXT PAGE.

PASSAGE III

Osmosis is the spontaneous movement of solvent molecules through a semi-permeable membrane into a region of higher solute concentration. The molecules move in the direction that tends to equalize solute concentration on both sides of the membrane.

Figure 1 shows a semi-permeable membrane between two sugar (sucrose) solutions of different concentrations. Osmosis occurs as the water molecules pass through the membrane to the side with higher sugar concentration. The sugar molecules, on the other hand, are too large to pass through the pore spaces in the semi-permeable membrane.

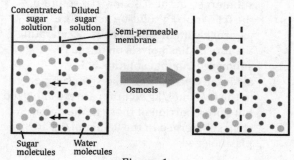

Figure 1

To observe the effect of osmosis, a group of students conducts experiments using plant tissues. In the experiments, the walls of the cells in the plant tissues function as the semi-permeable membrane separating regions of different solution concentrations.

Experiment 1

The students prepare shallow dishes with sugar solutions of varying concentrations. Using tweezers, the students gently pull off small strips of tissue, 3 to 10 millimeters in length and one cell layer thick, from the outer layer of an onion. Each strip is submerged in one of the prepared dishes.

After 45 minutes, the students mount the strips on slides and, using a microscope, examine the tissues for evidence of plasmolysis—the shrinkage of a cell's protoplasm and separation from the cell wall due to water loss from the cell. Forty to sixty-five cells from each onion strip are analyzed and scored as either plasmolyzed or not plasmolyzed. Any cells not clearly plasmolyzed are classified as not plasmolyzed. Table 1 summarizes the experimental results.

Table 1: Plasmolyzed Onion Cell Counts			
Sugar Solution Concentration (mol/kg)*	Number of Cells Analyzed	Number of Plasmolyzed Cells	Percentage of Plasmolyzed Cells
0.55	50	50	100
0.50	50	46	92.0
0.45	64	50	78.1
0.40	64	44	68.8
0.35	50	25	50.0
0.30	62	12	19.4
0.25	48	5	10.4
0.20	55	3	5.5
0.15	57	2	3.5
0.10	41	1	2.4
0.05	40	0	0.0
0.00	50	0	0.0

*moles of sugar per kilogram of water

Experiment 2

The students conduct a second experiment with beets. Beakers are prepared with sugar solutions of the same concentrations as in Experiment 1. Using an 8-millimeter diameter cork borer, cylinders of tissue are extracted from the beets. The tissue cylinders are sliced into disks approximately 3 millimeters thick. Each disk is weighed before being submerged in one of the prepared beakers.

After 75 minutes, the students extract, blot dry, and weigh each of the disks. The percentage of weight change in the disks are calculated. Table 2 summarizes the experimental results.

Table 2: Changes in Beet Tissue Weights			
Sugar Solution Concentration (mol/kg)	Original Weight (g)	Final Weight (g)	Percentage of Weight Change
0.55	2.865	2.460	−14.14
0.50	2.732	2.407	−11.90
0.45	2.807	2.666	−5.02
0.40	2.474	2.422	−2.10
0.35	3.101	3.152	+1.64
0.30	3.060	3.118	+1.90
0.25	2.549	2.642	+3.65
0.20	2.801	2.889	+3.50
0.15	2.357	2.428	+3.01
0.10	2.675	2.754	+2.95
0.05	2.413	2.528	+4.77
0.00	2.880	3.060	+6.25

GO ON TO THE NEXT PAGE.

15. In Experiment 1, osmosis proceeds due to the cell wall permitting:

    A.   sugar molecules but not water molecules to pass.

    B.   water molecules but not sugar molecules to pass.

    C.   neither sugar nor water molecules to pass.

    D.   certain water and certain sugar molecules to pass.

16. The purpose of Experiment 1 is to measure the:

    F.   solute concentrations of the solutions in which the onion strips are submerged.

    G.   quantity of water gained or lost by the onion cells due to osmosis.

    H.   number of cells plasmolyzed due to the effect of osmosis.

    J.   solute concentration threshold at which osmosis is triggered in onion cells submerged in a sugar solution.

17. Which of the following best explains why the students analyze 40 to 65 cells from each onion strip in Experiment 1?

    A.   The number of plasmolyzed cells in an onion strip ranges from 40 to 65 cells.

    B.   A sampling adequate to determine the effect of osmosis on onion cells requires 40 to 65 cells.

    C.   The average number of cells in an onion strip is 40 to 65 cells.

    D.   The unanalyzed cells of the onion strips do not show the effects of osmosis.

18. Which of the following best explains why no plasmolyzed cells are observed for the 0.05 mol/kg sugar solution?

    F.   The concentration of sugar inside the cells is greater than 0.05 mol/kg.

    G.   The concentration of sugar inside the cells is less than 0.05 mol/kg.

    H.   The concentration of sugar inside the cells is greater than 0.55 mol/kg.

    J.   The concentration of sugar inside the cells is less than 0.55 mol/kg.

19. The students identify the same number of plasmolyzed cells in both samples from the onion strips submerged in the 0.55 mol/kg and the 0.45 mol/kg sugar solutions yet calculate a value of "Percentage of Plasmolyzed Cells" of 100% for the 0.55 mol/kg solution but only 78.1% for the 0.45 mol/kg solution. This difference in percentage of plasmolyzed cells is due to the fact that:

    A.   the cells plasmolyzed by the 0.45 mol/kg solution are less completely depleted than those plasmolyzed by the 0.55 mol/kg solution.

    B.   the students analyzed 50 cells from the onion strip submerged in the 0.55 mol/kg solution and 64 cells from the onion strip submerged in the 0.45 mol/kg solution.

    C.   the 0.55 mol/kg solution acts more vigorously on the onion cells, accelerating the rate of plasmolysis on the cells submerged in that solution.

    D.   all of the cells in the onion strip submerged in the 0.45 mol/kg solution are plasmolyzed but only a portion of those in the onion strip submerged in the 0.55 mol/kg are are plasmolyzed.

20. Which of the following best explains the change in weight of the beet disk before and after submersion in the beaker containing the 0.00 mol/kg sugar solution?

    F.   The disk is dehydrated, causing it to absorb water while submerged in the solution.

    G.   The disk has a sugar concentration greater than 0.00 mol/kg of water, causing it to absorb water while submerged in the solution due to osmosis.

    H.   The disk has a sugar concentration less than 0.00 mol/kg of water and loses water while submerged in the solution due to osmosis.

    J.   No sugar molecules are available in the 0.00 mol/kg solution to migrate across the semi-permeable membranes of the cells in the beet disk.

GO ON TO THE NEXT PAGE.

21. Which of the following graphs best represents the percentage of weight change for the beet disks in Experiment 2?

A.

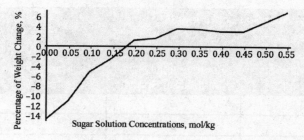

B.

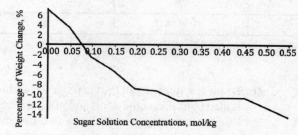

C.

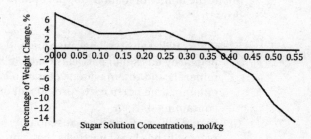

D.

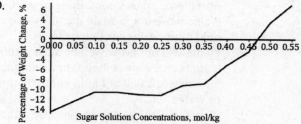

22. It can be inferred from the results of Experiment 2 that the average concentration of sugar per kilogram of water in the sampled beets is:

F. 0.45–0.50 moles.
G. 0.40–0.45 moles.
H. 0.35–0.40 moles.
J. 0.30–0.35 moles.

<u>PASSAGE IV</u>

The chart below shows various physical characteristics of soil components.

Physical Characteristics of Soil Components				
Soil Components	Diameter of Particles, d (μm)	Relative Ability* to Hold Positively Charged Minerals (Ca^{+2}, K^+, Mg^{+2})	Relative Ability* to Maintain Air Spaces	Relative Ability* to Retain Water
Clay	$d < 2$	1	4	1
Silt	$2 \leq d < 20$	2	3	2
Sand	$20 \leq d < 200$	3	2	3
Coarse Sand	$200 \leq d \leq 2{,}000$	4	1	4

*Relative abilities are rated from 1, indicating the most able, to 4, indicating the least able.

23. The soil type that is LEAST able to hold substances such as magnesium (Mg^{+2}) is:

A. sand.
B. coarse sand.
C. silt.
D. clay.

24. Based on the information in the chart, which of the following statements best describes the relationship between a soil's particle size and its other physical characteristics?

F. As particle size increases, the ability to hold positively charged minerals increases.
G. As particle size decreases, the ability to retain water decreases.
H. As particle size decreases, the ability to maintain air spaces increases.
J. As particle size increases, the ability to retain water decreases.

25. The size of particles in the soil type that is neither most able nor least able for any of the listed abilities must be:

A. less than 20 μm.
B. greater than or equal to 20 μm.
C. greater than or equal to 2 μm and less than 200 μm.
D. greater than or equal to 2 μm and less than or equal to 2,000 μm.

26. Loam is a type of soil that is mostly clay, but it also contains some sand and silt particles. Which prediction is most likely to be accurate about the ability of loam to support plant growth?

F. Plants will grow well because loam primarily has small particles that can hold minerals and retain water, yet it also has enough large particles to provide air spaces containing oxygen.
G. Plants will grow well because loam primarily has large particles that can provide air spaces containing oxygen, yet it also has enough small particles that can hold minerals and retain water.
H. Plants will not grow well because although loam is excellent at maintaining air spaces for oxygen, it will not hold enough minerals or water.
J. Plants will not grow well because although loam has enough minerals and air spaces for oxygen, it cannot retain enough water.

GO ON TO THE NEXT PAGE.

27. Based on the information provided in the chart, which of the following conclusions about soil types is NOT correct?

    A. Soils most able to retain water are also most able to hold positively charged minerals.
    B. No two soil types have the exact same combination of relative abilities.
    C. Clay and coarse sand are the soil types that are most different in every physical characteristic.
    D. No soil type is best for more than one category of relative ability.

PASSAGE V

Theory 1

The rate of a chemical reaction is defined as the number of moles of a specified product formed per unit of time. Reactants must collide in order for a reaction to occur. Therefore, at higher concentrations, the greater presence of particles increases the likelihood of effective collisions. For example, in the reaction: rate = $k[HCl]^2$, where k is the rate constant, and the exponents reflect the coefficients in front of the reactants in the reaction. The relationship between numbers of reactant particles and exponents in the rate law is a general one.

Theory 2

Theory 1 is sometimes true, for it expresses the reasonable insight that the greater the concentration of reactants, the greater the rate of a reaction. It has a great shortcoming, however, in its assumption that all reactions proceed in one fell swoop rather than in several skirmishes.

For example, let letters A and B stand for molecules. In the reaction $A + 2B \Rightarrow AB_2$, Theory 1 predicts a rate law as follows: rate = $k[A][B]^2$. However, if the reaction actually proceeds in two stages, the first one would be $A + B \Rightarrow AB$ (slow) and the second one would be $AB + B \Rightarrow AB_2$ (fast).

Thus, Theory 2 implies that one must understand the details of the reaction, including the relative speeds of the sub-reactions, in order to predict a rate law. For example, if in a three-stage reaction stage 1 and stage 2 are completed in seconds and stage 3 requires several hours to complete, then the reaction rate is primarily determined by the reaction rate of stage 3. Theory 1 is not completely wrong, just incomplete.

28. Theory 1 relates:

    F. reaction rate to the concentration of products.
    G. reaction rate to the concentration and coefficients of reactants.
    H. the relative amounts of products to one another.
    J. reaction rate to the individual rates of various stages of the reaction.

29. According to a proponent of Theory 2, Theory 1:

    A. can never give a correct prediction for a rate law.
    B. will give a correct result if the reactant coefficients are all equal to 1.
    C. will give a correct result only for a single-stage reaction.
    D. is in error because it claims that collisions are required for reactions to occur.

30. According to Theory 1, the rate of the reaction $3M + 2N \Rightarrow M_3N_2$ will be given by:

    F. $k[M][N]$.
    G. $k[M]^3[N]^2$.
    H. $k[M]^3[N]^2[P]^4$.
    J. $k([M]^3 + [N]^2)$.

31. A chemist studies the rate of the reaction $2NO_2 + F_2 \Rightarrow 2NO_2F$. According to Theory 1, the rate of the reaction is proportional to:

    A. the first power of $[NO_2]$ and the first power of F_2.
    B. the second power of $[NO_2]$ and the second power of $[NO_2F]$.
    C. the second power of $[NO_2]$ and the second power of $[F_2]$.
    D. the second power of $[NO_2]$ and the first power of $[F_2]$.

32. Supporters of Theory 2 would best be able to defend their positions if:

    F. they could show that a chemical reaction occurs in more than one stage.
    G. they could show that the rate of reaction speeds up with increasing concentration of products.
    H. they sped the reaction up with additional heat.
    J. they eliminated all collisions.

33. According to Theory 2, if in a two-stage reaction Stage 1 is much slower than Stage 2, then the overall reaction rate will be:

    A.   primarily determined by the rate of Stage 1.
    B.   primarily determined by the rate of Stage 2.
    C.   undeterminable unless all collisions are counted.
    D.   undeterminable unless the rate law is measured experimentally.

34. When discussing the rates of reactions that have more than one stage, Theory 2 would not be necessary if:

    F.   there were exactly two stages.
    G.   all stages had different rates.
    H.   the sum of the rates of each stage always equaled the rate of the reaction as a whole.
    J.   the sum of the rates of each stage was never equal to the rate of the reaction as a whole.

GO ON TO THE NEXT PAGE.

PASSAGE VI

Closely related species of butterflies are often found living in very different environments. A pair of experiments was performed in which butterfly species previously captured in either desert areas or mountain areas were tested in laboratory incubators to determine the conditions at which they could carry out important life functions such as mating, oviposition (egg-laying), and pupation (the stage in which the stationary cocoon undergoes its final development into an adult).

Experiment 1

Under conditions of 100% relative humidity (maximum moisture content of the air), 100 desert butterflies (Species D) and 100 mountain butterflies (Species M) were tested at temperature intervals of 2°C (from 0°C to 40°C) to determine if they could mate, oviposit, and pupate. Each species achieved at least 90% success at the following ranges of temperatures:

Table 1

	Temperature Ranges (°C)		
	Mating	Oviposition	Pupation
Species D	26–36	28–36	4–38
Species M	24–34	29–33	4–34

Experiment 2

The experiment was repeated at 50% relative humidity. Each species achieved at least 90% success at the following ranges of temperatures:

Table 2

	Temperature Ranges (°C)		
	Mating	Oviposition	Pupation
Species D	26–36	28–36	4–38
Species M	24–32	29–32	4–28

35. Results of Experiments 1 and 2 indicate that the life function with the narrowest range of temperature at which both species achieve 90% success is:

A. mating.
B. oviposition.
C. pupation.
D. different in Experiment 1 than it is in Experiment 2.

36. Which condition decreases the success of Species M in mating, oviposition, and pupation?

F. 100% relative humidity at low temperatures
G. 100% relative humidity at high temperatures
H. 50% relative humidity at low temperatures
J. 50% relative humidity at high temperatures

37. A third experiment was conducted at 100% relative humidity in which the temperature range for caterpillar survival (another life function) was tested in Species D and Species M. Species D achieved 90% success at 12–36 (°C), while Species M achieved 90% success at 8–30 (°C). Which temperature range is a good prediction of caterpillar survival in Species D at 50% relative humidity?

A. 8°C–30°C
B. 8°C–24°C
C. 12°C–36°C
D. 12°C–30°C

38. If an investigator wanted to set up an experiment to determine the effects of light and dark on mating ability in Species D and Species M at 100% relative humidity, which set of conditions would provide the most complete results?

F. Test both species at 20°C in the light and 20°C in the dark.
G. Test both species at 30°C in the light and 30°C in the dark.
H. Test both species at 34°C in the light and 34°C in the dark.
J. Test both species at 34°C in the light and 30°C in the dark.

GO ON TO THE NEXT PAGE.

39. Which hypothesis is NOT supported by the results of Experiment 1 and Experiment 2?

A. For all tested life functions, 50% relative humidity only affects Species M at the high end of its temperature ranges.

B. For all tested life functions, 50% relative humidity has no effect on the temperature ranges of the desert species.

C. Species D does better than Species M at high temperatures in all tested life functions.

D. Species M does better than Species D at low temperatures for pupation.

40. Which of the following statements best explains the broad range of temperatures for pupation observed in both butterfly species?

F. Since the cocoon is stationary, it must be able to survive changing temperature conditions until the adult butterfly emerges.

G. Deserts can get very hot and mountains can get very cold.

H. Mountain butterflies would not survive long in the desert, and desert butterflies would not survive long in the mountains.

J. The stationary cocoon must be able to survive under light and dark conditions until the adult butterfly emerges.

PRACTICE TEST I

5 5 5 5 5 5 5 5 5 5 5 5 5

SECTION 5: WRITING TEST (OPTIONAL)
40 Minutes—1 Essay Prompt

DIRECTIONS: You have 40 minutes to plan and write an essay. Read the prompt carefully and make sure you understand the instructions. A successful essay will have the following features: it will take a position on the issue presented in the writing prompt; it will maintain a consistent focus on the topic; it will use logical reasoning and provide supporting ideas; it will present ideas in an organized manner; and, finally, it will include clear and effective language in accordance with the conventions of standard written English. Sample essay responses begin on page 280.

I - intro
II - op 1 — 5 paragraph essay
III - op 2 — want your opinion
IV - op 3
V - conc.

Plastic Bag Use

Some countries and states have banned free plastic bags at grocery stores because of the environmental problems they cause. Plastic bags worsen communities' litter problems and can suffocate animals that come into contact with them. Some bags are also non-biodegradable and accumulate in landfills. Because of these environmental risks, some governments have required stores to sell paper or reusable bags to customers, instead of providing plastic bags for free. However, some argue that banning bags is impractical and would inconvenience customers. As more cities and states debate whether to ban free plastic bags, this issue will potentially affect millions of shoppers.

Perspective 1	Perspective 2	Perspective 3
It is impractical to ban free plastic bags in stores, and it will inconvenience shoppers who forget to bring reusable bags with them. Plastic bags can also be reused as trash bags at home.	Free plastic bags should be banned, but stores should have more paper or more durable plastic bags available for sale. Having to pay for bags will encourage shoppers to reuse them, either at home or on their next shopping trip.	Plastic bags should be banned at all stores, and shoppers should either buy recyclable paper bags or bring their own reusable bags. Although this may initially annoy consumers, the environmental risks outweigh the convenience of free plastic bags.

Essay Task

Write a unified, coherent essay in which you evaluate multiple perspectives on the issue of plastic bag use in grocery stores. In your essay be sure to:

- Analyze and evaluate perspectives given
- State and develop your own perspective
- Explain the relationship between your perspective and those given

Your perspective may be in full agreement with any of the others, in partial agreement, or wholly different. Whatever the case, support your ideas with logical reasoning and detailed, persuasive examples.

PRACTICE TEST II

DIRECTIONS

Practice Test II includes five subject tests: English, Mathematics, Reading, Science, and Writing. Calculator use is permitted on the Mathematics Test only.

Cambridge offers several services for schools utilizing our practice tests. Ask your teacher whether your school has decided to send your answers to Cambridge for scoring or to score your answers at your school. If Cambridge is scoring your test, you will use a Scantron™ form provided by your teacher, or you will enter your answers online. If your school is scoring your test, you may use a Scantron™ form provided by your teacher, or you may write your answers on paper.

If you are entering your test answers on a Scantron™ form, please be sure to include the following information on the Scantron™:

Book and Edition	*Victory for the ACT Test, 14th Edition*
Practice Test Number	**Practice Test II**

If you are only completing a single section of this practice test, make sure to also include the following information:

Subject	English, Mathematics, Reading or Science
Section Number	**Section 1, 2, 3 or 4**

The items in each multiple-choice test are numbered and the answer choices are lettered. The Scantron™ form has numbered rows that correspond to the items on the test. Each row contains lettered ovals to match the answer choices for each item on the test. Each numbered row has a corresponding item on the test.

For each item, first decide on the best answer choice. Then, locate the row number that corresponds to the item. Next, find the oval in that row that matches the letter of the chosen answer. Then, use a soft lead pencil to fill in the oval. DO NOT use a ballpoint pen.

Mark only one answer for each item. If you change your mind about an answer choice, thoroughly erase your first mark before marking your new answer.

Note that only responses marked on your Scantron™ form or written on your paper will be scored. Your score on each test will be based only on the number of items that are correctly answered during the time allowed for that test. You will not be penalized for guessing. Therefore, it is to your best advantage to answer every item on the test, even if you must guess.

On the Writing Test, write your response to the prompt using the essay response sheets or loose-leaf paper provided by your teacher. Your teacher might also direct you to enter your essay response online. (Note that the Writing Test is optional.)

You may work on each test only during the time allowed for that test. If you finish a test before time is called, use the time to review your answer choices or work on items about which you are uncertain. You may not return to a test on which time has already been called, and you may not preview another test. You must lay down your pencil immediately when time is called at the end of each test. You may not for any reason fill in or alter ovals for a test after time has expired for that test. Violation of these rules will result in immediate disqualification from the exam.

GO ON TO THE NEXT PAGE.

SECTION 1: ENGLISH TEST
45 Minutes—75 Items

DIRECTIONS: In the passages below, certain parts of the sentences have been underlined and numbered. In the right-hand column, you will find different ways of writing each underlined part; the original version is indicated by the "NO CHANGE" option. For each item, select the choice that best expresses the intended idea, is most acceptable in standard written English, or is most consistent with the overall tone and style of the passage.

There are also items that ask about a section of the passage or the passage as a whole. These items do not refer to an underlined portion of the passage; these items are preceded by statements that are enclosed in boxes.

Read the passage through once before you begin to answer the accompanying items. Finding the answers to certain items may depend on looking at material that appears several sentences beyond the item. So, be sure that you have read far enough ahead before you select your answer choice. Answers are on page 286.

<u>PASSAGE I</u>

The Philosophy of Botany

[1]

Botany is surely <u>the more gentler of</u> sciences.
                        1
The careful observation of a flower is a calm,

1. A. NO CHANGE
   B. the most gentle of
   C. the gentler of
   D. the gentlest in the

<u>ostentatious</u> action—the peaceful contemplation of a
   2

2. F. NO CHANGE
   G. unobtrusive
   H. violent
   J. chaotic

beautiful object. Reduced to its <u>essentials, it</u> requires
                                        3

3. A. NO CHANGE
   B. essentials; it
   C. essentials, botany
   D. essentials; botany

no laboratory <u>and the natural world is needed</u>, a few
                        4
tools, and the naked eye. Botany in its most scientific

4. F. NO CHANGE
   G. but you do need the natural world
   H. but the natural world
   J. but the natural world is necessary

GO ON TO THE NEXT PAGE.

or purest form <u>consists about</u> seeking to know
5
more about the plant simply for the sake of that

knowledge. Plants have not always been regarded as

worthy <u>of knowing</u> or studying in and of themselves,
6
not on their merits as sources of food or drugs but

as life-forms. In fact, the history of botany can be

viewed in terms of repeated rediscoveries of this one

theme—that plants are worthy of analysis <u>in and
7
of themselves</u>, quite apart from any use they might
7
have for mankind.

5. A. NO CHANGE
   B. consists of
   C. consists in
   D. consist of

6. F. NO CHANGE
   G. for knowledge
   H. of knowledge
   J. to know

7. A. NO CHANGE
   B. by themselves
   C. themselves
   D. by and for themselves

[2]

[8] The practical motives behind plant study

8. Beginning Paragraph 2 with which of the following might make the transition from Paragraph 1 to Paragraph 2 clearer?

   F. Since
   G. Heretofore
   H. However,
   J. Hence

should not be <u>disparaging—the</u> bulk of our medical
9
history, for instance, is made up of accounts of herbal

remedies. <u>Nonetheless,</u> the study of the medicinal
10
properties of plants contained a self-limiting

mechanism: if a plant seemed to have no utilitarian

value, it was disregarded, and no further study of it

<u>is made</u>. The Renaissance attitude towards nature
11
changed this overly practical bent and initiated the

scientific study of plants.

9. A. NO CHANGE
   B. disparaged—the bulk
   C. disparaged; the bulk
   D. disparaging, the bulk

10. F. NO CHANGE
    G. Consequently
    H. Thus
    J. Moreover

11. A. NO CHANGE
    B. had been made
    C. was made
    D. were made

GO ON TO THE NEXT PAGE.

[3]

Botany, as a pure science, has certain characteristics and makes certain assumptions that prove thought provoking and interesting. One of its unspoken or basic assumptions is an implicit
12
respect and regard for all living things. The botanist

who studies a plant's structure or tries to have
13
understood their functions confronts nature on its
13
own terms. Investigations of how a plant grows or reproduces, as well as studies of the purposefulness of a flower's coloration and structure, is self-
14

validating: the botanist studies the flower because it
15
exists; and because it exists, it is worthy of study.
15

12. F. NO CHANGE
    G. because
    H. and thus
    J. yet

13. A. NO CHANGE
    B. to understand its
    C. understanding their
    D. having understood its

14. F. NO CHANGE
    G. are
    H. being
    J. OMIT the underlined portion.

15. The distinction drawn in the underlined portion of the last sentence of the passage echoes which of the following points made earlier in the passage?

    A. The careful observation of a flower is a calm . . . action—the peaceful contemplation of a beautiful object
    B. . . . plants are worthy of analysis . . . quite apart from any use they might have for mankind
    C. . . . the bulk of our medical history, for instance, is made up of accounts of herbal remedies
    D. . . . the study of the medicinal properties of plants contained a self-limiting mechanism: if a plant seemed to have no utilitarian value, it was disregarded

Poverty in America

The main characteristic of poverty is, <u>of course</u>,
16
lack of money. A family is defined as poor when its

16. The use of the phrase "of course" is:

   F. appropriate because it is not obvious that someone who is poor lacks money.
   G. appropriate because it disrupts the flow of the sentence.
   H. appropriate because someone who is poor obviously lacks money.
   J. questionable since someone might be poor in spirit.

annual income <u>falls below a certain dollar amount,</u>
17
calculated by the US Federal Government to be

17. A. NO CHANGE
   B. falls and is under a certain dollar amount,
   C. is under a certain specified dollar amount,
   D. OMIT the underlined portion.

the minimum a family of <u>their</u> size would need to
18
maintain a minimally decent standard of living. In

18. F. NO CHANGE
   G. there
   H. its
   J. it's

certain areas of rural America, <u>consequently,</u> poverty
19
is the rule rather than the exception. As many as

19. A. NO CHANGE
   B. and therefore, as a result of this,
   C. moreover, due to this fact,
   D. OMIT the underlined portion.

50 percent of the families may earn <u>less than</u> the
20
poverty level, and some may manage to subsist

somehow on amounts even less than half the official

poverty level income. ☐21

20. F. NO CHANGE
   G. lower than
   H. less as
   J. lower as

21. The first paragraph provides which of the following?

   A. An argument
   B. A comparison
   C. A definition
   D. A narrative

<u>Although</u> lack of money is the defining
22
characteristic of poverty, poverty is more than

simply lack of money. Poverty is an entire complex

of symptoms. Low levels of formal schooling among

22. F. NO CHANGE
   G. (Do NOT begin a new paragraph) Although
   H. Since
   J. (Do NOT begin a new paragraph) Since

GO ON TO THE NEXT PAGE.

adults <u>parallel</u> low-income levels. Additionally, in
23
families below the poverty level, the number of

children and elderly who depend on those who work

is, in general, higher than the national average for all

families. <u>As a consequence</u>, fewer workers support a
24
greater number of non-workers than in other, more

prosperous families.

Often, the schooling provided in low-income

areas <u>are as inadequate like incomes</u>. In particular,
25
rural children get poorer schooling than city

children, and many rural poor are severely

handicapped by <u>it</u>. The general rural average is
26
only 8.8 years of school completed. Moreover, low

educational levels seem to <u>just keep repeating and
27
repeating themselves</u>. If the head of a rural poor
27

family <u>have</u> little schooling, the children are often
28
handicapped in their efforts to get an education. It is

especially difficult for people who are handicapped

educationally to acquire new skills, get new jobs, or

otherwise adjust to an increasingly urbanized society.

This is as true on the farm <u>rather than</u> in urban
29

industry, since modern farming <u>of the present day</u>
30

23. A. NO CHANGE
    B. go along with
    C. are a lot like
    D. very often go together with

24. F. NO CHANGE
    G. However
    H. Surprisingly
    J. Fortunately

25. A. NO CHANGE
    B. is—like family income, inadequate
    C. is so inadequate as family income
    D. is, like family income, inadequate

26. F. NO CHANGE
    G. education
    H. their education
    J. their lack of education

27. A. NO CHANGE
    B. be self-perpetuating of themselves
    C. be self-perpetuating
    D. cause the same thing to happen all over
        again

28. F. NO CHANGE
    G. have had
    H. has had
    J. was to have

29. A. NO CHANGE
    B. rather as
    C. as they are
    D. as it is

30. F. NO CHANGE
    G. of the present
    H. presently
    J. OMIT the underlined portion.

GO ON TO THE NEXT PAGE.

requires skills that <u>poor educated</u> people lack.
                          31

Lacking in education, the rural poor either take low-

paying jobs on the farm or elsewhere in rural areas

or swell the ranks of the unemployed or under-

employed.

31. A. NO CHANGE
    B. poorly educated
    C. educated poor
    D. poor education

Item #32 asks about the preceding passage as a whole.

---

32. The author does NOT use which of the following in the development of the essay?

    F. Definitions
    G. Personal experience
    H. Statistics
    J. Explanation

PASSAGE III

School Dropouts

One out of every four children who entered the

fifth grade in the fall of 1966 <u>fail to graduate</u> with his
                                      33

or her class. The total number <u>that should of</u>
                                    34

graduated was 4.1 million, but approximately

900,000 fell by the wayside.

Those who do not make it are called school

dropouts. (Official statistics define a dropout as a

person who has not yet attained the age of 16

and leaves school before graduation for any

reason except transfer.) School officials who

work with dropouts <u>who leave school</u> say a student
                        35

33. A. NO CHANGE
    B. failed to graduate
    C. failed graduation
    D. fails to graduate

34. F. NO CHANGE
    G. that should of been
    H. who should of
    J. who should have

35. A. NO CHANGE
    B. who have left school
    C. who are leaving school
    D. OMIT the underlined portion.

GO ON TO THE NEXT PAGE.

will usually starting thinking about dropping out
36

about two years before he or she ceases to attend

school: roughly at age 14. Absenteeism, class cutting,
37

lack of motivation, and lack of interest in school

is often early signs of the potential dropout. Also,
38   39

many students drop out mentally very early in their

school career, despite their physical presence until

graduation.

The dropout is most often a boy who mostly,
40

frequently leaves school at the age of 16 while in
40

the tenth grade. He is most likely than those who
41

stay in school to score low on an intelligence test

and is likely to be failing in school at the time of him
42

dropping out. Yet most dropouts are really not less
42   43

bright than students who remain in school until
43

graduation. The dropout typically comes from the

lower-income class and most often leaves school

for financial reasons. His absences from school

---

36. F. NO CHANGE
  G. usually will be starting thinking
  H. starts usually thinking
  J. usually starts to think

37. A. NO CHANGE
  B. school but roughly
  C. school and roughly
  D. school, roughly

38. F. NO CHANGE
  G. is oftentimes
  H. are often
  J. were often

39. A. NO CHANGE
  B. dropout also
  C. dropout
  D. dropout but also

40. F. NO CHANGE
  G. frequently and often
  H. frequently
  J. sometimes often

41. A. NO CHANGE
  B. more likely than those
  C. most likely as one
  D. more likely than one

42. F. NO CHANGE
  G. he drops out
  H. of his having dropped out
  J. he dropped out

43. A. NO CHANGE
  B. really they are no less bright than are the students who remain
  C. are, than the students who remain, really no less bright
  D. than the students who remain are really no less bright

GO ON TO THE NEXT PAGE.

<u>increasing noticeably</u> during the eighth grade and

44

he participates little <u>or none</u> in extra-curricular

45
activities. The reasons a student drops out of school

<u>goes deeper as</u> a mere desire to be rid of school.

46
Dropping out is a symptom; the roots of the problem

are usually below the surface. 47

44. F.　NO CHANGE

　　G.　increase so that

　　H.　increase noticeably

　　J.　increased to the point where it was noticed

45. A.　NO CHANGE

　　B.　and not at all

　　C.　or not much

　　D.　or not at all

46. F.　NO CHANGE

　　G.　go more deeply than

　　H.　go deeper as

　　J.　go deeper than

47. A logical continuation of the essay would be a discussion of:

　　A.　the financial reasons a student might leave school.

　　B.　a student's lack of motivation.

　　C.　possible extracurricular activities.

　　D.　why students might drop out of school.

> Item #48 asks about the preceding passage as a whole.

48. Is the use of the official definition of dropout in the second paragraph appropriate?

　　F.　Yes, because without a definition, the article would not be understandable.

　　G.　Yes, because the nature of a "dropout" is one of the central themes of the passage.

　　H.　No, because the definition has nothing to do with what the author is discussing in the second paragraph.

　　J.　No, because the author then redefines the word.

GO ON TO THE NEXT PAGE.

PASSAGE IV

Wind Machines

The idea of generating electricity with wind power is not new. But the kind of attention that idea is getting today, in terms of research and <u>development, are</u> both new and encouraging to
49

planners looking for renewable energy sources

<u>satisfying</u> growing national demands. An effort
50

is being made in the United States to use one of humankind's oldest energy sources to solve one of <u>its</u> most modern <u>problems, to find</u> reliable and
51   52

cost-effective ways to harness the wind to produce electricity.

Wind machines are not the simple devices <u>that</u>
53

<u>they may be appearing to be,</u> and the lessons they
53

teach seldom come easy. <u>On the other hand,</u> the
54

potential reward to a nation that needs more energy from a renewable source is beyond calculation.

Rewards for using wind power <u>have been gathered</u>
55

by civilizations and cultures since early in recorded history.

49. A. NO CHANGE
    B. development, is
    C. developing, is
    D. development are

50. F. NO CHANGE
    G. that would have satisfied
    H. to satisfy
    J. with the satisfaction of

51. A. NO CHANGE
    B. their
    C. it's
    D. your

52. F. NO CHANGE
    G. problems: to find
    H. problems, finding
    J. problems. To find

53. A. NO CHANGE
    B. they may be
    C. it may seem to be
    D. they may appear to be

54. F. NO CHANGE
    G. Therefore,
    H. As a consequence
    J. This means that

55. A. NO CHANGE
    B. has been gathering
    C. is gathering
    D. will have been gathered

GO ON TO THE NEXT PAGE.

No record survives of the earliest wind machine. It <u>may have been built</u> in China more than
56
three thousand years ago. It may have been built on the windy plains of Afghanistan. History hints at some sort of wind power used in the Pharaoh's Egypt <u>for the drawing of water</u> for agriculture,
57
long before the birth of Christ. Hammurabi may have taken time out from developing a legal code about 2,000 BCE to sponsor development of some sort of wind machine. The earliest confirmed wind machines are in that same region. Persian writers described gardens <u>irrigated through the means</u>
58
<u>of</u> wind-driven water <u>lifts several</u> centuries BCE.
58   **59**

Ultimately, <u>we can only guess at the origin of the</u>
60
<u>windmill.</u>
60

<u>Persian machines were horizontal devices,</u>
61
carousel-like contraptions that revolved around a center pole and caught the wind with bundles of

56. F. NO CHANGE
    G. may have been
    H. was being built
    J. has been building

57. A. NO CHANGE
    B. to draw water
    C. in order that water be drawn
    D. in order to draw water

58. F. NO CHANGE
    G. irrigated by means of
    H. which were then irrigated by means of
    J. irrigated by

59. A. NO CHANGE
    B. lifts several,
    C. lifts but several
    D. lifts and several

60. F. NO CHANGE
    G. the origin of the windmill can only be guessed at
    H. the origin of the windmill can only be guessed at by us
    J. the origin of the windmill could only be guessed at

61. A. NO CHANGE
    B. (Do NOT begin a new paragraph) Persian machines were horizontal devices,
    C. Since Persian machines were
    D. It was discovered that Persian machines were horizontal devices,

GO ON TO THE NEXT PAGE.

reeds. The carousel is perhaps the <u>more simple</u>

<u>design for capturing</u> the wind; it cares nothing for
62

the direction of the breeze, but revolves no matter

where on the compass the wind may originate. From

the Middle East, wind-machine technology may

have been carried to Europe by returning Crusaders.

Accurate records do not exist, but soon after the

Crusades, windmills appeared in northern Europe

and soon were found on the British Isles.

    For a while, windmills flourished in Europe, but

with the advent of steam power, they <u>come close to</u>
63

extinction, for the wind is <u>real iffy</u>. It can fail to blow
64

just when it is needed the most, or it can <u>rage into a</u>
65

<u>gale</u> when it is not needed at all.
65

62. F. NO CHANGE
    G. most simplest design for capturing
    H. simpler design to capture
    J. simplest design for capturing

63. A. NO CHANGE
    B. came close to
    C. are coming closer to
    D. come close upon

64. F. NO CHANGE
    G. likely to blow sometimes and not to others
    H. here today and gone tomorrow
    J. capricious

65. The author's use of the phrase "rage into a gale" is:

    A. inappropriate because images are out of place in scientific writing.
    B. inappropriate because wind is sometimes calm.
    C. appropriate because it creates a vivid image.
    D. appropriate because it minimizes the importance of weather.

PASSAGE V

The Development of Television Programming

    Television and its programs do not just happen.

<u>It is</u> planned products of a huge, wealthy, and highly
66

competitive commercial enterprise. The television

industry, which includes stations, networks,

66. F. NO CHANGE
    G. They are
    H. They would be
    J. It was

GO ON TO THE NEXT PAGE.

production companies, actors, and <u>writers, are</u>
₆₇
responsible for selecting, creating, and distributing

programs. The three most popular programs are the

<u>episodic series, the</u> made-for-television movie, and
₆₈
the mini-series.

    In the 1970s, the episodic series, both dramatic

and comic, <u>was the most</u> popular of these. <u>With the</u>
₆₉   ₇₀
<u>advent</u> of cable and pay television and of video disks
₇₀

and tapes, the television movie <u>is rapidly gaining in</u>
₇₁

popularity. The past ten years <u>have seen</u> several
₇₂
changes in television drama. The action-adventure

police drama has lost and the situation comedy <u>has</u>
₇₃
<u>grew</u> in popularity. Topics previously considered
₇₃

taboo have <u>emerged. Unmarried</u> couples living
₇₄
together, divorce, and single parents. Even topics

that are <u>politically controversy</u> can now be the focus
₇₅
of programs.

67. A. NO CHANGE
    B. writers, is
    C. writers are
    D. writers—is

68. F. NO CHANGE
    G. episodic series the
    H. episodic, series the
    J. episodic series the,

69. A. NO CHANGE
    B. was the more
    C. were the most
    D. were the more

70. F. NO CHANGE
    G. Including the advent
    H. Notwithstanding the advent
    J. With the beginning of the advent

71. A. NO CHANGE
    B. has rapidly gained in
    C. is rapidly gaining
    D. will rapidly gain in

72. F. NO CHANGE
    G. see
    H. will see
    J. would be seeing

73. A. NO CHANGE
    B. has grown
    C. grew
    D. grow

74. F. NO CHANGE
    G. emerged, unmarried
    H. emerged unmarried
    J. emerged: unmarried

75. A. NO CHANGE
    B. politically controversial
    C. politics controversy
    D. political controversy

END OF TEST 1
STOP! DO NOT TURN THE PAGE UNTIL TOLD TO DO SO.

NO TEST MATERIAL ON THIS PAGE

SECTION 2: MATHEMATICS TEST
60 Minutes—60 Items

DIRECTIONS: Solve each item and choose the correct answer choice. Then, fill in the corresponding oval on the bubble sheet.

Allocate time wisely. Try to solve as many items as possible, returning to skipped items if time permits.

Calculator use is permitted on this test; however, some items are best solved without the use of a calculator.

NOTE: All of the following should be assumed, unless otherwise stated.

1. Illustrative figures are NOT necessarily drawn to scale.
2. The word *average* indicates arithmetic mean.
3. The word *line* indicates a straight line.
4. Geometric figures lie in a plane.

Answers are on page 293.

1. $121,212 + (2 \times 10^4) = ?$

DO YOUR FIGURING HERE.

   A. 121,232
   B. 121,412
   C. 123,212
   D. 141,212
   E. 312,212

2. If $6x + 3 = 21$, then $2x + 1 = ?$

   F. 1
   G. 2
   H. 3
   J. 6
   K. 7

3. At a recreation center, it costs $3 per hour to rent a ping pong table and $12 per hour to rent a bowling lane. At the same cost as renting a bowling lane for 2 hours, for how many hours is it possible to rent a ping pong table?

   A. 4
   B. 6
   C. 8
   D. 18
   E. 36

GO ON TO THE NEXT PAGE.

4. If $q, r, s,$ and t are natural numbers and $q < r < s < t$, which of the following *could* be true?

   F. $r = r + s$
   G. $q = s + t$
   H. $q + r = s + t$
   J. $q + r + t = s$
   K. $q + t = r + s$

5. Which of the following is greater than $\frac{1}{2}$?

   A. $\dfrac{6}{11}$

   B. $\dfrac{9}{19}$

   C. $\dfrac{7}{15}$

   D. $\dfrac{4}{9}$

   E. $\dfrac{3}{7}$

6. Out of a group of 360 students, exactly 18 are on the track team. What percentage of the students are on the track team?

   F.   5%
   G. 10%
   H. 12%
   J.   20%
   K. 25%

7. In the figure below, 3 lines intersect as shown. Which of the following *must* be true?

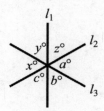

   I. $a = x$
   II. $y + z = b + c$
   III. $x + a = y + b$

   A. I only
   B. II only
   C. I and II only
   D. I and III only
   E. I, II, and III

DO YOUR FIGURING HERE.

GO ON TO THE NEXT PAGE.

8. In the figure below, $x = ?$

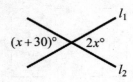

DO YOUR FIGURING HERE.

F. 15
G. 30
H. 45
J. 60
K. 90

9. Which of the following is the prime factorization of 60?

A. (2)(3)(10)
B. (3)(4)(5)
C. (2)(2)(3)(5)
D. (2)(2)(3)(6)
E. (3)(3)(3)(5)

10. The average height of 4 buildings is 20 meters. If 3 of the buildings are each 16 meters tall, what is the height, in meters, of the fourth building?

F. 32
G. 28
H. 24
J. 22
K. 18

11. In the figure below, $x = ?$

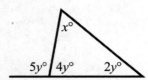

A. 15
B. 20
C. 30
D. 45
E. 60

GO ON TO THE NEXT PAGE.

12. In the figure below, what is the length of $\overline{PQ}$?

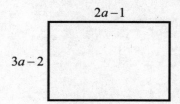

F. 0.09
G. 0.11
H. 0.12
J. 0.13
K. 0.16

13. What is the perimeter of the rectangle below?

$$2a-1$$

$$3a-2$$

A. $10a-6$
B. $10a-3$
C. $6a-3$
D. $5a-6$
E. $5a-3$

14. If the average of x, x, x, 56, and 58 is 51, then $x = ?$

F. 43
G. 47
H. 49
J. 51
K. 53

15. How many integers can x be if $-2 \leq 2x \leq 2$?

A. One
B. Two
C. Three
D. Four
E. Five

GO ON TO THE NEXT PAGE.

DO YOUR FIGURING HERE.

16. For all real numbers x, 8^x equals which of the following?

DO YOUR FIGURING HERE.

    F. $8x$

    G. x^8

    H. 2^{2x}

    J. $x^{\frac{2}{3}}$

    K. 2^{3x}

17. What is the sum of the areas, in square centimeters, of 2 squares with side lengths of 2 centimeters and 3 centimeters, respectively?

    A.   1

    B.   5

    C.   13

    D.   25

    E.   36

18. If the rectangular solid shown below has a volume of 54 cubic inches, what is the value of x, in inches?

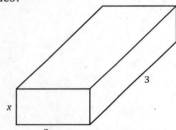

    F.   2

    G.   3

    H.   6

    J.   9

    K.   12

19. If x is 80% of y, then y is what percentage of x?

    A. $133\frac{1}{3}\%$

    B.   125%

    C.   120%

    D.   90%

    E.   80%

GO ON TO THE NEXT PAGE.

20. From which of the following statements can it be deduced that $m > n$?

DO YOUR FIGURING HERE.

    F. $m + 1 = n$
    G. $2m = n$
    H. $m + n > 0$
    J. $m - n > 0$
    K. $mn > 0$

21. If $f(x) = x^2 + x$, then what is the value of $f(f(2))$?

    A. 42
    B. 38
    C. 32
    D. 18
    E.   4

22. The circle below with center O has a radius with a length of 2. If the total area of the shaded regions is 3π, then $x = ?$

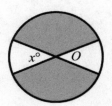

    F.   270
    G. 180
    H. 120
    J.   90
    K.   45

23. If a bar of metal alloy consists of 100 grams of tin and 150 grams of lead, what percentage of the entire bar, by weight, is tin?

    A. 10 %
    B. 15 %
    C. $33\frac{1}{3}$ %
    D. 40 %
    E. $66\frac{2}{3}$ %

GO ON TO THE NEXT PAGE.

DO YOUR FIGURING HERE.

24. If $\dfrac{1}{x} + \dfrac{1}{y} = \dfrac{1}{z}$, then $z = ?$

    F. $\dfrac{1}{xy}$

    G. xy

    H. $\dfrac{x+y}{xy}$

    J. $\dfrac{xy}{x+y}$

    K. $\dfrac{2xy}{x+y}$

25. $|-5| + |-12| - |-2| + (-6) = ?$

    A. 2
    B. 3
    C. 6
    D. 9
    E. 14

26. If the average of $2x$, $2x + 1$, and $2x + 2$ is $x - 1$, which of the following equations could be used to determine the value of x?

    F. $6x + 3 = x - 1$
    G. $6x + 3 = 3(x - 1)$
    H. $3(6x + 3) = x - 1$
    J. $(6x + 3) + (x - 1) = 3$
    K. $(6x + 3)(x - 1) = 3$

27. Participants in a community service project purchase boxes of candy for $1 each and sell them for $2 each. If no other expenses are incurred, how many boxes of candy must they sell to earn a net profit of $500?

    A. 250
    B. 500
    C. 1,000
    D. 1,500
    E. 2,000

28. $(-2)^2 - (-2)^3 = ?$

    F. 16
    G. 12
    H. 2
    J. -2
    K. -8

DO YOUR FIGURING HERE.

29. The sum, the product, and the average of 3 different integers are equal. If 2 of the integers are x and $-x$, the third integer is:

   A. $\dfrac{x}{2}$
   B. $2x$
   C. -1
   D. 0
   E. 1

30. In a school with a total enrollment of 360, 90 students are seniors. What percentage of all students enrolled in the school are seniors?

   F. 25%
   G. $33\dfrac{1}{3}$%
   H. 50%
   J. $66\dfrac{2}{3}$%
   K. 75%

31. What is the perimeter of the square in the figure below?

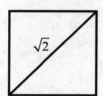

   A. 1
   B. $\sqrt{2}$
   C. 4
   D. $4\sqrt{2}$
   E. 8

32. If 2 straight line segments intersect as shown, what is the value of x?

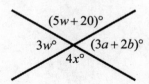

   F. 15
   G. 30
   H. 45
   J. 60
   K. 75

GO ON TO THE NEXT PAGE.

33. The figure below is a scale drawing of the floor of a dining hall. If 1 centimeter on the drawing represents 5 meters, what is the area, in square meters, of the floor?

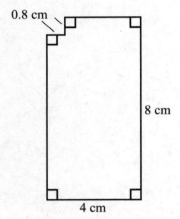

0.8 cm

8 cm

4 cm

DO YOUR FIGURING HERE.

A. 144
B. 156
C. 784
D. 796
E. 844

34. One side of a triangle has a length of 4 and another side has a length of 11. What are the *greatest* and *least* possible integer values for the length of the remaining side?

F. 7 and 4
G. 11 and 4
H. 14 and 8
J. 15 and 7
K. 16 and 7

35. Which of the following is the solution set for the equation $-x^2 = 3 - 4x$?

A. $\{-3, -1\}$
B. $\{-3, 1\}$
C. $\{1, 3\}$
D. $\{1, 4\}$
E. $\{3, 5\}$

GO ON TO THE NEXT PAGE.

36. The Global Exchange Club spends $\frac{2}{5}$ of its budget for one project and $\frac{1}{3}$ of what remains for another project. If the club's entire budget is $300, how much of the budget is left after the two projects?

F. $60
G. $90
H. $120
J. $180
K. $240

DO YOUR FIGURING HERE.

37. If the cost of n nails is c cents, which of the following equations could be used to determine d, the cost in dollars, of x nails?

A. $d = 100cnx$
B. $d = 100\dfrac{cx}{n}$
C. $d = \dfrac{100nx}{c}$
D. $d = \dfrac{nx}{100c}$
E. $d = \dfrac{cx}{100n}$

38. If a, b, and c are real numbers and $a^2 b^3 c < 0$, which of the following inequalities *must* be true?

F. $b^3 < 0$
G. $b^2 < 0$
H. $b < 0$
J. $c < 0$
K. $bc < 0$

39. If the figure below is an equilateral triangle, what is its perimeter?

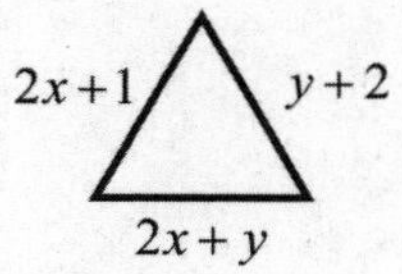

A.   1
B.   3
C.   9
D.   12
E.   15

DO YOUR FIGURING HERE.

40. In the *xy*-coordinate plane, what is the distance between the point with coordinates (2,1) and the point with coordinates (5,5)?

F. $\sqrt{3}$
G. $2\sqrt{3}$
H. $3\sqrt{2}$
J. 5
K. 6

41. $\sqrt{45} - \sqrt{20} + \sqrt{5} = ?$

A. $2 - \sqrt{5}$
B. 0
C. $2 + \sqrt{5}$
D. $2\sqrt{5}$
E. 10

42. What is the least positive integer *x* for which $12 - x$ and $15 - x$ will yield non-zero results with opposite signs?

F. 3
G. 4
H. 11
J. 12
K. 13

43. The solution set to the pair of equations $mx + ny = 15$ and $nx + my = 13$ is $x = 3$ and $y = 1$. What are the values of *m* and *n*?

A. $m = 5$; $n = 3$
B. $m = 4$; $n = 3$
C. $m = 3$; $n = 4$
D. $m = 3$; $n = 5$
E. $m = 2$; $n = 6$

GO ON TO THE NEXT PAGE.

44. In the figure below, line segments intersecting each other at right angles join equally spaced points. If the total length of all the small line segments joining two of these equally spaced points in the figure is 24, what is the area of the shaded part?

DO YOUR FIGURING HERE.

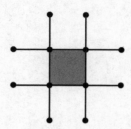

F.   1
G.   4
H.   8
J.   12
K.   16

45. All of the following are true for all real numbers EXCEPT:

A. $|a-b| = -|b-a|$
B. $|a-b| = |b-a|$
C. $|a-b| \le |a|+|b|$
D. $|a+b| \le |a|+|b|$
E. $|a| = |-a|$

46. $\mathrm{Arccos}\left(\cos\dfrac{\pi}{2}\right) = ?$

F.   0
G. $\dfrac{\pi}{4}$
H. $\dfrac{\pi}{2}$
J. π
K. $\dfrac{3\pi}{2}$

47. $\triangle ABC$ has coordinates $A\,(-1,-2)$, $B\,(0,4)$, and $C\,(3,-1)$. If $\triangle A'B'C'$ is the reflection of $\triangle ABC$ across the line $y=-x$, which of the following provides the coordinates of $\triangle A'B'C'$, respectively?

A. $(2,1)$, $(-4,0)$, $(1,-3)$
B. $(1,2)$, $(0,-4)$, $(-3,1)$
C. $(2,1)$, $(4,0)$, $(1,-3)$
D. $(3,2)$, $(5,1)$, $(2,-2)$
E. $(4,0)$, $(3,-1)$, $(-1,-2)$

48. If $\sin x = \cos x$, then x terminates only in:

F. quadrant I
G. quadrant I or quadrant III
H. quadrant II
J. quadrant II or quadrant III
K. quadrant II or quadrant IV

49. If the line $x=k$ is tangent to the circle $(x-2)^2+(y+1)^2=4$, then which of the following is the point of tangency?

A. $(-6,-1)$ or $(2,-1)$
B. $(-2,-1)$ or $(6,-1)$
C. $(0,-1)$ or $(4,-1)$
D. $(0,1)$ or $(4,1)$
E. $(2,1)$ or $(6,1)$

50. What is the last term in the expansion of $(2x+3y)^4$?

F. y^4
G. $9y^4$
H. $27y^4$
J. $81y^4$
K. $(xy)^4$

DO YOUR FIGURING HERE.

51. Which of the following could be a graph of the
equation $y = ax^2 + bx + c$, where $b^2 - 4ac = 0$?

DO YOUR FIGURING HERE.

A.

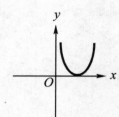

D.

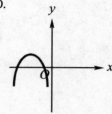

B.

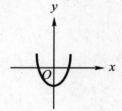

E.

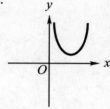

C.

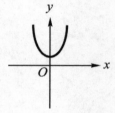

52. For any acute angle θ, which of the following is
equal to $\dfrac{\sin \theta}{\cos \theta}$?

F. $\tan \theta$
G. $\cot \theta$
H. $\sec \theta$
J. 1
K. 0.5

53. What is the degree measure of an angle that
measures $\dfrac{3}{2}\pi$ radians?

A. 60
B. 90
C. 120
D. 180
E. 270

GO ON TO THE NEXT PAGE.

54. What is the solution set for $|2x-1|=3$?

    F.   All real numbers

    G.   The empty set

    H. $\{-1\}$

    J. $\{2\}$

    K. $\{-1,2\}$

DO YOUR FIGURING HERE.

55. The end points of a line segment have coordinates $(2,5)$ and $(2,-4)$. What are the coordinates of the midpoint of the line segment?

    A. $(0,1)$

    B. $\left(2,\dfrac{1}{2}\right)$

    C. $(2,1)$

    D. $(2,9)$

    E. $(4,9)$

56. What is the slope of the line $2x+3y-2=0$?

    F. $-\dfrac{3}{2}$

    G. $-\dfrac{2}{3}$

    H. $\dfrac{2}{3}$

    J. 4

    K. 6

57. $\dfrac{1}{\sqrt{3}-1}=?$

    A. $\dfrac{\sqrt{3}-1}{4}$

    B. $\dfrac{\sqrt{3}-1}{3}$

    C. $\dfrac{\sqrt{3}-1}{2}$

    D. $\dfrac{\sqrt{3}+1}{2}$

    E. $\sqrt{3}+1$

GO ON TO THE NEXT PAGE.

58. $(-2)^2 - 2^{-2} = ?$

    F. -5

    G. -3

    H. 3

    J. $3\dfrac{3}{4}$

    K. $4\dfrac{1}{4}$

DO YOUR FIGURING HERE.

59. If $\dfrac{-3+\sqrt{5}}{2}$ is one root of the equation

$x^2 + 3x + 1 = 0$, then what is the other root?

    A. $\dfrac{-3-\sqrt{5}}{2}$

    B. $\dfrac{3-\sqrt{5}}{2}$

    C. $\dfrac{3+\sqrt{5}}{2}$

    D. $3-\dfrac{\sqrt{5}}{2}$

    E. $3+\dfrac{\sqrt{5}}{2}$

60. The figure below represents which of the following equations?

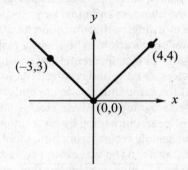

    F. $y = x$

    G. $y = -x$

    H. $y = |x|$

    J. $y = 2x$

    K. $y = x^2$

END OF TEST 2
STOP! DO NOT TURN THE PAGE UNTIL TOLD TO DO SO.
DO NOT RETURN TO THE PREVIOUS TEST.

3 3 3 3 3 3 3 3 3 3 3 3 3

SECTION 3: READING TEST
35 Minutes—40 Items

DIRECTIONS: Each passage below is followed by a set of items. Read each passage and choose the best answer for each item. Fill in the corresponding oval on your bubble sheet. You may refer to the passage as often as necessary to answer the items. Answers are on page 301.

PASSAGE I

PROSE FICTION: In this excerpt from Herman Melville's short story "Bartleby, the Scrivener," the narrator shares his exasperation with and sympathy for an employee.

Turkey was a short, pursy Englishman, of about my own age—that is, somewhere not far from sixty. In the morning, one might say, his face was of a fine florid hue. But after twelve o'clock,
5 meridian—his dinner hour—it blazed like a grate full of Christmas coals; and continued blazing—but, as it were, with a gradual wane—till six o'clock p.m., or thereabouts; after which, I saw no more of the proprietor of the face, which, gaining its
10 meridian with the Sun, seemed to set with, to rise, culminate, and decline the following day, with the like regularity and undiminished glory. There are many singular coincidences I have known in the course of my life. Not the least among these was the
15 fact that, exactly when Turkey displayed his fullest beams from his red and radiant countenance, just then, too, at that critical moment, began the daily period when I considered his business capacities as seriously disturbed for the remainder of the twenty-
20 four hours.

Not that he was absolutely idle, or averse to business then. Far from it. The difficulty was he was apt to be altogether too energetic. There was a strange, inflamed, flurried, flighty recklessness
25 of activity about him. He would be incautious in dipping his pen into his inkstand. All his blots upon my documents were dropped there after twelve o'clock, meridian. Indeed, not only would he be reckless, and sadly given to making blots
30 in the afternoon, but, some days, he went further, and was rather noisy. At such times, too, his face flamed with augmented blazonry, as if cannel coal had been heaped upon anthracite. He made an unpleasant racket with his chair; spilled his sand
35 box; in mending his pens, impatiently split them all to pieces, and threw them on the floor in a sudden passion; stood up, and leaned over his table, boxing the papers about in a most indecorous manner, very sad to behold in an elderly man like him.

40 Nevertheless, he was in many ways a most valuable person to me, and all the time before twelve o'clock, meridian, was the quickest, steadiest creature, too, accomplishing a great deal of work in a style not easily to be matched. For these reasons,
45 I was willing to overlook his eccentricities. Though, indeed, occasionally, I remonstrated with him. I did this very gently, however, because, though the civilest, nay, the blandest and most reverential of men in the morning, in the afternoon he was
50 disposed, upon provocation, to be slightly rash with his tongue—in fact, insolent. Now, valuing his morning services as I did, and resolved not to lose them—yet, at the same time, made uncomfortable by his inflamed ways after twelve o'clock—and
55 being a man of peace, unwilling by my admonitions to call forth unseemly retorts from him, I took upon me, one Saturday noon (he was always worse on Saturdays) to hint to him, very kindly, that perhaps, now that he was growing old, it might be well to
60 abridge his labors; in short, he need not come to my chambers after twelve o'clock, but, dinner over, had best go home to his lodgings, and rest himself till teatime. But no; he insisted upon his afternoon devotions. His countenance became intolerably
65 fervid. He oratorically assured me—gesticulating with a long ruler at the other end of the room—that if his services in the morning were useful, how indispensable, then, in the afternoon?

GO ON TO THE NEXT PAGE.

"With submission, sir," said Turkey, on this
70 occasion, "I consider myself your right-hand man. In
the morning I but marshal and deploy my columns;
but in the afternoon I put myself at their head, and
gallantly charge the foe, thus"—and he made a
violent thrust with the ruler.

75   "But the blots, Turkey," intimated I.

        "True; but, with submission sir, behold these
hairs! I am getting old. Surely, sir, a blot or two of a
warm afternoon is not to be severely urged against
gray hairs. Old age—even if it blot the page—is
80 honorable. With submission, sir, we *both* are getting
old."

        This appeal to my fellow-feeling was hardly to
be resisted. At all events, I saw that go he would not.
So, I made up my mind to let him stay. I resolved,
85 nevertheless, to see to it that, during the afternoon,
he had to do with my less important papers.

1. The narrator is Turkey's:

A. older brother.
B. physician.
C. co-worker.
D. employer.

2. The passage suggests that Turkey is a:

F. copyist.
G. painter.
H. fencing instructor.
J. sales clerk.

3. A logical explanation for Turkey's behavior is
that he:

A. becomes fatigued.
B. is growing old.
C. drinks alcohol.
D. dislikes the narrator.

4. The fellow-feeling mentioned in the final
paragraph is based on the fact that:

F. Turkey is the narrator's right-hand man.
G. Turkey and the narrator are the same age.
H. the narrator also makes ink blots.
J. the ink blots are not very serious.

5. The narrator's final resolution of the problem is
to:

A. find a replacement for Turkey.
B. give Turkey Saturdays off.
C. give Turkey afternoons off.
D. give Turkey less important work after noon.

6. According to the narrator, Turkey's face is
reddest:

F. in early morning.
G. shortly after noon.
H. in midafternoon.
J. in early evening.

7. It can be inferred that when cannel coal is
heaped on anthracite, a fire:

A. burns more intensely.
B. burns less intensely.
C. goes out altogether.
D. begins to sputter and spit.

8. The narrator's attitude toward Turkey's
afternoon behavior is one of:

F. amusement.
G. discomfort.
H. indifference.
J. outrage.

9. The narrator finds Turkey's work in the
mornings to be:

A. entirely satisfactory.
B. frequently unsatisfactory.
C. almost always unsatisfactory.
D. inconsistent.

10. Which of the following does NOT characterize
Turkey's behavior in the afternoon?

F. Frenzied activity
G. Excessive carelessness
H. Idleness
J. Verbal insolence

GO ON TO THE NEXT PAGE.

PASSAGE II

SOCIAL SCIENCE: This passage discusses punishment for individuals who have violated the law.

In the earliest attempts to articulate a theory of justice, justice is regarded as a form of equality. It is no accident that the modern symbol of the judicial system is the balance scale, but as early as Biblical
5 times, we find the principle set forth in writing. The most frequently quoted version is found in the book of Exodus, chapter 21, verse 24, but we also find similar statements in Leviticus, chapter 24, verse 20 and in Deuteronomy, chapter 19, verse 21. The
10 references are most often cited by "law and order advocates" seeking extremely harsh punishment for criminals, but the explicit statement and the intuition behind the statement does not support such a conclusion. "Eye for an eye, and a tooth for a
15 tooth" is a principle of equivalence: not only should there be punishment, but the punishment must be proportional to offense. Thus, it would be wrong to execute an offender for putting out an eye or cutting off a hand. The formulation in Leviticus makes this
20 abundantly clear by its use of the phrase "just as he has injured a man." Or as modern theorists might say, "The punishment must fit the crime."

We find similar expressions in the common law of Henry II, which had its origins in the blood
25 feud. Clan warfare characterized this period, and an injury to a member of one clan inevitably led to infliction of injury on a member of the other clan. In order to bring some measure of peace to the realm, the common law developed a system of
30 tariffs substituting money payments for injuries. Thus, a facial wound or a lost digit would require the payment of a predetermined amount. The entire system was an elaborate quid pro quo for violent injuries.

35 The notion of punishment as restoring a balance reaches its most abstract expression in the writings of the German idealist, G.W.F. Hegel. Hegel argued that society owed it to the criminal to administer a punishment equal to the crime
40 committed. The criminal has by his own actions denied his true self, and it is necessary to do something to restore the self that has been denied. To the murderer, nothing less than giving up his own life will pay his debt. The exaction of the death
45 penalty is a right the state owes the criminal, and it should not deny him his due.

Modern jurists have tried to replace retributive justice with the notion of corrective justice. The aim of the latter is not to abandon the concept of
50 equality but to find a more adequate way to express it. It tries to preserve the ideal of equal opportunity for each individual to realize the best that is in him. The criminal is regarded as being socially ill and in need of treatment that will enable him to become
55 a normal member of society. Before treatment can be administered, the causes that led to antisocial behavior must be found. If the causes can be removed, provisions must be made to have this done.

60 Only those criminals who are incurable should be permanently separated from the rest of society. This does not mean that criminals will escape punishment or be quickly returned to take up careers of crime. It means that justice is to heal
65 the individual, not simply to get even with him. If severe punishment is the only adequate means for accomplishing this, it should be administered. However, the individual should be given every opportunity to assume a normal place in society.
70 His conviction of crime must not deprive him of the opportunity to make his way in the society of which he is a part.

There are, of course, differing views of both retributive justice and corrective justice. On some
75 views, these two types of justice appear to overlap, even to be identical. Some views of retributive justice talk of "annulling" and "rectifying" wrongs, as do some views of corrective justice. However, though retributive and corrective justice are both
80 concerned with "annulling" or "rectifying" wrongs, their methods of doing so differ to the point that the two types of justice can hardly be confused for one another.

11. The best title for this selection is:

A. Fitting Punishment to the Crime.
B. Approaches to Just Punishment.
C. Improvement in Legal Justice.
D. Attaining Justice in the Courts.

12. Hegel would view the death sentence for murder as:

   F. inadequate justice.
   G. the best way for society to get revenge.
   H. the most efficient method of removing a known danger.
   J. an inalienable right of the murderer.

13. The author cites the three passages from the Old Testament in order to show that:

   A. the notion of justice evolved significantly during Biblical times.
   B. the three variations express substantially the same underlying moral intuition.
   C. justice is a concept that first originated in Biblical times.
   D. primitive notions of justice offend the moral sense of modern thinkers.

14. The punishment that would be most inconsistent with the views of corrective justice is:

   F. forced brain surgery.
   G. solitary confinement.
   H. life imprisonment.
   J. the electric chair.

15. The Biblical expression "an eye for an eye, and a tooth for a tooth" was presented in order to:

   A. justify the need for punishment as a part of law.
   B. give moral backing to retributive justice.
   C. show that humanity has long been interested in justice as a form of equality.
   D. indicate the lack of social development during Biblical times.

16. The concept of retributive justice still reflected in many modern legal codes is:

   F. giving the accused a fair trial.
   G. rehabilitating the criminal.
   H. separating incurable criminals from the rest of society.
   J. inflicting equal injury on the criminal.

17. A major goal of modern jurists is to:

   A. ensure that criminals do not escape punishment.
   B. preserve the notion of equality.
   C. restore states' rights.
   D. select an appropriate punishment for a crime.

18. Under the notion of corrective justice, assuming "a normal place in society" (line 69) most likely means:

   F. acting in one's best interests.
   G. denying one's true self.
   H. curing antisocial behavior.
   J. accepting punishment.

19. The author's tone in the passage is best described as:

   A. argumentative.
   B. sympathetic.
   C. explanatory.
   D. conciliatory.

20. According to the author, criminals cannot be treated until:

   F. they have been punished properly for their crime.
   G. they have received a fair trial.
   H. a legal code for treatment has been established.
   J. the causes of antisocial behavior have been found.

GO ON TO THE NEXT PAGE.

PASSAGE III

HUMANITIES: This passage describes events leading to and the effects of World War I.

The event that touched off World War I occurred in Sarajevo, the capital of the Austro-Hungarian province of Bosnia, on June 28, 1914. There the Archduke Francis Ferdinand, the
5 Hapsburg heir to the throne of the Austro-Hungarian Empire, and his wife, Sophie, were shot and killed by a young Serbian nationalist seeking revenge against the Austrians for their annexation of Bosnia. Austria issued an ultimatum to Serbia. The Serbians
10 acquiesced, in an attempt to stave off war. Austria, however, was intent on exacting retribution. In July of that year it declared war on Serbia.

For almost a century, since the Congress of Vienna in 1815, European diplomats had prevented
15 any real threat to the delicate balance of power achieved by the Congress. This time, though, they seemed powerless to stop the movement toward war. The assassination caused a fateful series of failed diplomatic attempts that led Russia to
20 mobilize its armed forces as Serbia's ally. Austria sought and gained the mobilization aid of its ally Germany. The other members of the Triple Entente, France and Great Britain, soon joined their ally Russia against Austria. In 1917, the United States
25 was drawn into the battle as an ally of France and Great Britain.

World War I was unlike any other war fought before or since. The nature of the warfare marked a dramatic departure from previous methods; while
30 the most iconic feature of this new warfare was the use of trench warfare, World War I also saw the first successful large-scale use of a traditional weapon of mass destruction on the battlefield (chemical, biological, or nuclear): chemical weapons. These
35 powerful new warfare tactics contributed to the striking casualty and fatality rates of World War I. The profound shock that the war generated dramatically affected life in Europe and America and changed the course of world politics. Moreover, the
40 war shocked millions of people throughout Europe into confronting the terrible losses and the grim and brutal realities of modern war. The few wars that had been fought since 1815 were distant colonial wars. Europeans had always been victorious. The
45 battles seemed nothing more than skirmishes that offered chances to experience adventure and to demonstrate bravery and heroism. The trenches and battlefields of Europe introduced millions of young men and women to a world of pain and death that
50 they had never imagined.

The war altered the social sensibility of the people of Europe. It destroyed the spirit of optimism that had prevailed in the nineteenth century. Civilized, polite behavior now seemed archaic and
55 hypocritical. Moreover, the impression that there appeared to be no sane way to end the carnage only added to the sense of futility. The war changed relationships between members of the same social class. Before the war, the upper classes of Europe
60 felt a bond that united them across national borders. After the war, national boundaries defined social consciousness in a way that destroyed the solidarity of class.

World War I produced several dramatic
65 changes in the political landscape of Europe. After four years of carnage and more than 16 million dead soldiers and civilians, three empires that had lasted for centuries—Austro-Hungarian, Russian, and Ottoman—gradually ceased to exist, and many
70 new nations emerged. The breakup of the Austro-Hungarian, Russian, and German empires led to the re-emergence of the state of Poland. The Austro-Hungarian Empire, the vast zone in the southern part of Europe, was divided into a range of smaller
75 states. The war also brought about the formation of new nation states in Europe. The Baltic republics of Latvia, Lithuania, and Estonia were established. The old empires had provided a degree of stability, so many people had trouble adjusting to life under
80 a different rule. Moreover, because borders that once seemed definitive now underwent significant re-mapping, many Europeans encountered tensions between their new place of legal citizenship and their place of cultural membership.

85 The war acted as a catalyst for European revolutionaries. The Russian Revolution of 1917 set the stage for the Bolshevik seizure of power. Total power was achieved by the Communist party. Stalin became the absolute dictator of the Russian state
90 (renamed the Union of Soviet Socialist Republics). World War I bore bitter fruit in Central and Southern Europe as well. The rise of Nazism in Germany and fascism in Italy led many historians to conclude that World War II, which was begun by Nazi Germany in
95 1939, was in fact the continuation of the Great War that destroyed the social fabric of Europe in 1914.

GO ON TO THE NEXT PAGE.

21. The precipitating cause of World War I was:

   A. an assassination.
   B. a coronation.
   C. a rebellion.
   D. a plebiscite.

22. The event occurred in the city of:

   F. Sarajevo in Bosnia.
   G. Vienna in Austria.
   H. Trieste in Italy.
   J. Budapest in Hungary.

23. Before World War I, a balance of power had existed for:

   A. nearly 15 years.
   B. almost a quarter century.
   C. almost 100 years.
   D. nearly 10 years.

24. The chief reason European countries other than Austria and Serbia were drawn into the conflict was that they:

   F. were members of the two alliance systems to which the combatants belonged.
   G. feared the Hapsburgs.
   H. wanted to ensure freedom of the seas.
   J. wanted the land of neighboring countries.

25. Mobilization for war resulted swiftly when:

   A. the United States declared war.
   B. attempts at diplomacy failed.
   C. Russia refused to help Serbia.
   D. Italy joined the conflict.

26. The way in which class relationships changed as a result of the outbreak of World War I suggests that:

   F. nationalism might have weakened had the war never occurred.
   G. the middle classes had no real love of country.
   H. the upper classes had eagerly anticipated war.
   J. everyone sanctioned the war.

27. The forces of militant nationalism that were unleashed during World War I culminated in the breakup of the Russian Empire and the German Empire. The political regimes that came to power in Germany and the Soviet Union before World War II were:

   A. democracies that isolated themselves from world politics.
   B. ruthless dictatorships dedicated to world conquest.
   C. weak states allied with the United States.
   D. members of a Europe-wide common market.

28. The sense of futility felt throughout Europe during and after World War I would be evident in a study of:

   F. American investment policies.
   G. statistics concerning foreign language study in America.
   H. the number of transatlantic voyages between 1920 and 1930.
   J. European literature of the 1920s, 1930s, and 1940s.

29. World War I and its aftermath suggest the idea that:

   A. nationalism has little to do with world conflict.
   B. war feeds on nationalist sympathies.
   C. the cause of peace is best aided by reinvigorating the spirit of nationalism.
   D. diplomacy never works.

30. Archduke Francis Ferdinand, as the heir to the Austro-Hungarian Empire, was a member of the:

   F. Hohenzollern family.
   G. Hanover family.
   H. Hapsburg family.
   J. Stuart family.

GO ON TO THE NEXT PAGE.

PASSAGE IV

NATURAL SCIENCE: This selection discusses the information gathered about the planet Uranus by the Voyager 2 spacecraft.

Voyager 2 is a space probe launched by NASA on August 20, 1977 to study the outer planets. Part of the Voyager program, it was launched 16 days before its twin, Voyager 1, on a trajectory that took
5 longer to reach Jupiter and Saturn but enabled further encounters with Uranus and Neptune. It is the only spacecraft to have visited either of the ice giants. When the Voyager 2 spacecraft flew past Uranus and its moons in 1986, it gathered startling
10 new information about these extraordinary celestial objects from an unprecedented distance. At nearly 3 billion kilometers away (1.8 billion miles from Earth), Uranus is so far away that scientists knew comparatively little about it before Voyager 2
15 undertook its historic first-ever encounter with the planet. At its closest, the spacecraft came within 81,500 kilometers (50,600 miles) of Uranus's cloud tops on January 24, 1986.

Uranus had long been known to be different
20 from all the other planets in one important respect: it lies tipped over on its side, with its rotational axis and its orbital path nearly at right angles. Instead of spinning like a top, it rolls like a ball along the path of its orbit. Its geographic poles, instead of being on
25 the top and bottom of the planet as Earth's are, are located on either side, one facing the Sun and one facing away—as if they were the ends of a gigantic axle. The reason for Uranus's strange tilt to its axis of rotation is not known, but the current hypothesis
30 is that during Uranus's formation, an Earth-sized space object collided with Uranus and caused the tilt. As a result, the northern and southern polar regions are alternatively exposed to sunlight or to the dark of space during the planet's 84-year orbit
35 around the Sun. Yet, strangely, Uranus is still warmer at its equator than the poles, even though the poles receive the direct sunlight with a very low sun angle over the equatorial region. In addition, unlike the other gas giants, Uranus does not radiate more heat
40 than it receives. This suggests that the planet may have a cold interior, lacking an internal heat source. This would differentiate it from Jupiter and Saturn, which, in contrast, each radiate away about twice as much energy as they receive from the sun due to
45 internal heating centers.

Voyager also found another oddity: Uranus' magnetic poles, instead of lying close to the geographic poles as Earth's do, are located not
50 far from the planet's equator, 60° away from the geographic poles. Still another discovery is that the clouds in the Uranian atmosphere move in the same direction as the planet rotates; that is, from top to bottom and back to top, rather than horizontally, as Earth's clouds move.

55 The Uranian moons proved to have equally striking features. The surface of Miranda, the moon nearest the planet, has patchwork regions of broken terrain indicating intense geological activity in Miranda's past, and is criss-crossed by huge canyons.
60 It also has the largest known cliff in the Solar System, Verona Rupes, which has a height of over 3.1 miles. Some of Miranda's terrain is possibly less than 100 million years old based on crater counts, which suggests that Miranda may still be geologically active
65 today. On Ariel, the next moon out, the landscape has been stretched apart, creating huge faults where the ground has broken apart and sunk inward. Its giant fault canyons are up to 12 times as deep as the Grand Canyon. However, there is no evidence of any
70 geological activity. Umbriel, the third moon, seems to be "painted" with some dark substance. On one side of Umbriel is a large, round bright marking called the "donut." It is presumably some type of impact crater. Each of Uranus' other 24 moons is equally odd and
75 unique in its own way. Furthermore, between the orbit of Miranda and Uranus' surface are up to one hundred charcoal-colored rings, ringlets, and bands of dust, and between some of these rings are still more tiny moonlets.

80 The moons and rings of Uranus are odd in still another way. Like the clouds in the planet's atmosphere, they circle Uranus in the same direction as the planet rotates. That is, they orbit over the top and bottom of the planet rather than around the
85 sides, as Earth's moon does.

The Voyager 2 spacecraft tripled the number of known Uranian moons, discovering 10 additional moons ranging from 26–154 km (16–96 miles) in diameter. Since then, astronomers using the Hubble
90 Space Telescope and improved ground-based telescopes have raised the total to 27 known moons.

31. Because of the odd way in which Uranus rotates, one geographic pole:

A. alternates between daylight and darkness.
B. receives only indirect sunlight.
C. varies between heat from the Sun and cold.
D. is always in darkness.

GO ON TO THE NEXT PAGE.

32. The warmest spot on Uranus would most likely be located at:

    F. one of the magnetic poles.
    G. the equator.
    H. one of the geographic poles.
    J. a spot midway between a geographic pole and the equator.

33. On Uranus, a surface location that receives sunlight:

    A. will alternate between daylight and darkness.
    B. will always be in daylight.
    C. will occasionally be in darkness.
    D. must be near one of the magnetic poles.

34. The Uranian equator extends:

    F. around the planet horizontally, as Earth's does.
    G. around the planet through the geographic poles.
    H. around the planet from top to bottom.
    J. around the planet through the magnetic poles.

35. An observer at the Uranian equator would most likely experience:

    A. a regular succession of days and nights.
    B. constant, indirect sunlight.
    C. a regular succession of warmth and cold.
    D. only darkness.

36. Auroras are sky phenomena that generally appear near a planet's magnetic poles. On Earth, auroras can be seen at extreme north or south latitudes. On Uranus, auroras would most likely:

    F. be visible near the planet's geographic poles.
    G. never be visible.
    H. be visible not far from the planet's equator.
    J. be visible from everywhere on the planet's surface.

37. On Earth, atmospheric circulation patterns are largely controlled by the varying amounts of sunlight received at different latitudes. On Uranus:

    A. atmospheric circulation functions in an identical way.
    B. there is no atmospheric circulation.
    C. the atmosphere circulates from one geographic pole to the other.
    D. some other factor besides sunlight controls atmospheric circulation.

38. According to the passage, which of the three Uranian moons closest to the planet exhibits features that can be attributed to geologic activity?

    F. Miranda only
    G. Miranda and Ariel only
    H. Ariel and Umbriel only
    J. Miranda, Ariel, and Umbriel

39. The great faults observed on the moon Ariel could have been caused by:

    A. moonquakes.
    B. continental drift.
    C. the gravitational pull of other nearby moons.
    D. volcanic activity.

40. Uranus has how many moons?

    F. 3
    G. 7
    H. 24
    J. 27

END OF TEST 3
STOP! DO NOT TURN THE PAGE UNTIL TOLD TO DO SO.
DO NOT RETURN TO THE PREVIOUS TEST.

PRACTICE TEST II

4 4 4 4 4 4 4 4 4 4 4 4 4

SECTION 4: SCIENCE TEST
35 Minutes—40 Items

DIRECTIONS: Each passage below is followed by several items. After reading a passage, choose the best answer for each item. Fill in the corresponding oval on your bubble sheet. You may refer to the passage as often as necessary. You are NOT permitted the use of a calculator on this test. Answers are on page 304.

PASSAGE I

The table below shows selected elements from the periodic table, together with atomic radii in angstrom units (Å) and electronegativities (second number).

H 0.37 Å 2.20						
Li 1.52 Å 0.98	Be 1.12 Å 1.57	B 0.85 Å 2.04	C 0.77 Å 2.55	N 0.75 Å 3.04	O 0.73 Å 3.44	F 0.72 Å 3.98
Na 1.86 Å 0.93	Mg 1.60 Å 1.31	A1 1.43 Å 1.61	Si 1.18 Å 1.90	P 1.10 Å 2.19	S 1.03 Å 2.58	C1 1.00 Å 3.16
K 2.27 Å 0.82						Br 1.14 Å 2.96
Rb 2.48 Å 0.82						I 1.33 Å 2.66

When two atoms of the same element form a covalent bond, the approximate bond length may be calculated by adding together the two atomic radii.

An atom's electronegativity is a measure of its relative ability to attract electrons. As atoms form chemical bonds, atoms with similar electronegativities compete more or less equally for the available electrons. This tug-o-war over electrons (which is often referred to as sharing) is a covalent bond. However, some bonds form between atoms with very different electronegativities. In this case, the more electronegative atom is able to completely remove the electron from the other atom creating ions. These ions are held together by electrostatic forces in what is called an ionic bond. The degree to which a bond behaves like an ionic bond or a covalent bond is called its ionic character.

GO ON TO THE NEXT PAGE.

1. Which of the following occur when moving down a column in the table?

   A. Radii decrease; electronegativities decrease or stay the same.
   B. Radii increase; electronegativities increase or stay the same.
   C. Radii decrease; electronegativities increase or stay the same.
   D. Radii increase; electronegativities decrease or stay the same.

2. The greatest electronegativity in the table is for the element:

   F. fluorine (F).
   G. chlorine (Cl).
   H. rubidium (Rb).
   J. hydrogen (H).

3. The bond length in a P-P bond is:

   A. 0.55 Å.
   B. 1.21 Å.
   C. 2.20 Å.
   D. 4.40 Å.

4. The bond between which of the following elements is likely to have the most covalent character?

   F. Sodium (Na) and iodine (I)
   G. Magnesium (Mg) and oxygen (O)
   H. Sulfur (S) and oxygen (O)
   J. Carbon (C) and nitrogen (N)

5. When the element fluorine (F) bonds with a second element in the table shown, the resulting bond generally has a greater ionic character:

   A. the closer the second element is to fluorine in the same row.
   B. the closer the second element is to fluorine in the same column.
   C. the farther the second element is from fluorine in the same row.
   D. the farther the second element is from fluorine in both a different row and a different column.

6. The element astatine (At) lies directly below iodine (I) in the periodic table. The electronegativity difference in HAt is likely to be:

   F. less than 0.46.
   G. greater than 0.46.
   H. equal to 0.46.
   J. Cannot be determined from the given information

PASSAGE II

A set of activities was carried out to investigate the relative sizes of the planets of our solar system and their relative distances from the sun. Table 1 was given to all students performing the activities.

Activity 1

Using a compass, ruler, and poster board (22 inches by 28 inches), students were asked to compare the sizes of the planets. Calling the size of Earth 1.00 (Earth diameter = 1 inch), a circle was made by inserting the point of the compass in the center of the poster board. The circle had a radius of 0.5 inches to produce a circle with a diameter of 1 inch representing Earth. All other planets were drawn to scale based on the size of their diameters relative to one Earth diameter (Table 1).

Table 1		
Planet	Approximate Diameter (in Earth diameters)	Approximate Distance from the Sun (A.U.)
Mercury	0.38	0.40
Venus	0.95	0.70
Earth	1.00	1.00
Mars	0.54	1.50
Jupiter	11.20	5.20
Saturn	9.50	9.50
Uranus	4.01	19.20
Neptune	3.88	30.00

Activity 2

Using the equipment from Activity 1, students were also asked to compare planetary distances from the sun. Earth is 93 million miles from the sun. This distance is called 1.00 astronomical unit (1 A.U. = 1 inch), and it was used as a reference distance when the other planets were drawn at their proper distances (Table 1) from the sun (a planet twice as far as Earth is from the sun would be drawn 2 A.U., or 2.0 inches, from the sun).

7. Based on Activity 1, which of the following pairs of planets are most similar in size?

   A. Earth and Venus.
   B. Mars and Mercury.
   C. Mars and Venus.
   D. Saturn and Jupiter.

8. In Activity 2, if the poster board were held the "long way" (landscape) and the left-hand edge represented the sun, which planet(s) would not fit on the paper?

   F. Saturn, Uranus, and Neptune
   G. Uranus and Neptune
   H. Neptune only
   J. All planets would fit on the paper.

9. Which of the following statements is supported by the data in Table 1?

   A. The larger the planet, the greater is its distance from the sun.
   B. The smaller the planet, the greater is its distance from the sun.
   C. Only planets larger than Earth are farther away from the sun.
   D. There is no consistent pattern between a planet's size and its distance from the sun.

10. A planet's "year" is how long it takes to orbit the sun, and it is related to the distance of that planet from the sun. If asteroids are found 2.8 A.U. from the sun, an "asteroid year" should be:

   F. longer than an "Earth year" but shorter than a "Mars year."
   G. longer than a "Jupiter year" but shorter than a "Mars year."
   H. longer than a "Mars year" but shorter than a "Jupiter year."
   J. longer than a "Neptune year" but shorter than a "Saturn year."

11. In Activity 1, how large would a circle representing the sun be if its diameter is approximately 110 times greater than that of Earth?

A. It would have a radius of approximately 55 inches.
B. It would have a diameter of approximately 55 inches.
C. It would have a radius of approximately 5.5 inches.
D. It would have a diameter of approximately 5.5 inches.

12. A third activity was conducted in which the mass of each planet was described relative to the mass of Earth (Jupiter had the greatest mass, Saturn had the next largest mass, Mercury and Mars had the smallest masses). If the planets were placed in an order based on how they compared to Earth for the variables measured in all three experiments, which two orders would be expected to be most similar?

F. Diameter and distance from the sun
G. Mass and distance from the sun
H. Diameter and mass
J. All three orders would be similar.

PASSAGE III

During photosynthesis, leaf pigments absorb light energy. Eventually, this process results in the production of glucose and other carbohydrates to be used by the green plant. Oxygen gas (O_2) is also produced during the process. Various factors affecting the rate of photosynthesis were investigated by measuring the oxygen concentration (using an oxygen sensor) produced by the conditions described in the following three experiments.

Experiment 1

A sample of leaf extract (a mixture of pigments previously separated from other leaf components) from the pond plant *Elodea* was placed in a beaker containing water and carbon dioxide (CO_2) at concentration 1.6 g/kg H_2O, both necessary ingredients for photosynthesis. Light of varying intensity was used to illuminate the beaker, and the number of oxygen bubbles emitted by the plant each minute was recorded. The results are summarized in Figure 1.

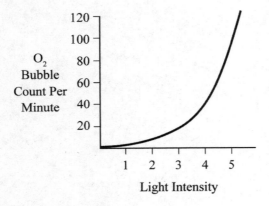

Figure 1

Experiment 2

An identical experiment was conducted in which the concentration of leaf extract was reduced four-fold (the mixture was one-fourth as concentrated as in Experiment 1). The results are summarized in Figure 2.

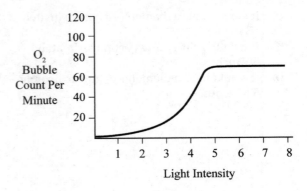

Figure 2

Experiment 3

Visible light consists of many different colors, or light wavelengths. Only those wavelengths that are absorbed by leaf pigments can provide the energy to maintain photosynthesis in the leaf. Different light wavelengths were used separately to illuminate two samples of leaf extract, each containing a different *Elodea* leaf pigment. Oxygen (O_2) bubbles were counted again as a measure of the rate of photosynthesis. The results are summarized in Figure 3.

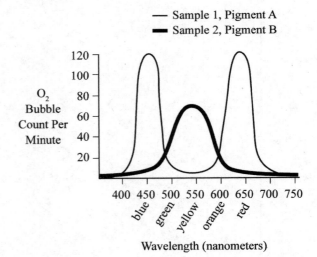

Figure 3

GO ON TO THE NEXT PAGE.

13. Which of the following changes in Experiment 1 would test the hypothesis that the level of carbon dioxide affects the rate of photosynthesis?

   A. Repeat the experiment, using the same concentration of carbon dioxide in the beaker of water, but with different species of green plants.
   B. Repeat the experiment, using no carbon dioxide as well as varying concentrations of carbon dioxide in the beaker of water.
   C. Repeat the experiment using different levels of water in the beaker containing a standard concentration of carbon dioxide.
   D. Repeat the experiment using additional light intensities.

14. The results from Experiments 1 and 2 demonstrate that maintaining a continued increase in the photosynthesis rate requires adequate amounts of:

   F. sensors.
   G. carbon dioxide.
   H. oxygen.
   J. leaf pigments.

15. Based on the information in Figure 3, which of the following statements is correct?

   A. Pigment A primarily absorbs light at 450 and 650 nanometers, while Pigment B absorbs light at 500–575 nanometers.
   B. Pigment B primarily absorbs light at 450 and 650 nanometers, while Pigment A absorbs light at 500–575 nanometers.
   C. Pigment A can influence the rate of photo-synthesis, while Pigment B cannot.
   D. Pigment B can influence the rate of photo-synthesis, while Pigment A cannot.

16. If the concentration of *Elodea* leaf extract were increased in Experiment 2, which of the following results could be expected with increasing light intensity?

   F. A decrease in the number of oxygen bubbles
   G. An increase in the number of oxygen bubbles
   H. No change in the number of oxygen bubbles
   J. A gradual dimming of light intensity

17. In Experiments 1 and 2, approximately how many oxygen bubbles per minute were produced at a light intensity level of 4?

   A. 0
   B. 20
   C. 40
   D. 80

18. According to the information in Figure 3, if an additional experiment were conducted, which condition would be LEAST effective in maintaining photosynthetic rate in *Elodea*?

   F. Using blue light only
   G. Using red light only
   H. Using yellow light only
   J. Using orange light only

PASSAGE IV

The accompanying figure shows how the world records for various footraces have improved during a portion of the twentieth century. Speeds are given in both meters per minute and minutes per mile.

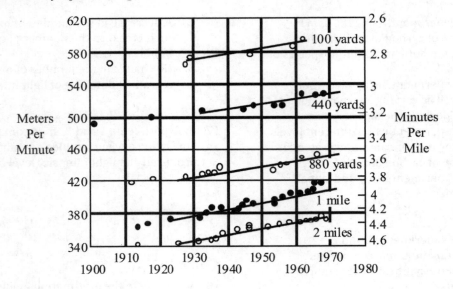

Modified from H.W. Ryder, H.J. Carr, and P. Herget, "Future performance in footracing," *Sci. Amer*. 234 (6): 109–114, 1976.

19. In what race and in what year was the greatest speed in meters per minute achieved?

A. The 440 yard dash in 1900
B. The 100 yard dash in 1930
C. The 100 yard dash in 1962
D. The 1 mile run in 1947

20. The trend in the graph of speed for the various distances shows:

F. roughly a linear increase.
G. roughly a linear decrease.
H. a linear increase for short distances and a linear decrease for long distances.
J. no systematic pattern.

21. For 1960, the ratio of speed in minutes per mile for the 1 mile run to speed in minutes per mile for the 440 yard dash is approximately:

A. $\dfrac{3}{4}$.

B. $\dfrac{4}{5}$.

C. $\dfrac{5}{5}$.

D. $\dfrac{4}{3}$.

22. The increase in speed, in meters per minute, for the 2 mile run from 1925 to 1967 is approximately:

F. 0.3.
G. 10.
H. 30.
J. 100.

23. If the trends shown can be expected to hold for later years, then the value of minutes per mile for the 880 yard run in 1980 is expected to be:

A. 3.5.
B. 3.8.
C. 420.
D. 460.

GO ON TO THE NEXT PAGE.

PASSAGE V

Two experiments were performed in which constant amounts of heat were added continuously to samples over a defined period of time. The temperatures of the samples were monitored while the heat was added. The results from the two experiments are shown below.

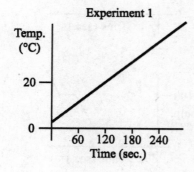

Experiment 1

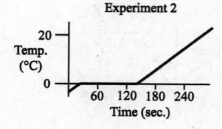

Experiment 2

24. The results of Experiment 1 may be interpreted to show that:

    F. it takes longer to heat a hot sample than a cold one.
    G. the temperature of the sample rises proportionately with time as heat is applied.
    H. temperature is not related to heat.
    J. temperature and time measure the same thing.

25. Experiment 2 differs from Experiment 1 in that:

    A. only the starting temperature is different in the two experiments.
    B. since the graph in Experiment 2 is not a straight line, there must have been experimental error.
    C. Experiment 2 has a lower starting temperature and a time period when the temperature does not rise.
    D. in Experiment 2, the heat was off for a while in the middle of the experiment.

26. The experimenter wants to explain the flat part of the graph from Experiment 2. It could represent:

    F. a period when the clock was turned off but heat was added as in Experiment 1.
    G. a period when the heat was turned off and the clock was turned off..
    H. a period when heat was added but some process occurred that did not occur in Experiment 1.
    J. a period when heat was added and the same processes occurred as in Experiment 1.

27. The "phase" of the sample changes (an example of a phase change is the melting of a solid, or the boiling of a liquid) in conjunction with the flat part of the graph in Experiment 2. From the temperature data given, the phase change might be:

    A. the melting of ice.
    B. the boiling of water.
    C. the condensation of steam.
    D. the freezing of water.

GO ON TO THE NEXT PAGE.

28. The results of these experiments demonstrate that:

    F. heat and temperature are the same.
    G. heat and temperature are not the same.
    H. a pause in heating can lead to a pause in temperature change.
    J. constant heating leads to constant change.

29. If the experimenter extends Experiment 2 to higher temperatures, using a sample with a phase change at 0°C and 100°C, which graph best illustrates the expected results?

A.
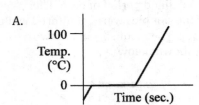

B.
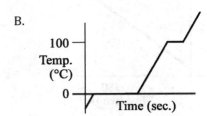

C.
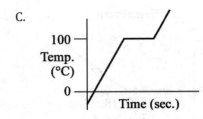

D
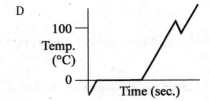

PASSAGE VI

The following chart shows the generalized sequence of early developmental stages (terms in boxes) observed in most vertebrates.

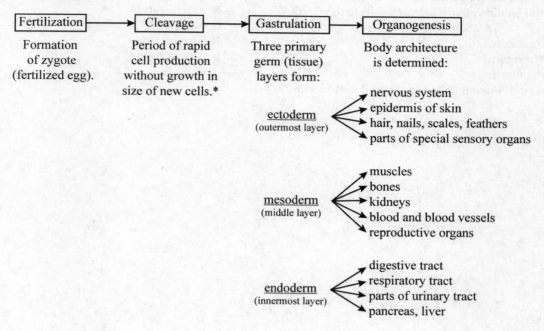

*New cells form as the zygote and its subsequent daughter cells divide and re-divide.

30. According to the chart, the stage of development when the three primary tissue layers form is:

F. fertilization.
G. cleavage.
H. gastrulation.
J. organogenesis.

31. Differentiation refers to a period of cell maturation during which time cells become specialized in structure and function. At which stage of development would most differentiation be expected to occur?

A. Fertilization
B. Cleavage
C. Gastrulation
D. Organogenesis

32. Based on the information in the diagram, which of the following conclusions is NOT correct?

F. Most bones develop from the innermost primary germ layer.
G. Vertebrates develop three primary germ layers.
H. Diverse structures such as scales, feathers, and hair always develop from the same primary germ layer.
J. Before an organism can form different primary tissue layers, it must go through a period of rapid cell production.

GO ON TO THE NEXT PAGE.

33. If a species of monkey were found to have extraordinary vision due to special receptor cells that were highly sensitive to different colors of light, from which primary germ layer(s) would you predict such cells to develop?

A. Endoderm
B. Mesoderm
C. Ectoderm
D. A combination of endoderm and mesoderm

34. On the basis of the information provided, the stage of development that probably has the smallest cells is:

F. fertilization.
G. cleavage.
H. gastrulation.
J. organogenesis.

GO ON TO THE NEXT PAGE.

PASSAGE VII

Before chemistry was well understood, there were two hypotheses regarding the proportions of chemicals that will react to form products.

Hypothesis 1

Although a chemical reaction is more than simple mixing, the two are similar in that any amounts of reactants may be brought together to form chemical products that contain the same elements as the reactants. For example, in the chemical reaction " hydrogen + oxygen ⇒ water ," we may use 1 mole of hydrogen and 1 mole of oxygen, or 2 to 1, or 1 to 2, etc. The reaction will adjust to the proportions given.

Hypothesis 2

Only certain proportions of reactants will combine chemically. For example, when hydrogen and oxygen are reacted, the amounts that will combine will be *exactly* 4 grams of hydrogen for every 32 grams of oxygen. We can show, using molecular weights, that these weights of reactants (which correspond to 2 moles of hydrogen and 1 mole of oxygen), imply the following reaction:

$$2H_2 + O_2 \Rightarrow 2H_2O$$

From this statement about the proportions of hydrogens and oxygens that react with each other, we can conclude that two hydrogen molecules must react with a single oxygen molecule to form two molecules of water.

35. Hypothesis 1 does NOT predict that:

   A.   reactions will adjust to the proportions given.
   B.   2 moles of zinc will react completely with 3 moles of sulfur.
   C.   7 moles of zinc will react completely with 4 moles of sulfur.
   D.   if 3 moles of zinc were mixed with 4 moles of sulfur, then 1 mole of sulfur would be left unreacted.

36. According to Hypothesis 1, how many moles of water would be produced by the reaction of 2 moles of hydrogen and 1 mole of oxygen?

   F.   1
   G.   2
   H.   4
   J.   Cannot be determined from the given information

Items #37–38 refer to the following:

An experimenter finds that when 170 grams of $AgNO_3$ is reacted with 58.5 grams of NaCl to form products, none of the original reactants remain in appreciable amounts. When the original amount of $AgNO_3$ is increased to 175 grams, then all of the NaCl is used up, but 5 grams of $AgNO_3$ remains.

37. The result described above is:

   A.   consistent with Hypothesis 1.
   B.   consistent with Hypothesis 2.
   C.   consistent with both Hypothesis 1 and Hypothesis 2.
   D.   not consistent with either hypothesis.

38. According to Hypothesis 2, how might the remaining 5 grams of $AgNO_3$ be used up?

   F.   Add more of the reactant NaCl.
   G.   Remove some of the reactant NaCl.
   H.   Add even more of the reactant $AgNO_3$.
   J.   There is no mechanism for using the 5 grams of $AgNO_3$.

39. An experimenter wishes to determine which theory better fits her data for an experiment in which iron is chemically combined with oxygen. She finds that 2 moles of iron will react completely with 2 moles of oxygen; she also finds that 2 moles of iron will react completely with 3 moles of oxygen. At this point she is confident that Hypothesis 1, which is in opposition to the idea of "definite proportions," is correct. What further experiment might she do to test the success of Hypothesis 1 over Hypothesis 2?

A. Add 1 mole of iron to 1 mole of oxygen.
B. Add 2 moles of iron to 4 moles of oxygen.
C. Add 3 moles of iron to 4.5 moles of oxygen.
D. Add 4 moles of iron to 4 moles of oxygen.

40. According to Hypothesis 1, the product of the reaction of hydrogen and oxygen:

F. is H_2O.
G. could be anything.
H. must contain hydrogen and oxygen, but lacks a specific formula.
J. has a definite proportion of hydrogen to oxygen.

NO TEST MATERIAL ON THIS PAGE

5 5 5 5 5 5 5 5 5 5 5 5 5

SECTION 5: WRITING TEST (OPTIONAL)
40 Minutes—1 Essay Prompt

DIRECTIONS: You have 40 minutes to plan and write an essay. Read the prompt carefully and make sure you understand the instructions. A successful essay will have the following features: it will take a position on the issue presented in the writing prompt; it will maintain a consistent focus on the topic; it will use logical reasoning and provide supporting ideas; it will present ideas in an organized manner; and, finally, it will include clear and effective language in accordance with the conventions of standard written English. Sample essay responses begin on page 307.

Social Activism Online

With the viral nature of online information, especially through social media, many people use social media to raise awareness or express support for various causes. Often, people post articles or sign online petitions to protest injustices. Others may start online campaigns about various social causes, encouraging people to spread the information or to donate to an organization. However, some call this form of activism "slacktivism," comparing it negatively to actions that require more time, effort, and sometimes risk, such as volunteering or protesting. Opponents of online activism question whether such activities really make a difference; furthermore, they argue that it could be counterproductive because "slacktivists" feel like they've done their part without ever leaving their chairs. As more citizens address social causes online, it is important to evaluate whether online activism can generate true social engagement.

Perspective 1	Perspective 2	Perspective 3
Online activism does not make people truly involved in social causes because it requires minimal time or effort and does not generate concrete results. It allows participants to feel involved in issues while doing little to nothing to help people who are suffering.	Online activism can be effective when it is combined with more direct forms of activism. For example, one could advertise activist organizations on social media to attract volunteers and increase donations.	Supporting or advertising a cause online is a valuable way to generate support for pressing social issues. When significant amounts of people are aware of social problems, it is more likely that governments or other organizations will address them.

Essay Task

Write a unified, coherent essay in which you evaluate multiple perspectives on the issue of social activism online. In your essay be sure to:

- Analyze and evaluate perspectives given
- State and develop your own perspective
- Explain the relationship between your perspective and those given

Your perspective may be in full agreement with any of the others, in partial agreement, or wholly different. Whatever the case, support your ideas with logical reasoning and detailed, persuasive examples.

END OF TEST 5
STOP! DO NOT RETURN TO ANY OTHER TEST.

PRACTICE TEST III

DIRECTIONS

Practice Test III includes five subject tests: English, Mathematics, Reading, Science, and Writing. Calculator use is permitted on the Mathematics Test only.

Cambridge offers several services for schools utilizing our practice tests. Ask your teacher whether your school has decided to send your answers to Cambridge for scoring or to score your answers at your school. If Cambridge is scoring your test, you will use a Scantron™ form provided by your teacher, or you will enter your answers online. If your school is scoring your test, you may use a Scantron™ form provided by your teacher, or you may write your answers on paper.

If you are entering your test answers on a Scantron™ form, please be sure to include the following information on the Scantron™:

Book and Edition	*Victory for the ACT Test, 14th Edition*
Practice Test Number	**Practice Test III**

If you are only completing a single section of this practice test, make sure to also include the following information:

Subject	English, Mathematics, Reading or Science
Section Number	**Section 1, 2, 3 or 4**

The items in each multiple-choice test are numbered and the answer choices are lettered. The Scantron™ form has numbered rows that correspond to the items on the test. Each row contains lettered ovals to match the answer choices for each item on the test. Each numbered row has a corresponding item on the test.

For each item, first decide on the best answer choice. Then, locate the row number that corresponds to the item. Next, find the oval in that row that matches the letter of the chosen answer. Then, use a soft lead pencil to fill in the oval. DO NOT use a ballpoint pen.

Mark only one answer for each item. If you change your mind about an answer choice, thoroughly erase your first mark before marking your new answer.

Note that only responses marked on your Scantron™ form or written on your paper will be scored. Your score on each test will be based only on the number of items that are correctly answered during the time allowed for that test. You will not be penalized for guessing. Therefore, it is to your best advantage to answer every item on the test, even if you must guess.

On the Writing Test, write your response to the prompt using the essay response sheets or loose-leaf paper provided by your teacher. Your teacher might also direct you to enter your essay response online. (Note that the Writing Test is optional.)

You may work on each test only during the time allowed for that test. If you finish a test before time is called, use the time to review your answer choices or work on items about which you are uncertain. You may not return to a test on which time has already been called, and you may not preview another test. You must lay down your pencil immediately when time is called at the end of each test. You may not for any reason fill in or alter ovals for a test after time has expired for that test. Violation of these rules will result in immediate disqualification from the exam.

GO ON TO THE NEXT PAGE.

PRACTICE TEST **III**

1 1 1 1 1 1 1 1 1 1 1 1

SECTION 1: ENGLISH TEST
45 Minutes—75 Items

DIRECTIONS: In the passages below, certain parts of the sentences have been underlined and numbered. In the right-hand column, you will find different ways of writing each underlined part; the original version is indicated by the "NO CHANGE" option. For each item, select the choice that best expresses the intended idea, is most acceptable in standard written English, or is most consistent with the overall tone and style of the passage.

There are also items that ask about a section of the passage or the passage as a whole. These items do not refer to an underlined portion of the passage; these items are preceded by statements that are enclosed in boxes.

Read the passage through once before you begin to answer the accompanying items. Finding the answers to certain items may depend on looking at material that appears several sentences beyond the item. So, be sure that you have read far enough ahead before you select your answer choice. Answers are on page 313.

PASSAGE I

Trade in the Northwest Territory

[1]

In 1849, San Francisco became the first official port of entry on the Pacific Coast. In 1851, on account of the rapid growth of the lumber
1
industry and a corresponding expansion of population in the Northwest Territory, the government established the Puget Sound District of the Bureau of Customs.

Nonetheless, smuggling grew rapidly, fostered
2
by the tempting proximity of British havens and the natural cover afforded by vast forested areas and by the coves and inlets of countless heavy timbered
3
islands.

1. A. NO CHANGE
   B. since
   C. because of
   D. for

2. F. NO CHANGE
   G. Therefore
   H. Consequently
   J. On the contrary

3. A. NO CHANGE
   B. countless, heavy
   C. countless, heavily
   D. countlessly heavy

GO ON TO THE NEXT PAGE.

[2]

Such fears were <u>well foundationed</u>. In
                    4

1851, US customers officers <u>seize</u> the Hudson Bay
                              5

Company's steamer *Beaver* <u>for a technical violation</u>
                            6

<u>of the revenue laws</u>. This incident signaled an
        6

end to the era of unrestricted trade in the Pacific

Northwest and drove some traders on both sides

of the international border into illicit commercial

arrangements. British wool, blankets, and liquor

<u>were the principle articles</u> of this trade.
        7

<u>In fact</u>, so much British wool was smuggled into
 8

the San Juan Islands <u>selling</u> as domestic wool by
                      9

American <u>sheepmen one</u> naive textbook writer
          10

credited San Juan sheep with a world's record

annual production of 150 pounds of wool per

animal.

---

4. F. NO CHANGE
   G. well founded
   H. founded well
   J. well found

5. A. NO CHANGE
   B. seized
   C. were seizing
   D. have seized

6. F. NO CHANGE
   G. on account of violating the revenue laws
   H. for technically being in violation of the revenue laws
   J. in that they were in technical violation of the revenue laws

7. A. NO CHANGE
   B. was the principle article
   C. were the principal articles
   D. was the principal article

8. F. NO CHANGE
   G. Furthermore
   H. Moreover
   J. On the contrary

9. A. NO CHANGE
   B. to sell
   C. and sold
   D. and would be sold

10. F. NO CHANGE
    G. sheepmen, one
    H. sheepmen that one
    J. sheepmen, and a

GO ON TO THE NEXT PAGE.

[3]

Although American settlers in the Northwest
11

Territory welcomed the assertion of national control
12

to the forty-ninth parallel, they were less amenable

to restrictions on trade with Vancouver Island. They

wanted the duty-free rum and woolens offered by

the British but were fearing that the imposition and
13

enforcement of permanent tariffs on goods from

British North America might be resulting in the
14

losing of British markets for American products.
14

11. A. NO CHANGE
B. Since
C. Therefore
D. Thus

12. F. NO CHANGE
G. welcoming
H. would welcome
J. were welcomed by

13. A. NO CHANGE
B. and were fearing
C. and was fearful
D. but feared

14. F. NO CHANGE
G. might result in the losing
H. might result in the loss
J. results in the loss

Items #15–16 ask about the preceding passage
as a whole.

15. Which of the following represents the most
logical order of the three paragraphs?

A. 1, 2, 3
B. 1, 3, 2
C. 2, 3, 1
D. 3, 1, 2

16. Which of the following does NOT represent a
technique used in the development of the essay?

F. Narrative
G. Example
H. Statistics
J. Quotations

GO ON TO THE NEXT PAGE.

Mapping the Cosmos

One of the beauties of astronomy <u>is that one does not have to be an expert to enjoy it</u>. Anyone
₁₇
can step outside on a clear, moonless night, gaze

at thousands of stars shining across the vast

interstellar <u>spaces, and then one can become</u>
₁₈
intoxicated by a heady mix of grandeur and

existential chill. The same questions come to mind

time and <u>again, how</u> far away are the stars? How
₁₉
many are there? Are they strewn endlessly through

space, or are we a part of an island universe of suns

<u>ending</u> abruptly somewhere out there in the black
₂₀
ocean of space?

It has been the sometimes heroic and often

frustrating task of astronomers since the dawn of

science <u>to chart</u> our position in the cosmic ocean. In
₂₁
the twentieth century, significant progress

<u>had been made</u> in constructing an accurate map of
₂₂
the cosmos. We know, for example, that our solar

system is part of a much larger system of hundreds

of billions of stars. <u>As such, this</u> system is the Milky
₂₃
Way Galaxy, a huge disk of stars and gas. We also

know that ours is not the only galaxy in the universe.

As far as the largest telescopes in the world can see,

17. A. NO CHANGE
B. is the not having to be an expert to enjoy it
C. is that the enjoying of it does not have to be done by an expert
D. is that one doesn't necessarily have to be an expert in order to derive some enjoyment from it

18. F. NO CHANGE
G. spaces—and became
H. spaces, and become
J. spaces and becomes

19. A. NO CHANGE
B. again and how
C. again how
D. again. How

20. F. NO CHANGE
G. that end
H. that ends
J. ended

21. A. NO CHANGE
B. charting
C. having charted
D. who charted

22. F. NO CHANGE
G. was made
H. is made
J. will be made

23. A. NO CHANGE
B. Obviously, this
C. Doubtless, this
D. This

GO ON TO THE NEXT PAGE.

there are galaxies in every direction. The nearest
24

galaxies to our own are the Magellanic Clouds; the
25

"crown jewels" of the southern skies.
25

Since they are so near, they offer a laboratory in which astronomers can study the evolution of stars and galaxies. The nearest large galaxy to the Milky Way is the Andromeda Galaxy, which is about two million light years away. It is a giant spiral galaxy, much like our own in size, shape, and number and
26

type of stars. This nearby sister galaxy provides to us
27
an opportunity to get a bird's eye view of a galaxy

much like our own—in effect, to see ourselves as
28

others do.
28

24. F.   NO CHANGE
    G.   These
    H.   (Begin a new paragraph here rather than after "skies") The
    J.   (Begin a new paragraph here rather than after "skies") As the

25. A.   NO CHANGE
    B.   Clouds, the crown jewels
    C.   Clouds which is the "crown jewels"
    D.   Clouds, the "crown jewels"

26. F.   NO CHANGE
    G.   much as
    H.   like much
    J.   much the same like

27. A.   NO CHANGE
    B.   provides us
    C.   provide us
    D.   providing to us

28. F.   NO CHANGE
    G.   to see ourselves the way other people tend to see us
    H.   so that we would be seeing ourselves the way other people would be seeing us
    J.   so that in this way we would see ourselves as others do

GO ON TO THE NEXT PAGE.

Item #29 asks about the preceding passage as a whole.

29. Which of the following is NOT one of the reasons the author poses a series of questions in the first paragraph?

   A. To give the reader a sense of the "grandeur and existential chill"
   B. To stimulate the reader's interest in astronomy
   C. To give specific examples of questions about the cosmos that are still unanswered
   D. To alert the reader that answers to these questions will follow later in the passage

PASSAGE III

A Brief History of the Mercury Space Program

The first astronauts entered the Mercury program in April 1959. They were volunteer, military <u>pilots, graduated</u> of test pilot schools.
                    30

Each <u>were required having</u> a bachelor's degree
            31
in engineering (or its equivalent) and at least 1,500 hours of jet time. Of the first group of sixty candidates called to Washington to hear about the program, more than 80 percent volunteered. Only seven <u>got</u> chosen. (Officials assumed that no more
        32

30. F. NO CHANGE
    G. pilots graduates
    H. pilots; graduates
    J. pilots, graduates

31. A. NO CHANGE
    B. was required to have
    C. required having
    D. had been required to have

32. F. NO CHANGE
    G. were
    H. had been
    J. has been

GO ON TO THE NEXT PAGE.

than seven men would have the opportunity to fly.)

[33] These men were true <u>pioneers, they</u> volunteered
                              34
at a time when the plans for space travel were only

on paper and no one knew what the chance of

success was.

<u>Scientists</u> were able to learn from each failure.
  35

<u>Fortunately they had these failures</u> early in the
            36
program. The astronauts and the animal passengers

as well were flown without mishap when <u>their time</u>
                                           37
<u>came for them.</u>
   37

---

33. Is the second use of parentheses in the first paragraph appropriate?

    A. Yes, because the information contained in the parentheses is irrelevant to the passage.

    B. Yes, because the information explains something the author said but is not vital to the understanding of the passage.

    C. No, because the material is vital to the understanding of the author's main argument.

    D. No, because an entire sentence should never be placed in parentheses.

34. F. NO CHANGE
    G. pioneers but
    H. pioneers yet
    J. pioneers. They

35. Which of the following phrases would best replace the word *scientists* to provide a transition from the first to the second paragraph?

    A. It was lucky that the men volunteered because scientists

    B. There were failures as well as successes in the Mercury program, but scientists

    C. Since the chances for success were unknown, scientists

    D. Since the volunteers were also engineers, scientists

36. F. NO CHANGE
    G. Fortunately, they had these failures occurring
    H. These failures occurred fortunately
    J. Fortunately, these failures occurred

37. A. NO CHANGE
    B. the time for them finally came
    C. their time finally came for them
    D. their time came

GO ON TO THE NEXT PAGE.

The most spectacular failure in the Mercury program came to be known as the "tower flight." 38 The escape tower, the parachutes, and the peroxide

fuel were all deployed on the launching pad in front of the domestic and international press. A <u>relatively</u>
39
<u>simple</u> ground-circuit defect in the Redstone launch
39
vehicle caused the main rocket engine to ignite

<u>and then shutting</u> down immediately after liftoff
40
from the launching pad. The "flight" lasted only a

second and covered a distance of only two inches. 41

<u>One of the requirements</u> of the Mercury
42

program was that an animal <u>had to precede man</u>
43
<u>into space</u>. The flight of Ham, the chimpanzee, was a
43
major milestone in the program. Again, there were

some problems. The pickup of the spacecraft was

38. Is the use of the word *spectacular* in the first sentence of the third paragraph appropriate?

    F.   Yes, because the author obviously disapproves of the Mercury program.
    G.   Yes, because the author is using the word in an ironic sense.
    H.   No, because the reader might be misled about the goals of the Mercury program.
    J.   No, because the failure cited was caused by a simple defect.

39. A. NO CHANGE
      B. relative and simple
      C. relative simple
      D. simple relatively

40. F. NO CHANGE
      G. and then will shut
      H. and then they shut
      J. and then to shut

41. The author put the word *flight* in quotation marks because:

    A. the author believes a flight must last for many miles.
    B. there was no real flight at all.
    C. the word is a technical term used by astronauts.
    D. the word is often repeated in the passage.

42. F. NO CHANGE
      G. (Do NOT begin a new paragraph) One of the requirements
      H. (Do NOT begin a new paragraph) One requirement
      J. (Do NOT begin a new paragraph) A requirement

43. A. NO CHANGE
      B. had to be the one to precede man in space
      C. was going to have to go into space before man
      D. needed to be the one to go into space before man did

GO ON TO THE NEXT PAGE.

delayed, and <u>water had leaked into</u> the capsule. Ham,
    44

however, was eventually rescued <u>unharmed</u>.
                            45

     Sending a man into zero gravity was among

the greatest medical experiments of all time.

Fortunately, all astronauts found the weightlessness

to be no problem. All <u>returning</u> to Earth with no
                        46
medical difficulties whatsoever. In this area, the only

question left unanswered by the Mercury program

was how long man <u>will tolerate</u> weightlessness.
                    47

It <u>seemed like</u>, however, that longer flights would
    48

require only that astronauts <u>to have</u> suitable
                            49

methods of exercise and nutrition. 50

44. F.   NO CHANGE
     G.   water leaked into
     H.   water leaks in
     J.   leaking water into

45. The best placement for the underlined portion would be:

     A.   where it is now.
     B.   before the word *was*.
     C.   before the word *eventually*.
     D.   before the word *rescued*.

46. F.   NO CHANGE
     G.   return
     H.   returned
     J.   will return

47. A.   NO CHANGE
     B.   will be able to tolerate
     C.   was able to tolerate
     D.   could tolerate

48. F.   NO CHANGE
     G.   seemed
     H.   seemed as
     J.   seemed to be

49. A.   NO CHANGE
     B.   have
     C.   had had
     D.   are sure to have

50. Which of the following might be an appropriate concluding sentence for the essay?

     F.   Although the Mercury program had some failures, it was on the whole a successful part of the space program.
     G.   Although the Mercury program had some successes, it was on the whole a failure.
     H.   Many people have objected to the use of animals in testing programs.
     J.   Science fiction writers have often written about space travel.

GO ON TO THE NEXT PAGE.

PASSAGE IV

Advances in Modern Medicine

It was not until the nineteenth century that

medicine was able, in any broad and real way, to
                                            51

help the suffering individual. During the nineteenth
51

century, technical advances aided the diagnostician

and also the surgeon, and the beginnings of an
52

understanding of the fundamental mechanisms

of disease had been emerging. All aspects of
                  53

medicine—from the research laboratory to the

operating table—was enjoying the benefits of the
                   54

rigorous application of the scientific method.

By the end of the nineteenth century, a person's

chances were fairly good that a doctor could not only

give a name to his medical complaint yet probably had
                                       55

an elementary understanding of what it was and

how it progressed. With somewhat more luck, the

doctor could select the proper treatment

and he could also mitigate the symptoms if not cure
       56

the disease altogether.

This transition to modern medicine depended

on three important advances. First, it required

an understanding of the true nature and origin of

disease. Second, it required that an organized body

51. A. NO CHANGE
    B. way of help
    C. way to help
    D. way, of helping

52. F. NO CHANGE
    G. as well as
    H. with
    J. as opposed to

53. A. NO CHANGE
    B. was emerging
    C. were emerging
    D. emerged

54. F. NO CHANGE
    G. were enjoying
    H. is enjoying
    J. enjoys

55. A. NO CHANGE
    B. but also probably had
    C. consequently probably has
    D. but also, probably would have

56. F. NO CHANGE
    G. but could mitigate
    H. and mitigate
    J. and can mitigate

GO ON TO THE NEXT PAGE.

of standard medical practice <u>be available to</u> guide
                             57
physicians in the diagnosis and treatment of disease.

Last, <u>it presupposes</u> a degree of medical technology
       58
never before available.

     <u>Among the more dramatic</u> nineteenth-century
           59
medical advances were those in the field of human

physiology. [60] In 1822, an obscure American army

camp surgeon practicing medicine <u>near where</u>
                                      61
<u>the Canadian frontier is</u> was transformed almost
        61
overnight into a specialist on the mechanism of

human digestion. The physician, William Beaumont,

was called to treat a young trapper who had been

accidentally shot in the stomach. <u>Beaumont's</u>
                                      62
<u>operating skill</u> saved the boy's life but the patient
    62
was left with an abnormal opening leading to the

stomach. To Beaumont's credit, he recognized this

unique opportunity to study the human digestive

57. A. NO CHANGE
     B. was available to
     C. is available for
     D. be available as

58. F. NO CHANGE
     G. it is presupposed
     H. it presupposed
     J. they presuppose

59. A. NO CHANGE
     B. (Do NOT begin a new paragraph) Among
         the more dramatic
     C. Since
     D. (Do NOT begin a new paragraph) Since

60. Which of the following correctly describes the
     function of the first sentence of this paragraph?

     F. It introduces a topic that has nothing to do
         with the material discussed in the first three
         paragraphs.
     G. It introduces material that will contradict
         what was discussed in the first three
         paragraphs.
     H. It provides a transition that sets up a
         contrast to the material that came before.
     J. It provides a transition that moves from a
         general discussion to a more specific yet
         related topic.

61. A. NO CHANGE
     B. near where the Canadian frontier is,
     C. near where the Canadian frontier was
     D. near the Canadian frontier

62. F. NO CHANGE
     G. (Begin a new paragraph) Beaumont's
         operating skill
     H. The skill of Beaumont at operating
     J. (Begin a new paragraph) The skill of
         Beaumont at operating

GO ON TO THE NEXT PAGE.

<u>process, but</u> for the next 10 years he conducted
63

hundreds of experiments with the reluctant

cooperation of his not-so-willing patient.

     From his experiments, Beaumont was able to

describe the physiology of digestion, demonstrating

the characteristics of gastric motility <u>and describe</u>
64

the properties of gastric juice. He determined that

the stomach contained hydrochloric acid and that it

broke down food by a chemical process and not by

maceration or putrefaction. Beaumont's pioneering

work made him a famous man. The young trapper

did not fare as well; he was forced to tour medical

schools as "the man with the window in his

stomach."

63. A. NO CHANGE
    B. process, and
    C. process,
    D. process. But

64. F. NO CHANGE
    G. to describe
    H. that describe
    J. and describing

PASSAGE V

All About Babies

     Newborn babies are not the passive creatures

most people assume <u>him to be</u>. Recent research
65

shows that the newborn comes well-endowed <u>of</u>
66

charm and full potential for social graces. His eyes

are equipped with surprisingly good vision. Shortly

after birth, he begins to watch his mother's face,

which he soon comes to recognize. He also learns

to know her voice and will turn toward her when

65. A. NO CHANGE
    B. he was
    C. them to be
    D. it is

66. F. NO CHANGE
    G. for
    H. with
    J. by

GO ON TO THE NEXT PAGE.

he hears it. This is about the time when affection
    67
begins. The infant's cry alerts the mother and causes

a biological including an emotional reaction. The
            68
infant's ability to cling and cuddle communicates a

pleasurable warmth to the mother, and the infant's

odor is pleasant and uniquely its own. The newborn

also smiles. The human infant, unfortunately,
                          69

is in possession of attributes that are guaranteeing
    70   71
its attractiveness.

   Although there is some argument about

whether the child sparks the development of love

or whether or not a special physiological state of
    72
the mother prompts her to interact with the new

infant. But most researchers agree that the newborn
    73
does mold or trigger adult behavior. The neonate

organizes the mother's behavior by crying and by

eye-to-eye contact. The newborn is not a passive

creature at all.

67. A. NO CHANGE
    B. it, this
    C. it this
    D. it

68. F. NO CHANGE
    G. and
    H. with
    J. but

69. A. NO CHANGE
    B. on the other hand
    C. nevertheless
    D. in fact

70. F. NO CHANGE
    G. possessed
    H. possesses
    J. are in possession of

71. A. NO CHANGE
    B. guaranteed
    C. guarantee
    D. guarantees

72. F. NO CHANGE
    G. or whether
    H. and whether if
    J. or whether if

73. A. NO CHANGE
    B. infant: but most
    C. infant. Most
    D. infant, most

GO ON TO THE NEXT PAGE.

Items #74-75 ask about the preceding passage as a whole.

74. Which of the following best describes the function of the last sentence of the essay?

    F. It introduces a new topic for the reader to investigate.
    G. It contradicts everything that was said before.
    H. It reiterates the main theme of the passage.
    J. It establishes the author as an authority.

75. Which of the following best describes the overall development of the essay?

    A. A comparison and contrast using anecdotes
    B. A narrative using examples
    C. A description using statistics
    D. An argument using examples

2 2 2 2 2 2 2 2 2 2 2 2

SECTION 2: MATHEMATICS TEST
60 Minutes—60 Items

DIRECTIONS: Solve each item and choose the correct answer choice. Then, fill in the corresponding oval on the bubble sheet.

Allocate time wisely. Try to solve as many items as possible, returning to skipped items if time permits.

Calculator use is permitted on this test; however, some items are best solved without the use of a calculator.

<u>NOTE:</u> All of the following should be assumed, unless otherwise stated.

1. Illustrative figures are NOT necessarily drawn to scale.
2. The word *average* indicates arithmetic mean.
3. The word *line* indicates a straight line.
4. Geometric figures lie in a plane.

Answers are on page 323.

---

1. Amanda has to arrange the five shapes below in a row. How many arrangements can Amanda make if the circle cannot be placed at the beginning or end of the row?

    A.   5
    B.   24
    C.   36
    D.   72
    E.   120

DO YOUR FIGURING HERE.

2. John is now three times Pat's age. Four years from now, John will be *x* years old. In terms of *x*, how old is Pat now?

    F. $\dfrac{x+4}{3}$

    G. $3x$

    H. $x+4$

    J. $x-4$

    K. $\dfrac{x-4}{3}$

GO ON TO THE NEXT PAGE.

3. If $\dfrac{3}{4}$ of x is 36, then $\dfrac{1}{3}$ of x = ?

DO YOUR FIGURING HERE.

    A.   9
    B. 12
    C. 16
    D. 24
    E. 42

4. In the figure below, what is the value of $x + y$?

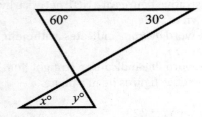

    F.   45
    G.   60
    H.   75
    J.   90
    K. 120

5. If n is a multiple of 3, which of the following expressions is also a multiple of 3?

    A. $2 + n$
    B. $2 - n$
    C. $2n - 1$
    D. $2n + 1$
    E. $2n + 3$

6. Which of the following is NOT equal to the ratio of 2 whole numbers?

    F. $\left(\dfrac{1}{5}\right)^2$

    G. 5%

    H. $\dfrac{1}{5}$

    J. 0.25

    K. $\dfrac{\sqrt{5}}{1}$

GO ON TO THE NEXT PAGE.

7. Nine playing cards from the same deck are placed as shown in the figure below to form a large rectangle with an area of 180 square inches. What is the perimeter, in inches, of this large rectangle?

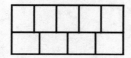

    A.   29
    B.   58
    C.   64
    D. 116
    E. 210

8. A train running between two towns arrives at its destination 10 minutes late when it travels at a constant rate of 40 miles per hour and 16 minutes late when it travels at a constant rate of 30 miles per hour. What is the distance, in miles, between the two towns?

    F. $8\frac{6}{7}$
    G.   12
    H. 192
    J. 560
    K. 720

9. What is the greatest factor of the expression $3x^2y^3z + 6x^3yz^3 + 2xy^2z^2$?

    A. $3x^2y^2z^2$
    B. $2x^2y^2z^2$
    C. $x^3y^3z^3$
    D. xyz
    E. xz

10. Depending on the value of k, the expression $3k + 4k + 5k + 6k + 7k$ may or may not be divisible by 7. Which of the terms, when eliminated from the expression, guarantees that the resulting expression is divisible by 7 for every positive integer k?

    F. $3k$
    G. $4k$
    H. $5k$
    J. $6k$
    K. $7k$

DO YOUR FIGURING HERE.

GO ON TO THE NEXT PAGE.

11. If $\dfrac{1}{3} < x < \dfrac{3}{8}$, which of the following is a possible value of x?

DO YOUR FIGURING HERE.

A. $\dfrac{3}{16}$

B. $\dfrac{17}{48}$

C. $\dfrac{9}{24}$

D. $\dfrac{5}{12}$

E. $\dfrac{1}{2}$

12. If $x^2 - y^2 = 3$ and $x - y = 3$, then $x + y = ?$

F. 0
G. 1
H. 2
J. 3
K. 9

13. If n is a positive integer, which of the following *must* be an even integer?

A. $n + 1$
B. $3n + 1$
C. $3n + 2$
D. $n^2 + 1$
E. $n^2 + n$

14. If the area of a square inscribed in a circle is 16 square centimeters, what is the area of the circle, in square centimeters?

F. 2π
G. 4π
H. 8π
J. 16π
K. 32π

15. Ellen bought a CD player on sale for 25% off the regular price of $120. If the store also collected an 8% sales tax on the sale price of the CD player, how much did Ellen pay for the CD player, including sales tax?

A. $106.30
B. $101.40
C. $97.20
D. $95.10
E. $88.44

GO ON TO THE NEXT PAGE.

16. A certain mixture of gravel and sand consists of 2.5 kilograms of gravel and 12.5 kilograms of sand. What percentage of the mixture, by weight, is gravel?

F.   10%

G. $16\frac{2}{3}\%$

H.   20%

J.   25%

K. $33\frac{1}{3}\%$

17. The figure below is the top-view of a folding room divider, hinged at P and Q. If sections $\overline{PR}$ and $\overline{QS}$ are moved as shown until R and S meet, what will be the enclosed area, in square feet? (Ignore the thicknesses of the hinges and the screen's sections.)

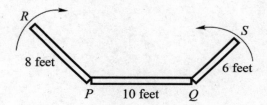

A.   6
B.   12
C. 6π
D.   24
E. 12π

18. Motorcycle A averages 40 kilometers per liter of gasoline while Motorcycle B averages 50 kilometers per liter. If the cost of gasoline is $2 per liter, what will be the difference in the cost of operating the two motorcycles for 300 kilometers?

F. $3
G. $6
H. $12
J. $15
K. $20

19. If $f(x) = x^2 - 2x + 1$, then $f(f(3)) = ?$

DO YOUR FIGURING HERE.

    A.   3
    B.   9
    C. 14
    D. 27
    E. 39

20. If $N! = N(N-1)(N-2)...[N-(N-1)]$, then

$$\frac{N!}{(N-2)!} = ?$$

    F. $N^2 - N$
    G. $N^5 + N^3 - N^2 + \dfrac{N}{N^2}$
    H. $N + 1$
    J.   1
    K.   6

21. Mailing a letter costs x cents for the first ounce and y cents for every additional ounce or fraction of an ounce. What is the cost, in cents, to mail a letter weighing a whole number of ounces, w?

    A. $w(x+y)$
    B. $x(w-y)$
    C. $x(x-1) + y(w-1)$
    D. $x + wy$
    E. $x + y(w-1)$

22. $|-3| \cdot |2| \cdot \left|-\dfrac{1}{2}\right| + (-4) = ?$

    F. -1
    G.   0
    H.   1
    J. $\dfrac{3}{2}$
    K.   4

GO ON TO THE NEXT PAGE.

23. In the figure below, the area of the square *OPQR* is 2 square inches, what is the area, in square inches, of the circle with center *O*?

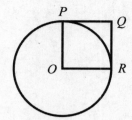

A. $\dfrac{\pi}{4}$

B. $\pi\sqrt{2}$

C. 2π

D. $2\pi\sqrt{2}$

E. 4π

24. Which of the following *must* be an odd number?

I. The product of a prime number and another prime number

II. The sum of a prime number and another prime number

III. The product of an odd number and another odd number

F. I only

G. III only

H. I and II only

J. II and III only

K. I, II, and III

25. What is the area of the shaded portion of the figure below, expressed in terms of *a* and *b*?

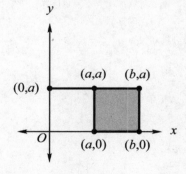

A. $a(b-a)$

B. $a(a-b)$

C. $b(a-b)$

D. $b(b-a)$

E. ab

GO ON TO THE NEXT PAGE.

26. $\sqrt{(43-7)(29+7)} = ?$

DO YOUR FIGURING HERE.

    F. $3\sqrt{3}$
    G.   6
    H.   36
    J.   42
    K. 1,296

27. A concrete mixture contains 4 cubic yards of cement for every 20 cubic yards of grit. If a mason orders 50 cubic yards of cement, how much grit, in cubic yards, should he order if he is to use all of the cement?

    A.   250
    B.   200
    C.   100
    D.   80
    E.   10

28. In the figure below, $\overline{QT} = \overline{QR}$. If $x° = 150°$, then $y = ?$

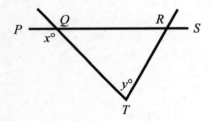

    F.   30
    G.   60
    H.   75
    J.   90
    K. 120

29. If $\dfrac{x}{y} = -1$, then $x + y = ?$

    A.   2
    B.   1
    C.   0
    D. -1
    E. -2

GO ON TO THE NEXT PAGE.

30. According to the table below, which fabric costs the LEAST per yard?

Fabric	Cost
F	3 yards for $8
G	2 yards for $6
H	4 yards for $9
J	5 yards for $7
K	8 yards for $10

F. F
G. G
H. H
J. J
K. K

31. For $\triangle PQR$ in the figure below, if $\overline{PQ} \parallel \overline{ST}$, then $y = ?$

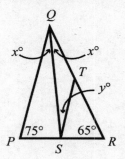

A. 20
B. 40
C. 45
D. 50
E. 55

32. $\dfrac{10^3(10^5 + 10^5)}{10^4} = ?$

F. $2(10^2)$

G. 10^4

H. $2(10^4)$

J. 10^6

K. $2(10^9)$

33. What is the solution set for the equation $x^2 - 5x + 4 = 0$?

A. $\{-4, -1\}$
B. $\{-3, -1\}$
C. $\{-1, 3\}$
D. $\{1, 4\}$
E. $\{2, 3\}$

GO ON TO THE NEXT PAGE.

34. The average of 7 different positive integers is 12. What is the greatest value that any one integer could have?

F. 19
G. 31
H. 47
J. 54
K. 63

35. If $x = b + 4$ and $y = b - 3$, then in terms of x and y, $b = ?$

A. $x + y - 1$
B. $x + y + 1$
C. $x - y - 1$
D. $\dfrac{x + y + 1}{2}$
E. $\dfrac{x + y - 1}{2}$

36. If $5x = 3y = z$, and x, y, and z are positive integers, all of the following must be an integer EXCEPT:

F. $\dfrac{z}{xy}$
G. $\dfrac{z}{5}$
H. $\dfrac{z}{3}$
J. $\dfrac{z}{15}$
K. $\dfrac{x}{3}$

37. What is the width of a rectangle with an area of $48x^2$ and a length of $24x$?

A. 2
B. $2x$
C. $24x$
D. $2x^2$
E. $3x^2$

DO YOUR FIGURING HERE.

GO ON TO THE NEXT PAGE.

38. If $x = \dfrac{1}{y+1}$ and $y \neq -1$, then $y = ?$

DO YOUR FIGURING HERE.

    F. $x + 1$

    G. x

    H. $\dfrac{x+1}{x}$

    J. $\dfrac{x-1}{x}$

    K. $\dfrac{1-x}{x}$

39. In the figure below, if the area of the triangle is 54, then $x = ?$

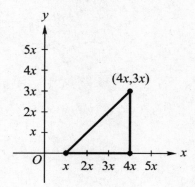

    A. $3\sqrt{3}$

    B. $2\sqrt{3}$

    C.   3

    D.   2

    E. $\sqrt{2}$

40. A drawer contains 4 green socks, 6 blue socks, and 10 white socks. If socks are pulled out of the drawer at random and not replaced, what is the minimum number of socks that must be pulled out of the drawer to *guarantee* that 2 of every color have been pulled out of the drawer?

    F.   6

    G.   7

    H.   11

    J.   12

    K.   18

GO ON TO THE NEXT PAGE.

DO YOUR FIGURING HERE.

41. In the figure below, the circle with center O has a radius 4 units long. If the area of the shaded region is 14π square units, what is the value of x?

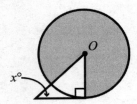

- A. 55
- B. 50
- C. 45
- D. 40
- E. 35

42. In the figure below, a circle is inscribed in a square that is in turn inscribed in a larger circle. What is the ratio of the area of the larger circle to the area of the smaller circle?

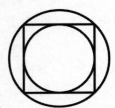

- F. $8:1$
- G. $4:1$
- H. $2\sqrt{2}:1$
- J. $2:1$
- K. $\sqrt{2}:1$

43. $2^0 + 2^3 - 2^{-2} = ?$

- A. 4
- B. $6\frac{1}{4}$
- C. 7
- D. $8\frac{3}{4}$
- E. $9\frac{3}{4}$

GO ON TO THE NEXT PAGE.

44. The graph of $y = x^2 - 3$ is a parabola with the axis of symmetry given by the equation $x = 0$. Which of the following are the (x, y) coordinates of the point on the parabola that is symmetric, with respect to the axis of symmetry, to the point with coordinates $(-1, -2)$?

F. $(-2, -1)$
G. $(-1, 2)$
H. $(0, -3)$
J. $(1, -2)$
K. $(1, 2)$

45. If two lines with equations $y = m_1 x + b_1$ and $y = m_2 x + b_2$ are perpendicular, which of the following *must* be true?

A. $m_1 = m_2$
B. $m_1 m_2 = 1$
C. $m_1 m_2 = -1$
D. $b_1 = b_2$
E. $b_1 b_2 = -1$

46. The figure below has lengths as marked, in inches. What is the area, in square inches, of the figure?

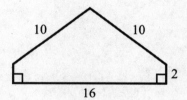

F. 36
G. 48
H. 56
J. 64
K. 80

47. For all $x > 0$ and $y > 0$, $\dfrac{\sqrt{x}}{2\sqrt{x} - \sqrt{y}}$ is equivalent to which of the following expressions?

DO YOUR FIGURING HERE.

A. $\dfrac{2x + \sqrt{xy}}{4x - y}$

B. $\dfrac{4x + \sqrt{xy}}{4x - y}$

C. $\dfrac{2\sqrt{x} + \sqrt{y}}{4xy}$

D. $\dfrac{2\sqrt{x} + \sqrt{xy}}{2x - y}$

E. $\dfrac{2\sqrt{x} - \sqrt{y}}{2}$

48. In the figure below, if $l_1 \parallel l_2$, then $x = ?$

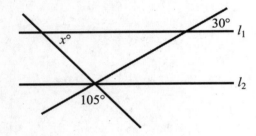

F. 20
G. 30
H. 45
J. 65
K. 130

49. The graph of $y = 2\cos(2x) + 2$ intersects the y-axis where $y = ?$

A. 0
B. 2
C. 3
D. 4
E. 5

50. In the figure below, *PQRS* is a square, and each of the 4 circles has a radius of *r*. What fractional part of the area of the square is shaded?

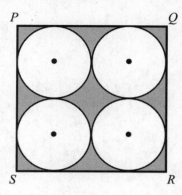

DO YOUR FIGURING HERE.

F. $\dfrac{\pi - 4}{2}$

G. $\dfrac{4 - \pi}{4}$

H. $\dfrac{\pi}{4}$

J. $\dfrac{4}{\pi}$

K. π

51. If $0° < \theta < 90°$, then $\dfrac{\sin^2\theta + \cos^2\theta}{\sin\theta} = ?$

A. $\sin\theta$
B. $\cos\theta$
C. $\csc\theta$
D. $\sec\theta$
E. $\cot\theta$

52. In the figure below, *ABC* is a right triangle. If $\sin 35° \approx 0.57$ and $\tan 55° \approx 1.4$, which of the following is the best approximation of the length of $\overline{AC}$?

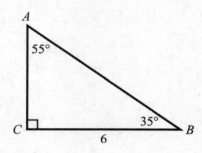

F. 3.42
G. 4.28
H. 8.57
J. 10.50
K. 12.25

GO ON TO THE NEXT PAGE.

53. For what value(s) of x is the function

$$f(x) = \frac{x(x+3)}{(x-1)(x+2)}$$ undefined?

    A. $\{-3\}$
    B. $\{-2\}$
    C. $\{1\}$
    D. $\{-2, 1\}$
    E. $\{-3, -2, 1\}$

DO YOUR FIGURING HERE.

54. What is the maximum value of $3y$ for x and y satisfying the system of inequalities below?

$$x \geq 0$$
$$y \geq 0$$
$$x + y \leq 6$$

    F. -3
    G. 0
    H. 6
    J. 12
    K. 18

55. Which of the following graphs correctly shows the points on the graph of $y(x) = |x^2 - 3|$ for $x = -1, 0,$ and 1?

DO YOUR FIGURING HERE.

A.

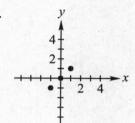

B.

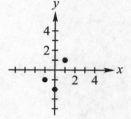

C.

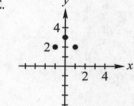

D.

E.

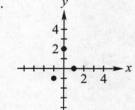

56. The figure below is a graph of which of the following equations?

DO YOUR FIGURING HERE.

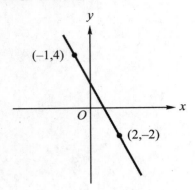

F. $y = -3x + 5$

G. $y = -2x + 2$

H. $y = -\dfrac{3}{2}x - 2$

J. $y = \dfrac{2}{3}x + 3$

K. $y = x + 2$

57. If the roots of the equation $ax^2 + bx + c = 0$

are $\dfrac{-3 + \sqrt{5}}{2}$ and $\dfrac{-3 - \sqrt{5}}{2}$, then which of the

following could be the equation?

A. $x^2 + 3x + 1 = 0$
B. $x^2 - 3x + 1 = 0$
C. $x^2 + 3x - 1 = 0$
D. $x^2 - 3x - 1 = 0$
E. $-x^2 + 3x + 1 = 0$

58. The relation defined by the set of ordered pairs
$\{(0,3), (2,1), (3,0), (-1,2), (0,5), (-2,5)\}$ is NOT
a function. Deleting which of the ordered pairs
will make the resulting set a function?

F. $(0,3)$
G. $(2,1)$
H. $(3,0)$
J. $(-1,2)$
K. $(-2,5)$

GO ON TO THE NEXT PAGE.

59. Trapezoid *ABCD* has lengths, in meters, and angle measures as marked in the figure below. What is the area, in square meters, of the trapezoid *ABCD*?

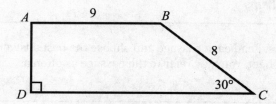

A. $18 + 8\sqrt{2}$
B. $18 + 8\sqrt{3}$
C. 42
D. $36 + 8\sqrt{2}$
E. $36 + 8\sqrt{3}$

60. If $\sin \theta = \dfrac{3}{5}$ and $\cot \theta = \dfrac{4}{3}$, then $\tan \theta = ?$

F. $\dfrac{3}{4}$

G. $\dfrac{4}{5}$

H. $\dfrac{7}{8}$

J. $\dfrac{5}{3}$

K. $\dfrac{20}{9}$

3 3 3 3 3 3 3 3 3 3 3 3 3

SECTION 3: READING TEST
35 Minutes—40 Items

> **DIRECTIONS:** Each passage below is followed by a set of items. Read each passage and choose the best answer for each item. Fill in the corresponding oval on your bubble sheet. You may refer to the passage as often as necessary to answer the items. Answers are on page 334.

PASSAGE I

PROSE FICTION: Passage A is adapted from Henry David Thoreau's *Walden* (1854) in which the author discusses his life of solitude in the New England woods. Passage B is adapted from *Public Opinion*, published in 1922 by Walter Lippman, a noted journalist and commentator.

Passage A

I am sure that I never read any memorable news in a newspaper. If we read of one man robbed or murdered or killed by accident, or one steamboat blown up, or one mad dog killed, or one lot of
5 grasshoppers in the winter—we never need read of another. One is enough. If you are acquainted with the principle, what do you care for a myriad instances and applications? All news, as it is called, is gossip, even though many people insist on hearing
10 it. If I should pull the bell-rope of the local church to sound a fire alarm, almost everyone in the entire area would stop everything and come running, not mainly to save property from the flames but to see the blaze, especially if it were the parish church itself
15 on fire.

After a night's sleep, the news is as indispensable to most people as breakfast: "Pray tell me everything important that has happened anywhere on this globe." They read over coffee
20 and rolls that a man has had his eyes gouged out the previous evening on the Wachito River. There was such a rush the other day at the railway office to learn the foreign news by the last arrival, that several large squares of plate glass were broken—
25 news that I seriously think a ready wit might have written a year or twelve years earlier with surprising accuracy. As for Spain, for instance, if you know how to throw in Don Carlos and the Infanta or Don Pedro and Seville and Granada from time to time
30 in the right proportions—they may have changed the names a little since I last saw the papers—and

serve up a bull-fight when other entertainments fail, it will be true to the letter and give as good an idea of the exact state of ruin of things in Spain
35 as the most succinct and lucid reports under this head in the newspapers. And as for England, almost the last significant scrap of news from that quarter was the revolution of 1649; and if you have learned the history of her crops for an average
40 year, you never need attend to that thing again, unless your speculations are of a merely pecuniary character. If one may judge who rarely looks into the newspapers, nothing new does ever happen in foreign parts, a French revolution not excepted.

Passage B

45 There is an island in the ocean, where in 1914 a few Englishmen, Frenchmen, and Germans lived. The island was not served by telegraph, and the British mail steamer came once every sixty days. On a day in mid-September, they learned of the start of the war
50 and that for over six weeks those of them who were English and those of them who were French had acted as if they were friends with those of them who were Germans, when in fact they were enemies.

Their plight was not so different from that
55 of most of the population of Europe. They had been mistaken for six weeks. There was a moment when the picture of Europe on which business was conducted as usual, and it did not correspond in any way to the Europe that was about to make a jumble
60 of so many lives. All over the world as late as July 25th people were making goods that they would not be able to ship, and buying goods that they would not be able to import. Then, over four years later, on a Thursday morning, came the news of an armistice,
65 and people gave vent to their unutterable relief that the slaughter was over. Yet, in the five days before the real armistice came, though the end of the war had been celebrated, several thousand young men died on the battlefields.

GO ON TO THE NEXT PAGE.

70   Looking back, we can see how indirectly we
know the environment in which we live. We can see
that the news of it comes to us sometimes quickly,
sometimes slowly, but whatever we believe to be a
true picture, we treat it as if it were the environment
75 itself. It is harder to remember that about the beliefs
upon which we are now acting, but in respect to
other peoples and other ages, we flatter ourselves
that it is easy to see when they were in deadly
earnest about ludicrous pictures of the world. We
80 insist, because of our superior hindsight, that the
world as they needed to know it and the world as
they did know it were often two quite contradictory
things. We can see, too, that while they governed and
fought, traded and reformed in the world as they
85 imagined it to be, they produced results, or failed to
produce any, in the world as it was. They started for
the Indies and found America.

Questions #1–5 ask about Passage A.

---

1. The newspaper report that a man has had his
eyes gouged out is included by the author of
Passage A as an example of:

A. a local event that affects people's lives
directly.
B. an insignificant incident that does not affect
the reader.
C. an unusual occurrence that merits special
coverage.
D. an international incident that warrants
detailed description.

2. The author mentions Don Carlos and the Infanta
in order to:

F. demonstrate a thorough familiarity with
current events in Spain.
G. familiarize the reader with recent events
that occurred in Spain.
H. explain how events in Europe affect people
all over the world.
J. illustrate the point that news from Spain
repeats itself.

3. The attitude of the author of Passage A towards
the news is:

A. ridicule.
B. admiration.
C. indifference.
D. confidence.

4. As used in this context, "attend to" (line 40)
means:

F. be present at.
G. be ignorant of.
H. be concerned with.
J. grow weary of.

5. The author adds "especially if it were the parish
church" (line 14) in order to:

A. emphasize that people are fascinated by the
bizarre.
B. prove that citizens do not care about public
property.
C. show that residents take an interest in local
events.
D. stress the importance of the church to
community.

Questions #6–8 ask about Passage B.

---

6. According to the author of Passage B, the people
on the island "acted as if they were friends" (line
52) because they:

F. originally came from European countries.
G. were isolated from the rest of the world.
H. disagreed over the outcome of the trial.
J. did not realize that war had started.

7. The "plight" to which the author refers in line 54
was:

A. incorrect reporting about the progress of
the war.
B. lack of accurate information about current
conditions.
C. an inability to obtain reports on a regular
basis.
D. slanted war news from the European front.

8. In line 83–86, the author implies that people of another time:

    F. accomplished something significant based upon wrong information.

    G. failed to realize that the information available was wrong.

    H. could have foreseen that America lay between Europe and India.

    J. realized only in hindsight that they had landed in America.

Questions #9–10 ask about both passages.

---

9. Which of the following best summarizes the different points of view of the two passages?

    A. The author of Passage B believes that news is important while the author of Passage A believes it is irrelevant.

    B. The author of Passage A believes that news is unreliable while the author of Passage B believes that it is accurate.

    C. The author of Passage A believes that newspapers provide critical information while the author of Passage B believes newspapers are too slow.

    D. The author of Passage A believes that news coverage could be improved while the author of Passage B believes that it is already adequate.

10. If the two authors had been able to write about the internet, they likely would:

    F. say that their points apply to the news content on the worldwide web.

    G. acknowledge that the new media makes reporting more relevant and more reliable.

    H. insist that newspapers remain a better source of information than electronic media.

    J. conclude that global news coverage gives readers a more accurate view of the world.

GO ON TO THE NEXT PAGE.

PASSAGE II

SOCIAL SCIENCE: This passage discusses the regulation of corporate takeovers.

There are a number of reasons why a company may wish to acquire another company. Some takeovers are opportunistic, that is, the target company may simply be very reasonably priced for
5 one reason or another and the acquiring company may decide that in the long run, it will end up making money by purchasing the target company. Berkshire Hathaway, a large holding company, has over the years made many profitable acquisitions by
10 simply buying other companies.

Other takeovers are strategic in that the acquiring company expects to obtain secondary benefits beyond the simple profitability of the target company. For example, an acquiring company may
15 purchase a company that is profitable and has good distribution capabilities in new areas which the acquiring company can use for its own products as well. A target company might be attractive because it has an established presence in a market
20 that the acquiring company wants to enter but without the risk and expense of starting from scratch. An acquiring company could even take over a competitor not only because the competitor is profitable, but in order to eliminate the competition
25 thus making it easier, in the long term, to earn a profit. Also, a takeover of a competitor could be advantageous to the acquiring company by permitting it to eliminate functions duplicated by the two companies prior to merger and thus reducing
30 expenses.

A "friendly takeover" is one that is approved by the management of the company to be acquired. In this case, the acquiring company usually first informs the other company's board of directors. If
35 the board feels that accepting the offer serves the shareholders better than rejecting it, it recommends the offer be accepted by the shareholders.

In a private company, because the shareholders and the board are usually the same people or closely
40 connected with one another, private acquisitions are usually friendly. If the shareholders agree to sell the company, then the board is usually of the same mind or sufficiently under the orders of the major shareholders to cooperate with the bidder.

45 Perhaps the most interesting type of acquisition, at least judging by the movies, is the hostile takeover; that is, an outside group or company trying to seize control of an existing company whose management opposes the takeover.

50 Most hostile takeovers begin with a tender offer in which the outside raiders offer to buy a sufficient amount of the company's outstanding stock at a stated price—usually well above the current market price. Another takeover strategy is to orchestrate
55 a proxy battle in which a vote of shareholders of record on a specific date is taken to approve or reject a new slate of directors put forth by the raiders. The aggressor company attempts to gather sufficient shareholder votes by promising a more profitable
60 return to oust the existing management and replace it with its own slate of directors. The word "proxy" indicates that the shareholders of record transfer their voting rights to one side or the other.

Regardless of the takeover strategy employed,
65 most raiders must purchase a significant portion of the company's stock at a price above its current market value. Outsiders usually finance such large purchases of stock through the sale of bonds that pay a very high rate of interest. The raiders argue
70 that the debt to be incurred can easily be paid off by selling parts of the targeted company or by drawing on the additional profits that the new management insists it can make.

Critics of hostile corporate takeovers believe
75 that the managers of the company to be taken over usually engage in short-term activities that have very negative long-term effects. In order to avoid hostile takeovers, managers of companies generally take measures to make the takeovers less
80 desirable. For instance, they may insert a golden parachute clause in employment contracts. This clause requires a company to pay very large bonuses to any management members who are fired after a takeover. Another tactic, the poison pill, restructures
85 the financial base of the corporation so that a takeover would make the company less profitable. Yet another anti-raid tactic is to pay greenmail to the raiders; that is, the target of the takeover pays the raiders to sell their shares back to the targeted
90 company at a much higher price. This prevents the takeover, but it usually adds a large sum to the company's debt.

Supporters of corporate raiders counter-argue that, in fact, it is the threat of a takeover that makes
95 managers more efficient. For instance, it may cause managers to sell parts of the company that they are not managing well in order to raise the money to fend off the takeover. In addition, those who believe that takeovers are good argue that the existing
100 shareholders always do better in a hostile takeover since they end up getting a higher price for each share of stock than the current market value.

GO ON TO THE NEXT PAGE.

11. Which statement expresses the main idea of this passage?

   A. Hostile corporate takeovers usually result in a detrimental long-term financial impact on the company that is taken over.
   B. A corporate takeover by one company of another can be initiated for any of several reasons using strategies appropriate to the relationship between the companies.
   C. Non-hostile acquisitions are economically preferable to hostile takeovers since the existing management of the acquired company retains corporate control.
   D. Corporate raiders planning a hostile takeover of a viable company must incur substantial debt to finance the takeover.

12. A corporation's board of directors votes to approve a new company policy. According to the plan, each member of the board and of upper management would receive severance of two to five years' pay if the new owner fired the member after a corporate takeover. This action would be considered:

   F. a poison pill.
   G. a golden parachute.
   H. greenmail.
   J. a hostile takeover.

13. What is the most important difference between a hostile and a non-hostile takeover?

   A. In a hostile takeover, stockholders must pay greenmail to the existing directors.
   B. In a non-hostile takeover, raiders sell bonds with high interest rates.
   C. In a hostile takeover, the existing management is opposed to the takeover.
   D. In a non-hostile takeover, the existing management uses golden parachutes.

14. According to the passage, which of the following parties in a hostile takeover will likely incur new debt?

   F. The raiders, because they need money to buy large blocks of stock
   G. The Securities and Exchange Commission, because it must oversee the transactions more closely
   H. The stockholders, because they must furnish additional funds
   J. The critics of hostile takeovers, because they make less money in the stock market

15. According to the passage, a poison pill strategy involves:

   A. paying the raiders high prices to buy back the company's stock from them.
   B. paying high bonuses to the members of the old management who are fired by the new management.
   C. more regulation by the Securities and Exchange Commission.
   D. restructuring the financial base of the company so that it will be less profitable or valuable to the raiders.

16. According to the passage, supporters of corporate takeovers believe that:

   F. the shareholders always lose money because a takeover profits only the raiders.
   G. fear of being targeted for a takeover makes managers more efficient.
   H. insider trading should be made legal.
   J. a proxy fight is the best way to win control.

17. According to the passage, in a proxy fight:

   A. the raiders sell bonds to buy the targeted company's stock.
   B. the raiders offer to buy stock at a higher-than-market price.
   C. insider information is traded illegally.
   D. the shareholders vote for approval or rejection of a new board of directors put forth by the raiders.

GO ON TO THE NEXT PAGE.

18. The management of a business recently
targeted for takeover decides to sell two of its
unprofitable subsidiaries to raise cash and cut
expenses. Supporters of corporate takeovers
would say that this action:

F. is an example of how the greenmail strategy
works.
G. is an example of how a golden parachute
strategy works.
H. is an example of how the fear of a takeover
makes managers more efficient.
J. is an example of how the poison pill strategy
works.

19. This passage cites Berkshire Hathaway as an
example of a holding company that:

A. was formed specifically for the purpose of
initiating hostile takeovers of companies
that presented profitable opportunities.
B. has enjoyed considerable financial success
locating and acquiring companies for less
than the companies are actually worth.
C. has repeatedly been targeted for hostile
takeover by larger companies but has
repelled them using the poison pill and
other strategies.
D. has a reputation as a corporate raider that
targets weaker companies and acquires
them by using its financial war chest.

20. According to the passage, a proxy battle for
control of a corporation attempts to:

F. acquire sufficient shareholder voting rights
to control the company..
G. conceal the identity of the hostile group
behind a facade of corporation.
H. threaten shareholders of the target
company with financial ruin.
J. drain the financial reserves of the target
company by cut-throat pricing.

GO ON TO THE NEXT PAGE.

PASSAGE III

HUMANITIES: This passage explores the contributions of Josquin des Prez to Western music.

Until Josquin des Prez (1440–1521), Western music was liturgical, designed as an accompaniment to worship. Like the intricate gargoyles perched atop medieval cathedrals beyond sight of any human,
5   music was composed to please God before anyone else; its main theme was reverence. Emotion was there, but it was the grief of Mary standing at the foot of the Cross, the joy of the faithful hailing Christ's resurrection. Even the secular music of the
10   Middle Ages was tied to predetermined patterns that sometimes seemed to stand in the way of individual expression.

While keeping one foot firmly planted in the divine world, Josquin stepped with the other into
15   the human world. He scored magnificent masses, but also newly expressive motets such as the *Lament of David* over his son Absalom or the *Deploration d'Ockeghem*, a dirge on the death of Ockeghem, the greatest master before Josquin. This motet
20   was written all in black notes and was one of the most profoundly moving scores of the Renaissance. Josquin was the first composer to set psalms to music. But alongside *Benedicite omnia opera Domini Domino* ("Bless the Lord, all ye works of the Lord")
25   he put *El Grillo* ("The cricket") and *Allegez moy* ("Solace me"). Martin Luther praised Josquin, for his music blends respect for tradition with a rebel's willingness to risk the horizon. What Galileo was to science, Josquin was to music. While preserving their
30   allegiance to God, both asserted a new importance for man.

Josquin dominated the musical world of his time, not only on account of his learning, skill, and originality, but because of his singular ability to
35   bring together the many streams of contemporary music. Musical styles were changing rapidly, in part owing to the movement of musicians between different regions of Europe. Many northern musicians moved to Italy, the heart of
40   the Renaissance, attracted by the Italian nobility's patronage of the arts; while in Italy, these composers were influenced by the native Italian styles, and often brought those ideas with them back to their homelands. The sinuous musical lines of the
45   Ockeghem generation, the contrapuntal complexity of the Netherlanders, and the homophonic textures of the Italian lauda and secular music began to merge into a unified style. During his lifetime, Josquin acquired immense popularity and fame and

50   was much in demand. Zarlino, writing in the 1580s, was still using examples from Josquin in his treatises on composition; and his fame was only eclipsed after the beginning of the Baroque era, with the decline of the polyphonic style.

55   In the twentieth century, there has been a revival of interest in his music in academic circles. A possible reason for his current popularity among students and teachers is that his music contains a direct emotional appeal to the listener. The
60   nineteenth century trend in musicology was to consider early music as moving from primitive forms to ever increasing perfection, and thus venerated later composers above Josquin. Contemporary musicology, however, tends to regard changes in
65   style not as progress towards perfection but simply as trends. Thus, Josquin is regarded as someone who simultaneously brought together most of the contemporary trends, made significant innovations, and was also able to express intense emotion.

70   Still, outside of the conservatory Josquin is not particularly well known. Why then should he, Josquin, languish in popular obscurity? The answer has to do with the separation of concept from performance in music. In fine art, concept and
75   performance are one; both the art lover and the art historian have thousands of years of paintings and sculptures to study and enjoy. Similarly with literature: poetry, fiction, and criticism survive on the printed page or in manuscript for judgment
80   and admiration by future generations. But musical notation on a page is not art, no matter how lofty or excellent the composer's conception; it is, crudely put, a set of directions for making art.

Being highly symbolic, musical notation
85   requires training before it can even be read, let alone performed. Moreover, because the musical conventions of other days are not ours, translation of a Renaissance score into modern notation brings difficulties of its own. For example, the Renaissance
90   notation of Josquin's day did not provide the tempo at which the music should be played or sung. It did not indicate all flats or sharps; these were sounded in accordance with musician rules, which were capable of changing major to minor, minor to major,
95   diatonic to chromatic sound, and thus affect melody, harmony, and musical expression. A Renaissance composition might include several parts— but it did not tell which were to be sung or played, or whether instruments were to be used at all.

100   Thus, Renaissance notation permits many interpretations. A creative musician may give an

GO ON TO THE NEXT PAGE.

interpretation that is a revelation. But no matter how creative, few modern musicians can offer any interpretation of Renaissance music. The public
105 need for it is small, limiting the number of musicians who can afford to learn, rehearse, and perform it. Most of those who attempt it at all are students organized in *collegia musica* whose memberships have a habit of changing every semester. This
110 prevents directors from maintaining the year-in, year-out continuity required to achieve excellence of performance. Finally, the instruments used in Renaissance times—krummhorns, rauschpfeifen, shawms, sackbuts—must be specially procured.

21. The primary purpose of the passage is to:

   A. introduce the reader to Josquin and account for his relative obscurity.
   B. describe the main features of medieval music and show how Josquin changed them.
   C. place Josquin's music in an historical context and show its influence on later composers.
   D. enumerate the features of Josquin's music and supply critical commentary.

22. The passage contains information that would help answer all of the following items EXCEPT:

   F. What are the titles of some of Josquin's secular compositions?
   G. What are the names of some Renaissance musical instruments?
   H. Who was the greatest composer before Josquin?
   J. What are the names of some of Josquin's most famous students?

23. It can be inferred from the passage that modern musical notation has which of the following characteristics?

   I. The tempo at which a composition is to be played is indicated in the notation.
   II. Whether a note is a sharp or a flat is indicated in the notation.
   III. The notation indicates which parts of the music are to be played by which instruments.

   A. I only
   B. II only
   C. I and III only
   D. I, II, and III

24. The author would most likely agree with which of the following statements?

   F. Music is a better art form than painting or sculpture.
   G. Music can be said to exist only when it is being performed.
   H. Josquin was the greatest composer of the Middle Ages.
   J. Renaissance music is superior to music produced in modern times.

25. The passage leads most logically to a proposal to:

   A. establish more *collegia musica*.
   B. study Josquin's compositional techniques in greater detail.
   C. include Renaissance music in college studies.
   D. provide funds for musicians to study and play Josquin.

26. The author cites all of the following as reasons for Josquin's relative obscurity EXCEPT:

   F. the difficulty one encounters in attempting to read his musical notation.
   G. the inability of modern musicians to play instruments of the Renaissance.
   H. the difficulty of procuring the unusual instruments needed to play the music.
   J. the lack of public interest in Renaissance music.

GO ON TO THE NEXT PAGE.

27. The author's attitude toward Galileo can best be described as:

    A. admiring.
    B. critical.
    C. accepting.
    D. analytical.

28. Which of the following statements about liturgical music is consistent with the selection?

    F. It is lacking in any emotion.
    G. It is written to entertain people.
    H. It is intended to be reverential.
    J. It treats primarily nonreligious themes.

29. Which of the following is NOT an example of fine art as that term is used in the passage?

    A. A ballet
    B. A novel
    C. A poem
    D. A mural

30. Josquin des Prez is important in the history of music because he:

    F. wrote motets using only black notes.
    G. wrote only nonliturgical music.
    H. wrote both liturgical and nonliturgical music.
    J. invented new musical instruments for his music.

PASSAGE IV

NATURAL SCIENCE: This passage discusses supernova explosions and their effects.

A high energy universe is almost by definition a violent one, but violence has its uses—even for a species as fragile as our own. Without the violence of volcanoes, for example, life might never have spread
5 across the face of Earth. Looking at things from a somewhat larger perspective, it is probable that the Sun and all the planets of the solar system would not be here but for violence on a much grander scale. The vast amorphous cloud of dust and gas from
10 which our solar system was formed might still be a formless mass if an interstellar shock wave had not triggered the collapse of the cloud.

About twice every century, one of the massive stars in our galaxy blows itself apart in a supernova
15 explosion. The force of the explosion hurls vast quantities of radiation and matter into space and generates shock waves that sweep through the arms of the galaxy. The shock waves heat the interstellar gas, evaporate small clouds, and compress larger
20 ones to the point at which they collapse under their own gravity to form new stars. The general picture that has been developed for the supernova explosion and its aftermath goes something like this. Throughout its evolution, a star is much like a leaky
25 balloon; it keeps its equilibrium figure through a balance of internal pressure against the tendency to collapse under its own weight. The pressure is generated by nuclear reactions in the core of the star that must continually supply energy to balance
30 the energy that leaks out in the form of radiation. Eventually, the nuclear fuel is exhausted, and the pressure drops in the core. With nothing to hold it up, the matter in the center of the star collapses inward, creating higher and higher densities and
35 temperatures, until the nuclei and electrons are fused into a super-dense lump of matter known as a neutron star.

As the overlying layers rain down on the surface of the neutron star, the temperature rises
40 until, with a blinding flash of radiation, the collapse is reversed. A thermo-nuclear shock wave runs through the now expanding stellar envelope, fusing lighter elements into heavier ones and producing a brilliant visual outburst that can be as intense as the
45 light of 10 billion suns.

The shell of matter thrown off by the explosion plows through the surrounding gas, producing an expanding bubble of hot gas, with gas temperatures in the millions of degrees. This gas will emit most
50 of its energy at X-ray wavelengths, so it is not surprising that X-ray observatories have provided some of the most useful insights into the nature of the supernova phenomenon. More than twenty supernova remnants have now been detected
55 in X-ray studies. Studies of these sources have provided the best estimates of the energy released in a supernova explosion. High Energy Astrophysics Observatories have gathered information that should clarify our understanding of the interaction
60 of the expanding shell with the surrounding interstellar gas and the mechanism for producing cosmic rays.

Recent discoveries of meteorites with anomalous concentrations of certain isotopes
65 indicate that a supernova might have precipitated the birth of our solar system more than four and a half billion years ago. Although the cloud that collapsed to form the Sun and the planets was composed primarily of hydrogen and helium, it also
70 contained carbon, nitrogen, and oxygen, elements essential for life as we know it. Elements heavier than helium are manufactured deep in the interior of stars and would, for the most part, remain there if it were not for the cataclysmic supernova explosions
75 that blow giant stars apart. Additionally, supernovas produce clouds of high-energy particles called cosmic rays. These high-energy particles continually bombard the Earth and are responsible for many of the genetic mutations that are the driving force of
80 the evolution of species.

Supernovas are the creative flashes that renew the galaxy. They seed the interstellar gas with heavy elements, heat it with the energy of their radiations, stir it up with the force of their blast waves, and
85 cause new stars to form. Some of these stars will be massive. They will rush through their life cycle, explode, dump a new supply of heavy elements into the gas, and quite possibly trigger the formation of other stars to make other supernovas in a chain of
90 violence that links the rise of life on Earth to events billions of years and half a galaxy away.

31. According to the passage, we can expect to observe a supernova in our galaxy about:

A. twice each year.
B. 100 times each century.
C. once every 50 years.
D. once every other century.

GO ON TO THE NEXT PAGE.

32. According to the passage, all of the following are true of supernovas EXCEPT:

    F. they are extremely bright.
    G. they are an explosion of some sort.
    H. they are emitters of large quantities of X-rays.
    J. they are caused by the collision of large galaxies.

33. The author employs which of the following to develop the second paragraph?

    A. Analogy
    B. Irony
    C. Statistics
    D. Example

34. It can be inferred from the passage that the meteorites mentioned by the author (line 63):

    F. contain dangerous concentrations of radioactive materials.
    G. give off large quantities of X-rays.
    H. include material not created in the normal development of our solar system.
    J. are larger than the meteorites normally found in a solar system like ours.

35. The author implies that:

    A. it is sometimes easier to detect supernovas by observation of the X-ray spectrum than by observation of visible wavelengths of light.
    B. life on Earth is endangered by its constant exposure to radiation forces that are released by a supernova.
    C. recently discovered meteorites indicate that the Earth and other planets of our solar system survived the explosion of a supernova several billion years ago.
    D. lighter elements are formed from heavier elements during a supernova as the heavier elements are torn apart.

36. According to the passage, what is the first event in the sequence that leads to the occurrence of a supernova?

    F. An ordinary star begins to emit tremendous quantities of X-rays.
    G. A superheated cloud of gas envelops a neutron star.
    H. An imbalance between light and heavy elements causes an ordinary star to collapse.
    J. An ordinary star exhausts its supply of nuclear fuel and begins to collapse.

37. According to the passage, a neutron star is:

    A. a gaseous cloud containing heavy elements.
    B. an intermediate stage between an ordinary star and a supernova.
    C. the residue that is left by a supernova.
    D. the core of an ordinary star that houses the thermonuclear reactions.

38. The author is primarily concerned with:

    F. speculating about the origins of our solar system.
    G. presenting evidence proving the existence of supernovas.
    H. discussing the nuclear reaction that occurs in the core of a star.
    J. describing a theory about the causes and effects of supernovas.

39. How long ago was our galaxy formed?

    A. 100 million years
    B. 1 billion years
    C. 2 billion years
    D. Over 4.5 billion years

40. What is the connection between supernovas and the evolution of species on Earth?

    F. There is no connection.
    G. Cosmic radiation from supernovas retards evolution.
    H. Cosmic radiation from supernovas drives evolution.
    J. Evolution makes future supernovas possible.

END OF TEST 3
STOP! DO NOT TURN THE PAGE UNTIL TOLD TO DO SO.
DO NOT RETURN TO THE PREVIOUS TEST.

SECTION 4: SCIENCE TEST
35 Minutes—40 Items

DIRECTIONS: Each passage below is followed by several items. After reading a passage, choose the best answer for each item. Fill in the corresponding oval on your bubble sheet. You may refer to the passage as often as necessary. You are NOT permitted the use of a calculator on this test. Answers are on page 339.

PASSAGE I

Before making their historic first powered flight, the Wright Brothers made extensive lift tests in 1901 using a glider. Their data differed from that obtained twelve years earlier by the German, Otto Lilienthal.

Results of both tests (Wright: thin line; Lilienthal: thick line) are shown below. "Lift" is the force that pulls the wing away from the earth, in a direction perpendicular to the flight path, and the "angle of incidence" is the angle that the flight path makes with the horizon.

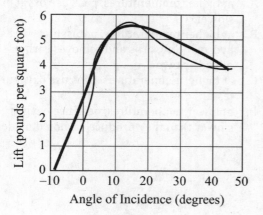

Modified from Culick, F.E.C, "The Wright 'Flyer' was the outcome of an intensive program of research." *Sci. Amer. 241* (1): 86–100, 1979.

1. The two curves differ chiefly in that:

    A. the Wrights' data were more accurate.
    B. lift was generally greater in Lilienthal's experiments.
    C. lift was generally greater in the Wrights' experiments.
    D. the peak value for lift was greater in Lilienthal's experiments.

2. In the Wrights' experiments, the greatest lift occurred at an angle of incidence of about:

    F. −5.5 degrees.
    G. 0 degrees.
    H. 14 degrees.
    J. 46 degrees.

3. At an angle of incidence of 50°, by how much would you expect the two experiments to show a difference in lift?

    A. 0–1 pounds per square foot.
    B. 1–2 pounds per square foot.
    C. 2–3 pounds per square foot.
    D. 3–4 pounds per square foot.

4. The two sets of experiments differed most in lift at which of the following angles?

    F. 10°
    G. 15°
    H. 30°
    J. 40°

5. The widest range of angles, in degrees, over which the Lilienthal values for lift continuously exceeded the Wrights' values was:

    A. 43.
    B. 25.
    C. 19.
    D. 10.

GO ON TO THE NEXT PAGE.

PASSAGE II

Two experiments were performed to determine the effects of temperature on the rate of cellular respiration* in germinating peas.

*Summary Equation:

consumed   produced

$$\underset{\text{(glucose)}}{C_6H_{12}O_6} + \underset{\text{(oxygen)}}{6O_2} \Rightarrow \underset{\text{(carbon dioxide)}}{6CO_2} + \underset{\text{(water)}}{6H_2O}$$

Experiment 1

A simple respirometer was used, primarily consisting of a large test tube partially filled with germinating peas. The peas were covered with a layer of cotton and a small amount of potassium hydroxide (KOH), a substance that can absorb and remove carbon dioxide from the tube. The remainder of the tube, with its starting volume of air sealed inside, was closed to the outside with a rubber stopper. Attached was a meter designed to detect and measure any changes in pressure in the tube during the experiment. The experiment was conducted at room temperature (22°C), and the respirometer was monitored for 15 minutes. At the end of 15 minutes, the pressure inside the tube had *decreased* from its starting pressure of 760 torr to 722 torr.

Experiment 2

An identical experiment was conducted at 30°C. At this temperature, the pressure inside the tube after 15 minutes had decreased from 786 torr (starting pressure) to 707 torr.

6. Separate control experiments were performed alongside Experiments 1 and 2. The control contained plastic beads (the same size as peas) instead of germinating peas. All other conditions were identical. Any decrease in pressure inside the control tube would suggest that:

F. plastic beads utilize oxygen at approximately the same rate as germinating peas.
G. plastic beads produce carbon dioxide at about the same rate as germinating peas.
H. plastic beads carry out all aspects of cellular respiration at approximately the same rate as germinating peas.
J. factors having nothing to do with cellular respiration must be responsible.

7. In both experiments, the decrease in pressure in the tube was mainly due to a change in the abundance of what specific gas?

A. Oxygen
B. Carbon dioxide
C. Potassium hydroxide
D. All of the above

8. If potassium hydroxide (KOH) were not included in the tubes, what would happen to the pressure during each experiment?

F. Final pressure would be approximately the same as starting pressure.
G. Final pressure would be higher than starting pressure.
H. Final pressure would decrease faster than what was observed in Experiments 1 and 2.
J. Results would not be different from what was observed in Experiments 1 and 2.

9. Experiment 2 showed a greater decrease in pressure in the tube because:

A. at higher temperatures, peas use oxygen slower.
B. at higher temperatures, potassium hydroxide absorbs and removes carbon dioxide slower.
C. at higher temperatures, peas use oxygen faster.
D. at lower temperatures, peas use oxygen slower than they produce carbon dioxide.

10. An additional set of experiments with germinating peas is conducted in the dark at 22°C and 30°C. All other conditions are identical to those in Experiments 1 and 2. After 15 minutes, if the final pressure inside the tube at 22°C is 722 torr, and the final gas volume inside the tube at 30°C is 707 torr, which hypothesis best explains the results?

F. Darkness affects cellular respiration in germinating peas the same way that a rise in temperature affects cellular respiration in germinating peas.
G. Light/dark conditions have little or no effect on cellular respiration in germinating peas.
H. Cellular respiration in germinating peas occurs faster in the light than in the dark.
J. Cellular respiration in germinating peas occurs faster in the dark than in the light.

11. The summary equation in the passage shows that during cellular respiration, germinating peas must consume glucose. In Experiments 1 and 2, glucose molecules:

A. were in the peas.
B. were not available.
C. were consumed at equal rates.
D. were available but not consumed at all.

PASSAGE III

Two different views of Earth's past are presented below.

Scientist 1

The history of our planet has been marked by sudden spectacular events that have no counterpart in the natural processes observed today (catastrophism). Today's valleys formed during periods of downward slippage by fragments of the earth's crust. Mountains rose due to gigantic upheavals of land during Earth's beginnings. The three major types of rock formed when one worldwide ocean precipitated out great masses of different materials during three sudden and separate events. Substances such as granite were precipitated first (today's igneous rocks), while materials in the flat upper layers precipitated last (today's sedimentary rocks). This was followed by the disappearance of much of this great ocean's water (perhaps by evaporation during years of intensive heat). Distinct assemblages of animal and plant fossils, found in successive rock layers of a region, can be explained by local catastrophic events, such as massive fires or floods. Old forms were wiped out, and eventually new forms replaced them as foreign species immigrated from other geographic areas.

Scientist 2

Processes now in operation are adequate to account for changes in Earth's past (principle of uniform change). Although today's processes seem to have negligible effects on the landscape, great changes can result from ongoing processes, if given long enough periods of time. Valleys form as flowing water cuts through the sides and bottom of the land and rock they pass across. Rocks and mountains can be formed, destroyed and reformed by processes still going on today. Volcanic activity, heat and pressure under Earth's surfaces, erosion, weathering, and even shifts and movements can lift massive areas below the land and ocean surfaces to high elevations. Different fossil types in successive layers of rocks represent the changes in form that can take place among related organisms as a result of evolutionary processes over vast periods of time.

12. One major difference between the views of Scientist 1 and Scientist 2 relates to:

F. where fossils are found.
G. the rate of change of Earth's landscape.
H. the size of mountain ranges.
J. whether water played a role in forming any of Earth's characteristics.

13. Which of the following provides the strongest evidence against Scientist 1's point about mountain formation?

A. The beginnings of Earth are not well documented.
B. Floods and fires have never been massive enough to eliminate fossils from all mountain areas.
C. Volcanic activity, weathering, and erosion are believed to be less common today than in years past.
D. Fossils of recent sea creatures can be found in rocks on mountain peaks.

14. Which of the following best characterizes the main difference between catastrophism and the principle of uniform change?

F. Catastrophism maintains that violent changes in the relatively recent past shaped Earth's landscape while the principle of uniform change holds that gradual changes over an enormous span are responsible.
G. Catastrophism predicts that sudden, violent events will soon reshape Earth's landscape while the principle of uniform change expects the landscape to remain mostly unchanged.
H. Catastrophism theorizes that the landscape was largely shaped by cataclysmic events in the distant past while the principle of uniform change holds that the landscape is the result of a steady transformation over a long time.
J. Catastrophism holds that relatively recent events of enormous magnitude created the landscape while the principle of uniform change holds that the landscape has remained relatively unchanged since Earth's formation.

GO ON TO THE NEXT PAGE.

15. According to Scientist 1, which of the major types of rocks should be found at the lowest levels?

A. Igneous (granite)
B. Metamorphic (marble)
C. Sedimentary (limestone)
D. Cannot be determined from the given information

16. According to the views of Scientist 1, the number of major rock types will most likely:

F. remain unchanged.
G. decrease.
H. increase.
J. Cannot be determined from the given information

17. To refute Scientist 2's point of view about strictly uniform processes of change, Scientist 1 could argue that:

A. the streams of today are measurably effective in cutting through the sides and bottoms of rock they pass across.
B. fossils are not found everywhere today.
C. at some early point in time, the actual formation of Earth had to involve very different processes than those now in evidence.
D. mountain ranges formed gradually.

18. Which argument does NOT support the views of Scientist 2?

F. There are many regions of lava where no volcanoes are present today.
G. There are three major types of rock that exist today.
H. Many rivers today are flowing far below their former channels.
J. Distinctive fossils in upper layers of rock show similarities to those in lower layers, yet they are never found in any other geographic areas.

Poikilothermic (cold-blooded) animals cannot regulate their body temperatures internally. Their body temperature varies as the environmental temperature varies. Consequently, the rates of many bodily processes also vary as outside temperatures change (as environmental temperatures increase, body temperature as well as the rates of bodily processes may also increase). Homeothermic (warm-blooded) animals, on the other hand, can maintain their body temperatures internally. Therefore, the rates of their bodily processes can remain relatively stable when environmental temperatures change.

Experiments were set up to determine how heart rate, a bodily process, may be affected by different temperatures in two species of live laboratory animals.

Experiment 1

In this experiment, 10 individuals from Species A and 10 individuals from Species B were kept in 20 separate containers at room temperature (22°C) for 30 minutes. Their heart rates (heart beats/minute) were recorded every 10 minutes starting 10 minutes into the experiment. Average heart rates for the entire experiment were calculated for each species: Species A had an average heart rate of 150 beats/minute, while Species B averaged 100 beats/minute.

Experiment 2

Identical procedures were used to repeat the original experiment except that the containers holding the individuals of each species were placed in an incubator set at 35°C. At the end of 30 minutes, the average heart rate for both species was 148 beats/minute.

19. How many values were used to calculate the average heart beats for each species in each of these experiments?

   A. 1
   B. 10
   C. 20
   D. 30

20. Which of the following hypotheses is supported by the results of both experiments?

   F. Species A is most likely poikilothermic.
   G. Species B is most likely poikilothermic.
   H. Both species are most likely poikilothermic.
   J. Neither species is poikilothermic.

21. Which of the following statements best explains why 10 individuals of each species were used in each of the experiments?

   A. In case a few died, there would still be others available for testing.
   B. If only one individual was used, it would be lonely.
   C. An average value for 10 individuals reduces the chance of getting an extreme value based on any one individual.
   D. If only one individual was chosen from each species, it would be difficult to show differences.

22. If a third experiment were conducted at 6°C, which set of results for average heart rates (in beats/minute) is closest to what might be expected?

   F. Species A: 146; Species B: 146
   G. Species A: 50; Species B: 146
   H. Species A: 50; Species B: 50
   J. Species A: 146; Species B: 50

23. Which statement is accurate concerning Species A and Species B?

   A. At 22°C, Species A has a higher average heart rate than Species B.
   B. Species A has a larger average size than Species B.
   C. As environmental temperature increases, average heart rate increases more for Species A than Species B.
   D. As environmental temperature decreases, average heart rate increases more for Species A than Species B.

24. If the average body temperature for 10 individuals of each species was recorded during Experiments 1 and 2, which results would be expected?

F. Species A: Temperature stays the same in both experiments. Species B: Temperature increases in Experiment 2.
G. Species A: Temperature increases in Experiment 2. Species B: Temperature stays the same in both experiments.
H. Both Species: Temperature increases in Experiment 2.
J. Both Species: Temperature stays the same in both experiments.

The chart below shows a set of "energy levels" that an electron in atom X can occupy. The value of the energy in each level is shown to the right.

Energy Level	Energy Value
E_5	2.07 eV
E_4	1.75 eV
E_3	1.52 eV
E_2	1.20 eV
E_1	0.60 eV

An electron can move from one level to the next (transition) in two ways:

(1) The molecule can absorb a particle of light, called a "photon," of just the right energy to lift the electron to a higher level. For example, an electron in level 4 can be raised to level 5 if the molecule absorbs a photon whose energy is 0.32 eV.

(2) The molecule can emit, or give off, a photon of just the right energy necessary to lower an electron to another level. For example, an electron in level 4 can move to level 2 if the molecule emits a photon whose energy is 0.55 eV.

25. A sample containing many X molecules absorbs light, each photon of which carries 0.60 eV. As each photon is absorbed an electron:

A. moves from level 1 to level 2.
B. occupies level one.
C. moves from level 2 to level 3.
D. moves from level 2 to level 4.

26. A sample containing many X molecules emits light, each photon of which carries 0.32 eV. As each photon is emitted, an electron moves from:

F. level 3 to level 2.
G. level 2 to level 3.
H. level 5 to level 4.
J. level 3 to level 2 or from level 5 to level 4.

27. A sample of molecule X emits light, each photon of which carries 0.92 eV. As each photon is emitted an electron moves from:

A. level 5 to level 2.
B. level 1 to level 5.
C. level 1 to level 3.
D. level 3 to level 1.

28. Suppose that in a sample containing many X molecules, all of the electrons are in level 5. Based on the information in the chart, the sample could emit photons of how many different energies, if each emission resulted in an electron transitioning to a new level?

F. One
G. Two
H. Three
J. Four

29. Assume that each of the molecules in a sample containing many X molecules has two electrons, and those two electrons are on the same level, but the level is not known. Light is passed through the sample, and photons, each of energy 0.23 eV, are absorbed. A very short time later, photons of the same energy are emitted. It is likely that:

A. electrons are moving from level 1 to level 2.
B. electrons are moving from level 4 to level 3, then back again to level 4.
C. electrons are moving from level 3 to level 4, then back again to level 3.
D. electrons are moving from level 5 to level 4.

30. If photons whose individual energies are each 2.07 eV encounter a sample containing many X molecules, then:

F. electrons will be promoted from level 1 to level 5.
G. electrons will be promoted from all levels to level 5.
H. electrons will drop from level 5 to level 1.
J. no electron transitions will occur between levels 1 and 5.

PASSAGE VI

A student performs three experiments in which a light beam passes through water and air. The "refraction angles" are the angles that the light beam makes with a line perpendicular to the surface of the water or air. In the water, this angle is called θ_1. When the beam leaves the water and passes into air, a second angle, θ_2, can be measured. Figure 1 illustrates θ_1 and θ_2.

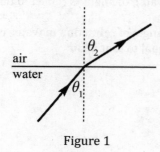

Figure 1

Experiment 1

The entry angle, θ_1, and the exit angle, θ_2, are both equal to zero.

Experiment 2

The angles observed are shown in Figure 2.

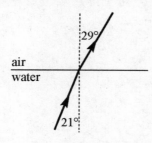

Figure 2

Experiment 3

The angles observed are shown in Figure 3.

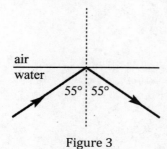

Figure 3

31. Which of the following diagrams could represent the observations of Experiment 1?

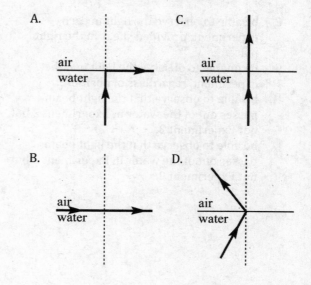

32. The student attempts to draw a conclusion from Experiments 1 and 2. Which of the following is justified by the data?

F. Refraction angles in water are greater than those in air.
G. Refraction angles in water are less than those in air.
H. Refraction angles are equal in air and in water.
J. Refraction angles in water are equal to or less than those in air.

33. In Experiment 3, the beam travels through the water and:

A. is reflected back down from the surface of the water.
B. enters the air.
C. is absorbed completely.
D. is reflected back on itself.

GO ON TO THE NEXT PAGE.

34. An observer in the air attempts to see the beam of light in Experiments 2 and 3. She will:

    F. be able to observe the light in each experiment, provided she is in the right place.
    G. be unable to observe the light in either experiment, regardless of position.
    H. be able to observe that the light beam passes out of the water in Experiment 2 but not Experiment 3.
    J. be able to observe that the light beam passes out of the water in Experiment 3 but not Experiment 2.

35. A student attempts to summarize the results of all three experiments. Which of the following is most consistent with the observations?

    A. The angle of refraction in water is less than that in air.
    B. The angle of refraction in air is less than that in water.
    C. The angle of refraction in water is less than or equal to that in air, but at high angles in the water, the light is reflected back into the water.
    D. The angle of refraction in water is less than or equal to that in air.

GO ON TO THE NEXT PAGE.

PASSAGE VI

The table below presents the results of a study in which butterflies of different size and color were captured in flight for marking with a chemical, and then recaptured in flight a few weeks later.

Size	White		Tan		Dark Brown	
	Marked	Recaptured	Marked	Recaptured	Marked	Recaptured
Small (less than 20 mm)	35	30	40	10	20	10
Medium (20-40 mm)	30	15	40	20	20	10
Large (greater than 40 mm)	50	25	60	30	30	10

36. For all sizes of butterflies, the color that seems most difficult to capture for marking is:

    F. white.
    G. tan.
    H. dark brown.
    J. Both tan and dark brown are almost equally difficult.

37. The specific type of butterfly that is easiest to recapture after being marked is:

    A. between 10–20 mm and tan.
    B. greater than 40 mm and tan.
    C. greater than 40 mm and dark brown.
    D. less than 20 mm and white.

38. Based on the information in the table, which statement best represents the relationship between a butterfly's size and its tendency to be captured for marking?

    F. The larger the butterfly, the harder it is to be captured for marking.
    G. The larger the butterfly, the easier it is to be captured for marking.
    H. Medium-sized butterflies are consistently the easiest to capture for marking.
    J. The smaller the butterfly, the easier it is to be captured for marking.

39. The chemical used to mark all the butterflies was found to be poisonous to one specific type because it was being absorbed through the wings. Based on the data in the table, which type of butterfly appears most likely to have suffered from the effects of the marking chemical?

    A. Greater than 40 mm and white
    B. Less than 20 mm and tan
    C. Greater than 40 mm and dark brown
    D. Less than 20 mm and white

40. Which conclusion is correct concerning the information in the table?

    F. For tan butterflies, the proportion of individuals that are recaptured always stays the same.
    G. For medium-sized butterflies, the proportion of individuals that are recaptured always stays the same.
    H. For small-sized butterflies, the proportion of individuals recaptured always stays the same.
    J. For all sizes of butterflies, the darker the color the easier it is to recapture an individual.

END OF TEST 4
STOP! DO NOT TURN THE PAGE UNTIL TOLD TO DO SO.
DO NOT RETURN TO THE PREVIOUS TEST.

PRACTICE TEST |||

5 5 5 5 5 5 5 5 5 5 5 5 5

SECTION 5: WRITING TEST (OPTIONAL)
40 Minutes—1 Essay Prompt

DIRECTIONS: You have 40 minutes to plan and write an essay. Read the prompt carefully and make sure you understand the instructions. A successful essay will have the following features: it will take a position on the issue presented in the writing prompt; it will maintain a consistent focus on the topic; it will use logical reasoning and provide supporting ideas; it will present ideas in an organized manner; and, finally, it will include clear and effective language in accordance with the conventions of standard written English. Sample essay responses begin on page 342.

Online Voting Systems

Homes, schools, libraries, and churches all have Internet access. With the broad availability of Internet access, the problem of voter turnout can be addressed and effectively solved. In America's last national election, less than 40% of the eligible voters cast ballots. Internet access can be used to theoretically double voter turnout and maybe even increase it to 100%. The technology exists to allow each American to register and vote from a computer terminal of his or her choosing. Such a move would certainly increase democratic voice and popular participation in our elections, but would it lead to more voters who are uninformed about candidates and issues? It is important to address this controversy, as future generations of voters will be increasingly technology-oriented.

Perspective 1	Perspective 2	Perspective 3
Informed voters are the heart of democracy. Simply providing mechanical solutions that add quantity to the voter turnout would not necessarily lead to an educated electorate to shape our future.	This type of voting system is risky because it will be difficult to determine who will monitor the electronic machines that are used. We cannot trust the security systems to protect our most precious right when these very same systems regularly fail to protect our credit cards.	Voter turnout is supremely important to a democracy. A country needs the participation of its citizens to realize its fondest hopes and dreams. We need to get more people to vote to help America reach its potential.

Essay Task

Write a unified, coherent essay in which you evaluate multiple perspectives on the issue of online voting systems. In your essay be sure to:

- Analyze and evaluate perspectives given
- State and develop your own perspective
- Explain the relationship between your perspective and those given

Your perspective may be in full agreement with any of the others, in partial agreement, or wholly different. Whatever the case, support your ideas with logical reasoning and detailed, persuasive examples.

ANSWERS AND EXPLANATIONS

ENGLISH

QUIZ I (p. 2)

1. **(B)** *English/Conventions of Standard English/Grammar and Usage/ Pronoun Usage*

   The original sentence is incorrect because the pronoun "one" does not agree with its antecedent "most people." (B) corrects this problem. (C) is wrong because, like the original, it uses a singular pronoun, not a plural one. Additionally, "that" should be used instead of "which" since the introduced material specifies the type of crime. Finally, (D) is wrong because it creates a shifting point of view.

2. **(H)** *English/Conventions of Standard English/Grammar and Usage/Diction*

   The contraction of "it is" is written as "it's." "Its" is a possessive pronoun, and "its'" does not exist in English. (G) is wrong because "they" is intended to refer to "a certain crime," which is singular.

3. **(B)** *English/Production of Writing/ Strategy/Effective Transitional Sentence*

   "Moreover" is not a logical transitional word choice. It signals a continuation of a thought, while the author clearly implies a contrast. (B) makes the appropriate correction by using "however" to signal a contrast. (C) is wrong for the same reason that the original sentence is wrong. (D) is wrong because "therefore" is used to signal a logical deduction rather than a contrasting idea.

4. **(F)** *English/Production of Writing/No Change*

   The original sentence is correct; "odd" logically functions to demonstrate that the "confidence scheme" would not normally be viewed as the worst crime.

5. **(C)** *English/Conventions of Standard English/Sentence Structure/Fragments*

   The underlined portion of the original sentence creates a sentence fragment. "Although" is a subordinate conjunction used to introduce a dependent clause, and a dependent clause is not a complete sentence. (C) corrects this problem by replacing "although" with the coordinate conjunction "but" and creates a correctly punctuated compound sentence. (B) eliminates the sentence fragment problem but makes the mistake of illogical subordination. The intended meaning of the original sentence requires that the second idea (the crime is heartless) has the same emphasis as the first idea (the crime is nonviolent). However, "though" is used to introduce a subordinate idea. (D) eliminates the fragment problem and creates a proper compound sentence in which the two ideas are given equal importance, but it is incorrect since "and" signals a similarity of ideas.

6. **(F)** *English/Conventions of Standard English/No Change*

   The original sentence is correct. (G) is wrong because "it" does not agree with its antecedent, "con artists." Both (H) and (J) are awkward. Additionally, (H) is wrong because "its" does not have an antecedent. (J) is also wrong because the possessive pronoun "their," not the objective pronoun "them," must modify the gerund.

7. **(C)** *English/Conventions of Standard English/Punctuation/Commas*

The original sentence is incorrect because the punctuation disrupts the parallel direct objects "honesty and trust." (C) appropriately punctuates the sentence. (B) fails to eliminate the incorrect punctuation. As for (D), a comma is necessary to set off the parenthetical phrase describing honesty and trust.

8. **(H)** *English/Conventions of Standard English/Punctuation/Commas*

The original sentence runs together two ideas: "simplistic" and "almost infantile." (H) correctly separates them with a comma.

9. **(D)** *English/Knowledge of Language/Style/ Idiomatic Expression*

The use of "on account of" to indicate a causal relationship is informal usage and unacceptable in standard written English. (B) fails to correct the error and creates an awkward sentence. (C) is awkward and substitutes another unacceptable phrase ("owing to"). (D) expresses the correct causal relationship by using the word "because."

10. **(J)** *English/Conventions of Standard English/Sentence Structure/Faulty Parallelism*

The original underlined portion is incorrect because it does not maintain the parallel structure of the sentence. The auxiliary verb "can" governs the other verbs in the sentence, so the form of the verb "to dangle" must be parallel to both "win" and "talk." Only (J) provides the necessary verb form.

11. **(C)** *English/Conventions of Standard English/Grammar and Usage/Sequence and Verb Tense*

The use of the future tense in the original sentence conflicts with the other present tense verbs in the paragraph. (B) is wrong because the use of the infinitive verb form eliminates the only conjugated verb in the clause, thus reducing the clause to a fragment. (D) is wrong because "is" is singular and does not agree with the plural noun "targets."

12. **(G)** *English/Conventions of Standard English/Grammar and Usage/Pronoun Usage*

The underlined material in parentheses is not incidental to the passage's development—it has the same status as "the primary targets...are the elderly and women." Therefore, it should be incorporated into the main body of the passage. Additionally, it is not clear whether "they" refers to women, criminals, or the elderly. The use of "con artists" in (G) corrects this ambiguity.

13. **(A)** *English/Production of Writing/ Strategy/Main Idea*

(B), (C), and (D) are assertions that can be empirically verified. (A), on the other hand, expresses an opinion.

14. **(F)** *English/Production of Writing/ Organization/Passage-Level Structure*

A striking feature of the passage is its generality. An example or two would help the reader appreciate the points that the author makes.

15. **(C)** *English/Production of Writing/ Strategy/Appropriate Supporting Material*

An illustration would be helpful. A specific example of how a con game preys on and breaks a person's trust would strengthen the author's argument.

16. **(J)** *English/Knowledge of Language/Style/ Conciseness*

The underlined material is irrelevant to the discussion of Elizabeth's character—it should be deleted.

17. **(C)** *English/Conventions of Standard English/Grammar and Usage/Subject-Verb Agreement and Sequence and Verb Tense*

The original sentence is incorrect because the verb "is" is singular and must be plural to agree with "splendor and pleasure." In addition, the past tense is needed in order to agree with the other past tense verbs in the passage.

18. **(J)** *English/Conventions of Standard English/Sentence Structure/Fragments*

The original sentence is incorrect because the material following "age" creates a fragment. Additionally, the comma after "even" is incorrect because "even" is intended to be a part of the parenthetical phrase "even to old age." (G) is wrong because the use of the present tense conflicts with the past tense verbs in the rest of the paragraph. (H) also fails because it is in the present tense and because a second comma is required after "age" to complete the parenthetical expression. (J) is correct because its verb is in the past tense and because the parenthetical expression is correctly set off by two commas.

19. **(C)** *English/Conventions of Standard English/Grammar and Usage/Pronoun Usage*

The original sentence is incorrect because the object pronoun "whom," not "who," is required (she outwitted "them," not "they"). (B) is wrong because the pronoun "that" should not be used to refer to people. (D) is wrong because "whom," not "who," is required, and the past progressive tense is awkward.

20. **(F)** *English/Production of Writing/No Change*

The original sentence is correct. The underlined phrase should not be omitted since it describes an important trait of Elizabeth's character. Therefore, (J) is wrong. (G) and (H) are awkward.

21. **(A)** *English/Conventions of Standard English/No Change*

The original sentence is correct. (B) is wrong because it is not idiomatic. (C) is wrong because the tense is incorrect—it suggests that Elizabeth was "being" before and up to the time the statesman saw her. The original sentence indicates that she was "being" Elizabeth at the same time they saw her. Additionally, omitting the gerund changes the meaning of the sentence. (D) suggests "far" in the sense of distance, which makes little sense in this context.

22. **(G)** *English/Conventions of Standard English/Grammar and Usage/Diction*

The idiomatic form of comparison in English is "as...as," (G).

23. **(A)** *English/Production of Writing/No Change*

The original sentence is correct. The other choices are needlessly wordy or awkward.

24. **(G)** *English/Conventions of Standard English/Grammar and Usage/Verb Tense*

The original sentence is incorrect because the past perfect tense is wrong and because the past participle should be "become," not "became." (H) is wrong because it suggests an ongoing state of affairs, but the sentence intends that the transformation occurred and was completed at a certain point in time. (J) is wrong because the switch to the present tense creates a conflict of tenses. (G) correctly provides the past tense.

25. **(A)** *English/Conventions of Standard English/No Change*

The original sentence is correct. (B) is wrong because it is not idiomatic. In English, the correct phrasing is to say that someone has "superiority over" someone or that someone is "superior to" someone. Both (C) and (D) are not idiomatic.

26 . **(H)** *English/Conventions of Standard English/Grammar and Usage/Diction*

The original sentence is incorrect because "more nobler" is not idiomatic since "nobler" is already the comparative form of the adjective. (G) is wrong because the comma illogically separates the noun from its corresponding prepositional phrase. (J) fails to correct the original error and suffers from the same punctuation defects as (G). (H) correctly omits "more" and does not include a comma.

27. **(C)** *English/Conventions of Standard English/Sentence Structure/Run-On Sentences*

The original sentence is incorrect because it is a run-on sentence. The comma after "genius" is not enough to separate the two independent clauses—it is preferable to start a new sentence.

28. **(J)** *English/Conventions of Standard English/Sentence Structure/Faulty Parallelism*

The original sentence is incorrect because it fails to preserve the sentence's parallel construction. (G) is wrong because it changes the meaning of the sentence. It implies that Elizabeth endeavored to keep her throne and to keep England out of war because she wanted to restore civil and religious order. (H) is wrong because it does not maintain the parallelism of the sentence. (J) correctly preserves the sentence's parallel construction.

29. **(A)** *English/Production of Writing/ Organization/Passage-Level Structure*

The passage is a discussion of Elizabeth's character. Some biographical background might have provided the reader with a context in which to place the later discussion.

30. **(G)** *English/Production of Writing/ Strategy/Audience*

Since the passage is a discussion of Elizabeth's character, the information was most likely excerpted from a biographical information source.

31. **(B)** *English/Production of Writing/ Strategy/Appropriate Supporting Material*

The passage speaks in general terms about Elizabeth's character. Some specific incidents would help the reader appreciate what the author means by those descriptions.

QUIZ II (p. 7)

1. **(C)** *English/Conventions of Standard English/Sentence Structure/Faulty Parallelism*

   The sentence should read: "for her luminous beauty, for her acclaimed acting ability, and for her humanitarian work with organizations." (B) fails to address the problem of parallelism. Additionally, "humanitarian organizations work" is awkward.

2. **(J)** *English/Conventions of Standard English/Sentence Structure/Incomplete Split Constructions*

   The problem with the original is the improperly completed split construction: "as great or greater...than." (J) corrects this by substituting "at least as great...as," which is logically equivalent to "as great as or greater than." (G) and (H) fail to correct the original error.

3. **(D)** *English/Conventions of Standard English/Sentence Structure/Misplaced Modifiers*

   The original contains an ambiguity. It is not clear whether "caused by" is supposed to modify "increase" or "churn"; consequently, the reader must work to determine whether it is the churn or the increase in the churn that is the problem that results from the greater customer willingness to switch providers. Of course, it is the increase that is caused by customer willingness to switch, and you can figure this out for yourself; but, in general, a properly written sentence should not require so much work of the reader. (D) is better because it avoids the ambiguity. (B) is wrong because it fails to remove the ambiguity and introduces a new error. (B) implies that the offers switch the customers rather than provide a reason to switch. (C) fails to correct the original problem and makes things worse by suggesting that customer willingness is caused by switching.

4. **(H)** *English/Conventions of Standard English/Grammar and Usage/Verb Tense and Diction*

   The original sentence contains two similar errors. First, the use of the present participle "originating" fails to show that the action of "originating" is completed and in the past. To reflect the correct sequence of events, the sentence should use a verb to show past action. Second, there is an error of diction. To show bloodlines, the sentence needs the word "descended," not "descending." "Descending" used here suggests the dog is walking down a staircase. (G) makes the first correction but not the second. (J) makes both needed changes, but the way in which the first change is made changes the intended meaning of the original sentence. (J) implies that it is "the water spaniel" that "originated in ancient times in the Mediterranean area," but in the original, this phrase modifies "Bichon Frisé." Only (H) makes both needed changes without introducing another error.

5. **(D)** *English/Conventions of Standard English/Sentence Structure/Faulty Parallelism*

   In the original, the phrase "after drawing trumps" cuts off the remainder of the sentence from the main body of the sentence, so "was able..." has no clear logical connection with any other element in the sentence. The sentence intends, however, for "was able..." to be the third element in a series of parallel verbs: "ruffed," "sloughed," and "was able to score." The "and" in (D) provides the logical connection to bring the orphan phrase back into the sentence. "And" creates a compound verb consisting of the three elements just mentioned.

6. **(J)** *English/Conventions of Standard English/Grammar and Usage/Verb Tense*

   The original contains two errors. One, the use of "discovering" suggests that "discovering" is intended to be an adjective modifying "Lincoln," but the speaker really intends for "discovering" to be a verb showing some action taken by Lincoln. Two, the use of "has" creates an illogical sequence of verb tenses by implying that the action of the Yankee peddler began before Lincoln's act of discovering but continued through that time of discovery. (G) changes the order of the elements in the sentence but doesn't correct either error. (H) corrects the second error but not the first. Only (J) corrects both errors adequately.

7. **(D) *English/Conventions of Standard English/Grammar and Usage/Adjectives versus Adverbs* and *Sentence Structure/Unintended Meanings***

The original sentence contains two errors. First, "inadvertent" is intended to modify the action of leaving the portfolio, so the adverb "inadvertently" is needed. Second, the use of "including" illogically implies that the uncompleted sketches were examples of watercolors. (B) corrects the first error but not the second. (C) corrects the first error but not the second and introduces yet another problem: "containing" seems to modify "bus." Thus, (C) implies that it was the bus that contained the art and not the portfolio. Only (D) corrects both the errors of the original without introducing any new problems.

8. **(H) *English/Knowledge of Language/Style/Clarity of Meaning***

The difficulty with the original is that two ideas are run together in the underlined portion in such a way that the significance of neither is clear. Some device—a word, a phrase, or punctuation—needs to be used to separate those two ideas and make clear their significance. (H) does this with the word "or." (G) fails because the ideas are still not distinguished. (J) fails to separate the ideas clearly; plus, it changes the meaning of the original.

9. **(C) *English/Knowledge of Language/Style/Conciseness***

The original sentence runs together two ideas and is needlessly wordy. (C) correctly contrasts the two ideas (brought up in one language but wrote in another) and eliminates the excess verbiage. (B) is wrong because it introduces an illogical verb tense. (D) is needlessly wordy.

10. **(G) *English/Conventions of Standard English/Grammar and Usage/Subject-Verb Agreement* and *Production of Writing/Style/Idiomatic Expression***

The original sentence is incorrect because the verb "have" does not agree with the subject "relationship." Additionally, it is not idiomatic to say "the relationship of x and y." The correct expression is "the relationship of x to y." (H) corrects that mistake but introduces a logical error. It now says that the warnings jeopardize health. (J) is not idiomatic.

11. **(D) *English/Conventions of Standard English/Sentence Structure/Misplaced Modifiers***

This sentence is afflicted by the notorious dangling modifier. As written, the sentence implies that the "prima ballerina" was thrown onto the stage by the adoring fans. To avoid this ambiguity, the modifier should be placed closer to what it modifies, "the bouquets." (D) not only solves the problem of the dangling modifier, but it is also a more direct way of rendering the thought.

12. **(F) *English/Conventions of Standard English/No Change***

The original is correct as written. The other choices involve verb tense errors. The problem with both (G) and (H) is that the use of "could" implies that there is an event that might have occurred, but did not occur, that would have made the Battle of Fort Ann the most significant event: the battle could have been the most significant event if only something else had happened. The use of "leading" in (J) makes it seem as though the Battle of

Fort Ann was significant only as an event leading up to the engagement at Saratoga.

13. (B) *English/Conventions of Standard English/Sentence Structure/Problems of Coordination and Subordination and Unintended Meanings*

The original is wrong because the coordinating conjunction "and" does not create a logical connection between the two ideas that are expressed. In this case, the writer intends to say that poor driving conditions did not result in any car accidents even though one might have expected accidents to occur. So, a contrast must be made between the two ideas (what was expected and what actually occurred). The coordinating conjunction "but" provides the necessary contrast.

14. (G) *English/Conventions of Standard English/Grammar and Usage/Faulty or Illogical Comparisons*

The original contains a faulty comparison. It seems to compare the movie industry in India with the United States. (J) does not address this problem; (G) and (H) do. But (H) is wrong because "on account of" is not an acceptable alternative to "because."

15. (D) *English/Conventions of Standard English/Sentence Structure/Unintended Meanings*

The problem with the original is that the relationship between the two clauses is upside-down. The author means to express a causal connection in which the dropped baton is the cause and the failure to qualify is the effect. (D) makes the needed correction.

16. (F) *English/Production of Writing/No Change*

The original is correct as written; the other choices introduce idiomatic expression errors or change the intended meaning of the original. (G) is wrong because "released new worm" is not idiomatic. (H) is wrong for the same reason and for the additional reason that

the change in the order of words in the latter part of the underlined segment changes the meaning of the original. (J) is wrong because "on account of" is not an acceptable substitute for "because."

17. (D) *English/Knowledge of Language/Style/ Clarity of Meaning*

The original is wrong because it is illogical. It compares sanitation workers to other city agencies instead of to other city workers. (B) repeats this error and adds a new one. The possessive case is needed when a pronoun modifies the "-ing" form of verbs. Therefore, "their being underpaid," not "them being underpaid," is correct. (C) repeats the illogical comparison. So, (D) is the correct answer choice.

18. (H) *English/Conventions of Standard English/Sentence Structure/Misplaced Modifiers*

The original contains a misplaced modifier. As written, the sentence implies that it was the failure of the crusading movement that learned of the fall of Constantinople. Each of the other choices corrects this error. (G), however, is wrong because the placement of the final clause is incorrect. (What is "which" intended to modify?) (J) changes the intended meaning of the original; it implies that Christian Europe reached its realization while ignoring earlier defeats, but the original means to say that Christian Europe only then realized that the movement had failed.

19. (D) *English/Knowledge of Language/ Style/Idiomatic Expression and Clarity of Meaning*

The original has two faults. "Insofar as" is used incorrectly, and "a good bargain" and "less than a dollar a pound" are too loosely connected. Only (D) corrects both faults.

20. (J) *English/Knowledge of Language/ Style/Idiomatic Expression* and *Clarity of Meaning*

The original contains two errors. First, the phrase "more percentage" is not idiomatic. The correct idiom is "greater percentage" or "higher percentage." Second, the original creates an illogical comparison between the population of Boston and other cities. (G) fails to eliminate either error and introduces a new mistake. Without "other," the sentence seems to include Boston itself in the comparison. (H) eliminates the incorrect idiom but introduces a new one: "greater...as." Only (J) corrects both errors in the original sentence.

READING

1. **(A)** *Reading/Craft and Structure/ Vocabulary*

   The word "nomological" will not be familiar to most students. The item illustrates, however, that it is possible to use the context in which the word appears to arrive at a good guess as to its meaning. In this case, the Hempel model views history as a science and claims that it can produce conclusions that can be logically deduced from laws. These two elements, logic and laws, are the heart of the theory. Since "deductive-nomological" is intended to describe this view, and since deduction describes the "logical" element, we can infer that "nomological" describes the "law-like" element.

2. **(J)** *Reading/Craft and Structure/ Vocabulary*

   The burden of Passage A is that it is not reasonable to expect historical explanations to be as good as scientific explanations because there are so many variables that must be taken into account. However, according to the author of Passage A, if it were possible to capture and account for all the variables, then a scientifically valid historical conclusion could be drawn—the "if" being an "adequately articulated" set of empirical laws. Thus, in this case, the phrase means "sufficiently detailed," (J). Eliminate (F) as this is the primary and most obvious definition. As for (G) and (H), these choices are not related to the ideas discussed.

3. **(C)** *Reading/Key Ideas and Details/ Application*

   In the second paragraph of Passage A, the author notes that history may seem to be different from the natural sciences because it does not allow for laboratory experiments. Then, the author mentions a series of revolutions. We can infer that the author thinks that a series of observed historical events can confirm a hypothesis in the same way that a series of laboratory experiments can.

4. **(G)** *Reading/Key Ideas and Details/Explicit Detail*

   In lines 37–38, the author of Passage A specifically states that it is "difficult to find a sufficiently large number of revolutions" to test the validity of a scientific hypothesis, (G). While (F) is true, it does not respond to the question asked. (H) and (J) are both incorrect since they are not mentioned in Passage A.

5. **(C)** *Reading/Craft and Structure/ Development*

   In the second paragraph, the author argues that historical explanations would seem more scientific if data from other disciplines were incorporated into its explanations. To use the example of a revolution, we might expect that a "complete" historical explanation might include information from psychology about something such as a "frustration threshold." For example, the average person is ready to revolt when the standard of living drops by 25 percent. So, the author apparently believes that these disciplines are able to provide reliable data.

6. **(G)** *Reading/Key Ideas and Details/Main Idea*

What is the main theme of the selection? The burden of the author's argument is to demonstrate that history, when properly understood, is as much a science as physics or chemistry.

7. **(B)** *Reading/Key Ideas and Details/Explicit Detail*

Passage B mentions *Verstehen* in the third paragraph as the technique that is used by historians to get at the "inside" of an event—the "why," or the motives and intentions, of the actors, (B). (A) is incorrect because "understanding" would not apply to the "outside" or physical aspect of an event. As for (C), while psychology and sociology study intentions and motives, they do not employ *Verstehen*. Rather, those disciplines emulate the hard sciences. (D) is incorrect since the whole point of *Verstehen* is that historical laws simply do not exist.

8. **(J)** *Reading/Key Ideas and Details/Application*

The author of Passage A argues that both human actions and strictly physical events are governed by scientific laws; the author of Passage B argues that human actions are not governed by scientific laws, though purely physical events are. Thus, despite their disagreement, both authors would share the intuition that purely physical events are law-like.

9. **(B)** *Reading/Key Ideas and Details/Explicit Detail*

The author argues that the friendship coupled with prevailing attitudes about Dutch origins of New York institutions helps to explain the Dutch influences in "A Visit," thereby dating it to the time of "Dutch Revival" around 1822, which is found in paragraph 6.

10. **(H)** *Reading/Craft and Structure/Main Idea*

The passage provides an overview of the debate concerning the authorship of "A Visit." The author of the passage presents evidence on both sides and offers analysis and even rebuttal to the evidence. The overall objective is to weigh the evidence and draw a conclusion as to which side of the debate is more persuasive.

11. **(B)** *Reading/Key Ideas and Details/Explicit Detail*

This item asks about the function of the detail in the debate. One problem with attributing the poem to Moore is that Moore did not make such a claim himself at the time the poem was first published. Why didn't he? He wasn't aware the poem had been made public.

12. **(G)** *Reading/Craft and Structure/Voice*

After rehearsing the arguments for Livingston's authorship, the author of the passage presents a counterargument that the poem includes features pointing to Moore's authorship; and while Livingston seems likelier to have written in anapestic form, there is no evidence that Moore never wrote in that form. The best word to describe the evidence then is inconclusive, (G).

13. **(C)** *Reading/Key Ideas and Details/Implied Idea*

The author considers the significance of the names in paragraphs four and five. Scholars who support Livingston's authorship see the Dutch names used in the original publication as evidence that the author knew Dutch. The author of the passage rejects this theory, holding that Moore, who actually wrote the poem, used the German equivalents. This counter-theory is supported by the fact that in anticipation of a reprint Moore changed the originally printed version back to the German. Where did the original Dutch names come from? According to the passage, they were inserted by an editor at the newspaper, (C).

14. (J) *Reading/Craft and Structure/Voice*

The author is generally skeptical of the Livingston claim, emerging as it does so many years after the poem's original publication and reprint in anthology form. Additionally, the main support for the claim is the recollections of Livingston's heirs, many years removed.

15. (A) *Reading/Craft and Structure/ Vocabulary*

The author is being generous to the Livingston family in trying to explain how it could, in good faith, have claimed authorship of the poem when so much evidence points to Moore. The author theorizes that Livingston's children may have made an honest mistake. The holiday poems written and read by their father would quite naturally have been similar to "A Visit," so it is forgivable that they would combine or confuse the two, (A).

16. (J) *Reading/Key Ideas and Details/Main Idea*

This is a main idea question that asks about the final paragraph. The author's goal in that paragraph is to explain how the Livingston family could have made their claim when so much evidence points to Moore as the poet. The passage states that the similarity between the Moore poem and Livingston holiday tradition would have made it easy to think that "A Visit" was one of those holiday poems written by Livingston, (J).

17. (C) *Reading/Craft and Structure/ Development*

This is a development question. The use of "claimed" and "allegedly" make a big difference in how the supposed loss of the manuscript in a fire should be interpreted. The author uses those words to indicate that the claim is doubtful.

18. (J) *Reading/Key Ideas and Details/Explicit Detail*

This is a detail question. The first three choices are taken by the author as firmly established. The original date of publication was 1823 (line 5); Moore was good friends with Washington Irving (lines 76–77); and Dunder and Blixem appeared in the original newspaper version of the poem (lines 61–62). But whether it was the housekeeper who sent the poem to the paper is an idea not embraced by the author in the first paragraph. The author allows that the poem was sent by an unknown third party who acted without Moore's knowledge (lines 17–18), but that person was the housekeeper is not accepted or denied. In fact, the identity of the third party is pretty much irrelevant to the author's case. All that the author needs to prove his point is that someone, anyone but Moore, sent the poem to the newspaper without his knowledge.

QUIZ II (p. 17)

1. **(D)** *Reading/Key Ideas and Details/Main Idea*

   The author begins by stating that the Agricultural Adjustment Act of 1933 was declared unconstitutional; then, the author describes the administration's reaction to that decision. Specifically, the author details the difficulties of the administration in working out a second and permanent agricultural policy, the Agricultural Adjustment Act of 1938. This development is correctly described by (D). (A) is wrong for two reasons. First, the author doesn't really analyze the connection between changes in the weather and fluctuations in farm prices. Second, the connection is only a part of the overall discussion. (B) is wrong because, while the reader might learn something about farmers during the Great Depression, this is not the *author's* purpose in writing the passage. Finally, (C) is wrong because, while the passage might be used to argue that Roosevelt's policy had some weaknesses, finding weaknesses is not the main point of the passage.

2. **(J)** *Reading/Key Ideas and Details/Explicit Detail*

   The phrase "statement made" identifies this as an Explicit Detail item, and the item stem includes the thought-reverser "NOT," so the correct choice is NOT explicitly stated in passage. (F), (G), and (H) are all mentioned in the first paragraph: one aim of the law was conservation, but it was also intended to reduce output by taking land out of use; it was considered a stopgap or temporary measure. Only (J) is not mentioned in the passage; in fact, (J) represents a misreading of the passage—it was the Agricultural Adjustment Act of 1938, not the Soil Conservation and Domestic Allotment Act, that was drafted largely by members of the Farm Bureau.

3. **(C)** *Reading/Key Ideas and Details/Explicit Detail*

   The phrase "according to" identifies this as an Explicit Detail item, and the item stem includes the thought-reverser "EXCEPT," so the correct choice is NOT explicitly stated in the passage. (A) is mentioned in the middle of the first paragraph. (B) and (D) are mentioned in the final sentence of the passage. (The idea of the "ever-normal granary" is explained in greater detail in the second paragraph.) Only (C) is not mentioned in the passage; in fact, in the final sentence of the second paragraph, the author states that one of the criticisms leveled at the new act was the wastefulness of the existing AAA—it is inferable from this that the new act continued the AAA.

4. **(J)** *Reading/Key Ideas and Details/Explicit Detail*

   The phrase "according to" identifies this as an Explicit Detail item, and the item stem includes the thought-reverser "EXCEPT," so the correct choice is NOT explicitly stated in the passage. (F) is mentioned in the second paragraph. (G) is developed in the final paragraph. (H) is found in the second paragraph. Only (J) is not mentioned in the passage: while the passage states that the administration wanted a bill that would not be struck down, it does not indicate that constitutional concerns were an impediment to the bill's passage.

5. **(A)** *Reading/Key Ideas and Details/Implied Idea*

   The word "implies" identifies this as an Implied Idea item, so the correct answer is not directly stated in the passage but is inferable. In the final paragraph, the author describes the sequence of events that led to the passage of the 1938 legislation, and he shows how Roosevelt used the changing economic conditions to his advantage. In this discussion, the author implies that the changing economic conditions were a critical factor in the passage of the bill. Therefore, (A) is the best choice. (B) is wrong because, while the author does state that some farm groups were displeased with the new bill, as it was written primarily by members of the Farm Bureau, it is not inferable that the Secretary of Agriculture was blamed for this. (C) is wrong because it represents a confused reading of the passage: the author never states why the 1933 Act was voided but later does say that it was the new legislation (which would finally become the 1938 Act) that was written by members of the Farm Bureau. (D) is wrong because, while there are two references to the CCC making loans, it is not inferable that the CCC encouraged taking land out of production—this confuses the Soil Conservation and Domestic Allotment Act with the CCC.

6. **(G)** *Reading/Key Ideas and Details/Implied Idea*

In the second paragraph, the author states that *since* ten members of the Committee of Eighteen were members of the American Farm Bureau Federation, the bill was labeled a Farm Bureau Bill and opposed by the Farmer's Holiday Association. Therefore, it is inferable that the Farmer's Holiday Association opposed the American Farm Bureau Federation, (G). (F) is wrong because, while the passage does state that the bill was not, at first, strongly supported by Roosevelt, the author does not give that as the reason for the opposition to the bill by the Farmer's Holiday Association. (H) is wrong because, while the passage does state that some groups opposed the bill for this reason, the author does not give this as the reason for the FHA's opposition; in fact, it seems more likely that the FHA would favor a bill for farmers even if it did entail government spending. (J) is wrong because, while the author does mention that opponents of the bill charged that it favored large-scale farmers, the passage does not imply that this was the reason for the FHA's opposition.

7. **(D)** *Reading/Key Ideas and Details/ Implied Idea*

Under Wallace's plan, the CCC would grant farmers loans that could be repaid in the future when the grain was sold. It is inferable that the loans were intended to be a substitute for the revenue generated by the immediate sale of the grain. So, in essence, the loan simply postponed the farmer's sale of grain and eventual financial gain. (A) is wrong because the loan in no way provided an incentive to take land out of production. If anything, when guaranteed some sort of a return, farmers would have an incentive to increase acreage. (B) is wrong because the passage does not mention the successful enactment of a mandatory soil conservation program. (C) is wrong because everything in the passage says that the voluntary programs, like the Agricultural Adjustment Administration program, were ineffective.

8. **(H)** *Reading/Key Ideas and Details/Explicit Detail*

This is another explicit detail question. In the opening sentence of the second paragraph, the name of the Secretary of Agriculture is given, so (I) must be part of the correct answer. The name of Roosevelt's opponent in 1936 is given in the first paragraph, so (II) must be a part of the correct response. The passage does not mention anyone from the Farm Bureau by name, so (III) cannot be part of the answer.

9. **(A)** *Reading/Craft and Structure/Voice*

Eliminate (D) because the tone of the passage is neutral, like a scholarly journal. The first words of the remaining choices seem correct. One might describe the passage as scholarly, objective, or analytical. Eliminate (B), however, because the author doesn't offer a negative assessment of the policies; and eliminate (C) because the tone of the passage is not abrasive. Therefore, by the process of elimination, (A) is the correct choice. Indeed, "appreciative" is supported by the author's reference to Roosevelt's "adroit" political maneuver, which indicates that the author appreciates the significance of that move.

10. (H) *Reading/Key Ideas and Details/Main Idea*

(H) correctly identifies the author's primary concern: to explain the evolution of the idea that alcoholism is a disease. (F) is wrong because the author never denies the seriousness of the problem. (G) is wrong because the author does not compare the seriousness of the problem at two different times. (J) is wrong because, while the passage provides an example of changing medical terminology, this is not the author's main point.

11. (A) *Reading/Key Ideas and Details/Explicit Detail*

In lines 22–25, the author states, "the Temperance Movement stressed that alcohol itself was the cause of drunkenness and advocated its control and eventually its prohibition." Therefore, the members of the Temperance Movement agreed with doctors that alcohol abuse was a serious problem, (A). (B) is wrong because the passage states that the Temperance Movement solution was to ban alcohol altogether. (C) is wrong because the Temperance Movement didn't share this view. (D) is wrong because the Temperance Movement did agree with doctors on this point.

12. (F) *Reading/Craft and Structure/ Development*

The author states that Rush developed the disease concept of alcoholism, (F). (G) and (H) are both wrong because they incorrectly identify the author's purpose in mentioning Rush. As for (J), physicians already treat alcoholism as a physical disease.

13. (D) *Reading/Key Ideas and Details/ Implied Idea*

In the third paragraph, the author says that the identification of the physical effects of alcoholism initiated the understanding of alcoholism as a disease, (D). (A) is wrong because the concept

of alcoholism as a manifestation of a fundamental personality disorder— mentioned later in the third paragraph—is only something that the National Council on Alcoholism was thinking about. (B) is wrong because it refutes, rather than supports, the argument. (C), discussed in the first paragraph, precedes the author's explanation of the disease model of alcoholism.

14. (J) *Reading/Key Ideas and Details/Voice*

The "Drunkenness a Vice, Not a Disease" pamphlet is over 100 years old, and the author says that its publication "perhaps does not surprise us" (line 83) so (J) is the best choice. (F) is wrong because the author might say the other book mentioned in the last paragraph is misguided and dangerous, not the pamphlet. (G) is wrong because the author would probably say the essay is wrong but doesn't seem to think something written over 100 years ago is still harmful. (H) is wrong because the author fairly clearly thinks that the essay is wrong.

15. (A) *Reading/Key Ideas and Details/Implied Idea*

The author specifically states in the final paragraph that the view of alcoholism as a moral problem has not been discredited, (A). (B) is wrong because the author discusses beliefs about the role of the will in the first paragraph. (C) is wrong because the author does refer to several modern definitions of alcoholism. (D) is wrong because, in the last paragraph, the author discusses the fact that some people use the terms "alcoholic" and "drunkard" interchangeably, which indicates that the public may not fully understand medical terminology.

16. (G) *Reading/Key Ideas and Details/Explicit Detail*

(G) correctly identifies that the early drafts of the 1980 version and the 1993 version described tolerance and dependence as important but not essential. (F) is wrong because, according to paragraph five, the 1993 version did not require tolerance and withdrawal symptoms. (H) is wrong because it incorrectly identifies the source of the idea that alcoholism might be a generic, biological disorder, which is attributed to the National Council on Alcoholism report in paragraph three. (J) is wrong because it is not mentioned in the passage.

17. (C) Reading/Key Ideas and Details/Application

In the first sentence of the passage, the author says that the shift to "alcoholism as a disease" was not a medical discovery but a thesis, and in the second paragraph, the author says that the modern notion was motivated by treatment concerns. Therefore, (C) is the best choice. (A) is wrong because the author seems secure in the idea that the medical community agrees that alcoholism is a disease. (B) is wrong because the most recent version of the *Diagnostic and Statistical Manual of Mental Disorders* leaves diagnosis of alcoholism up to the doctor and "the clinician is not required to find whether either [dependence or tolerance] is present or to what degree in order to make the diagnosis" (lines 76–79). (D) is wrong because it is a misstatement of the timing of events as laid out by the author.

18. (F) Reading/Craft and Structure/Voice

The passage is mostly expository in describing the theories of Burnham. However, the author also criticizes Burnham for being hypocritical and for making predictions based on existing conditions. Therefore, (F) is the best choice. (G) is wrong because, while the author is insightful, he is not neutral. (H) is wrong because the author is not speculative, but analytical: Burnham speculates and Burnham is perhaps jaded, but the author of the passage is not. (J) is wrong because the author is not cynical.

19. (A) Reading/Craft and Structure/Implied Idea

The author states that most thinkers identify three political entities, beginning with the individual, and consider society an embodiment of the individual and the state a logical outgrowth of the individual and the society. Burnham inverts that sequence and theorizes that the state is the logical beginning and individuals are merely parts of the state, (A).

20. (F) Reading/Key Ideas and Details/Explicit Detail

The author mentions Burnham's irrepressible tendency to project existing conditions into the indefinite future in lines 14–16 and lines 62–64. In lines 64–70, the author explains that this is why many of Burnham's predictions proved wrong. Therefore, (F) is the best choice. As for (G), though the author believes that Burnham was wrong in his predictions, this is not a criticism he aims at Burnham. As for (H), the author specifically states that Burnham failed to defend democracy—not that Burnham preferred democracy. As for (J), though Burnham inverts the traditional relationship between the individual and state in his writings, the author does not criticize him on this score. The author apparently accepts the validity of making the alternative assumption for purposes of argument.

21. (A) Reading/Key Ideas and Details/Explicit Detail

The phrase "According to" identifies this as an Explicit Detail item, so the correct choice is explicitly stated in the passage (lines 39–43). (B) and (C) are both wrong because, while mentioned in the passage, they are not mentioned in the second paragraph where the author talks about the end of history. (D) is wrong because it is not specifically stated in the passage. Therefore, (A) is the best choice: apparently, what the author means is that history will end because there will no longer be any change; instead, the state will prescribe certain forms to which individuals must conform.

22. (H) *Reading/Key Ideas and Details/Main Idea*

(H) is the best choice: the author describes Burnham's theories and then criticizes them. (F) is wrong because the author does not present his own vision. (G) is wrong because, although he mentions the fact that Burnham's predictions were false, this observation is only a part of his criticism of Burnham's views. (J) is wrong because the author never mentions Burnham's literary style.

23. (B) *Reading/Key Ideas and Details/Implied Idea*

Given that the author mentions *We* only in passing and then only to show in what way it differed from *The Managerial Revolution*, we can infer that *We* was in many respects similar to *The Managerial Revolution*. However, the passage does not state which of the two works came first, and there is nothing to suggest that Zamyatin's work was based on Burnham's, so (I) is incorrect. By the same reasoning, we can conclude that (II) is a correct statement. Since Burnham's idea of three super powerful states is compared to Zamyatin's idea of one state, we can infer that the two ideas are similar. (III) is incorrect because these works predicted an outcome of world history, and although the ideas about the outcome of history were based on current political and social conditions, the books do not describe these conditions; rather, they describe the future conditions.

24. (G) *Reading/Key Ideas and Details/Main Idea*

One of the striking features about the passage is that the author does not first produce a contention and then offer facts to support it. Rather, the author's method is to produce the facts and then ask what conclusions might be drawn, (G). (F) is wrong because the author is not arguing for a single conclusion but is instead working toward a conclusion by exploring data. (H) is wrong for the same reason as (F): the author does answer some objections along the way, but that is not the main purpose. (J) is wrong because, while the final paragraph does seem to be a sort of challenge, there is a lot more going on in the passage than (J) suggests.

25. (A) *Reading/Key Ideas and Details/Implied Idea*

How do we know that the meteor is from Mars? The answer is found in the first paragraph, where the passage implies that oxygen isotopes found in the group of meteorites match the analysis of the Martian atmosphere. Therefore, (A) is the best choice. As for the remaining choices, while they mention ideas from the passage, each of them proves something different; many serve as evidence of microorganisms rather than as evidence of where the meteorite originated.

26. (F) *Reading/Key Ideas and Details/Explicit Detail*

This is an Explicit Detail item. All of the ideas given are mentioned in the passage, but (G), (H), and (J) all provide evidence that ALH84001 may show signs of life. As for (G), the PAHs, while possibly produced by inorganic processes, might have been produced by living matter. As for (H) and (J), the odd deposits suggest chemical processes. (F), however, suggests only that the rock came from Mars, not that it contains signs of extinct life.

27. (B) *Reading/Key Ideas and Details/Explicit Detail*

The passage specifically states that the carbonate deposits might have come from inorganic processes (line 33), but they seem more likely to have been deposited by a microorganism (lines 43–45). Similarly, the PAHs are different from the byproducts of ordinary combustion (lines 49–50), but, according to the author, they might conceivably be the result of inorganic reactions (lines 52–53).

28. (F) *Reading/Craft and Structure/
Development*

This item asks about the connection
between the two ideas mentioned in
the stem and the larger argument. Why
does the author mention gravitation and
space? Well, there are some shapes in
the meteorite that seem to be bacteria,
or at least they have the right shape, but
they are very, very small compared to any
bacteria we actually know. So, the author
suggests that the unique conditions on
Mars (weaker gravitational field) and
the conditions in the rock (small spaces)
might mean that the bacteria would be
small.

29. (D) *Reading/Key Ideas and Details/
Application*

The author seems to be inclined toward
the view that the scientific evidence is
at least consistent with the possibility of
life on Mars, even if the passage does not
affirmatively support the conclusion that
life once existed on Mars. Of course, the
author does not go so far as to say that the
data prove the existence of life on Mars,
but, on balance, that would seem to be the
author's view.

WRITING

QUIZ I *(p. 28)*

Above Average Response

A quick glance at an online forum or a website's comment section reveals the offensive, and often abusive language that is sometimes used online. Website moderators should be allowed to monitor commenters' language on their sites, and threatening comments that would have legal repercussions in real life should have legal consequences online. Eliminating profanity and threatening speech would allow the website to foster respectable dialogue and would provide its writers with a safe space to express their opinions. Furthermore, by taking online threats as seriously as "real life" threats, law enforcement could prevent serious crimes.

Although one may argue that filtering offensive language is an attack on free speech online, forcing people to speak respectfully would actually help build constructive debate. I agree with Perspective 1 that filtering language is a slippery slope and should not lead to narrowing of opinions expressed online. However, there is a difference between censoring ideas and setting guidelines for how they are expressed. A website, for example, could set up a program that blocks posts with certain profane words. This would allow for debate without regressing to obscenity. I am not arguing for a universal ban on profanity on the Internet, but I think that individual websites should have the discretion to monitor their users' language. Just as print media have the right to choose whether to print letters to the editor, online media should have the right to choose what appears on their websites.

Furthermore, abusive language online could actually curb writers' freedom of speech. As Perspective 2 argues, writers could be intimidated into silence by threats from commenters, which would stifle certain viewpoints and limit the diversity of writers. For example, recent articles about online harassment have reported that many female bloggers quit writing because of sexual harassment and even death threats from their readers. Also, as said in Perspective 3, the anonymity of posting online may allow commenters to speak more offensively than they would in person. Certain websites should be safe spaces where writers can share a variety of ideas without worrying about threats. In "real life," free speech does not allow for bullying and harassment, and these behaviors should not be protected online.

Finally, people's language should be held to the same legal standards online as it would be in personal interactions. If writers receive violent threats, those threats should be investigated. I also think that, in general, police should investigate threats that Internet users make on platforms such as forums or social media because such investigations could prevent violent crime. Last year, two female students were murdered at the University of California Santa Barbara, and the murderer had posted online videos where he threatened to kill women. If his online actions had legal consequences, his victims might still be alive. I recognize that this legal issue is not black and white; for example, I don't think that someone who writes a violent work of fiction and posts it online must be investigated. However, cases that could clearly be interpreted as threats should be reported to the police.

Monitoring speech online is a complicated issue, but I think that certain forms of speech can be limited without censoring ideas. Eliminating profane and vulgar language online could promote a respectful exchange of ideas and make writers feel safe to express a variety of opinions. Furthermore, law enforcement could prevent tragedies by investigating online threats.

Ideas and Analysis: In the introduction, the writer clearly states his or her position on the essay topic. In this essay, the writer does not argue for one of the given perspectives, but the thesis combines elements from Perspectives 2 and 3. The writer also gives a preview of all the main points that will support the thesis statement. In the first and third body paragraphs, the writer also acknowledges opposing viewpoints and uses these oppositions to clarify his or her own opinion.

Development and Support: The introduction states the thesis and previews the arguments that will support it. The writer presents these arguments in a thorough and logical manner:

- The body paragraphs begin with topic sentences that clearly state the main point or argument to be made in the paragraph.

- The body paragraphs are well developed. Each body paragraph includes several examples and details to support the arguments being made in it. The writer also strengthens his or her argument by engaging with opposing viewpoints.

- The body paragraphs do not include any sentences that are unrelated to the main argument.

Organization:

- The writer uses transitions to link sentences together and to draw connections between paragraphs. The writer introduces each paragraph with topic sentences and uses transitions to link each paragraph with previous ideas. For example, the second body paragraph begins with the transition "furthermore" because the paragraph provides an additional argument on how abusive language online can limit others' freedom of speech.

- The writer logically builds the argument throughout the essay. In the introduction, he or she opens with a hook and states the thesis in the second sentence. The rest of the introduction previews the essay's main topics. The body paragraphs address progressively harmful consequences of unlimited freedom for online speech. The first body paragraph argues that websites could foster more respectful debate by filtering profanity. The second body paragraph describes how harassment threatens writers' freedom of speech and sense of safety, and the third body paragraph addresses the crimes that could occur if violent threats are not investigated.

- In the third body paragraph, the writer should make a stronger connection between the prompt and his or her argument. The prompt asks how websites should monitor users' speech. Instead of saying, "in general, police should investigate threats that Internet users make on platforms such as forums or social media," he or she could argue that websites should report such language to legal authorities.

Language Use and Conventions:

The essay contains at least three principal strengths in this area:

- The essay does not have any mechanics/usage errors. As a result, the reader's attention is not distracted from the substance of the essay.

- The writer does not use any informal language.

- Stylistically, the writer varies sentence structures and includes vivid examples to keep the reader's attention focused on the page.

- The writer uses the first person to clarify his or her views, but does so without using slang or informal language.

Summary and Conclusions: This essay demonstrates writing skills that are very well developed and analyzes multiple viewpoints of the issue. The writer engages with all perspectives on the issue. This essay would likely receive a score of 10. (Remember that the Writing Test is scored on a scale of 2 to 12.)

Below Average Response

I agree with Perspectives 2 and 3 and agree that certain types of speech should be limited online. Mean speech online is called cyber-bullying and can cause lots of harm for it's victims. If certain websites are dominated by hateful speech, people might be afraid to express controversial ideas. Parents should also monitor their children's behavior online.

On websites, it is easy to bully others because you do not have to reveal your identity. Even if you do not know who your attacker is, cyber-bullying can have harmful consequences, just like being bullied in person. Online, you can also insult people unfairly for everything from their opinions to their appearance, in the past, this has led to depression or eating disorders.

Offensive language on websites could also scare writers into not expressing their believes. Sometimes, people say really angry things in the comments section and even threaten writers if they don't agree with what they said. I'm not saying that people shouldn't be able to argue back at what the writer says, but they should argue in a polite way. The website should be able to remove comments with things like swear words or insults to the writer that have nothing to do with the article.

Parents should supervise their children's behavior online. Kids sometimes go onto websites where theirs a lot of offensive language, and they learn to speak like that. Teenagers especially sometimes say violent things online, and if parents find this, they should figure out what is causing this behavior.

The Internet could be a safer place for everyone if people limited offensive speech, especially cyber-bullying, and if parents watched their kids' behavior.

Ideas and Analysis: The writer clearly states his or her thesis in the first sentence of the introduction. However, the thesis is formulated in a very simplistic way and unnecessarily repeats the word "agree." Instead of saying "I agree with Perspectives 2 and 3," the writer should explain his or her own thesis more thoroughly. The writer also previews the main arguments but should use transitions to link these arguments more logically. Finally, the writer briefly acknowledges Perspectives 2 and 3, but the essay does not address the opposing viewpoint in Perspective 1.

Development and Support: The essay contains a clear thesis and supporting arguments, but he or she does not effectively link the arguments to the prompt.

- The paragraph on cyber-bullying could be a strong argument for limiting free speech online. However, the writer does not say how limiting offensive speech on websites can stop cyber-bullying.

- The second body paragraph introduces several arguments without developing them. The paragraph mentions that offensive language could intimidate writers, that people should still be able to argue on websites, and that websites should limit profanity. For a more effective paragraph, the writer should elaborate on one or two of these points.

- Although the third body paragraph relates to Internet use, it does not relate to the prompt. The prompt asks what websites (not parents) should do to monitor offensive language.

- The writer fails to mention the prompt's main question: what should website managers do about profanity on their sites?

Organization:

- The writer uses a few transitional words, such as "also," but the essay would flow better with a more effective use of transitions. None of the topic sentences use transitions. The paragraphs all discuss offensive behavior online, but they do not build on ideas previously mentioned in the essay.

- The writer needs to incorporate the prompt's perspectives into the arguments of the essay.

- The writer should write a less generic opening sentence to "hook" the reader. The conclusion is underdeveloped. It should summarize the thesis and main ideas more thoroughly, without repeating the exact wording in the introduction.

Language Use and Conventions:

The essay contains several weaknesses in this area that distract from its content.

- The essay contains some usage and mechanics errors:

  - Introduction: "harm for it's victims" should be "harm for its victims."

  - Body paragraph 1: The last sentence contains a comma splice and should be divided into two sentences.

  - Body paragraph 2: In the first sentence, "their believes" should be "their beliefs."

  - Body paragraph 3: In the second sentence, "theirs" should be "there's" or "there is."

- The writer uses informal language, such as "really" and "lots."

- The writer sometimes uses vague language that adds no value to the essay. For example, in body paragraph 2, the phrase "comments with things like swear words" should just say "comments like swear words."

Summary and Conclusions: The writer has a clear thesis and supporting arguments, but not all the arguments are well developed or relevant to the prompt. The writer also needs to address opposing viewpoints. This essay would likely receive a score of 5. (Remember that the Writing Test is scored on a scale of 2 to 12.)

MATH

QUIZ I (p. 32)

1. **(C)** *Mathematics/Statistics and Probability/Measures of Center*

   A calculator makes the calculation of the average easy:
   $$\frac{6+7+8+9+10+11+12+13+14+15}{10}$$
   $$= 10.5$$

   Alternatively, it is faster to note that the average of an even number of consecutive integers is the average of the first and last numbers: $\frac{6+15}{2} = 10.5$.

2. **(F)** *Mathematics/Number and Quantity/Scientific Notation*

   This item is simplified by rewriting the numerator without a decimal: $3.2 \times 10^5 = 32 \times 10^4$. Next, use the rules for exponents to simplify the expression:
   $$\frac{32 \times 10^4}{8 \times 10^8} = \frac{32}{8} \times 10^{4-8} = 4 \times 10^{-4}.$$

3. **(E)** *Mathematics/Geometry/Rectangles and Squares*

   Write an equation for the area and solve for x:
   $$\text{area}_{\text{rectangle}} = (l)(w) = (x+3)(x-3) = 72 \Rightarrow$$
   $$x^2 - 3x + 3x - 9 = 72 \Rightarrow x^2 = 81 \Rightarrow$$
   $(x+9)(x-9) = 0$. Therefore, $x = 9$ or -9; x is a length, so it must be 9.

   Alternatively, "test-the-test" by plugging the answer choices for x into the equation for the area of the rectangle. The correct choice will return a value of 72.

4. **(G)** *Mathematics/Number and Quantity/Rates and Proportions*

   Machine X produces 3 more units per minute than does Machine Y. Thus, in 1 hour, Machine X produces $(3)(60) = 180$ more units than does Machine Y.

5. **(D)** *Mathematics/Statistics and Probability/Data Representation/Pie Charts*

   The total budget is $720, and each sector of the pie charts reflects the fraction of that expenditure of the total budget.

   Transportation ($240) is $\frac{240}{720} = \frac{1}{3}$.

   Lodging ($360) is $\frac{360}{720} = \frac{1}{2}$. Meals ($120)

   is $\frac{120}{720} = \frac{1}{6}$. Since lodging accounts for half of the budget, eliminate any answer choice that does not have a gray sector equal to half of the pie. Only (D) remains.

6. **(G)** *Mathematics/Number and Quantity/Basic Arithmetic Manipulations*

   Let T be the total number of pages in the assignment. After the first day, $\left(T - \frac{T}{2}\right)$ pages remain in the assignment. After the second day, $\left(T - \frac{T}{2}\right) - 3$ pages remain. We are given that there are six pages remaining after the second day. Set $\left(T - \frac{T}{2}\right) - 3$ equal to six and solve for T:
   $$\left(T - \frac{T}{2}\right) - 3 = 6 \Rightarrow \frac{T}{2} = 9 \Rightarrow T = 18.$$

Alternatively, "test-the-test," beginning with (H): if the assignment was 24 pages, then the student had 12 left after the first day and 9 left after the second day. Since 9 pages is too many, try (G) next: $\frac{1}{2}(18) = 9$, and $9 - 3 = 6$. Therefore, the answer is (G).

7. **(B) Mathematics/Statistics and Probability/Measures of Center**

The average of the first two scores is 78, so set them both equal to 78 in the average of the three tests. Solve for the value of the third test: average $= \frac{78 + 78 + x}{3} = 80 \Rightarrow$ $78 + 78 + x = 240 \Rightarrow x = 84$.

8. **(F) Mathematics/Geometry/Lines and Angles**

Opposite angles created by two intersecting lines are equal, so $a = c$ and $b = d$. Therefore, $a + c = a + a = 2a$, and $a + c - b = 2a - d$.

9. **(D) Mathematics/Algebra and Functions/ Manipulating Algebraic Expressions/ Evaluating Expressions**

This item has two variables and only one equation, so there is no way to find the value of a or b. However, it is not necessary to find these values because the item asks for the value of $a + 2b$. Since $3a + 6b = 12$, $a + 2b = \frac{3a + 6b}{3} = \frac{12}{3} = 4$.

10. **(J) Mathematics/Geometry/Circles**

The area of a circle is πr^2, so area$_{\text{large circle}}$ − area$_{\text{small circle}} = \pi(r + 3)^2 - \pi r^2 = 15\pi \Rightarrow (r + 3)^2 - r^2 = 15 \Rightarrow 6r = 6 \Rightarrow r = 1$.

11. **(D) Mathematics/Number and Quantity/ Properties of Numbers**

The direct solution requires recognizing that for x to have the greatest possible value, y and z must have the smallest possible values. The smallest integer greater than 1 is 2, so $z = 2$. The next smallest integer greater than 2 is 3, so $y = 3$. Therefore, $xyz = (x)(3)(2) = 144 \Rightarrow$ $x = \frac{144}{6} = 24$.

12. **(F) Mathematics/Algebra and Functions/ Expressing and Evaluating Algebraic Functions/Function Notation**

Complete the indicated operations in each statement, and check for equality. (I) is part of the correct answer since $2(3) + 3(2) = 12$; eliminate (J). (II) is not part of the correct answer: since $x \, \Phi \, y = 2x + 3y$, $y \, \Phi \, x = 2y + 3x$, but $2x + 3y \neq 2y + 3x$. Thus, eliminate (G) and (K). Finally, (III) cannot be part of the correct answer: $0 \, \Phi \, (1 \, \Phi \, 2) = 0 \, \Phi \, [2(1) + 3(2)] = 0 \, \Phi \, 8 = 2(0) + 3(8) = 24$, $(0 \, \Phi \, 1) \, \Phi \, 2 = 3 \, \Phi \, 2 = 2(3) + 3(2) = 12$, but $24 \neq 12$. Therefore, the answer is (F), (I) only.

13. **(A) Mathematics/Algebra and Functions/ Coordinate Geometry/Slope of a Line**

This item can be solved by using the formula for finding the slope of a line $\left(m = \frac{y_2 - y_1}{x_2 - x_1} \right)$: $\frac{0 - (-2)}{2 - 0} = \frac{2}{2} = 1$.

Alternatively, recall some of the general rules about slopes to help identify the correct answer. First, a line that runs "up" the graph from left to right has a positive slope; a line that runs "down" the graph from left to right has a negative slope. Thus, eliminate (D) and (E). Second, the line $x = y$ and the line $x = -y$ intersect the x-axis at 45° angles and have slopes of 1 and −1, respectively. Lines that are "steeper" have slopes greater than 1 or less than −1, and lines that are "less steep" have slopes that are fractions. Eyeballing the given graph, the line appears parallel to $x = y$, so (A) is a good choice.

14. **(F)** *Mathematics/Algebra and Functions/ Evaluating, Interpreting, and Creating Algebraic Functions/Functions as Models*

Instead of deriving the necessary algebraic equation, simply plug in some numbers. If Yuriko is 20 years old now, then 10 years ago Lisa was $\dfrac{20}{2} = 10$ years old, and so now Lisa is 20 years old. Substitute 20 for n in the answer choices; the correct choice will return a value of 20, (F): $\dfrac{20}{2} + 10 = 20$.

15. **(C)** *Mathematics/Geometry/Complex Figures* and *Rectangles and Squares* and *Circles*

The width of the rectangle is equal to the radius of the circle, 2, and the length of the rectangle is equal to the diameter of the circle, 4. Thus, the area of the rectangle is $wl = (2)(4) = 8$. The shaded region is the difference between the area of the rectangle and the area of one-half of the circle. The area of the semicircle is $\dfrac{\pi r^2}{2} = \dfrac{\pi (2)^2}{2} = 2\pi$. Thus, $\text{area}_{\text{shaded region}} = \text{area}_{\text{rectangle}} - \text{area}_{\text{semicircle}} = 8 - 2\pi$.

16. **(G)** *Mathematics/Number and Quantity/ Properties of Numbers*

The sum of two consecutive integers, if the larger of the two is x, is written as $(x - 1) + x$. Set this equal to n and solve for x: $(x - 1) + x = n \Rightarrow 2x - 1 = n \Rightarrow x = \dfrac{n + 1}{2}$.

Alternatively, "test-the-test." If 2 and 3 are the two integers, $n = 5$. Plug 5 into each of the answer choices. The correct answer will return a value of 3:

F. $\dfrac{n - 1}{2} = \dfrac{5 - 1}{2} = \dfrac{4}{2} = 2$ ✘

G. $\dfrac{n + 1}{2} = \dfrac{5 + 1}{2} = \dfrac{6}{2} = 3$ ✔

17. **(C)** *Mathematics/Statistics and Probability/Data Representation/Tables* and *Number and Quantity/Rates and Proportions*

Set up a direct proportion. The Old Scale has a 100-point range and the New Scale has a 60-point range: $\dfrac{60}{100} = \dfrac{x}{60}$, where x is the number of points above the 120-point minimum that the new minimum score will be. Solve for x: $100x = (60)(60) \Rightarrow x = 36$. Therefore, the new equivalent minimum score is $120 + 36 = 156$.

Alternatively, simple common sense applies here too: 60 is slightly above the midpoint of the Old Scale, so the correct answer choice will be slightly above the midpoint of the New Scale.

18. **(G)** *Mathematics/Geometry/Complex Figures* and *Lines and Angles*

The vertices of the polygon divide the circumference of the circle into equal parts. Since a circle has 360 degrees, the correct answer is the only one that does not evenly divide into 360: 25, (G).

19. **(E)** *Mathematics/Statistics and Probability/Probability*

If the probability of picking a red marble is 1 out of 4, then $\dfrac{1}{4}$ of the marbles in the jar must be red marbles. The total number of marbles is $5 + 25 + x$, where x is the number of red marbles. Therefore, $\dfrac{x}{5 + 25 + x} = \dfrac{1}{4} \Rightarrow 4x = 30 + x \Rightarrow 3x = 30 \Rightarrow x = 10$.

Alternatively, "test-the-test," beginning with (C): if $x = 15$, then the total number of marbles is 45, and the probability of drawing a red marble is $\frac{15}{45} = \frac{1}{3}$. Since $\frac{1}{3} > \frac{1}{4}$, the number of red marbles must be less than 15. Therefore, try (D) next: $\frac{12}{42} = \frac{2}{7}$. Since $\frac{2}{7} > \frac{1}{4}$, (E) must be the correct answer.

20. **(H) *Mathematics/Geometry/Trigonometry/ Definitions of the Six Trigonometric Functions* and *Triangles/45°-45°-90° Triangles***

Since $\cos 45° \approx 0.7$, and $\cos 45° = \dfrac{\overline{BC}}{\overline{AB}}$, $\dfrac{\overline{BC}}{\overline{AB}} \approx 0.7$, $\overline{AB} = 2$, and so

$$\frac{\overline{BC}}{\overline{AB}} = \frac{\overline{BC}}{2} \approx 0.7 \Rightarrow \overline{BC} \approx 2(0.7) \approx 1.4.$$

Alternatively, use the properties of a 45°-45°-90° right triangle:
$(\text{side})(\sqrt{2}) = \text{hypotenuse} \Rightarrow$
$(\overline{BC})(\sqrt{2}) = 2 \Rightarrow$
$(\overline{BC})(\sqrt{2})(\sqrt{2}) = 2\sqrt{2} \Rightarrow (\overline{BC})(2) = 2\sqrt{2} \Rightarrow \overline{BC} = \sqrt{2} \approx 1.4$.

QUIZ II (p.36)

1. **(C)** *Mathematics/Number and Quantity/ Basic Arithmetic Manipulations and Algebra and Functions/Solving Algebraic Equations or Inequalities with One Variable/Simple Equations*

Historical novels account for $\frac{1}{4}T$, where T is the total number of books. Of the remaining books, $\frac{3}{4}T$, classics account for one-half, or $\frac{1}{2}\left(\frac{3}{4}T\right) = \frac{3}{8}T$. The remainder of the books are travel books, or $T - \left(\frac{1}{4}T + \frac{3}{8}T\right) = T - \frac{5}{8}T = \frac{3}{8}T$. Since there are 30 travel books, $\frac{3}{8}T = 30 \Rightarrow$

$$T = \frac{(30)(8)}{3} = 80.$$

2. **(F)** *Mathematics/Number and Quantity/ Percentages and Statistics and Probability/Data Representation/Tables*

The item stem asks for the percent increase, so use the "change-over-original" equation: $\frac{\text{Change}}{\text{Original}} = \%\ \text{Change}$.

Immediately eliminate (G) and (H) because these changes are significantly less than for (F) and (J). Eliminate (K) because it is not an increase in enrollment. From 2006 to 2007, (F), the percent increase was $\frac{15,100 - 14,000}{14,000} = \frac{1,100}{14,000} \approx 0.078 \approx 7.9\%$. From 2009 to 2010, (J), the percent increase was $\frac{17,600 - 16,500}{16,500} = \frac{1,100}{16,500} \approx 0.066 \approx 6.7\%$.

Therefore, the greatest percent increase in enrollment was from 2006 to 2007.

3. **(E)** *Mathematics/Algebra and Functions/ Expressing and Evaluating Algebraic Functions/Function Notation*

First, substitute -2 for x in the function $f(x)$ and evaluate:

$$f(x) = \frac{x^2 + x}{x - 1} \Rightarrow f(-2) =$$

$$\frac{(-2)^2 + (-2)}{(-2) - 1} = \frac{4 - 2}{-3} = -\frac{2}{3}.$$

Next, substitute $-\frac{2}{3}$ for x in the function $g(x)$ and evaluate:

$$g(f(-2)) = g\left(-\frac{2}{3}\right) = 2\left(-\frac{2}{3}\right) + 3 \Rightarrow$$

$$-\frac{4}{3} + \frac{9}{3} = \frac{5}{3}.$$

4. **(H)** *Mathematics/Number and Quantity/ Properties of Numbers and Statistics and Probability/Sets*

Set A is the positive factors of 24: {1, 2, 3, 4, 6, 8, 12, 24}. Set B is all prime numbers less than 20: {2, 3, 5, 7, 11, 13, 17, 19}. Therefore, there are two numbers common to both sets: 2 and 3.

5. **(D)** *Mathematics/Algebra and Functions/ Evaluating, Interpreting, and Creating Algebraic Functions and Solving Algebraic Equations or Inequalities with One Variable/Simple Inequalities*

For the model to be within the height requirements, his or her height, x, must be within 70 ± 2 inches. Therefore, $70 - 2 < x \Rightarrow -2 < x - 70$ and $x < 70 + 2 \Rightarrow x - 70 < 2$, which combined is the same as $-2 < x - 70 < 2 \Rightarrow |x - 70| < 2$.

Alternatively, simply note that the conditions state that the difference between x and 70 must be less than 2. The difference between x and 70 is written as $|x - 70|$, so $|x - 70| < 2$.

6. **(F)** *Mathematics/Algebra and Functions/ Solving Simultaneous Equations and Evaluating, Interpreting, and Creating Algebraic Functions*

Translate the given information into a system of simultaneous equations. Let b, g, and r represent the number of blue, green, and red marbles, respectively: $b + g = 25$; $b + r = 30$; and $r = 2g$. Substitute $2g$ for r in the second equation and subtract the result from the first equation to eliminate the b variable:

$$b + g = 25$$
$$- (b + 2g = 30)$$
$$-g = -5 \Rightarrow g = 5$$

7. **(D)** *Mathematics/Number and Quantity/ Matrices and Vectors*

First, convert the percentages in the second matrix to decimals:

$\begin{bmatrix} 20\% \\ 50\% \\ 75\% \end{bmatrix} = \begin{bmatrix} 0.2 \\ 0.5 \\ 0.75 \end{bmatrix}$. To find the number of

potatoes for each entree, find the product of the given matrices: $\begin{bmatrix} 85 & 58 & 68 \end{bmatrix} \begin{bmatrix} 0.2 \\ 0.5 \\ 0.75 \end{bmatrix} =$

$[85(0.2) \; 58(0.5) \; 68(0.75)]$. Therefore, the total number of potatoes sides is the sum of the values in the matrix: $17 + 29 + 51 = 97$.

8. **(G)** *Mathematics/Geometry/Lines and Angles*

When two parallel lines are cut by a transversal, opposite exterior angles are equal. And the sum of the angles in a straight line is $180°$. Therefore, $y = 4x$ and $y + 2x = 180 \Rightarrow 4x + 2x = 180 \Rightarrow 6x = 180 \Rightarrow x = 30$.

9. **(E)** *Mathematics/Algebra and Functions/ Manipulating Algebraic Expressions/ Factoring Expressions*

The trick to solving this item is to recognize that both x and y can be factored:

$$\frac{x}{y} = \frac{a^2 - b^2}{a^2 + 2ab + b^2}$$
$$= \frac{(a+b)(a-b)}{(a+b)(a+b)} = \frac{a-b}{a+b} \; .$$

10. **(H)** *Mathematics/Geometry/Triangles/ Pythagorean Theorem*

Draw a figure:

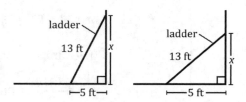

First, find the original height of the ladder on the wall using the Pythagorean theorem: $13^2 = 5^2 + x^2 \Rightarrow x^2 = 169 - 25 = 144 \Rightarrow x = \sqrt{144} = 12$ feet. Next, find the new height of the ladder on the wall after it has slid to its new position: $13^2 = 8^2 + y^2 \Rightarrow y^2 = 169 - 64 = 105 \Rightarrow y = \sqrt{105}$, or a little over 10 feet. Therefore, the ladder slid just a little less than 2 feet.

11. **(C)** *Mathematics/Geometry/Complex Figures and Triangles/30°-60°-90° Triangles*

In order to find the area of the shaded portion, which is a triangle, the length of the base $\overline{EC}$ must be determined. Since $\overline{AD} = 2$, $\overline{BC} = 2$ and $\overline{DE} = 2$. Also, $\angle BAC = 30°$, so $\triangle ABC$ is a 30°-60°-90° triangle ($\overline{BC} = \dfrac{\overline{AC}}{2}$ and $\overline{AB} = \dfrac{\sqrt{3}}{2}\overline{AC}$).

Solve for $\overline{AB}$: $\overline{AC} = 2\overline{BC} = 2(2) = 4$ and

$\overline{AB} = \dfrac{\sqrt{3}}{2}(4) = 2\sqrt{3}$. Since $\overline{AB} = \overline{DE} + \overline{EC}$,

$\overline{EC} = \overline{AB} - \overline{DE} = 2\sqrt{3} - 2$. Therefore, the

area of the triangle is

$$\frac{(\overline{AD})(\overline{EC})}{2} = \frac{2(2\sqrt{3} - 2)}{2} = 2\sqrt{3} - 2 \ .$$

12. (G) *Mathematics/Geometry/Circles*

The sector is $\frac{40°}{360°} = \frac{1}{9}$ of a circle, so the circumference of the circle is $9(\overgroup{DE}) = 9(2\pi) = 18\pi$. From the circumference, determine the radius, r: $C = 2\pi r \Rightarrow 18\pi = 2\pi r \Rightarrow r = 9$. Therefore, the area of the circle is $\pi r^2 = \pi(9)^2 = 81\pi$, and the area of the sector is $\frac{81\pi}{9} = 9\pi$.

13. (D) *Mathematics/Number and Quantity/ Properties of Numbers*

The prime factorization of 24 is $(3)(2)(2)(2)$, so the greatest prime factor of 24 is 3. The prime factorization of 80 is $(5)(2)(2)(2)(2)$, so the greatest prime factor of 80 is 5. Therefore, $ab = 3(5) = 15$.

14. (J) *Mathematics/Algebra and Functions/ Evaluating, Interpreting, and Creating Algebraic Functions and Statistics and Probability/Measures of Center*

Translate the given information into an algebraic expression: $\frac{a + b + c}{3} = z \Rightarrow a + b + c = 3z$. Therefore, the average of a, b, c, and d is $\frac{a + b + c + d}{4} = \frac{3z + d}{4}$.

15. (B) *Mathematics/Number and Quantity/ Properties of Numbers*

Two positive integers yield a remainder of 5 when divided by a positive integer: $\frac{21}{16} = 1$ plus remainder 5 and $\frac{21}{8} = 2$ plus remainder 5.

16. (H) *Mathematics/Algebra and Functions/ Evaluating, Interpreting, and Creating Algebraic Functions/Function Notation*

Substitute 2 for x, 3 for y, and 1 for z in the given functions and evaluate: $2 \ ✪ \ 3 = 2(3) + 3 = 9$ and $z \ ✪ \ 1 = z(1) + 1$. Since $2 \ ✪ \ 3 = z \ ✪ \ 1$, $9 = z + 1 \Rightarrow z = 8$.

17. (B) *Mathematics/Algebra and Functions/ Coordinate Geometry/The Coordinate System and Geometry/Circles*

Since the circle only touches the y-axis once, it is tangent to the y-axis, and the center of the circle is 3 coordinate spaces away from the y-axis, which means that the radius is 3. Therefore, the diameter of the circle is twice the radius, or 6.

18. (F) *Mathematics/Algebra and Functions/ Solving Quadratic Equations and Relations*

Solve the quadratic equation by factoring: $x^2 + 3x - 18 = 0 \Rightarrow (x - 3)(x + 6) = 0$. So, $x - 3 = 0 \Rightarrow x = 3$ or $x + 6 = 0 \Rightarrow x = -6$. Therefore, possible values of m are $\frac{x}{2} = \frac{3}{2}$ and $\frac{x}{2} = \frac{-6}{2} = -3$.

19. (E) *Mathematics/Algebra and Functions/ Coordinate Geometry/Graphs of Quadratic Equations and Relations* and *Distance and Midpoint Formulas*

The equation $x^2 + y^2 = 36$ can be rewritten as $x^2 + y^2 = 6^2$, which is the standard form of the equation of a circle $(x^2 + y^2 = r^2)$, so it is clear that the circle is centered at the origin with radius 6. Test each of the coordinate pairs given in the answer choices in the distance formula, measuring the distance from the origin:

$$\sqrt{(x-0)^2 + (y-0)^2} = \sqrt{x^2 + y^2}.$$

For a point inside the circle, the distance will be less than 6:

A. $(6, 0)$: $\sqrt{6^2 + 0^2} = 6$ ✗

B. $(0, -6)$: $\sqrt{0^2 + (-6)^2} = 6$ ✗

C. $(-4, 5)$: $\sqrt{(-4)^2 + 5^2} = \sqrt{16 + 25} = \sqrt{41} > 6$ ✗

D. $(2, 7)$: $\sqrt{2^2 + 7^2} = \sqrt{4 + 49} = \sqrt{53} > 6$ ✗

E. $(4, 4)$: $\sqrt{4^2 + 4^2} = \sqrt{16 + 16} = \sqrt{32} < 6$ ✓

Alternatively, sketch the circle and plot the points to estimate which will be inside the circle.

20. (F) *Mathematics/Algebra and Functions/ Manipulating Algebraic Expressions/ Factoring Expressions*

The key to solving this item is to recognize that $x^2 - y^2$ can be factored as $(x - y)(x + y)$. Therefore, $(x - y)(x + y) = 35 \Rightarrow 7(x + y) = 35 \Rightarrow x + y = 5$.

21. (C) *Mathematics/Number and Quantity/ Complex Numbers*

Imaginary numbers are manipulated like variables. So, $(2i - 1)(i + 3) = 2i^2 + 6i - i - 3 = 2i^2 + 5i - 3$. Since $i^2 = -1$, reduce the expression: $2i^2 + 5i - 3 = -2 + 5i - 3 = -5 + 5i$.

22. (H) *Mathematics/Geometry/Trigonometry/ Trigonometric Relationships*

The Pythagorean identity states that $\sin^2 x + \cos^2 x = 1$, so $\cos^2 x - 7 + \sin^2 x = \sin^2 x + \cos^2 x - 7 = 1 - 7 = -6$.

23. (A) *Mathematics/Algebra and Functions/ Solving Algebraic Equations or Inequalities with One Variable/Equations Involving Logarithms*

To determine the value of x, ask, "what x raised to -4 equals $\dfrac{1}{81}$?":

$$x^{-4} = \frac{1}{81} \Rightarrow x^{-4} = 81^{-1} \Rightarrow$$
$$x^{-4} = (3^4)^{-1} \Rightarrow x = 3.$$

24. (J) *Mathematics/Geometry/Trigonometry/ Definitions of the Six Trigonometric Functions and Triangles/Pythagorean Theorem*

Since $\frac{\pi}{2} < \theta < \pi$, the angle is in Quadrant II. Use the definition for cosine ($\cos \theta = \dfrac{\text{side adjacent } \theta}{\text{hypotenuse}} = -\dfrac{3}{5}$) to construct a triangle in Quadrant II:

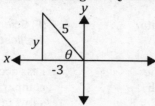

Use the Pythagorean theorem to find the missing side of the triangle: $5^2 = y^2 + (-3)^2 \Rightarrow y^2 = 25 - 9 = 16 \Rightarrow y = 4$. (Or, recognize that the triangle is a 3-4-5 triangle.) The definition for sine is $\sin \theta = \dfrac{\text{side opposite } \theta}{\text{hypotenuse}}$. Therefore, $\sin \theta = \dfrac{4}{5}$.

25. (C) *Mathematics/Algebra and Functions/ Manipulating Algebraic Expressions/ Factoring Expressions and Solving Quadratic Equations and Relations and Number and Quantity/Complex Numbers*

If $x = -4$ is a root of the equation, then $x + 4$ is a factor. Therefore, divide $x + 4$ out of the equation using synthetic division:

$$-4 \begin{array}{|rrrr} 3 & 12 & 2 & 8 \\ & -12 & 0 & -8 \\ \hline 3 & 0 & 2 & 0 \end{array}$$

Therefore, $\dfrac{3x^3 + 12x^2 + 2x + 8}{x + 4} = 3x^2 + 2$.

Now, solve the quadratic equation using the quadratic formula (if $ax^2 + bx + c = 0$, then $x = \dfrac{-b \pm \sqrt{b^2 - 4ac}}{2a}$):

$$\frac{0 \pm \sqrt{0^2 - 4(3)(2)}}{2(3)} =$$

$$\pm \frac{\sqrt{-24}}{6} = \pm \frac{2i\sqrt{6}}{6} = \pm \frac{i\sqrt{6}}{3}.$$

SCIENCE

QUIZ (p. 42)

1. **(C)** *Science/Interpretation of Data/ Analysis*

   For each element in the table, the ionization energy increases with increasing energy level: $E_1 < E_2 < E_3$.

2. **(G)** *Science/Interpretation of Data/ Comprehension*

   Of the four answer choices, only C, carbon, doubles in ionization energy with each successive energy level.

3. **(C)** *Science/Interpretation of Data/ Analysis*

   The data trend for the ionization energy of the second energy level as a function of increasing atomic number is to increase for a few values, then to suddenly decrease, followed by another increase, etc.

4. **(F)** *Science/Interpretation of Data/ Application*

   For an atom to be ionized by the electron beam, the first ionization energy of the element must be less than 200 kcal/mol. There are seven elements listed in the table with values of E_1 below 200 kcal/ mole: Li, B, Na, Mg, Al, Si, and K.

5. **(A)** *Science/Interpretation of Data/ Analysis*

   Air resistance slows the stone relative to its speed in a vacuum chamber, causing it to take a longer time to reach the ground.

6. **(F)** *Science/Scientific Investigation/ Application*

   Less acceleration means less speed at comparable times, so the lunar photos will show images of the stone that are more bunched up.

7. **(C)** *Science/Evaluation of Models/Analysis*

   In a vacuum, objects of equal mass fall at the same rate, regardless of size, shape, or density. On the other hand, the resistance of air on a falling object will cause a decrease in its acceleration. Cork has a much lower density than stone—a piece of cork with the same mass as the stone will be much larger. The larger the surface area of an object, the more air resistance it encounters when falling in air, and thus the slower it will fall in air when compared to a denser object of equal mass.

8. **(G)** *Science/Interpretation of Data/ Application*

   Since the stone moves faster as it drops due to acceleration, it will fall farther in each 0.1-second interval.

9. **(D)** *Science/Scientific Investigation/ Application*

   At the 0.2-second point, the stone's speed becomes constant, covering equal distance in equal time. It does not stop, as in (A), since it needs no gravitational acceleration to help it continue with the speed that it already has.

10. **(H)** *Science/Scientific Investigation/ Application*

Since the moon's gravity is one-sixth of Earth's gravity, the cork will accelerate more slowly on the moon. Yet, the moon has no atmosphere, so the cork will fall at the same rate as a stone of equal mass when dropped on the moon.

11. **(B)** *Science/Interpretation of Data/ Analysis*

Compare the section of the acceleration data with positive slope with the displacement data sets for the same period: 0.375 seconds to 0.75 seconds. At 0.375 seconds, the mass is at its highest position (maximum displacement above resting position) and at 0.75 seconds, the mass is at its lowest position (maximum displacement below resting position). This represents the period in which the mass is moving downward. It speeds up to a maximum velocity (in the negative direction) and then slows down to a velocity of 0 m/s when the mass is at its lowest point, so it is speeding up and then slowing down.

12. **(G)** *Science/Evaluation of Models/Analysis*

According to the first paragraph of the passage, the period is the time it takes the mass to complete one complete cycle of motion: from its resting point to its maximum height, back to its resting point, to its minimum height, and back to its resting point again. The dashed line in Figure 1 shows the position of the mass at times 0 to 1 second. One period can be measured from the first resting point (0.19 seconds) through a full cycle to the second resting point (0.94 seconds). A complete cycle, or period, is 0.94 – 0.19 = 0.75 seconds. As the first paragraph states, a period can be measured from any starting point. Resting position is a convenient *y*-value to use as a starting point.

13. **(C)** *Science/Evaluation of Models/Analysis*

The velocity (solid line) and displacement (dashed line) are both negative from

0.56 seconds to 0.75 seconds. During this time period, the mass is already below the resting point (0 m). Even though the velocity is negative, it is returning to 0, which means the mass is still moving downward but at a slower speed.

14. **(J)** *Science/Interpretation of Data/Analysis*

The best approach to this item is to check each answer choice against the experimental data. When the mass is at its maximum positive displacement (its highest point), its velocity is zero. As the mass moves toward its resting position, its velocity magnitude increases to –3 m/s, so (F) is wrong. As for (G), the velocity is least (0 m/s) when the mass is at its maximum positive or negative displacement. (H) is wrong because the data clearly shows that velocity is not constant at any point of the cycle. Only (J) is supported by the data: the maximum velocity, whether positive (mass is moving upward) or negative (mass is moving downward) corresponds to where the displacement data crosses the *x*-axis, that is, when the mass passes through the resting position.

15. **(A)** *Science/Interpretation of Data/ Analysis*

The dashed line in Figure 1 shows that the resting point occurs at 0.19 seconds, and the next resting point occurs at 0.56 seconds. At these same points, acceleration (the dashed line with alternating dash lengths) also equals 0.

16. **(F)** *Science/Scientific Investigation/ Application*

The key to answering this item is to carefully read the passage. The end of the first paragraph states that the period of an object in periodic motion is unaffected by how much the spring is initially stretched. Therefore, (G) is wrong and (F) is right. (H) is wrong because doubling the distance that the spring is stretched would double the amplitude. (J) is wrong because if the distance traveled were twice as far but the period were the same, the maximum velocity would increase, not decrease.

PRACTICE TEST I

MULTIPLE-CHOICE ANSWER KEYS

DIRECTIONS: For each <u>correct</u> answer, check the corresponding box. Then, total the number of checkmarks to determine the raw score for that test.

Section 1: English (Student Text, p. 51)

	Correct		Correct		Correct		Correct		Correct
1. B		16. H		31. B		46. F		61. C	
2. J		17. D		32. H		47. D		62. H	
3. D		18. G		33. A		48. J		63. D	
4. G		19. A		34. J		49. C		64. G	
5. A		20. F		35. A		50. F		65. D	
6. H		21. C		36. F		51. B		66. F	
7. A		22. H		37. B		52. F		67. A	
8. G		23. A		38. H		53. B		68. F	
9. A		24. G		39. B		54. J		69. C	
10. G		25. C		40. H		55. D		70. J	
11. C		26. J		41. D		56. G		71. A	
12. J		27. D		42. H		57. D		72. G	
13. B		28. G		43. A		58. H		73. B	
14. H		29. C		44. F		59. A		74. J	
15. A		30. G		45. C		60. J		75. B	

Raw Score: _____ /75

Section 2: Mathematics (Student Text, p. 62)

	Correct		Correct		Correct		Correct
1. A		16. H		31. A		46. J	
2. K		17. B		32. H		47. A	
3. C		18. K		33. A		48. F	
4. K		19. E		34. K		49. C	
5. E		20. F		35. D		50. K	
6. H		21. D		36 J		51. C	
7. D		22. G		37. C		52. J	
8. H		23. C		38. G		53. A	
9. D		24. F		39. C		54. F	
10. G		25. E		40. G		55. D	
11. B		26. G		41. D		56. H	
12. F		27. C		42. K		57. B	
13. C		28. J		43. A		58. K	
14. G		29. E		44. G		59. A	
15. D		30. H		45. C		60. J	

Raw Score: _____ /60

Section 3: Reading (Student Text, p. 80)

	Correct		Correct		Correct		Correct
1. D		11. B		21. A		31. B	
2. J		12. G		22. J		32. H	
3. B		13. D		23. B		33. A	
4. J		14. G		24. H		34. J	
5. A		15. C		25. A		35. C	
6. G		16. G		26. H		36. F	
7. A		17. B		27. C		37. A	
8. F		18. H		28. J		38. G	
9. B		19. D		29. A		39. B	
10. F		20. F		30. H		40. H	

Raw Score: _____ /40

Section 4: Science (Student Text, p. 90)

	Correct		Correct		Correct
1. B		15. B		28. G	
2. H		16. H		29. C	
3. C		17. B		30. G	
4. H		18. F		31. D	
5. C		19. B		32. F	
6. J		20. G		33. A	
7. A		21. C		34. H	
		22. H			
8. F				35. B	
9. B		23. B		36. J	
10. F		24. J		37. C	
11. A		25. C		38. G	
12. H		26. F		39. D	
13. C		27. D		40. F	
14. J					

Raw Score: _____ /40

MULTIPLE-CHOICE EXPLANATIONS

Section 1: English

1. **(B)** (p. 51) *English/Knowledge of Language/Style/Conciseness*. The original sentence is needlessly repetitious: "to begin" means "to start." (B) eliminates the unnecessary repetition.

2. **(J)** (p. 51) *English/Conventions of Standard English/Grammar and Usage/Diction*. The original sentence contains an error of diction. The correct word for making the comparison intended by the original is "from," not "than." ("Than" is a conjunction, and conjunctions are used to introduce clauses. What follows the underlined part of the sentence is a noun phrase, not a clause.) (G) fails to make the needed correction. (H) makes the needed correction but introduces a new error. In general, a modifier should be placed as close as possible to what it modifies. Here, "fundamentally" must modify "are different," but the placement of "fundamentally" after "from" suggests that it is intended to modify "weapons." Thus, (H) would result in an ambiguous sentence.

3. **(D)** (p. 51) *English/Knowledge of Language/Style/Conciseness*. The underlined material is needlessly repetitious. A weapon of "mass destruction" is one "that could do a lot of harm." Eliminate the surplus material.

4. **(G)** (p. 52) *English/Conventions of Standard English/Sentence Structure/Run-On Sentences*. The original sentence is a run-on sentence. (G) solves the problem by starting a new sentence at an appropriate point. Neither (H) nor (J) solve the problem of the run-on sentence.

5. **(A)** (p. 52) *English/Production of Writing/No Change*. The original sentence is correct. (B) destroys the logic of the sentence. (C) ambiguously implies that injuries are unavailable. (D) is needlessly wordy.

6. **(H)** (p. 52) *English/Conventions of Standard English/Grammar and Usage/Diction*. The original sentence is not idiomatic. (H) is idiomatic with "resulting from." (G) and (J) are not idiomatic.

7. **(A)** (p. 52) *English/Conventions of Standard English/No Change*. The original sentence is correct as written. The use of the subjunctive "would" correctly suggests that a nuclear war might or might not occur. (B) and (C) are both wrong because the indicative mood ("is" and "are") does not have this meaning. Additionally, (B) must be wrong because the subject of the sentence is the compound subject "number of deaths . . . and economic damage," and a compound subject requires a plural verb. (C) is also wrong because "as" makes the answer unidiomatic. In (D), although "might" preserves the element of contingency suggested by the subjunctive "would," the phrasing "more devastating even as" is not idiomatic.

8. **(G)** (p. 52) *English/Production of Writing/Strategy/Effective Concluding Sentence*. In the second paragraph, the author is arguing that nuclear weapons are fundamentally different from conventional weapons because of their massive destructive power on multiple levels. (G) correctly summarizes this point.

9. **(A)** (p. 52) *English/Conventions of Standard English/No Change*. The original sentence is correct. The other choices introduce errors in modification.

10. **(G)** (p. 52) *English/Conventions of Standard English/Sentence Structure/Run-On Sentences and Grammar and Usage/Pronoun Usage*. The original sentence has two mistakes. First, it is a run-on sentence. Also, "it" is singular but refers to "weapons," which is plural. (G) makes both the needed corrections.

11. (C) (p. 52) *English/Conventions of Standard English/Grammar and Usage/Diction*. The original sentence is not idiomatic as written. The correct idiom is "neither . . . nor," not "neither . . . but."

12. (J) (p. 53) *English/Production of Writing/Organization/Paragraph-Level Structure*. The original sentence is incorrect because a new paragraph should begin here. In the opening paragraph, the author announces that he or she will make three points. The second paragraph is devoted to the first point—the other two points should be presented in separate paragraphs.

13. (B) (p. 53) *English/Knowledge of Language/Style/Conciseness*. The original sentence is awkward. (B) is more concise and reads better than the original sentence. (C) is incorrect because the subject of the sentence is the singular noun "step," so the singular verb "has," not the plural verb "have," is needed. (D) has the errors of the original sentence and inappropriately includes a plural verb.

14. (H) (p. 53) *English/Conventions of Standard English/Grammar and Usage/Pronoun Usage*. The ubiquitous "they" makes the original sentence ambiguous. Who are they? The other choices eliminate the ambiguous pronoun, but (H) is the most direct and concise.

15. (A) (p. 53) *English/Production of Writing/Organization/Passage-Level Structure*. In the initial paragraph, the author announces that three considerations should guide our formulation of a defense policy. The author then proceeds to address each consideration.

16. (H) (p. 53) *English/Production of Writing/Strategy/Main Idea*. Again, the author argues that three principles should guide our defense policy.

17. (D) (p. 53) *English/Conventions of Standard English/Sentence Structure/Fragments*. The original sentence lacks a main verb. (C) and (D) supply the verb, but (B) does not. ("Having viewed" is a participle form and cannot be a main verb.) In (C), "its" is intended to refer to "founders," but "founders" is plural, so the plural "their" is needed.

18. (G) (p. 54) *English/Conventions of Standard English/Grammar and Usage/Diction*. The original sentence is not idiomatic. The correct idiom is "rather than," not "rather as." Both (H) and (J) are wrong because they too are not idiomatic.

19. (A) (p. 54) *English/Production of Writing/Strategy/Effective Transitional Sentence*. This question tests understanding of the relationship between ideas in the passage. The idea discussed in the second sentence of the passage is the result or effect of the idea discussed in the first sentence. "Therefore" is then the best choice to show this relationship.

20. (F) (p. 54) *English/Conventions of Standard English/No Change*. The original sentence is correct as written. (G) is needlessly wordy, so the original sentence is preferable. (H) destroys the logical structure of the sentence. (J) changes the intended meaning of the sentence by implying that the founders could have chosen to view education "as" academic excellence, rather than "as a means to" academic excellence.

21. (C) (p. 54) *English/Conventions of Standard English/Sentence Structure/Fragments*. The problem with the sentence as originally written is that it lacks a conjugated or main verb. "Talking" is a participle and cannot function as a main verb. Only (C) supplies a conjugated verb form.

Use the Process of Elimination

Pay careful attention to the variations offered in the answer choices—do any of them change things that do not need to be changed? For example, in item #13, do not worry about changing the subject to plural. Eliminate the plural answer choices to get to the root of the problem.

22. (H) (p. 54) *English/Conventions of Standard English/Punctuation/Commas.* The original sentence is not punctuated correctly. "Goals" is an appositive that refers to "liberty," "equality," etc. The correct punctuation is a comma preceding the appositive. (G) is wrong because the period completely isolates the appositive from the sentence that supports it and turns everything following the comma into a sentence fragment. (J) is also incorrectly punctuated. The semicolon is too powerful—it signals that an independent clause will follow. An appositive, however, is dependent for its existence on the nouns that come before it, so a comma provides enough separation from the main body of the sentence without being too powerful.

23. (A) (p. 54) *English/Conventions of Standard English/No Change.* The original sentence is correct as written. To "take precedence over" is an English idiom meaning to be more important than something else. (B) distorts the intended meaning of the original sentence. To "precede" means to come before in time, so the resulting sentence would make no sense. (C) and (D) are simply not idiomatic.

24. (G) (p. 54) *English/Conventions of Standard English/Punctuation/Commas and Grammar and Usage/Subject-Verb Agreement and Pronoun Usage.* The original sentence contains three errors. First, a comma, not a dash, must close the parenthetical expression signaled by the comma following "generation." (Dashes or commas may be used to set off such remarks, but not a mixture of both.) Second, the subject of the sentence is "generation," which is singular. So, the plural noun "assert" is wrong. Third, "their" refers to "generation" and so fails to agree in number with its referent. (G) makes all three changes. (H) makes two of the changes, but the semicolon is a mistake. The semicolon would be used to separate two clauses, but what follows the semicolon used in (H) is not a clause. Finally, (J) fails to correct the third error mentioned above and is incorrectly punctuated (a second comma is needed). Additionally, (J) uses the present tense verb "asserts," which is inconsistent with the other verbs in the selection.

25. (C) (p. 54) *English/Conventions of Standard English/Grammar and Usage/Subject-Verb Agreement.* The verb "was" is singular and fails to agree with its plural subject, "ingredients." (C) corrects this problem. (B) eliminates the problem of agreement. "Being" is a participle and does not show number. Unfortunately, since "being" is a participle, the resulting construction lacks a main verb, and the sentence becomes a sentence fragment. Finally, (D) distorts the intended meaning of the original sentence. The author does not mean to say that the principal ingredients of a civic education were similar to literacy and inculcation of patriotic and moral virtues.

26. (J) (p. 54) *English/Conventions of Standard English/Sentence Structure/Run-On Sentences.* The original sentence is a run-on, with two clauses that run together without any punctuation or conjunction. (J) is one way of solving the problem: use a semicolon to separate the two clauses. (A comma and a coordinate conjunction such as "and" could also be used.) The dash cannot be used to separate two clauses, so (G) is wrong. As for (H), a comma by itself is just not strong enough to do the job.

27. (D) (p. 55) *English/Conventions of Standard English/Sentence Structure/Problems of Coordination and Subordination.* The original sentence contains an error of illogical subordination, compounded by a punctuation mistake. The two ideas joined at the underlined part have equal importance. One should not be subordinated to the other, but "since" always signals a subordinate idea. Additionally, a semicolon cannot be used to join a subordinate clause to an independent or main clause. (B) solves the subordination problem, but "and" signals a continuation of a thought. The second idea here contrasts with the first and should be signaled by a word like "but." (C) eliminates the punctuation mistake but creates a sentence fragment in the second half of the sentence. "Since" introduces a subordinate clause that must be joined to an independent or main clause.

28. **(G)** (p. 55) *English/Conventions of Standard English/Grammar and Usage/Diction*. The original sentence is not idiomatic. The correct idiom requires the use of the infinitive "to be" rather than the gerund "being." (H) and (J) both correct this error, but they also eliminate the only conjugated verb in the clause. The result is a fragment rather than a complete sentence. (G) correctly uses "to be" without introducing another error.

29. **(C)** (p. 55) *English/Conventions of Standard English/Grammar and Usage/Diction*. The placement of "almost" is not idiomatic. Given its proximity to "agreed," "almost" seems to modify "agreed" rather than "universally." The intended meaning of the sentence is that "almost" modifies "universally." (C) provides the correct and idiomatic placement of "almost." (B) is also not idiomatic. As for (D), although the words are in the correct order, the comma between "universally," an adverb, and the word it modifies, "agreed," disrupts the logical flow of the sentence.

30. **(G)** (p. 55) *English/Conventions of Standard English/Sentence Structure/Faulty Parallelism*. The underlined part is incorrect because it destroys the parallelism of the sentence. The sentence has a series of three elements: "emphasized," "put," and "attempt." However, the third element is a noun rather than a verb. (G) restores the parallelism of the sentence by supplying a verb. (H) fails to provide a verb. Finally, although (J) includes a verb, it also includes a subject. The result is a clause that is not parallel to the verb forms.

31. **(B)** (p. 55) *English/Production of Writing/Organization/Paragraph-Level Structure*. The final paragraph contains a new thought that extends the logical development of the essay.

32. **(H)** (p. 55) *English/Production of Writing/Strategy/Audience*. The passage is a discussion of old textbooks. Surely educators would be most interested in old textbooks.

33. **(A)** (p. 56) *English/Production of Writing/No Change*. The original sentence is correct. (B) destroys the logic of the sentence. (C) and (D) are illogical because the sentence intends to refer generally to "the contribution of women" as a whole—not to the contribution of any particular individual.

34. **(J)** (p. 56) *English/Conventions of Standard English/Grammar and Usage/Diction*. The original sentence is non-idiomatic. (J) provides the correct idiom: "range . . . from . . . to." (G) and (H) fail to correct the problem, though (H) does change the noun "operation" to the verb "operating," creating parallelism with "knitting."

35. **(A)** (p. 56) *English/Production of Writing/No Change*. The original sentence is correct as written. It is idiomatic, and the past tense verb "marked" is consistent with the other past tense verbs in the selection. (B) is wrong because the present perfect "has marked" implies an action that began in the past but continues into the present. (C) is wordy and awkward. As for (D), the use of the passive voice completely destroys the logic of the sentence.

36. **(F)** (p. 56) *English/Conventions of Standard English/No Change*. The original sentence is correct as written: "effort was made . . . to utilize." (G) and (H) are not idiomatic—"effort was made . . . being able to utilize" and "effort was made . . . utilizing." Finally, (J) destroys the logical structure of the sentence: "effort was made . . . and utilize."

37. **(B)** (p. 56) *English/Conventions of Standard English/Grammar and Usage/Sequence and Verb Tense*. The original sentence uses an incorrect verb tense. The present tense "falls" conflicts with the other past tense verbs of the selection. (B) and (D) both make the needed correction, but (D) is not idiomatic in this context. The correct idiom is "falls within" a category. (C) is grammatically incorrect because it eliminates the only conjugated verb in the clause introduced by "while."

38. (H) (p. 56) *English/Conventions of Standard English/Grammar and Usage/Diction.* The original sentence is not idiomatic. The correct idiom is "reserved for," not "reserved by." "Reserved by" has a meaning that is not appropriate here. (G) is needlessly wordy and ambiguous because it is not clear what the phrase is intended to modify. It seems to modify "women," but the intent of the sentence is for the phrase to modify "work." (J) is also wordy and awkward.

39. (B) (p. 56) *English/Conventions of Standard English/Sentence Structure/Unintended Meanings.* The original sentence uses an illogical transition word. "However" is used to signal a contrast, but the sentence that is introduced by "however" is actually a continuation of the thought contained in the previous sentence. (B) is correct; since there is no transition word, the reader will naturally assume that the next sentence will continue the train of thought. (C) is wrong because the use of "but" tells the reader to expect a contrasting thought. Finally, (D) is a fragment rather than a complete sentence.

40. (H) (p. 56) *English/Conventions of Standard English/Punctuation/Colons.* The original sentence is incorrectly punctuated. Since there is no punctuation between "activity" and "knitting," a reader will not pause after "activity." Consequently, "knitting" seems to be a participle that somehow modifies "activity." The author intends for "knitting" to be a gerund in the series including "knitting," "canning," and "planting." The correct punctuation in this series is the colon.

Use the Process of Elimination

Crossing off answer choices is invaluable in questions that ask for the best order or sequence for paragraphs or that ask you to determine where a sentence or paragraph would best be placed (there is usually at least one of these in the ACT English section). Notice that in item #45, the only answer choice that places Paragraph 4 at the end of the passage is (C). If you immediately determine that Paragraph 4 is the best summary or conclusion for the passage, you can cross off (A), (B), and (D), landing on (C) quickly.

41. (D) (p. 57) *English/Conventions of Standard English/Grammar and Usage/Pronoun Usage.* The original sentence contains an error of pronoun usage. The pronoun "their" refers to "homemaker"—the singular "her" should be used. (B) eliminates the problem by using no pronoun at all. The resulting structure is a bit awkward ("could be demonstrating patriotism") but not incorrect. However, the verb in (B) is not acceptable. "Could be demonstrating" is inconsistent with the other verbs in the paragraph. (C) is incorrect— the verb "could have demonstrated" implies that a woman might or might not have demonstrated her patriotism, but this is not the intended meaning. The author means to assert definitely that women did demonstrate their patriotism. (C) is also wrong because it fails to correct the pronoun problem.

42. (H) (p. 57) *English/Conventions of Standard English/Punctuation/Commas.* The original sentence is incorrectly punctuated. The colon seems to signal a clarification of the idea of hostessing at canteens. Instead, hostessing is one of a group of activities women volunteered to do. The correct punctuation is a comma.

43. (A) (p. 57) *English/Production of Writing/No Change.* The material between the commas is an adjective phrase: "Army, dressed . . . and armed . . . 'with the Musket,' was dispatched." The other choices destroy this logic.

44. (F) (p. 57) *English/Conventions of Standard English/No Change.* The original sentence is correct as written. The other choices disrupt the parallelism of the sentence. Since the two verbs "performed" and "laid" have a similar function in the sentence, they should both have similar forms. (G) and (H) use the passive voice and are not parallel to the active voice "performed." (J) is the participle and is not parallel to "performed," a conjugated verb.

45. (C) (p. 57) *English/Production of Writing/Organization/Passage-Level Structure.* A way to fix the order of the paragraphs is to recognize that neither [2] nor [3] can be the first paragraph. "While" in the first sentence of [2] clearly refers to something that has come before.

Similarly, the phrase "much of the work" in the first sentence of [3] also refers to something that has come before. [1] appears to be the best choice for the first paragraph because [4] seems to be a summary or conclusion. Only (C) has [4] as the conclusion, so it is the correct answer.

As for [2] and [3], [2] must follow [3] because [2] is intended to contrast with [3]: most of the work was traditional, but some was not. A reader cannot understand the importance of the contrast suggested by [2] without the information provided by [3].

Master Moves

Keep an eye out for thought-reversers—phrases or sentences that present a shift in thought or meaning. Item #49 for provides an example of a thought-reverser.

46. (F) (p. 57) *English/Production of Writing/Strategy/Appropriate Supporting Material.* Examples are often helpful, as they enable readers to understand a general point in a more concrete fashion. In this instance, the slogan helps the reader understand the motivation and purpose behind the Women's Land Army.

47. (D) (p. 58) *English/Conventions of Standard English/Sentence Structure/Fragments.* "Undertaken" is the past participle of the verb "to undertake." A past participle is not itself a complete verb. (D) solves this problem by creating a sentence that uses the passive voice: "changes were undertaken."

48. (J) (p. 58) *English/Conventions of Standard English/Grammar and Usage/Diction.* The original sentence is not idiomatic. The sentence means to say that some people embraced the new values, and that is the sense of (J). (G) introduces an error in diction, substituting "excepted" for the intended word choice "accepted," as well as using the wrong preposition for "excepted." (H) is wrong for the same first reason that (G) is wrong.

49. (C) (p. 58) *English/Conventions of Standard English/Sentence Structure/Problems of Coordination and Subordination.* The two ideas joined at the underlined part contrast with each other: these did something; the others did not. To signal this contrast, something other than "and" must be used. "But" is an acceptable choice, so (C) is correct. (B) and (D) are incorrect because "since" and "consequently" signal a relationship in which one idea follows from or is the consequence of another.

50. (F) (p. 58) *English/Production of Writing/No Change.* The original sentence is correct. By comparison, the other choices are needlessly wordy and awkward.

51. (B) (p. 58) *English/Conventions of Standard English/Sentence Structure/Fragments.* The comma and the conjunction "and" signal that the last half of the sentence is a clause. Yet, the original contains no main verb. (B) supplies a main verb in the right tense that also agrees in number with its subject, "notions."

52. (F) (p. 58) *English/Production of Writing/No Change.* The original sentence is correct. This is the proper place at which to begin a new paragraph since the author is shifting from talking about the past to a discussion of the present. Since a new paragraph is needed here, (G) and (J) are wrong. (J) is wrong for two additional reasons: "Today, owing to the fact that . . . political life" is an incomplete sentence; and the use of "owing to the fact that" makes "democratic processes" the new subject, which will no longer agree with the verb "is." "Triumph" is the necessary subject. Finally, (H) illogically isolates the subject of the sentence from its verb.

Use Your Test Booklet

You may find it helpful to circle the subject and put a square around the predicate in sentences dealing with subject-verb agreement. See item #56 for an example of when this technique can come in handy.

53. (B) (p. 58) *English/Knowledge of Language/Style/Conciseness.* In the original sentence, "clear" is intended to modify "evident." However, that is a job that can be done only by the adverb "clearly." In any event, "clear" and "evident" are synonyms, so both are not needed. (B) is the best choice because it eliminates the redundant term "clear."

54. (J) (p. 58) *English/Production of Writing/Strategy/Effective Transitional Sentence.* The transitional word must signal a contrast between two ideas. The best choice is "yet."

55. (D) (p. 59) *English/Knowledge of Language/Style/Conciseness.* "Being" is a participle that can function as an adjective. However, there is no noun that can logically be modified by "being." What the sentence means to assert is that the lack of a stable value system is due to the influence of Western ideas. The word "since" in (D) is sufficient by itself to give the reason for the preceding part of the sentence. Both (B) and (C) are wrong because they are awkward.

56. **(G)** (p. 59) *English/Conventions of Standard English/Sentence Structure/Unintended Meanings.* "And so" distorts the logical structure of the sentence. It seems to introduce another clause, but what follows lacks a main verb. By eliminating "and so," (G) allows "emphasizing," a participle, to function as an adjective modifying "principles." (H) results in a sentence that is distorted because "and" seems to join another verb to the first verb, "expound." However, "emphasis" is a noun, so the sentence reads: "textbooks expound . . . and the emphasis." In (J), "that" seems to introduce a relative clause, but no verb follows.

57. **(D)** (p. 59) *English/Knowledge of Language/Style/Conciseness.* "Often sometimes" is not a possible phrase because the words have contradictory meanings. One of the words must be eliminated. All of the choices make this correction. (B), however, uses a verb tense that is inconsistent with the other tenses in the paragraph. In (C), "misinterpreted" and "distorted" are past participles and cannot stand alone. They require another verb such as "are."

58. **(H)** (p. 59) *English/Conventions of Standard English/Grammar and Usage/Sequence and Verb Tense and Pronoun Usage.* The original sentence contains two errors. The past tense "translated" is inconsistent with the present tense verbs in the rest of the paragraph. Also, "who" should replace "that" since the author is referring to people. Only (H) makes both corrections.

59. **(A)** (p. 59) *English/Production of Writing/Strategy/Appropriate Supporting Material.* At the end, the author introduces the topic of Japanese youth; it would be appropriate for the discussion to continue along these lines.

60. **(J)** (p. 59) *English/Conventions of Standard English/Grammar and Usage/Diction.* The original sentence does not contain a grievous error, but it is not as idiomatic as (J). The placement of "always" directly before the main element of the verb, instead of before "has," is preferable to the original. (G) is wrong because "have" does not agree with the singular "humankind." (H) is wrong as the present tense is inconsistent with the introductory phrase "from the beginning."

61. **(C)** (p. 59) *English/Conventions of Standard English/Grammar and Usage/Faulty or Illogical Comparisons.* In English, if an adjective has more than one syllable, the comparative is generally formed by using "more" rather than by adding "-er."

62. **(H)** (p. 59) *English/Conventions of Standard English/Punctuation/Commas.* The comma following "agriculture" has no logical function in the sentence. (H) solves this problem by allowing the comma to mark the close of a parenthetical expression introduced by the first comma in front of "along." (G) attempts the correction but is wrong because the resulting phrase has no clear logical connection with the rest of the sentence. (H) does not have this problem. In (H), the noun "discovery" is the object of a preposition, and the prepositional phrase is connected to the rest of the sentence as a modifier of "domestication." (J) destroys the logical structure of the sentence by isolating the subject from the verb. The semicolon is too strong.

63. **(D)** (p. 60) *English/Knowledge of Language/Style/Conciseness.* The underlined material is repetitious and therefore should be omitted.

64. **(G)** (p. 60) *English/Conventions of Standard English/Sentence Structure/Faulty Parallelism and Grammar and Usage/Pronoun Usage.* The original sentence contains two errors. First, it lacks parallelism. As written, it reads: "between regarding . . . and to consider." Second, the pronoun "them" does not agree in number with its antecedent, "animal." Only (G) corrects both of these problems. (H) solves the problem of parallelism but fails to eliminate the wrong pronoun. (J) does not correct either mistake.

65. **(D)** (p. 60) *English/Conventions of Standard English/Sentence Structure/Misplaced Modifiers and Grammar and Usage/Sequence and Verb Tense.* The original sentence contains two errors. First, the placement of "seemingly" is incorrect. It is intended to modify "every," which in turn modifies "subject." However, its placement in front of the

verb seems to suggest that Aristotle "seemingly" wrote. Second, the present tense "writes" is inconsistent with the other verbs describing Aristotle's actions, which took place in the past. Present tense verbs would only be used to describe the author's current opinions about Aristotle's writings. (B) corrects the second problem but not the first. Simply putting "seemingly" into parentheses does not clarify what the word is supposed to modify. As for (C), while it eliminates the problem of verb tense by reducing the verb to a participle modifying "Aristotle," there is still the ambiguity created by "seemingly."

The Cambridge Edge

Remember that double quotation marks, the kind used for setting off a quoted section of the sentence, always come in pairs. See item #69 for an example of an item that tests this rule.

66. **(F)** (p. 60) *English/Conventions of Standard English/No Change.* The original sentence is correct as written. The comma following "subject" marks the end of the introductory dependent clause. Since punctuation is needed at that point, (H) is wrong. The correct punctuation is a comma. The semicolon and the colon are both too powerful, so (G) and (J) are wrong as well. (H) also uses the possessive apostrophe incorrectly and (G) is missing it altogether.

67. **(A)** (p. 60) *English/Conventions of Standard English/Sentence Structure/Problems of Coordination and Subordination.* The transition word here must connect the two ideas: Aristotle was interested in all life; he was particularly interested in marine life. "And" correctly coordinates these two ideas. Had the passage gone on to discuss marine life in particular, then the contrast set up by "but" in (C) would make it the better choice.

68. **(F)** (p. 60) *English/Production of Writing/No Change.* The original sentence is correct as written. "Wedding" is a participle that modifies "observer." (G) distorts the intended meaning by suggesting that Aristotle himself was joined to something. The sentence means to say that Aristotle joined two ideas. (H) is needlessly wordy and awkward. Finally, (J) creates a prepositional phrase that does not clearly modify any other element in the sentence.

69. **(C)** (p. 60) *English/Conventions of Standard English/Punctuation/Quotation Marks.* The original sentence is incorrectly punctuated. Quotation marks must be used to indicate the start of the quotation. (B) fails to make this correction and makes another error of punctuation. A dash cannot be used instead of a period. (D) is wrong because the adverb "simply" cannot be used as a predicate complement; that is, "simply" cannot modify the subject of the sentence.

70. **(J)** (p. 60) *English/Knowledge of Language/Style/Conciseness.* The underlined material is repetitious and therefore should be omitted.

71. **(A)** (p. 61) *English/Production of Writing/No Change.* The original sentence is correct. By comparison, the other choices are needlessly wordy and awkward.

72. **(G)** (p. 61) *English/Production of Writing/Strategy/Appropriate Supporting Material.* The author's use of Aristotle's own words is particularly forceful. It lets Aristotle make the point for himself.

73. **(B)** (p. 61) *English/Production of Writing/Strategy/Audience.* The passage is expository but not overly technical, so (A) and (D) are wrong. Since the main topic is Aristotle, (B) is the best choice.

74. **(J)** (p. 61) *English/Production of Writing/Strategy/Main Idea.* As stated in the first sentence of the second paragraph of the passage, the essay intends to show how the animal world became a source of serious study because of Aristotle.

75. **(B)** (p. 61) *English/Production of Writing/Organization/Paragraph-Level Structure.* The first paragraph doesn't pose any questions, (A); introduce an argument, (C); or provide an anecdote, (D). Its function is to place Aristotle in a certain context. It gives a kind of history of the link between humans and animals that segues into Aristotle's interest in the subject.

Section 2: Mathematics

1. **(A)** (p. 62) *Mathematics/Algebra and Functions/Solving Algebraic Equations or Inequalities with One Variable/Equations Involving Rational Expressions.* Solve for x:
$$\frac{1}{x} + \frac{1}{x} = 8 \Rightarrow \frac{2}{x} = 8 \Rightarrow x = \frac{1}{4}.$$

   Alternatively, one can reason that $\frac{1}{x}$ and $\frac{1}{x}$ are equal, and since their sum is 8, $\frac{1}{x}$ equals 4. Thus, $x = \frac{1}{4}$.

2. **(K)** (p. 62) *Mathematics/Algebra and Functions/Manipulating Algebraic Expressions/Basic Algebraic Manipulations.* Substitute the given values for x and y in the given expression and evaluate: $3x - 4y = 3(2) - 4(-1) = 6 + 4 = 10$.

3. **(C)** (p. 62) *Mathematics/Number and Quantity/Percentages.* First, 20% of 600 boys equals $0.20(600) = 120$ boys on the honor roll. Second, 30% of 400 girls equals $0.30(400) = 120$ girls on the honor roll. Therefore, there are 120 boys $+ 120$ girls $= 240$ students on the honor roll.

4. **(K)** (p. 63) *Mathematics/Number and Quantity/Properties of Numbers.* Since the variable t is outside the brackets and parentheses, it must be multiplied by everything within the brackets and parentheses. And since an even number times any other whole number yields an even number, t must be even. None of the other letters being even guarantees an even result.

5. **(E)** (p. 63) *Mathematics/Statistics and Probability/Data Representation/Tables.* The data in the table represents an arithmetic sequence: the number of flies in each successive week is four times the number in the previous week. The final count should be $4 \cdot 192 = 768$.

6. **(H)** (p. 63) *Mathematics/Number and Quantity/Basic Arithmetic Manipulations* and *Statistics and Probability/Counting Methods.* Use the formula for finding the number of permutations: $3! = 3 \cdot 2 \cdot 1 = 6$.

7. **(D)** (p. 64) *Mathematics/Algebra and Functions/Coordinate Geometry/The Coordinate System.* Since the x-coordinate of both points is 2, the line runs parallel to the y-axis, and the x-coordinate of the midpoint will also be 2. As for the y-coordinate, the midpoint is halfway between 2 and -2: 0.

8. **(H)** (p. 64) *Mathematics/Algebra and Functions/Solving Algebraic Equations or Inequalities with One Variable/Equations Involving Absolute Value.* Since the absolute value of xy is positive, xy itself must be positive (since $|xy| = xy$). Therefore, both x and y have the same sign: they might both be positive, or they might both be negative, so (F), (G), (J), and (K) can all be true. However, (H) cannot be true because x and y cannot have different signs, as a positive times a negative yields a negative result.

   Alternatively, substitute some numbers. If $x > 0 > y$, then x could be 1 and y could be -1, and $(1)(-1) = -1$.

9. **(D)** (p. 64) *Mathematics/Geometry/Rectangles and Squares.* Convert the dimensions shown to real dimensions. Since 1 centimeter is equal to 4 meters, the width of the room is 4 meters and the length is 4.8 meters. Thus, the area of the room is $4 \cdot 4.8 = 19.2$ square meters.

10. **(G)** (p. 64) *Mathematics/Number and Quantity/Scientific Notation.* First, perform the indicated multiplication: $30,000 \times 20 = 600,000$. And convert 600,000 to scientific notation by increasing the power of 10 once for each zero to the right of the leading digit before the decimal place: $600,000 = 6 \times 10^5$.

11. **(B)** (p. 65) *Mathematics/Number and Quantity/Rates and Proportions* **and** *Algebra and Functions/Solving Simultaneous Equations.* Use simultaneous equations to solve this problem. If x is the quantity of chocolates and y is the quantity of caramels, then $x + y = 4$ and $3x + 2y = 10$. Substitute $4 - x$ for y in the second equation and solve for x: $3x + 2(4 - x) = 10 \Rightarrow 3x + 8 - 2x = 10 \Rightarrow x = 10 - 8 = 2$.

Alternatively, test the answer choices, starting with (C). If Karen bought 2.5 pounds of chocolates, she bought $4 - 2.5 = 1.5$ pounds of caramels and the total cost is $(2.5 \cdot 3) + (1.5 \cdot 2) = 7.50 + 3 = \$10.50$. This is too much money. Since chocolates are more expensive than caramels, Karen bought less than 2.5 pounds of chocolates. Try (B): 2 pounds of chocolates and 2 pounds of caramels cost $(2 \cdot 3) + (2 \cdot 2) = 6 + 4 = 10$.

12. **(F)** (p. 65) *Mathematics/Statistics and Probability/Measures of Center.* Set up an equation for the average and solve for the missing element. Since the average of two of the tests is 77, they can both be set equal to 77 in the average for all three: $\dfrac{77 + 77 + x}{3} = 80 \Rightarrow x = 86$.

13. **(C)** (p. 65) *Mathematics/Number and Quantity/Rates and Proportions.* Only the ratio in (C), $5:2$, is impossible because the number of photographs, 10, would not be evenly divisible by the total number of ratio parts: $5 + 2 = 7$.

14. **(G)** (p. 65) *Mathematics/Algebra and Functions/Solving Algebraic Equations or Inequalities with One Variable/Simple Equations.* Solve for x: $\dfrac{4}{5} = \dfrac{x}{4} \Rightarrow 4(4) = 5x \Rightarrow x = \dfrac{16}{5}$.

Know Thyself

Use the strategies you feel most comfortable and confident with in order to get to the solution. Notice in item #14, for example, that you can use various different approaches:

1) Rearrange the equation to get x alone and then solve directly for x.

2) Cross-multiply and then solve for x using the new equation.

3) Plug and chug using the different answer choices, starting with (H).

Unlike tests you took in Math class, the ACT does not check your work—it does not matter how you come to the solution as long as you arrive at the right one. Especially in math, arrive at the solution in the way that works most effectively for you.

15. **(D)** (p. 66) *Mathematics/Geometry/Lines and Angles* **and** *Triangles/Properties of Triangles.* Label the unlabeled angles:

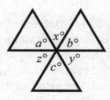

Since the measure of the degrees in a circle is 360, the sum of $x, y,$ and z plus the sum of $a, b,$ and c is 360. What is the value of the angles inside the triangles? Since they are equilateral triangles, each angle is 60°: $3(60) + x + y + z = 360 \Rightarrow x + y + z = 180$.

Alternatively, since you can determine from the given figure that the unlabeled angles each measure 60 and therefore total 180, you can use vertical angles to solve this item. After labeling the unlabeled angles, as done above, simply recognize that $a = y$, $b = z$, and $c = x$. So, $x + y + z = a + b + c = 180$.

Master Moves

For items like #16, it can be incredibly helpful to just choose a starting number, x, and perform the indicated calculations on x. Notice that fractions are not affected by the specific quantity you pick as your starting point, but you can make it easier on yourself to perform the calculations by choosing a number that suits the fractions. In item #16, numbers that are multiples of both 3 and 4 (such as 24) can lead to values that are easy to work with.

16. **(H)** (p. 66) *Mathematics/Number and Quantity/Basic Arithmetic Manipulations.* If Peter spent $\frac{1}{4}$ of his allowance on Monday, he had $\frac{3}{4}$ of his allowance left. Then, he spent $\frac{1}{3}$ of that $\frac{3}{4}$ on Tuesday: $\frac{1}{3} \cdot \frac{3}{4} = \frac{1}{4}$. After spending the additional $\frac{1}{4}$, he was left with $\frac{3}{4} - \frac{1}{4} = \frac{1}{2}$ of the original allowance. Substitution of numbers would also work, but the arithmetic would be the same.

Read Twice, Answer Once

When reading an item like #16, don't fall into the trap of thinking that both fractions are referring to the same amount, x. Read the question again carefully, noting that the 1/3 refers to the amount that remains after subtracting 1/4 of the original amount. In other words, note that Peter spent 1/3 times 3/4 of the original amount, and calculate what fraction of the original amount remains.

17. **(B)** (p. 66) *Mathematics/Number and Quantity/Rates and Proportions.* There are three ways to solve the problem. The simplest and most direct is to reason that if 100 bricks weigh p pounds, 20 bricks, which is $\frac{1}{5}$ of 100, must weigh $\frac{1}{5}$ of p. This same reasoning can be expressed using a direct proportion. The fewer the bricks, the lesser the weight, so

$$\frac{x}{p} = \frac{20}{100} \Rightarrow 100x = 20p \Rightarrow x = \frac{20p}{100} \Rightarrow x = \frac{p}{5}.$$

Alternatively, substitute some numbers. Assume that 100 bricks weigh 100 pounds, which is 1 pound each, so 20 bricks weigh 20 pounds. Only the correct formula will generate the number 20 when 100 is substituted for p in the answer choices.

18. **(K)** (p. 67) *Mathematics/Geometry/Circles and Triangles/Properties of Triangles.* The following drawings show that (I), (II), and (III) are all possible:

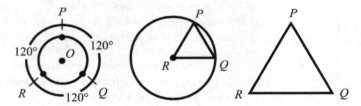

19. **(E)** (p. 67) *Mathematics/Number and Quantity/Percentages and Statistics and Probability/Data Representation/Tables.* This problem can be solved with the "change-over" principle, but that would require five different calculations. It is always easier and faster to find the greatest ratio of the increased value to the original value. Therefore, look at the successive ratios. The price doubles during the first 5-year period. However, it less than doubles during the periods in B, C, and D. In E, the price increases by more than double. Thus, the answer is (E).

20. **(F)** (p. 67) *Mathematics/Algebra and Functions/Manipulating Algebraic Expressions/Factoring Expressions.* The easiest approach is to multiply the binomials given in the answer choices to find the one that is equivalent to the given expression:

F. $(x-2)(x+6) = x^2 + 4x - 12$ ✔
G. $(x-4)(x+3) = x^2 - x - 12$ ✘
H. $(x-6)(x+2) = x^2 - 4x - 12$ ✘
J. $(x+2)(x+6) = x^2 + 8x + 12$ ✘
K. $(x+3)(x+4) = x^2 + 7x + 12$ ✘

21. **(D)** (p. 67) ***Mathematics/Algebra and Functions/Solving Algebraic Equations or Inequalities with One Variable/Simple Equations.*** Since the average of $3x - 2$ and $2x - 3$ is 10, the sum is 20: $3x - 2 + 2x - 3 = 20 \Rightarrow 5x - 5 = 20 \Rightarrow 5x = 25 \Rightarrow x = 5$. One package weighs $3(5) - 2 = 13$ pounds and the other package weighs $2(5) - 3 = 7$ pounds. The weight difference is $13 - 7 = 6$ pounds.

22. **(G)** (p. 68) ***Mathematics/Statistics and Probability/Measures of Center.*** This question is a variation on the theme of an average with missing elements. Since 10 students have scores of 75 or more, the total of their scores is at minimum $10 \cdot 75 = 750$. Then, even assuming the other 5 students each scored zero, the average for the 15 would be at least $750 \div 15 = 50$.

23. **(C)** (p. 68) ***Mathematics/Algebra and Functions/Manipulating Algebraic Expressions/ Manipulating Expressions Involving Exponents.*** Since $16 = 4^2$, $16^x = (4^2)^x = 4^{2x}$. This problem is also solvable by assuming a value for *x*. If $x = 1$, $16^x = 16^1 = 16$.

The correct answer choice will yield the value 16 when 1 is substituted for *x*:

A. $1^{16} = 1$ ✘
B. $2^{3(1)} = 2^3 = 8$ ✘
C. $4^{2(1)} = 4^2 = 16$ ✔
D. $8^{2(1)} = 8^2 = 64$ ✘
E. $8^{4(1)} = 8^4 = 4,096$ ✘

24. **(F)** (p. 68) ***Mathematics/Geometry/Rectangles and Squares.*** The figure is a square, so the two sides are equal: $2x + 1 = x + 4 \Rightarrow x = 3$. One side is $x + 4 = 3 + 4 = 7$. Since all four sides are equal, the perimeter is $4 \cdot 7 = 28$.

25. **(E)** (p. 68) ***Mathematics/Geometry/Rectangles and Squares*** and ***Triangles/45°-45°-90° Triangles*** and ***Properties of Triangles.*** If *w* is the width of the rectangle, the length is $2w$ and the rectangle has an area of $w \cdot 2w = 2w^2$. Then, *w* is also the length of the hypotenuse of a 45°-45°-90° triangle. Each of the other two sides forming the right angle (which also represent the altitude and base) is $\frac{1}{2} \cdot w \cdot \sqrt{2} = \frac{\sqrt{2}\,w}{2}$. The area of the triangle is $\frac{1}{2} \cdot \text{altitude} \cdot \text{base} = \frac{1}{2} \cdot \frac{\sqrt{2}\,w}{2} \cdot \frac{\sqrt{2}\,w}{2} = \frac{1}{2} \cdot \frac{2w^2}{4} = \frac{w^2}{4}$. The ratio of the area of the rectangle to that of the triangle is $\dfrac{2w^2}{\dfrac{w^2}{4}} = \dfrac{2}{\dfrac{1}{4}} = \dfrac{8}{1}$.

The above explanation is difficult to follow without a diagram, so draw one:

Plug-and-Chug

Item #23 can strike many students as intimidating. However, remember that even if all the exponent rules you know go out the window under pressure on test day, you can still plug in values for *x* in the original value, 16^x, and check to see which of the answer choices, when you fill in the same value for *x*, produces the same result as 16^x.

Master Moves

If a figure isn't provided, draw one. For example, draw a figure to solve item #25.

The explanation will not only be easier to follow, but it can be dispensed with altogether. The rectangle is obviously bigger than the triangle, so eliminate (A), (B), and (C). Adding to the figure shows that the area of the triangle is less than $\frac{1}{4}$ of the area of the rectangle. Approximating all of the triangles shows it is $\frac{1}{8}$ the area:

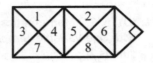

26. **(G)** (p. 69) *Mathematics/Algebra and Functions/Coordinate Geometry/The Coordinate System.* No diagram is provided, so sketch one:

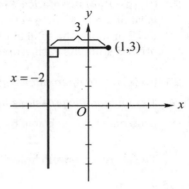

27. **(C)** (p. 69) *Mathematics/Number and Quantity/Rates and Proportions.* Determine how much coffee costs per pound: $\frac{\$12}{5 \text{ pounds}} = \$2.40$ per pound. Therefore, $30 buys $\frac{\$30}{\$2.40 / \text{pound}} = 12.5$ pounds.

Alternatively, the process can be represented in a single direct proportion:
$$\frac{\text{Cost } X}{\text{Cost } Y} = \frac{\text{Pounds } X}{\text{Pounds } Y} \Rightarrow \frac{\$30}{\$12} = \frac{x}{5} \Rightarrow 12x = 150 \Rightarrow x = \frac{150}{12} = 12.5.$$

28. **(J)** (p. 69) *Mathematics/Geometry/Triangles/Properties of Triangles.* Since the triangles are equilateral, the ratio of their perimeters is the same as the ratio of their sides. Thus, the ratio of their perimeters is also $\frac{3}{12} = \frac{1}{4}$.

Alternatively, find the perimeter of each triangle. Since the triangles are equilateral, the smaller one has a perimeter of $3 + 3 + 3 = 9$, and the larger one has a perimeter of $12 + 12 + 12 = 36$. Therefore, the ratio is $\frac{9}{36} = \frac{1}{4}$.

29. **(E)** (p. 70) *Mathematics/Algebra and Functions/Expressing and Evaluating Algebraic Functions/Function Notation.* Substitute -2 for x in the given function:
$f(-2) = -3(-2)^3 + 3(-2)^2 - 4(-2) + 8 = -3(-8) + 3(4) - (-8) + 8 = 24 + 12 + 8 + 8 = 52.$

30. **(H)** (p. 70) *Mathematics/Number and Quantity/Percentages.* Add 40% to the $60 wholesale price: $\$60 + (0.40 \cdot \$60) = \$60 + \$24 = \$84$. Then, find the 30% off sale price: $\$84 - (0.30 \cdot \$84) = \$84 - \$25.20 = \$58.80$.

Master Moves

It can be tempting to do all the calculations at once in problems such as item #30. However, expert test-takers know that it pays off (in points and in time) to go one step at a time. Factor in the markup first as one equation, then the sale price reduction in another equation using the markup value only.

31. **(A)** (p. 70) *Mathematics/Algebra and Functions/Manipulating Algebraic Expressions/Basic Algebraic Manipulations*. Translate the given information: $\frac{1}{3}$ of the number equals $\frac{1}{5}$ of the number plus 2, so $\frac{1}{3}x = \frac{1}{5}x + 2 \Rightarrow \frac{1}{3}x - \frac{1}{5}x = 2$.

32. **(H)** (p. 70) *Mathematics/Geometry/Complex Figures* and *Triangles/Properties of Triangles* and *Rectangles and Squares*. This is a composite figure: one side of the equilateral triangle is also a side of the square. The triangle has a perimeter of 12, so each side is 4. If the square has a side of 4, then the perimeter is $4 + 4 + 4 + 4 = 16$.

33. **(A)** (p. 71) *Mathematics/Algebra and Functions/Solving Algebraic Equations or Inequalities with One Variable/Simple Equations*. Substitute $\frac{2}{3}$ for x in the equation and solve the resulting linear equation for k: $6 = 12\left(\frac{2}{3}\right)^2 + k\left(\frac{2}{3}\right) \Rightarrow 6 = 12\left(\frac{4}{9}\right) + k\left(\frac{2}{3}\right) = 4\left(\frac{4}{3}\right) + k\left(\frac{2}{3}\right) = \frac{16}{3} + k\left(\frac{2}{3}\right) \Rightarrow \frac{18}{3} - \frac{16}{3} = k\left(\frac{2}{3}\right) \Rightarrow k = 1$.

Plug-and-Chug

Item #33 is a clear plug-and-chug question—in fact, the question even tells you what value to plug in for x. Plug in that value and set up an equation to solve for the only remaining variable, k.

34. **(K)** (p. 71) *Mathematics/Algebra and Functions/Manipulating Algebraic Expressions/Basic Algebraic Manipulations* and *Geometry*. The perimeter is equal to the sum of the lengths of the sides: $2(x - 2y) + 4(2x + y) = 2x - 4y + 8x + 4y = 10x$.

35. **(D)** (p. 71) *Mathematics/Number and Quantity/Basic Arithmetic Manipulations* and *Algebra and Functions/Evaluating, Interpreting, and Creating Algebraic Functions*. Let x be the number of packages in the van before the first delivery: $\left(x - \frac{2}{5}x\right) - 3 = \frac{1}{2}x \Rightarrow \frac{3}{5}x - 3 = \frac{1}{2}x \Rightarrow \frac{3}{5}x - \frac{1}{2}x = 3 \Rightarrow \frac{1}{10}x = 3 \Rightarrow x = 30$.

36. **(J)** (p. 71) *Mathematics/Algebra and Functions/Manipulating Algebraic Expressions/Basic Algebraic Manipulations*. Perform the indicated operations in the answer choices to determine which one is equal to the expression in the stem $\left(12x^3y^2 - 8x^2y^3\right)$:

F. $2x^2y^2(4x - y) = 8x^3y^2 - 2x^2y^3$ ✗
G. $4x^2y^2(2xy) = 8x^3y^3$ ✗
H. $4x^2y^2(3xy) = 12x^3y^3$ ✗
J. $4x^2y^2(3x - 2y) = 12x^3y^2 - 8x^2y^3$ ✓
K. $x^3y^3(12xy - 8xy) = 12x^4y^4 - 8x^4y^4$ ✗

37. **(C)** (p. 72) *Mathematics/Algebra and Functions/Manipulating Algebraic Expressions/Basic Algebraic Manipulations*. The fastest way to solve this problem is to simplify the expression by getting rid of the fraction in the denominator: $\dfrac{1}{1 + \frac{1}{x}} = \dfrac{1}{\frac{x+1}{x}} = 1\left(\frac{x}{x+1}\right) = \frac{x}{x+1}$.

Alternatively, substitute numbers into the expression. If $x = 1$, then

$$\frac{1}{1+\dfrac{1}{x}} = \frac{1}{1+\dfrac{1}{1}} = \frac{1}{1+1} = \frac{1}{2}.$$ If $x = 1$, both (B) and (C) generate $\dfrac{1}{2}$. Therefore, try another

number. If $x = 2$, the correct answer should generate the value $\dfrac{2}{3}$; (B) is eliminated and (C)

must be correct.

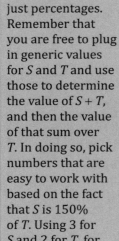

Plug–and–Chug

Item #38 can feel tricky because it uses two variables and no quantities—just percentages. Remember that you are free to plug in generic values for S and T and use those to determine the value of $S + T$, and then the value of that sum over T. In doing so, pick numbers that are easy to work with based on the fact that S is 150% of T. Using 3 for S and 2 for T, for example, can lead you straight to the fraction you need. Then just convert the fraction to a percentage.

38. (G) (p. 72) *Mathematics/Number and Quantity/Percentages*. The percentage of $S + T$

that is T is equal to $\dfrac{T}{S+T}(100)$. Since S is 150 percent of T, $S = 1.5T$. Substitute $1.5T$ for S:

$$\frac{T}{1.5T + T}(100) = \frac{T}{2.5T}(100) = \frac{1}{2.5}(100) = 40\%.$$

Alternatively, substitute real numbers. Let S be 15 and T be 10; then,

$$\frac{T}{S+T} = \frac{10}{10+15} = \frac{10}{25} = 40\%.$$

39. (C) (p. 72) *Mathematics/Geometry/Lines and Angles*. No figure is provided, so sketch one:

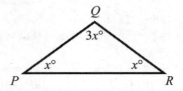

The sum of the interior angles in a triangle is $180°$, so
$x° + x° + 3x° = 180° \Rightarrow 5x° = 180° \Rightarrow x = 36$.

40. (G) (p. 72) *Mathematics/Number and Quantity/Rates and Proportions*. The greater the number of books, the greater the cost, so use a direct proportion:

$$\frac{\$C}{x \text{ books}} = \frac{\$d}{b \text{ books}} \Rightarrow Cb = dx \Rightarrow C = \frac{dx}{b}.$$

Plug–and–Chug

An ambush of variables to work with can be confusing. Item #40 is a question in which it might be faster to plug in values for b, d, C, and x, and to check which of the answer choices offered works with those values.

41. (D) (p. 73) *Mathematics/Number and Quantity/Percentages*. First, find the reduced price: $\$64 - (25\% \text{ of } \$64) = \$64 - (0.25 \cdot \$64) = \$64 - \$16 = \$48$. Next, calculate the sales tax on $\$48$: 5% of $\$48 = 0.05 \cdot \$48 = \$2.40$. Now, find the total cost: $\$48.00 + \$2.40 = \$50.40$.

42. (K) (p. 73) *Mathematics/Algebra and Functions/Solving Simultaneous Equations*. Use

the method for solving simultaneous equations: $\dfrac{y}{z} = k - 1 \Rightarrow k = \dfrac{y}{z} + 1$. Since $\dfrac{x}{z} = k$:

$$\frac{x}{z} = \frac{y}{z} + 1 \Rightarrow x = z\left(\frac{y}{z} + 1\right) = y + z.$$

43. (A) (p. 73) *Mathematics/Number and Quantity/Percentages* and *Algebra and Functions/ Evaluating, Interpreting, and Creating Algebraic Functions*. If $x = 0.25y$, then

$$y = \frac{x}{0.25} = 4x.$$ Thus, y is 400 percent of x.

44. (G) (p. 73) *Mathematics/Number and Quantity/Properties of Numbers.* Since 3 is a factor of 9 and 5 is a factor of 5, any multiple of both 9 and 5 will be a multiple of $3(5) = 15$; (II) belongs in the correct choice. (I), however, is not correct: x could be any multiple of 45, e.g., 90, which also proves that (III) does not belong in the correct choice.

45. (C) (p. 74) *Mathematics/Geometry/Complex Figures* and *Triangles/Pythagorean Theorem.* The neat thing about a cube is that if given any one feature (e.g., volume, edge, diagonal of a face, diagonal of the cube, surface area), every other feature can be calculated. This is why cubes are often the focus of test problems. The edge has a length of 2:

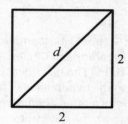

Use the Pythagorean theorem to find the length of the diagonal of a face:
$d^2 = 2^2 + 2^2 = 4 + 4 = 8 \Rightarrow d = 2\sqrt{2}$:

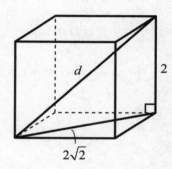

Now, find the length of the diagonal of the cube: $d^2 = 2^2 + (2\sqrt{2})^2 = 4 + 8 = 12 \Rightarrow d = 2\sqrt{3}$. The point that is the center of the cube is the midpoint of the diagonal of the cube and is $\sqrt{3}$ units of length from each vertex.

46. (J) (p. 74) *Mathematics/Geometry/Solids.* The volume of the large cylinder is $\pi r^2 h$.

Redefine the dimensions of the smaller cylinder in terms of r and h: $r = kr'$, so $r' = \dfrac{r}{k}$ and $h = kh'$, so $h' = \dfrac{h}{k}$. The volume of the small cylinder is $\pi \left(\dfrac{r}{k}\right)^2 \left(\dfrac{h}{k}\right) = \dfrac{\pi r^2 h}{k^3}$. The ratio of the volume of the small cylinder to the volume of the large cylinder is $\dfrac{\dfrac{\pi r^2 h}{k^3}}{\pi r^2 h} = \dfrac{1}{k^3}$, or $1 : k^3$.

Alternatively, assume some numbers. Let the radius and height of the larger cylinder be 4 and 4, and those of the smaller cylinder be 2 and 2. Since $r = kr'$ and $h = kh'$, k must be 2. The volume of the large cylinder is $\pi (4)^2 (4) = 64\pi$. The volume of the smaller cylinder is $\pi (2)^2 (2) = 8\pi$. The ratio of the volume of the smaller cylinder to that of the larger cylinder is $\dfrac{8\pi}{64\pi} = \dfrac{1}{8}$. Use $k = 2$ to find the answer that has a value of $\dfrac{1}{8}$:

F. $1 : \pi = \dfrac{1}{\pi}$ ✗

G. $\pi : 1 = \dfrac{\pi}{1} = \pi$ ✗

H. $k\pi : 1 = \dfrac{k\pi}{1} = 2\pi$ ✗

J. $1 : k^3 = \dfrac{1}{k^3} = \dfrac{1}{2^3} = \dfrac{1}{8}$ ✓

K. $k^3 : 1 = \dfrac{k^3}{1} = \dfrac{2^3}{1} = \dfrac{8}{1} = 8$ ✗

Master Moves

Use what you know about geometric figures and all the information given to find the best approach to solving item #47. You know that you have a right triangle (indicated by right angle Q), that $PQ = QR$, and that the triangle has an area of 1 square unit. What can you do with this information, and how can it lead you to the area of the circle?

47. (A) (p. 74) *Mathematics/Geometry/Complex Figures* and *Triangles/Pythagorean Theorem* and *Circles*. Triangle PQR is a right triangle, so $\angle PQR$ intercepts an arc of $180°$. (The inscribed angle $\angle PQR$ is equal to half its intercepted arc.) The arc is $180°$, so the hypotenuse of the triangle, $\overline{PR}$, is also the diameter of the circle. From any bit of information about a right isosceles triangle (e.g., either side lengths, the hypotenuse, or the area), the other information can be found. Using the two adjacent sides as the altitude and the base, $\text{area}_{\text{triangle}} = \dfrac{1}{2}(s)(s) \Rightarrow 1 = \dfrac{1}{2}s^2 \Rightarrow s^2 = 2$. Now, use the Pythagorean theorem to solve for $\overline{PR}$: $s^2 + s^2 = \overline{PR}^2 \Rightarrow 2 + 2 = \overline{PR}^2 \Rightarrow 4 = \overline{PR}^2 \Rightarrow \overline{PR} = 2$. Since $\overline{PR} = 2$, the radius of the circle is 1, and $\text{area}_{\text{circle}} = \pi(1)^2 = \pi$.

The same conclusion can be arrived at in a slightly different manner:

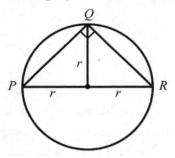

Based on the figure, r is the length of the altitude of the triangle and $2r$ is the length of the base, so $\text{area}_{\text{triangle}} = \dfrac{1}{2}(2r)(r) = r^2$ and $r^2 = 1 \Rightarrow r = 1$. Thus, $\text{area}_{\text{circle}} = \pi r^2 = \pi(1)^2 = \pi$.

Finally, a little common sense can solve this problem without any math. The triangle, which has an area of 1, takes up slightly less than half the circle:

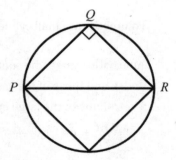

The correct answer must be a bit larger than 2, and only one choice qualifies: (A) is π and π is slightly larger than 3. Therefore, (A) is reasonable. All of the other choices are too large to be reasonable.

48. (F) (p. 75) *Mathematics/Geometry/Complex Figures* and *Circles* and *Triangles/Properties of Triangles*. This is a good exercise in organized problem-solving. Look at the figure and ask what is known: the radius of the circle, and that the perimeter of the shaded area consists of two arcs. There must be some way to use the information about the radius to find the length of the arcs. Arcs can be measured in terms of length or in terms of degrees.

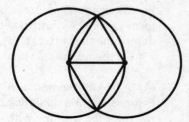

Since the sides of the triangles are all radii, the triangles must be equilateral, and the degree measure of each arc is 120. The circles have radii of 1, so they have circumferences of $2\pi(1) = 2\pi$. Each arc is a third of that length: $\dfrac{2\pi}{3}$. Since there are two such arcs, the perimeter of the shaded area is $2 \cdot \dfrac{2\pi}{3} = \dfrac{4\pi}{3}$.

49. (C) (p. 75) *Mathematics/Statistics and Probability/Measures of Center*. For the first six tests, the student has a total point count of $(6)(83) = 498$. If the student scores a zero on each of the four remaining tests, the total point count will remain 498 and the average will be $\dfrac{498}{10} = 49.8$. If the student scores 100 on each of the four remaining tests, the total point count will be 898 and the average will be $\dfrac{898}{10} = 89.8$. Therefore, $49.8 \le x \le 89.8$.

50. (K) (p. 75) *Mathematics/Number and Quantity/Complex Numbers*. The product of a complex number and its multiplicative inverse is 1. Let x be the multiplicative inverse of $2 - i$: $x(2 - i) = 1 \Rightarrow x = \dfrac{1}{2-i} \Rightarrow x = \dfrac{1}{2-i} \cdot \dfrac{2+i}{2+i} = \dfrac{2+i}{4-i^2}$. Since $i = \sqrt{-1}$, $i^2 = -1$. Thus, $x = \dfrac{2+i}{4-(-1)} = \dfrac{2+i}{5}$.

51. (C) (p. 76) *Mathematics/Algebra and Functions/Manipulating Algebraic Expressions/Logarithmic Expressions*. From the exponential concept of logarithms, if $a^x = b$, then the equation can be written in logarithmic form as $\log_a b = x$. Let $\log_3 \sqrt{3} = x$; then $3^x = \sqrt{3} \Rightarrow 3^x = 3^{\left(\frac{1}{2}\right)}$. Thus, $x = \dfrac{1}{2}$.

52. (J) (p. 76) *Mathematics/Algebra and Functions/Evaluating, Interpreting, and Creating Algebraic Functions/Concepts of Domain and Range*. Study the structure of f. When will the function be at its minimum value? This is like asking for the minimum value of $(x - 1)^2$. Squaring any positive number yields a positive number; squaring any negative number yields a positive number; and squaring zero yields zero. Since zero is less than any positive number, we want $x - 1$ to equal zero, and this occurs when $x = 1$. Now, plug in 1 for x in the given function and solve to find the minimum value of the function: $f(1) = (x - 1)^2 + 2 = (1 - 1)^2 + 2 = 2$.

Alternatively, test the answer choices. Plug each answer choice into the given function; the correct choice will be the lowest value:

F. $(-3-1)^2 + 2 = (-4)^2 + 2 = 16 + 2 = 18$ ✗
G. $(-2-1)^2 + 2 = (-3)^2 + 2 = 9 + 2 = 11$ ✗
H. $(0-1)^2 + 2 = (-1)^2 + 2 = 1 + 2 = 3$ ✗
J. $(1-1)^2 + 2 = (0)^2 + 2 = 0 + 2 = 2$ ✓
K. $(2-1)^2 + 2 = (1)^2 + 2 = 1 + 2 = 3$ ✗

Finally, if you recognized the function $f(x) = (x-1)^2 + 2$ as a parabolic equation in the form $(x-h)^2 + k$ with a vertex of (h, k), you could simply plug in the values of h and k to determine the vertex: $(1,2)$. Which means $x = 1$ is the minimum value of x.

53. **(A) (p. 76) *Mathematics/Algebra and Functions/Manipulating Algebraic Expressions/Manipulating Expressions Involving Exponents*.** Simply use the rules for working with exponents to solve the given equation for x:

$2^n + 2^n + 2^n + 2^n = x(2^{n+1}) \Rightarrow (4)(2^n) = x(2^{n+1}) \Rightarrow (2)(2^1)(2^n) = x(2^{n+1}) \Rightarrow$
$2(2^{n+1}) = x(2^{n+1}) \Rightarrow 2 = x$.

54. **(F) (p. 76) *Mathematics/Algebra and Functions/Evaluating, Interpreting, and Creating Algebraic Functions*.** The value(s) of k for which $f(k)$ equals $f(-k)$ occur when

$(k)^2 + 2(k) + 1 = (-k)^2 - 2k + 1 \Rightarrow k^2 + 2k + 1 = k^2 - 2k + 1 \Rightarrow 2k = -2k \Rightarrow 4k = 0 \Rightarrow k = 0$.

Another approach is to work backward from the answer choices. First, use the value 0: $(0)^2 + 2(0) + 1 = (-0)^2 - 2(0) + 1 \Rightarrow 1 = 1$. Thus, 0 is part of the solution set; eliminate (G), (H), and (J). The only question that remains is whether the correct answer is (K). Take another value, say 1. If $k = 1$, $f(1) = (1)^2 + 2(1) + 1 = 4$ and $f(-1) = (-1)^2 - 2(1) + 1 = 0$, so $f(1) \neq f(-1)$, and (K) is eliminated. This proves that the answer is (F).

55. **(D) (p. 76) *Mathematics/Algebra and Functions/Evaluating, Interpreting, and Creating Algebraic Functions/Concepts of Domain and Range*.** Factor the function:

$f(x) = \dfrac{x^2 - 1}{x - 1} = \dfrac{(x+1)(x-1)}{x-1} = x + 1$. Therefore, as x approaches 1, $f(x) = x + 1$ approaches 2.

56. **(H) (p. 77) *Mathematics/Geometry/Trigonometry/Graphs of Trigonometric Functions*.** Given the restrictions on x and since $\cos x = -1$, x must equal π and $\cos \dfrac{\pi}{2} = 0$.

Alternatively, visualize the graph of the cosine function (or graph it on a calculator).

57. **(B) (p. 77) *Mathematics/Algebra and Functions/Evaluating, Interpreting, and Creating Algebraic Functions*.** The domain of a function is the set of all possible x values; the range of a function is the set of all possible y values. This item can be solved algebraically by solving for x. Since $f(x) = \dfrac{1-x}{x}$, $x[f(x)] = 1 - x \Rightarrow x[f(x)] + x = 1 \Rightarrow x[f(x) + 1] = 1 \Rightarrow x = \dfrac{1}{f(x) + 1}$.

The range of the function is the set of all possible values for $f(x)$. Since division by zero is undefined, $f(x) + 1 \neq 0 \Rightarrow f(x) \neq -1$. Thus, $f(x)$ can be any value except -1.

Alternatively, use your calculator to graph the function:

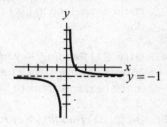

From the graph, it is obvious that the y-values both approach, but never actually reach, -1. Therefore, the range is defined by all real numbers except -1.

58. (K) (p. 77) **Mathematics/Geometry/Trigonometry/Trigonometric Relationships.** Since

$x = 3(\sin\theta)$ and $y = 2(\cos\theta)$, so $\sin\theta = \dfrac{x}{3}$ and $\cos\theta = \dfrac{y}{2}$. According to the Pythagorean identity, $\sin^2\theta + \cos^2\theta = 1$, so $\left(\dfrac{x}{3}\right)^2 + \left(\dfrac{y}{2}\right)^2 = 1 \Rightarrow \dfrac{x^2}{9} + \dfrac{y^2}{4} = 1$ is the equation of

an ellipse with center $(0,0)$ that passes through the points $(3,0)$ and $(0,2)$.

Alternatively, plug in values for θ. For $\theta = 0$, $x = 3[\sin(0)] = 3(0) = 0$, and $y = 2(\cos(0)) = 2(1) = 2$. For $\theta = \dfrac{\pi}{2}$, $x = 3\left(\sin\dfrac{\pi}{2}\right) = 3(1) = 3$ and $y = 2\left(\cos\dfrac{\pi}{2}\right) = 2(0) = 0$. Therefore, the graph must include the points $(3,0)$ and $(0,2)$. The only graph given that contains both of these points is (K).

59. (A) (p. 78) **Mathematics/Geometry/Trigonometry/Definitions of the Six Trigonometric Functions.** Sine and cosecant are reciprocal functions, so the product of the sine of any angle and the cosecant of that angle is 1. This fact can quickly be derived from the definitions of sine and cosecant. Given a triangle with sides a and b and hypotenuse c, let θ be opposite side b, so $\sin\theta = \dfrac{b}{c}$ and $\csc\theta = \dfrac{c}{b}$. Therefore, $\sin\theta \cdot \csc\theta = 1$.

60. (J) (p. 78) **Mathematics/Geometry/Trigonometry/Definitions of the Six Trigonometric Functions.** There are several different ways of expressing the length of $\overline{BC}$: as a number, as a function of $\angle ACB$, and as a function of $\angle CAB$. "Test-the-test" is the easiest option, and some exam wisdom will help. First, do not fall for (F) or (G). Test-takers are not expected to know values of trigonometric functions at particular angles. Since 40° and 50° are not easily remembered values, the answer is not going to be 4 or 5. The answer will be expressed using a trigonometric function. (J) is correct: $\tan A = \dfrac{\overline{BC}}{\overline{AB}} \Rightarrow \overline{BC} = \overline{AB}(\tan A) = 3(\tan 50°)$.

Section 3: Reading

1. (D) (p. 81) **Reading/Key Ideas and Details/Implied Idea.** In the final paragraph, the young man, Robin, is trying to explain to himself why the barbers laughed at him. Thus, he is talking to himself.

2. (J) (p. 81) **Reading/Key Ideas and Details/Explicit Detail.** The five shillings were not enough to satisfy the ferryman for having to make a special trip. The young man was forced to pay an additional three pence, bringing the total fare to five shillings and three pence.

3. **(B)** (p. 81) *Reading/Key Ideas and Details/Implied Idea.* Just after the young man gets off the ferryboat, he finds himself in a neighborhood of hovels and old houses that, he concludes, could not belong to his relative. Therefore, the young man must think his relative is well-to-do.

4. **(J)** (p. 81) *Reading/Key Ideas and Details/Implied Idea.* The scene is at night: the boat crosses at nine o'clock in the evening, the lights are on in the barber shop, and the stranger in the coat threatens to have the young man put in the stocks by morning.

5. **(A)** (p. 81) *Reading/Key Ideas and Details/Implied Idea.* In the first paragraph, the narrator remarks that the young man sets off on foot with a light step—as though he had not already traveled more than thirty miles. Thus, thirty miles is a long way to travel in a day.

6. **(G)** (p. 81) *Reading/Key Ideas and Details/Explicit Detail.* The young man finally concludes that the barbers laugh at him for approaching the stranger in the coat because it should have been obvious to him that the stranger in the coat would not know the Major.

7. **(A)** (p. 81) *Reading/Key Ideas and Details/Implied Idea.* The currency used to pay the ferryman and the length of a day's journey is suggestive. The reference to a "New England colony" clearly places the action sometime before the end of the eighteenth century.

8. **(F)** (p. 81) *Reading/Key Ideas and Details/Implied Idea.* The young man bows to the stranger and addresses him as "honored sir" in order to show respect.

9. **(B)** (p. 81) *Reading/Key Ideas and Details/Implied Idea.* The passage states that nine o'clock in the evening was an "unusual hour." Such language implies that nine o'clock was an unusual time for anyone to be using the ferryboat. This is why the young man was its only passenger.

10. **(F)** (p. 81) *Reading/Key Ideas and Details/Implied Idea.* The phrase "small and mean wooden buildings" characterizes the neighborhood near the ferry landing. The next paragraph also mentions a hovel and an old house.

11. **(B)** (p. 83) *Reading/Key Ideas and Details/Explicit Detail.* In the last paragraph, and the last sentence in particular, the author of the first passage states that the interdisciplinary approach used by Turner was a new technique. (B) best captures this idea. As for (A), the same paragraph states specifically that the reliance on political history was characteristic of history prior to Turner. As for (C), although Turner made the original presentation at a conference, the passage does not say that presenting was a technique of study. While Turner used the opportunity to present his new theory, he could equally well have published an article or made an informal presentation to colleagues. As for (D), the first passage doesn't enter into such a debate, though you will find some mention of this in the second passage. But because the information appears in the second passage, it cannot be an answer to this Explicit Detail item about the first passage.

12. **(G)** (p. 83) *Reading/Key Ideas and Details/Implied Idea.* Passage A notes even some students of Turner demonstrated that some of his points were wrong. There would have been no reason to use "even" unless one would ordinarily expect for students to support the work of a professor. And in the development of the passage, the author is pointing out that even though Turner's thesis was criticized by some scholars who might otherwise have been supporters, the thesis still remains important. As for (F), the passage implies that the students did scholarly work on the thesis, not that they were ignorant of it. As for (J), there is no support for this conclusion in the text. (H) is wrong because there is nothing to support this conclusion.

13. **(D)** (p. 83) *Reading/Key Ideas and Details/Voice.* The author of Passage A evidently approves of Turner's work. The passage says that it had great influence, that it was original, and that it used a novel approach. That's a pretty good review. As for (A), while the author allows that Turner's thesis was not immune to debate or even criticism, this does not mean that

the author was "suspicious" of the work itself. After all, it could turn out to be that Turner's conclusions are ultimately false, but the groundbreaking approach and radical theory would still have value. As for (B), the thesis is not treated negatively, so "condescending" can't be used to express the author's attitude. Finally, as for (C), the author takes a pretty strong position, so "undecided" is not a good description.

14. **(G)** (p. 83) *Reading/Craft and Structure/Vocabulary*. Because "grand" is a word with some common meanings, you can pretty much discount any choices that use these more common synonyms. That would certainly eliminate (H). Instead, the author is using the word "grand" in a derivative sense to mean large or great or overall. Turner's thesis did try to be comprehensive, accounting for the uniquely American character. As for (F), though the author allows that Turner's thesis was not perfect, line 14 is not where that discussion occurs. And (J) must be wrong since Turner's thesis was not tentative.

15. **(C)** (p. 83) *Reading/Key Ideas and Details/Development*. The author of Passage B discusses the limitations of Turner's theory, and one of the most important of these is its attempt to explain everything American in terms of the frontier. At the referenced lines, the author lists some other very important historical factors in order to show that the frontier could not have been the entire story. As for (A), this is the topic introduced at the end of that paragraph and developed in the following paragraphs, but it is not an answer to this question. As for (B), even granting that this statement is correct, it is not an answer to this question. For example, the author mentions the Civil War in order to show that Turner's thesis was too limited, not that traditional histories were too limited. As for (D), this is a point that is raised in the fifth paragraph, so it is not an answer to the question asked about the third paragraph.

16. **(G)** (p. 83) *Reading/Craft and Structure/Development*. At the end of the third paragraph, the author of Passage B states that Turner's thesis, in addition to failing as a comprehensive theory of American history, does not do an adequate job of explaining the frontier. The next three paragraphs are the specific points to support this argument: (i) land wasn't free, (ii) frontier is a dubious concept, and (iii) groups as well as individuals were important. The information about wagon trains supports this last point: it was groups, not loners, who moved into the westward regions and stayed. As for (F), (H), and (J), these are ideas that are mentioned, but they do not explain the significance of the wagon trains.

17. **(B)** (p. 83) *Reading/Key Ideas and Details/Voice*. The author of Passage B is critical of the frontier thesis, but you'll notice that the criticisms all deal with Turner's ideas. For example, Turner thought that the frontier offered free land, but the author of Passage B argues that he was wrong because the land was already used by indigenous peoples. So, while the passage criticizes Turner's idea, it doesn't criticize Turner himself. Thus, (C) and (D) are wrong, and (B) is correct. As for (A), the author says that the thesis has "rightfully" been abandoned because of its weaknesses.

18. **(H)** (p. 84) *Reading/Craft and Structure/Vocabulary*. You get the information you need to answer the question from the discussion about the significance of the Indian Wars. Turner claimed that the land was free, but in reality, it was necessary to pursue a policy of military aggression to secure the land. So, when the author writes that the wars "belie" the free land theory, the author means "prove false," (H). (F) is a distracting choice, but don't be misled by the superficial connection between "lie" and "untruth." In this context, the phrase is "prove to be false," not "lie about." As for (G) and (J), while these are phrases that relate generally to the idea of debating the merits of a theory, they don't focus on the connection between the wars and the free land thesis.

19. **(D)** (p. 84) *Reading/Integration of Knowledge and Ideas/Explicit Detail*. The key word other than "EXCEPT" in this item is "both;" therefore, the correct answer choice is the only one that is *not* mentioned in *both* passages. Both authors mention (A), (B), and (C). However, "nationalism" is only mentioned in the first passage.

20. (F) (p. 84) *Reading/Integration of Knowledge and Ideas/Application.* To a certain extent, any weakening of Turner's theory would have implications for all aspects of the theory. So, you might argue that the referenced evidence, in some way, tends to show that people from different regions did not mix at the frontier because the frontier was not quite as well-defined as Turner thought. But that's a pretty feeble point, and so (J) is wrong. You can apply similar reasoning to (G) and (H). The best answer here is (F). The "safety valve" point, as explained in Passage A, maintained that people who were dissatisfied with life in the urban areas could simply pack up and move to the country because there was land for the claiming. If the "free land" thesis is false, then the "safety valve" thesis must also be false.

21. (A) (p. 85) *Reading/Craft and Structure/Development.* At the end of the first paragraph, the author raises a question, which he then proceeds to answer. (A) describes this development. (B) is incorrect because the author does not present a theory as such. A theory is a hypothetical explanation of phenomena; the author instead presents his viewpoint about what is important in life. Also, while the author offers many opinions, none "prove" his viewpoint. As for (C), the author does not contrast his own views with other views. As for (D), the author does not define a term.

22. (J) (p. 85) *Reading/Craft and Structure/Vocabulary.* In the final paragraph, the author explains that life is much too short. The author introduces the discussion by stating that experience is the end goal of life—to get the most out of life, one must pack it with "as many pulsations as possible." One can infer that the author means experiences.

23. (B) (p. 86) *Reading/Key Ideas and Details/Explicit Detail.* The discussion of art is found in the closing sentences of the passage. Having said that the best life is one packed with experiences (pulsations), the author goes on to say how one can have these intense experiences. This is one function of art, he says—to do nothing but provoke feelings—not to depict reality, (A); not to encourage reform, (C); not as a means of expression, (D).

24. (H) (p. 86) *Reading/Key Ideas and Details/Application.* Experience is everything according to the author, so he would probably agree with (H). It is the feeling of the moment that is important, not the memory of the feeling. Once the feeling is past, you should be looking for new feelings, not thinking about past ones.

25. (A) (p. 86) *Reading/Craft and Structure/Voice.* The writing is highly impassioned. The intensity of the writing is evident in every sentence. The issues are those of life and death. The author uses phrases such as "passionate attitude," "tragic dividing," "awful brevity," and "splendor of our experience."

26. (H) (p. 86) *Reading/Craft and Structure/Implied Idea.* In the second paragraph, the author argues that the best life is one filled with experiences of every sort. Not to seek after a variety of experiences is, in the author's words, "on this short day of the frost and sun, to sleep before evening." The phrase "to sleep before evening" must mean to stop living even before death. Thus, the "short day of the frost and sun" refers to a person's life.

27. (C) (p. 86) *Reading/Craft and Structure/Implied Idea.* The author emphasizes the importance of living life to the fullest. In line 34, "awful brevity" refers to the shortness of life.

28. (J) (p. 86) *Reading/Key Ideas and Details/Explicit Detail.* In the final paragraph, the author contrasts those who are listless with those who are the children of the world. The children of the world are high in passion, wise, and in love with art and song.

29. (A) (p. 86) *Reading/Key Ideas and Details/Implied Idea.* Line 67 says that the desire for beauty has the most power to quicken our sense of life.

30. (H) (p. 86) *Reading/Craft and Structure/Implied Idea*. The author says that we are all under a sentence of death with an indefinite reprieve, meaning that we are all mortal. We have an "interval," meaning our life; and then "our place knows us no more," meaning we are gone from the earth; that is, we are dead.

31. (B) (p. 88) *Reading/Key Ideas and Details/Explicit Detail*. Lines 3–4 read, in part: "energy, which is the capacity for doing work."

32. (H) (p. 88) *Reading/Key Ideas and Details/Explicit Detail*. The second paragraph states that the result of the process is a mix of sugar and oxygen. O_2 names oxygen, and H_2O names water, so $C_6H_{12}O_6$ names a sugar.

33. (A) (p. 88) *Reading/Key Ideas and Details/Explicit Detail*. Lines 18–21 define both terms. Reduction is the addition of electrons, and oxidation is the removal of electrons.

34. (J) (p. 88) *Reading/Key Ideas and Details/Explicit Detail*. Lines 18–20 state that photosynthesis involves the addition of electrons, making (I) correct. Lines 24–27 state that photosynthesis involves action on hydrogen, meaning that (II) is also correct. Lines 21–22 state that "Reduction stores energy, while oxidation releases it," and line 18 states that "Photosynthesis is a reduction reaction." So, (III) cannot be correct. Since (I) and (II) are correct, the answer is (J).

35. (C) (p. 88) *Reading/Key Ideas and Details/Main Idea*. The fifth paragraph gives a systematic analysis of the process defined in preceding paragraphs, which is photosynthesis.

36. (F) (p. 88) *Reading/Key Ideas and Details/Explicit Detail*. (G) is supported by lines 54–56, (H) is supported by lines 68–71, and (J) is stated in lines 53–54. (F) states the reverse of the truth; it is ADP that is mixed with phosphate to form ATP (see lines 49–52).

37. (A) (p. 88) *Reading/Key Ideas and Details/Implied Idea*. A careful reading of lines 73–76 can lead to no other conclusion. A five-carbon sugar (RuDP) is combined with carbon dioxide (CO_2), ultimately resulting in the formation of a three-carbon sugar (PGAL).

38. (G) (p. 88) *Reading/Key Ideas and Details/Implied Idea*. Growing periods, (J), are never discussed. Higher temperatures, (H), as indicated in the final paragraph, can lead to disagreeable conditions. Lines 77–83 state that the photorespiration, with its seemingly wasteful result, occurs when CO_2 levels are low, suggesting that a higher level of CO_2 would be a more agreeable condition. Also, more agreeable conditions facilitate carboxylation. This process involves combining CO_2. Therefore, more CO_2 means an increase in carboxylation.

39. (B) (p. 88) *Reading/Key Ideas and Details/Explicit Detail*. As stated in line 18, photosynthesis is a reduction reaction, which makes (III) an incorrect choice. Lines 71–73 and lines 77–81 indicate that RuDP is used in carboxylation and photorespiration, making (I) correct. Another difference, as stated in lines 80–81, is that no ATP is created via photorespiration, (II).

40. (H) (p. 89) *Reading/Key Ideas and Details/Main Idea*. The angiosperm plants discussed in the final paragraph *do* photosynthesize, so (F) is incorrect. They do it in an unusual way, using their specialized leaf structure (H). According to the paragraph, Kranz plants have a method of maintaining carbon dioxide levels; they do not transform carbon dioxide into carbohydrate.

Section 4: Science

1. (B) (p. 91) *Science/Interpretation of Data/Comprehension*. As the table shows, with each additional carbon atom, the boiling point of the compound increases. For example, from methane (1 carbon atom) to ethane (2 carbon atoms), the boiling point increases from −162°C to −89°C, and from ethane to propane (3 carbon atoms), from −89°C to −42°C. Note that although it is true that the melting point decreases from ethane to propane, that is not the overall trent, so (C) is incorrect.

2. (H) (p. 91) *Science/Interpretation of Data/Analysis*. Butane has four carbon atoms. This means that it has ten hydrogen atoms. Both (G) and (H) have chains with ten hydrogen, but only (H) is similar to the propane example, with CH_3 on the end and CH_2 in the middle.

3. (C) (p. 91) *Science/Interpretation of Data/Application*. This item is answered by looking at the values in the table. Boiling points for the compounds shown increase as the number of carbon atoms increase.

4. (H) (p. 91) *Science/Interpretation of Data/Application*. This item tests information provided in the passage. The passage states that alkanes that differ by one carbon atom differ in molecular mass by 14u: 142 + 14 = 156.

5. (C) (p. 91) *Science/Interpretation of Data/Application*. According to the passage, the number of hydrogen atoms can be found using the formula $2n + 2$, where n is the number of carbon molecules: 2(12) + 2 = 26.

6. (J) (p. 91) *Science/Interpretation of Data/Application*. The graph shows that the boiling points of the first four alkanes are below room temperature (about 20°C). So methane, ethane, propane, and butane are all gases at that temperature. Hexane, however, is still a liquid. It boils and becomes a gas between 50°C and 100°C.

7. (A) (p. 91) *Science/Interpretation of Data/Analysis*. The graph in (A) shows the correct values for density; as the number of atoms in the carbon backbone increases, the density of the alkane increases. The other answer choices do not show a constant increase in density.

8. (F) (p. 93) *Science/Interpretation of Data/Comprehension*. According to the explanation provided in the first paragraph, the flag leaves penetrate the top of the coleoptile once it has reached the surface and continue to grow. The feature corresponding to that description is the plumule.

9. (B) (p. 93) *Science/Scientific Investigation/Comprehension*. The paragraph following Table 1 states that the greater growth rate for the coleoptiles with tips exposed to the air is explained by the production of additional growth substance. Those coleoptiles completely immersed in water had available only the growth substance left over from before the clipping.

10. (F) (p. 93) *Science/Scientific Investigation/Comprehension*. The first experiment immersed the coleoptiles in water, though in the second test the tops were allowed to extend into the air. But in neither test was anything but water used. Experiments 2 and 3 used growth solution.

11. (A) (p. 93) *Science/Interpretation of Data/Analysis*. The numbers in the table represent the average growth per hour as a percentage of the original length of the coleoptile segment. The values decrease as time increases and after hours 6 and 7, the values are the same. Therefore, (A) must be the correct graph.

12. (H) (p. 93) *Science/Interpretation of Data/Comprehension*. The greatest cumulative growth after 24 hours was 31.0%, associated with a concentration of 10 units per cm^3.

13. **(C)** (p. 94) *Science/Interpretation of Data/Analysis.* Table 2 shows that the solution of 40 units grew 8.0% longer than the original length after 4 hours, but after 24 hours it had only grown 7.2% longer than the original length. Therefore, it showed shrinkage.

14. **(J)** (p. 94) *Science/Scientific Investigation/Application.* The introductory material for Table 3 explains that cyanide would interfere with a metabolic process. The data in the table clearly shows that the greater the concentration of KCN, the lower the growth rate.

15. **(B)** (p. 96) *Science/Interpretation of Data/Comprehension.* According to the introductory paragraph, osmosis occurs when solvent molecules pass through a semi-permeable membrane to dilute the solute concentration on the other side of the membrane. In Experiment 1, the water (solvent) passes through the membrane from the side with lower sugar concentration to the side with higher sugar concentration—no sugar (solute) molecules pass through the membrane. This is also explained in the second paragraph, which introduces the figure illustrating the process of osmosis with sugar solutions.

16. **(H)** (p. 96) *Science/Scientific Investigation/Comprehension.* The purpose of Experiment 1 is to determine how many cells in a representative sample undergo plasmolysis—an effect of osmosis—after being submerged in sugar solutions of varying solute concentrations, (H). The solute concentrations of the solutions, (F), is a controlled variable. The quantity of water lost due to osmosis, (G), is beyond the scope of the experiment. Finally, although the data do show the threshold at which osmosis is first observed, (J), locating that point is not the purpose of the experiment.

17. **(B)** (p. 96) *Science/Scientific Investigation/Comprehension.* The description of Experiment 1 states that "[f]orty to sixty-five cells from each onion strip are analyzed and scored." The statement is part of the experimental setup and not tied with any experimental outcome. The best approach to an item like this is to eliminate the wrong choices. Nothing is known about the number of plasmolyzed cells, (A), or average total, (C), in an onion strip—what is known is the number of plasmolyzed cells in a sample consisting of 40 to 65 cells. As for (D), nothing can be known about the unanalyzed cells of the onion strips simply because they are unanalyzed. Therefore, by the process of elimination, the correct choice must be (B). Indeed, the purpose of analyzing 40 to 65 cells from each strip is to provide a representative snapshot of the cells in an onion without having to count endlessly.

18. **(F)** (p. 96) *Science/Scientific Investigation/Analysis.* According to the passage, osmosis is the movement of solvent (e.g., water) from an area of lesser solute (e.g., sugar) concentration to one of higher concentration. In Experiment 1, osmosis results in plasmolyzed cells because the cells lose water (solvent) to regions of higher sugar (solute) concentration. When immersed in the 0.05 mol/kg sugar solution, the cells do not lose water—that is, there is no evidence of plasmolysis—because the sugar concentration inside the cells is greater than that of the surrounding solution.

19. **(B)** (p. 96) *Science/Interpretation of Data/Analysis.* The difference in percentage of plasmolyzed cells is accounted for by the number of cells analyzed in each case. For the

onion strip submerged in the 0.55 mol/kg sugar solution, 50 of the 50 analyzed cells are

plasmolyzed: $\frac{50}{50} = 100\%$. For the onion strip submerged in the 0.45 mol/kg sugar solution,

50 of the 64 analyzed cells are plasmolyzed: $\frac{50}{64} \approx 78.1\%$.

20. **(G)** (p. 96) *Science/Evaluation of Models/Analysis.* According to Table 2, the beet disk submerged in the
0.00 mol/kg sugar solution increases in weight. A solution concentration of 0.00 moles of sugar per kilogram of water indicates that there is no sugar in the solution—the beaker contains only water. Therefore, any sugar in the cells of the beet disk triggers osmosis and water molecules moved across the semi-permeable cell walls into the beet cells, adding weight to the disk.

21. **(C)** (p. 97) *Science/Interpretation of Data/Application.* According to Table 2, as the sugar solution concentration increases, the percentage of weight change decreases. Therefore, eliminate (A) and (D). The graphs in (B) and (C) are similar for high and low values but different for values in the middle of the graph, so compare the values in Table 2 for a sugar solution concentration of 0.25 mol/kg. According to the table, the percentage of weight change in the disk submerged in the 0.25 mol/kg sugar solution is +3.65%, so (C) is the correct choice.

22. **(H)** (p. 97) *Science/Evaluation of Models/Analysis.* According to Table 2, the beet disk submerged in the 0.35 mol/kg sugar solution increases in weight, while the beet disk submerged in the 0.40 mol/kg sugar solution decreases in weight. Thus, the concentration of sugar in the beet cells must be between 0.35 moles and 0.40 moles per kilogram of water.

23. **(B)** (p. 98) *Science/Interpretation of Data/Comprehension.* Magnesium is a positively charged mineral (Mg^{+2}). The soil that has the worst relative ability to hold such minerals is coarse sand.

24. **(J)** (p. 98) *Science/Interpretation of Data/Analysis.* As particles get larger (from less than 2 micrometers to 200–2,000 micrometers), their relative ability to retain water decreases (from 1 to 4).

25. **(C)** (p. 98) *Science/Interpretation of Data/Comprehension.* Soils that are neither most able nor least able for any ability cannot be ranked 1 or 4. The only soils that are never ranked 1 or 4 are silt (greater than or equal to 2 μm and less than 20 μm) and sand (greater than or equal to 20 μm and less than 200 μm). The total size range, therefore, is greater than or equal to 2 μm and less than 200 μm.

26. **(F)** (p. 98) *Science/Scientific Investigation/Application.* Since loam is mostly clay, it primarily has small particles that hold minerals and water well. The larger silt and sand particles in loam are adequate at maintaining air spaces containing oxygen. None of the other predictions fit the data in the chart.

27. **(D)** (p. 99) *Science/Evaluation of Models/Analysis.* (A), (B), and (C) are all true. However, (D) is NOT true: clay is most able (relative ability is 1) to both hold positively charged minerals and retain water, so there is a soil type that is best for more than one category of relative ability.

28. **(G)** (p. 100) *Science/Evaluation of Models/Comprehension.* Concentrations of reactants, not products, determine rate in both theories.

29. **(C)** (p. 100) *Science/Evaluation of Models/Comprehension.* This question tests critical comprehension of the passage, and it requires an understanding of the relationship between the two theories. According to the passage, Theory 2 explains that Theory 1 is based upon an incomplete understanding of the details of chemical reactions, assuming that all reactions operate by a single-step mechanism. Therefore, one can conclude that a proponent of Theory 2 believes that Theory 1 can be used for single step reactions, but should not be used for more complex reactions.

30. **(G)** (p. 100) *Science/Interpretation of Data/Comprehension.* This question tests understanding of the relation of numbers of reactants in the overall equation to exponents in the rate law. For the reaction $Mg + 2HCl \Rightarrow MgCl_2 + H_2$, Theory 1 states that rate $= k[HCl]^2$, where k is the rate constant and the exponents are the coefficients in front of the reactants in the reaction. Using this formula, the rate equation for $3M + 2N \Rightarrow 4P$ must be $k[M]^3[N]^2$.

31. **(D)** (p. 100) *Science/Interpretation of Data/Analysis.* The coefficients of the reactants determine their exponents in the rate law.

32. **(F)** (p. 100) *Science/Evaluation of Models/Analysis.* This question tests understanding of the differences between the theories. Theory 2 disagrees with Theory 1 on the grounds that chemical reactions do not all occur in one stage. Therefore, Theory 2 may be best supported by evidence that proves that some reactions occur in more than one stage.

33. **(A)** (p. 101) *Science/Interpretation of Data/Comprehension.* If the first stage is very slow and the second stage is much quicker, the overall rate is essentially that of the first stage.

34. **(H)** (p. 101) *Science/Evaluation of Models/Analysis.* If the sum of the rates of each stage always equaled the rate of the reaction taken as a whole, there would be no need to analyze each sub-reaction.

35. **(B)** (p. 102) *Science/Interpretation of Data/Comprehension.* Temperature range for a life function is the high temperature minus the low temperature. For both species and both humidity conditions, oviposition always has the narrowest range.

36. **(J)** (p. 102) *Science/Interpretation of Data/Comprehension.* For each life function, Species M achieved 90% success at the same low temperatures in either humidity. At high temperatures, however, 50% humidity was detrimental. (Under 50% humidity, 90% success was not achieved at the same high temperatures as 100% relative humidity.)

37. **(C)** (p. 102) *Science/Scientific Investigation/Analysis.* Since humidity levels had no effect on Species D for mating, oviposition, or pupation, it is likely that 50% relative humidity will have little effect on caterpillar survival in Species D as well. The temperature range would, therefore, be the same as observed at 100% relative humidity: 12°C–36°C.

38. **(G)** (p. 102) *Science/Scientific Investigation/Analysis.* Mating success in the light and in the dark should be compared at the same temperature. It should be a temperature at which both species can successfully mate. Otherwise, additional variables confuse the issue. (30°C is an optimum temperature for both species under all conditions presented.)

39. **(D)** (p. 103) *Science/Evaluation of Models/Analysis.* Species M and Species D are both equally successful at low temperatures for pupation.

40. **(F)** (p. 103) *Science/Evaluation of Models/Analysis.* (G) and (H) are not relevant to the question. (J) only refers to light conditions. (F) is a hypothesis supported by the results.

SAMPLE ESSAY RESPONSES AND ANALYSES

Section 5: Writing

Above-Average Response

If you walk through a suburban parking lot, on a city street, or even along a beach, you are likely to see grocery bags littering the ground. Because of the environmental risks they pose, free plastic and paper bags should be eliminated and be replaced with cloth bags or purchased bags that are designed for reuse. Non-reusable bags have a harmful impact on the environment, and consumers needlessly accumulate them. Although eliminating free grocery bags would be an unwelcome change for some consumers and manufacturers, it is a long-term change that needs to be made for the good of the environment.

The production and use of both plastic and paper bags have a negative impact on the environment. As litter, plastic bags are more dangerous than paper because often, they are not biodegradable. They accumulate in landfills and can kill animals that attempt to eat them or that become entangled in them and suffocate. Plastic bags can be especially harmful in coastal cities because they can float into bodies of water, where they are difficult to recover and can kill marine life. Paper bags, however, require more energy to manufacture, which produces more greenhouse gases. Unless paper bags are made from recycled material, trees must be cut down to manufacture them. Paper bags are also harder to reuse because some plastic bags are waterproof and more durable. Because both types cause environmental problems, it is best to shop with reusable, cloth bags.

Grocery bags are also an example of waste because Americans accumulate more bags than necessary. One may argue that some sources of pollution, such as gasoline, cannot be eliminated because there is no widely available substitute. However, paper and plastic bags can easily be replaced with more environmentally-friendly products. It is wasteful to manufacture a product that harms the environment and that is used for about 20 minutes before being thrown out. Because these bags are so rapidly disposed of, they accumulate in shoppers' homes, or worse, outside. Some California cities, for example, have banned plastic bags because of the pollution they cause when they accumulate in natural environments. Stores should cut down on the number of non-reusable bags they distribute by charging for paper and plastic bags and also by having cloth bags available for sale.

Opponents of banning plastic bags claim that a ban would be inconvenient for consumers and would harm manufacturers. For consumers, however, the ban would cease to be an annoyance once they adjusted to bringing their own bags. Shoppers could keep bags in their cars or backpacks for last-minute trips to the store, and initially, stores could reward customers who bring their own bags. For example, some stores enter shoppers with their own bags in a raffle for free groceries. Some consumers argue that they reuse plastic bags for garbage; however, they would still be able to purchase durable plastic bags at a low cost. The biggest challenge to eliminating plastic bags would be the threat to bag manufacturers. In California, a statewide ban was delayed because it would have eliminated manufacturers' jobs. Before implementing a ban, states should devise plans to minimize job loss; for example, factories could transition into making fewer, more durable bags.

Although eliminating free grocery bags would be an adjustment for many Americans, it would be worth the long-term environmental benefits. The large quantities of bags that Americans currently use are wasteful, and their convenience does not justify the threat they pose for the environment.

Ideas and Analysis: The writer clearly states his or her thesis in the introduction: free, non-reusable shopping bags are a threat to the environment and should be banned. The writer's thesis largely agrees with Perspective 2, but the writer adds that paper bags can also harm the environment. The author addresses Perspective 3's argument by arguing that both paper and plastic bags can be harmful, and the quantity of bags overall should be reduced. The essay also counters Perspective 1's claim that the convenience of free bags makes them necessary for consumers.

Development and Support:

- The introduction opens with a hook, and the description of litter in different environments illustrates that it is a widespread problem.

- The writer clearly states the thesis in the second sentence of the introduction and previews the three main arguments.

- The body paragraphs begin with topic sentences that state the main point or argument to be made in the paragraph.

- The body paragraphs include concrete examples to support the writer's opinions.

  ○ Body paragraph 1: The writer describes specific effects of both paper and plastic bags on the environment.

  ○ Body paragraph 2: The writer argues that the accumulation of non-reusable bags is harmful and unnecessary and uses the California ban to illustrate this claim.

  ○ Body paragraph 3: The writer acknowledges the opposing viewpoint. Although the writer does not have specific, proven examples of how to prevent job loss when fewer bags are manufactured, he or she provides practical advice on how to make the transition easier for consumers.

Organization:

- The writer introduces each paragraph with a topic sentence.

- The writer uses transitions to connect ideas between and within paragraphs. See, for example, the first sentence of the second body paragraph: "Grocery bags are also an example of waste because Americans accumulate more bags than necessary."

- The main ideas are arranged in a logical progression:

  1) Non-reusable bags are harmful for the environment.

  2) These risks are unnecessary because non-reusable bags can be replaced with products that are more environmentally friendly.

  3) Consumers and companies can think of solutions to make the elimination of non-reusable bags easier for customers and manufacturers.

- The second body paragraph becomes slightly repetitive because both the first and second body paragraphs mention the accumulation of paper and plastic bags.

Language Use and Conventions: The essay contains at least three principal strengths in this area:

- The essay does not have any mechanics/usage errors. As a result, the reader's attention is not distracted from the substance of the essay.

- The essay does not have any informal language.

- Stylistically, the writer varies sentence structures throughout most of the essay.

Summary and Conclusions: This essay demonstrates writing skills that are well developed and provides arguments, as well as practical suggestions for eliminating non-reusable shopping bags. The writer also addresses all three perspectives throughout the essay. This essay would likely receive a score of 10.

Below-Average Response

Eliminating paper and plastic bags might be good for the environment but its just not doable in America. Shopping bags are really convenient for shoppers and can be used around the house. Also, we do other things also have a bad affect on the environment, so I don't see why people have to care so much about plastic bags.

Shopping bags are very convenient, and it would be too much of a burden on customers if they were eliminated. Often, my parents just stop by the store on the way home from work to pick up a few things they need. They would never remember to bring a reusable bag with them to work in case they needed to go shopping afterwards. I think it would be unfair to consumers to have to buy bags every single time they went shopping because the reality is that shoppers aren't used to bringing bags with them, and it would take a long time for them to get used to this.

Also, plastic bags can be used around the house. I often use them as trash bags, since they're waterproof, they're very useful for this purpose. Sometimes when it's raining, I also use them to protect my books and my calculator because my backpack isn't completely waterproof.

Also, it is impossible not to harm the environment. So many things that we do harm the environment, like driving, taking long showers, and using gas stoves. However, theres never going to be a law banning these activities, so why should shopping bags be banned?

Although in an ideal world we'd be able to ban non-reusable shopping bags, this wouldn't work in the US. It would be too hard for Americans to adjust to the change.

Ideas and Analysis: The writer has a clear thesis and three main supporting arguments. However, while the essay defends Perspective 1, it does not take into account the opposing arguments in Perspectives 2 and 3. The writer's analysis of the situation is weak because he or she claims to speak for all "Americans" but only offers arguments and examples from his or her personal life. The essay would be stronger if it analyzed a wider range of viewpoints, instead of relying on generalizations.

Development and Support:

- The writer states his or her thesis in the first sentence of the introduction, and the introduction also previews the three main supporting arguments.

- In the body paragraphs, the writer uses several personal examples, but he or she generalizes from these examples and claims that banning plastic bags would be difficult for everyone.

- The second body paragraph does not develop the writer's argument well. The writer provides two examples of uses of plastic bags but does not explain that these activities make plastic bags a less wasteful product.

- The third body paragraph, in particular, contains a superficial argument. The writer does not acknowledge that activities like driving and cooking are necessary parts of one's daily life, whereas there is a feasible alternative to using plastic bags.

Organization:

- The organization of the essay is clear and easy to follow. The writer states his or her thesis in the introduction, and each body paragraph has a topic sentence.

- The writer uses transitions, but the transitions sometimes sound repetitive and awkward. For example, both the second and third body paragraphs begin with the transition "also." The writer needs to vary transitions to make the essay flow more smoothly.

Language Use and Conventions: The essay contains several weaknesses in this area:

- The essay contains some usage and mechanics errors.
    - Introduction: In the first sentence, "its" should be changed to "it's." (Explain that "its" is the possessive form, and "it's" means "it is.")

    - Introduction: In the last sentence, "affect" should be changed to "effect." (Explain that usually, "affect" is a verb and "effect" is a noun.)

    - Body paragraph 2: The second sentence has a comma splice. (I often use them as trash bags, since they're waterproof, they're very useful for this purpose.) The writer should begin a new sentence after "bags" or replace the comma with a semicolon.

    - Body paragraph 3: In the final sentence, "theres" should be changed to "there's."

- The essay contains many examples of informal language. For example, in the conclusion, the writer says, "this wouldn't work in the US." Instead, the writer should say, "banning non-reusable bags would not be practical in the US."

- The essay also uses repetitive language. For example, the introduction states that "Shopping bags are really convenient for shoppers." The writer should use a synonym for "shoppers," such as "consumers," to avoid sounding repetitive.

Summary and Conclusions: The essay has a clear thesis and three main arguments. However, the writer does not use developed reasoning or a variety of examples to support these arguments. Furthermore, the writer does not consider the opposing viewpoints. This essay would likely receive a score of 5.

PRACTICE TEST II

MULTIPLE-CHOICE ANSWER KEYS

DIRECTIONS: For each <u>correct</u> answer, check the corresponding box. Then, total the number of checkmarks to determine the raw score for that test.

Section 1: *English* (Student Text, p. 107)

	Correct		Correct		Correct		Correct		Correct
1. B		16. H		31. B		46. J		61. A	
2. G		17. A		32. G		47. D		62. J	
3. C		18. H		33. B		48. G		63. B	
4. H		19. D		34. J		49. B		64. J	
5. B		20. F		35. D		50. H		65. C	
6. F		21. C		36. J		51. A		66. G	
7. A		22. F		37. D		52. H		67. B	
8. H		23. A		38. H		53. D		68. F	
9. C		24. F		39. A		54. F		69. A	
10. F		25. D		40. H		55. A		70. F	
11. C		26. J		41. B		56. F		71. B	
12. J		27. C		42. G		57. B		72. F	
13. B		28. H		43. A		58. J		73. B	
14. G		29. D		44. H		59. A		74. J	
15. B		30. J		45. D		60. F		75. B	

Raw Score: _____ /75

Section 2: *Mathematics* (Student Text, p. 120)

	Correct		Correct		Correct		Correct
1. D		16. K		31. C		46. H	
2. K		17. C		32. G		47. A	
3. C		18. G		33. C		48. G	
4. K		19. B		34. H		49. C	
5. A		20. J		35. C		50. J	
6. F		21. A		36. H		51. A	
7. C		22. K		37. E		52. F	
8. G		23. D		38. K		53. E	
9. C		24. J		39. C		54. K	
10. F		25. D		40. J		55. B	
11. E		26. G		41. D		56. G	
12. K		27. B		42. K		57. D	
13. A		28. G		43. B		58. J	
14. G		29. D		44. G		59. A	
15. C		30. F		45. A		60. H	

Raw Score: _____ /60

Section 3: *Reading* (Student Text, p. 136)

	Correct		Correct		Correct		Correct
1. D		11. B		21. A		31. D	
2. F		12. J		22. F		32. G	
3. C		13. B		23. C		33. B	
4. G		14. J		24. F		34. H	
5. D		15. C		25. B		35. B	
6. G		16. J		26. F		36. H	
7. A		17. B		27. B		37. D	
8. G		18. F		28. J		38. F	
9. A		19. C		29. B		39. C	
10. H		20. J		30. H		40. J	

Raw Score: _____ /40

Section 4: *Science* (Student Text, p. 144)

	Correct		Correct		Correct
1. D		13. B		30. H	
2. F		14. J		31. D	
3. C		15. A		32. F	
4. J		16. G		33. C	
5. D		17. C		34. G	
6. F		18. J			
				35. D	
7. A		19. C		36. J	
8. H		20. F		37. B	
9. D		21. D		38. F	
10. H		22. H		39. B	
11. A		23. A		40. H	
12. H					
		24. G			
		25. C			
		26. H			
		27. A			
		28. G			
		29. B			

Raw Score: _____ /40

MULTIPLE-CHOICE EXPLANATIONS

Section 1: *English*

1. **(B)** (p. 107) *English/Conventions of Standard English/Grammar and Usage/Faulty or Illogical Comparisons.* The original sentence is incorrect for two reasons. First, the phrase "more gentler" is wrong. "More" is redundant of the "-er" suffix. Second, the rest of the passage makes it clear that the author means to say that botany is the most gentle of sciences. (C) is wrong because the passage makes it clear that the author intends the superlative "most." (D) is not idiomatic.

2. **(G)** (p. 107) *English/Conventions of Standard English/Grammar and Usage/Diction.* The word "ostentatious" means "showy" and is not appropriate here. "Unobtrusive" is a better fit.

3. **(C)** (p. 107) *English/Conventions of Standard English/Grammar and Usage/Pronoun Usage.* The original sentence is incorrect because the pronoun "it" does not have a clear and unambiguous referent. Although it must refer to "botany," on first reading it seems that it might refer to "flower." (C) eliminates the potential for misreading. (B) and (D) are incorrectly punctuated.

4. **(H)** (p. 107) *English/Knowledge of Language/Style/Conciseness.* The original sentence is incorrect because the phrasing is awkward and wordy. (H) provides the most direct and concise phrasing: "but the natural world." (G) and (J) are incorrect for the same reason as the original.

5. **(B)** (p. 108) *English/Conventions of Standard English/Grammar and Usage/Diction.* The original sentence is not idiomatic. The correct idiom is "consists of," not "consists about." (C) is wrong because it is not idiomatic. (D) is wrong because it uses a plural verb with a singular subject.

6. **(F)** (p. 108) *English/Conventions of Standard English/No Change.* The original sentence is correct as written. The other choices are not idiomatic and destroy the parallelism between "knowing" and "studying."

7. **(A)** (p. 108) *English/Production of Writing/No Change.* The original sentence is the best phrasing. The phrase "in and of themselves" serves to emphasize the thought that plants are intrinsically worth studying.

8. **(H)** (p. 108) *English/Production of Writing/Strategy/Effective Transitional Sentence.* The second paragraph sets up a contrast with the first. In the first paragraph, the author states that plants are intrinsically worthy of study. Here, the author says that we should not entirely discount their practical value.

9. **(C)** (p. 108) *English/Conventions of Standard English/Grammar and Usage/Verb Tense and Punctuation/Semicolons.* The original sentence contains two errors. First, the past participle "disparaged" is needed rather than the present participle following "should." Second, the dash disrupts the logical flow of the sentence. It seems to signal an aside or a clarifying remark, but what follows is actually another clause. (C) is the best choice; it uses the correct verb form, and the semicolon is a correct choice of punctuation to separate two clauses when no coordinate conjunction is used. (B) corrects the verb but not the punctuation error. (D) contains both errors.

10. **(F)** (p. 108) *English/Production of Writing/No Change.* "Nonetheless" sets up a contrast between the idea that plants have practical value and the idea that this very fact imposes limits on the study of plants.

11. (C) (p. 108) *English/Conventions of Standard English/Grammar and Usage/Sequence and Verb Tense.* The present tense conflicts with the other verbs in the sentence. They are all in the simple past tense. Only (C) makes the required change. (B) is wrong because there is no reason to use the past perfect. ("Had been made" suggests that one past event occurred and was completed before another past event, but that is not the intended meaning of the original.) (D) is wrong because the subject is "study," a singular noun.

12. (J) (p. 109) *English/Conventions of Standard English/Sentence Structure/Problems of Coordination and Subordination.* "Or" implies that the two ideas are alternatives. However, an assumption can be basic and still unspoken. What the author intends to say is that these ideas are very basic but no one ever makes them explicit.

13. (B) (p. 109) *English/Conventions of Standard English/Grammar and Usage/Sequence and Verb Tense and Pronoun Usage.* The original sentence contains two mistakes. First, "to have understood" is inconsistent with the other verb forms in the paragraph, for it suggests something that will occur at a future time before some other action. (e.g., John hopes to have finished his homework before his mother comes home.) Additionally, "their" is a plural pronoun and cannot substitute for the singular "plant." (B) makes both of the needed corrections.

14. (G) (p. 109) *English/Conventions of Standard English/Grammar and Usage/Subject-Verb Agreement.* The subject of the sentence is plural, so you need the plural verb "are." Deleting the main verb or changing the form to "being" results in a sentence fragment.

15. (B) (p. 109) *English/Production of Writing/Strategy/Appropriate Supporting Material.* The question asks about the development of the passage. In paragraph two, the author makes the point that plants are worthy of study in and of themselves and that botany has, throughout its history, rediscovered this truth. In the underlined part of the final sentence, the author makes the same point.

16. (H) (p. 110) *English/Production of Writing/Strategy/Appropriate Supporting Material.* The author inserts "of course" to acknowledge that the point being made is an obvious one: of course, poverty means lack of money.

17. (A) (p. 110) *English/Production of Writing/No Change.* The original sentence is correct. (B) and (C) are awkward or wordy by comparison. (D) destroys the structure of the sentence.

18. (H) (p. 110) *English/Conventions of Standard English/Grammar and Usage/Pronoun Usage.* The original sentence contains an error of pronoun usage. "Their" is intended to refer to "family," which might be either plural or singular. However, there is already another pronoun in the sentence that refers to "family," and it is singular. Thus, the first "its" determines that the author will treat "family" as a singular noun. (G) is wrong because "there" is not a pronoun. Finally, (J) is the contraction for "it is" and not a pronoun at all.

19. (D) (p. 110) *English/Production of Writing/Strategy/Effective Transitional Sentence.* The logic of the sentence does not support the use of the transitional word "consequently." "Consequently" is used to show that one idea follows logically from another idea or that one event follows from another event as a matter of causality. Neither of these notions is implied by the sentence. The author has not yet explained why one would find more poverty in rural America than in other regions. The best course is simply to drop the word entirely.

20. (F) (p. 110) *English/Conventions of Standard English/No Change.* The original sentence is correct as written. (G) is wrong because "lower" cannot be substituted for "less." The phrase "may earn lower than" is not idiomatic. (H) is wrong because the correct idiom for making a comparison like this is "less than," not "less as." Finally, (J) combines the errors of both (G) and (H).

21. (C) (p. 110) *English/Production of Writing/Organization/Paragraph-Level Structure*. In the first paragraph, the author provides the definition of "poor."

22. (F) (p. 110) *English/Production of Writing/No Change*. The original sentence is correct as written. A new paragraph is needed here because the author is taking up a new topic. Thus, (G) and (J) are wrong. As for (H), "since" destroys the logic of the sentence.

23. (A) (p. 111) *English/Production of Writing/No Change*. The single word "parallel" nicely expresses the thought that lack of education is associated with low income. By comparison, the alternatives are wordy. Notice also that the wrong choices use phrases that would seem out of place given the formal style of the passage.

24. (F) (p. 111) *English/Production of Writing/No Change*. The last sentence of the paragraph expresses an idea that follows from, or is the result of, the idea that precedes it. The phrase "as a consequence" signals the reader that the second idea is the result of the first.

25. (D) (p. 111) *English/Conventions of Standard English/Grammar and Usage/Subject-Verb Agreement* and *Diction*. The original sentence contains two errors. First, the plural verb "are" does not agree with its subject, "schooling." Second, the phrase "as inadequate like" is not idiomatic. (B) corrects both errors but is punctuated incorrectly. One can treat the phrase "like family income" as an aside, but the limits of the aside cannot be marked with one dash and one comma. Either two dashes or two commas must be used. (C) is guilty of illogical expression, because it seems to imply that schooling is supposed to function "as" family income. (D) is the right choice because it corrects the problems of the original and is correctly punctuated.

26. (J) (p. 111) *English/Conventions of Standard English/Grammar and Usage/Pronoun Usage*. "It" has no antecedent. (J) corrects this by supplying a noun. (G) and (H) make illogical statements.

27. (C) (p. 111) *English/Knowledge of Language/Style/Conciseness*. The original sentence is needlessly wordy. (C) is more concise and more in keeping with the formal tone of the selection.

28. (H) (p. 111) *English/Conventions of Standard English/Grammar and Usage/Subject-Verb Agreement*. The original sentence is incorrect because the plural verb "have" does not agree with its singular subject, "head." (G) fails to correct this problem. (H) and (J) are both singular verbs, but "was to have" in (J) implies a condition that was never fulfilled. This suggestion of an unfulfilled condition is out of place here. (H) is the correct choice. The present perfect is acceptable because it indicates an action that occurred at some unspecified time in the past (the head of the family had some schooling). It would also be acceptable to use the present tense: "If the head...has little schooling, the children are...."

29. (D) (p. 111) *English/Conventions of Standard English/Grammar and Usage/Diction*. The original sentence is incorrect because the expression "as...rather than in" is not idiomatic. An idiomatically correct alternative is supplied by (D): "is as true...as." (B) fails to correct the problem of the original sentence. Although (C) is idiomatic, "they" does not agree with the demonstrative pronoun, "this," to which it refers.

30. (J) (p. 111) *English/Knowledge of Language/Style/Conciseness*. The underlined phrase is redundant of "modern." Just omit it.

31. (B) (p. 112) *English/Conventions of Standard English/Grammar and Usage/Adjectives versus Adverbs*. The original sentence is incorrect because the adjective "poor" cannot be used to modify another adjective (educated). The adverb "poorly" is needed for that. (B) makes the correction. (C) is wrong because it changes the intended meaning of the sentence. The author is talking about poor people who are not well educated, not "educated poor people." Finally, (D) is grammatically incorrect. The noun "education" cannot modify a noun.

The Cambridge Edge

The correct answer, if the original contains an error, will make needed corrections without introducing new errors. In item #25, you might choose (B) because it corrects both of the original errors. However, (B) introduces a new error of punctuation. Double-check for any new errors before making your final selection.

32. (G) (p. 112) *English/Production of Writing/Organization/Passage-Level Structure*. The author supplies a definition and statistics in the first paragraph. Throughout the selection the author offers explanations.

33. (B) (p. 112) *English/Conventions of Standard English/Grammar and Usage/Sequence and Verb Tense*. The original sentence is wrong because the present tense "fail" is not consistent with the other verb in the sentence. The other verb describes a past action. Additionally, "fail" is a plural verb, but the subject of the sentence is "one," a singular noun. (B) corrects the problem of tense (and the problem of agreement since there is only one form in the simple past). (C) makes the needed corrections, but the resulting phrase is not idiomatic. Finally, (D) addresses the problem of agreement, but there is still the problem of tense.

34. (J) (p. 112) *English/Conventions of Standard English/Grammar and Usage/Pronoun Usage and Diction*. The original sentence contains two errors. First, it uses "that" rather than "who" to refer to people. Second, it is not idiomatic. The correct idiom is "should have," not "should of." "Should of" is never correct diction because "of" is not a verb. (G) corrects neither of these errors. (H) corrects the first but not the second. Only (J) corrects both errors.

35. (D) (p. 112) *English/Knowledge of Language/Style/Conciseness*. The underlined phrase is redundant of "dropouts." It should be deleted.

36. (J) (p. 113) *English/Conventions of Standard English/Grammar and Usage/Verb Tense and Diction*. The original sentence is both grammatically incorrect and not idiomatic. First, "will starting" is not an English verb form at all. Second, an infinitive is used after a verb ending in "-ing" rather than the gerund. Thus, "starting to think" is more idiomatic than "starting thinking." (J) corrects both the problems of the original sentence. (G) does not solve the idiom problem, and (H) is ambiguous. The placement of "usually" suggests that it is intended to modify "thinking" rather than "starts."

37. (D) (p. 113) *English/Conventions of Standard English/Punctuation/Commas*. The original sentence is incorrectly punctuated; if, for clarity, the final prepositional phrase is set apart, a comma must be used. The colon is too powerful and isolates the prepositional phrase from the rest of the sentence. (B) and (C) are wrong because connecting the prepositional phrase to the rest of the sentence with a coordinate conjunction gives it an importance equal to that of the verb: "he or she ceases...and roughly at age 14."

38. (H) (p. 113) *English/Conventions of Standard English/Grammar and Usage/Subject-Verb Agreement*. The original sentence is incorrect because the singular verb "is" does not agree with its subject. The subject is a compound subject (a series of elements joined by "and"), which is plural. (G) fails to correct this mistake. (H) and (J) correct the error, but the use of the past tense in (J) is incorrect. The author is describing a current problem using the present tense.

39. (A) (p. 113) *English/Conventions of Standard English/No Change*. The original sentence is correct. Each of the wrong answer choices creates a run-on sentence. In general, when there are two independent clauses, one of three things is done: the clauses are joined together using a comma and a coordinate conjunction such as "and" or "but"; the clauses are joined together using a semicolon; or the clauses are put in separate sentences.

40. (H) (p. 113) *English/Knowledge of Language/Style/Conciseness*. "Most often" and "mostly" have the same meaning. (H) eliminates the needless repetition.

41. (B) (p. 113) *English/Conventions of Standard English/Grammar and Usage/Faulty or Illogical Comparisons*. The original sentence contains a grammatical mistake. It uses "most" rather than "more" to compare two things. Both (B) and (D) make the needed correction. (D) is wrong, however, because the singular "one" does not agree with its verb "stay."

42. **(G)** (p. 113) *English/Conventions of Standard English/Grammar and Usage/Pronoun Usage.* The original sentence is wrong for two reasons. First, it uses the objective case pronoun "him" to modify the gerund "dropping." Instead, the possessive case "his" must be used. Second, the use of the gerund is awkward. It is much more direct to simply say "at the time he drops out." (G) corrects the original sentence and is more direct and concise as well. (J) would be correct except that it uses the past tense. The author uses present tense verbs to describe an ongoing problem, so the present tense should also be used here.

43. **(A)** (p. 113) *English/Production of Writing/No Change.* The original sentence is the best version. The other choices are awkward and wordy.

44. **(H)** (p. 114) *English/Conventions of Standard English/Sentence Structure/Fragments.* The original sentence is incorrect because the sentence lacks a conjugated or main verb. "Increasing" is a participle and cannot function as a main verb. Each of the other choices uses a conjugated form of "to increase" and so avoids this error. (G), however, is incorrect because "so that" seems to introduce a clause, but what follows is not a clause: "so that during the eighth grade...." (J) is wordy and indirect. Additionally, the past tense in (J) is inconsistent with the other verbs in this paragraph.

45. **(D)** (p. 114) *English/Conventions of Standard English/Grammar and Usage/Diction.* In the original sentence, "none" is a pronoun. What is required, however, is an adverb to explain how the dropout participates in activities: not at all. (B) uses the correct idiom, but the "and" results in a contradictory statement. How could one participate a little and not at all? (C) is incorrect because "not much" is equivalent to "little," so the resulting statement does not create the either/or situation intended by the original sentence.

46. **(J)** (p. 114) *English/Conventions of Standard English/Grammar and Usage/Subject-Verb Agreement and Diction.* The original sentence contains two errors. First, "goes" is a singular verb and does not agree with the subject of the sentence, "reasons." Second, the phrase "goes deeper as" is not idiomatic. (J) corrects both of these problems. (G) and (H) do correct the problem of subject-verb agreement, but they are not idiomatic.

47. **(D)** (p. 114) *English/Production of Writing/Strategy/Appropriate Supporting Material.* In the final sentence, the author notes that dropping out is a symptom that has other root causes. It would be appropriate for the author to continue talking about those causes.

48. **(G)** (p. 114) *English/Production of Writing/Strategy/Appropriate Supporting Material.* The word "dropout" is familiar, so the passage would not be incomprehensible without the definition. However, the definition serves to tighten up the discussion.

49. **(B)** (p. 115) *English/Conventions of Standard English/Grammar and Usage/Subject-Verb Agreement.* In the original sentence, the verb "are" does not agree with its subject, "kind." Both (B) and (C) make the needed correction, but (C) makes a change that disrupts the parallelism of the sentence: "research and developing." Since "research" and "development" have similar functions in the sentence (they are both objects of the preposition "of"), the noun "development" should be used.

50. **(H)** (p. 115) *English/Conventions of Standard English/Grammar and Usage/Diction.* The original sentence is not idiomatic. The correct idiom is "look for something to do something" (to satisfy), not "look for something doing something." (G) is incorrect because the subjunctive "would have" suggests that an anticipated past event did not occur because of some other event. (John would have come to the party, but he was taken ill.) Finally, (J) is ambiguous. "With the satisfaction of" is a prepositional phrase, but it is not clear what the phrase is supposed to modify.

51. **(A)** (p. 115) *English/Conventions of Standard English/No Change.* The original sentence is correct as written. "Its" refers to "humankind." (B) is incorrect because "humankind" is singular. (C) is wrong because "it's" is the contraction of "it is" and is not a pronoun at all. Finally, "your" cannot be substituted for "humankind."

52. **(H)** (p. 115) *English/Conventions of Standard English/Grammar and Usage/Diction.* In the original sentence, the infinitive "to find" does not have a clear logical relationship to any other part of the sentence. (H) solves this problem by turning "to find" into "finding," which can then function as an appositive for "one" ("one of the problems"). (G) doesn't solve the problem of the orphaned phrase and, if anything, makes matters worse since a colon is more powerful than a comma. Finally, (J) just creates a sentence fragment of everything that follows the period.

53. **(D)** (p. 115) *English/Knowledge of Language/Style/Conciseness.* The original sentence is wordy. (D) is more concise and more direct. (B) is very concise, but (B) destroys the sense of the sentence: what may they be? (C) is wrong because "it" is a singular pronoun and cannot refer to "machines."

54. **(F)** (p. 115) *English/Production of Writing/No Change.* The author intends here to contrast two ideas: wind is difficult to harness, but it is valuable. (G), (H), and (J) signal a cause-effect relationship, when a contrast is needed instead.

55. **(A)** (p. 115) *English/Conventions of Standard English/No Change.* The original sentence is correct as written. (B) is wrong because the singular "has" does not agree with the subject "rewards." (C) is wrong for this reason and also because the author clearly intends to make a statement about the past, not the present. Finally, (D), which uses the future tense, must be wrong as well.

56. **(F)** (p. 116) *English/Conventions of Standard English/No Change.* The original sentence is correct. Notice how the next sentence parallels the structure of this sentence. (G) is wrong because it eliminates this stylistic feature and also because the resulting sentence is ambiguous. Does the author mean to say the machine was located in China, was built in China, or was simply in China one day passing through? (H) is wrong for the same reasons as (G) and also because the verb tense is illogical. Finally, (J) is wrong because "has" switches to the active voice and implies that the machine was building something.

57. **(B)** (p. 116) *English/Knowledge of Language/Style/Conciseness.* The original sentence does not contain a grammatical mistake, but it is awkward. By comparison, (B) is more concise and more direct than any of the other choices.

58. **(J)** (p. 116) *English/Knowledge of Language/Style/Conciseness.* The original sentence does not contain an error but is needlessly wordy. By substituting "by" for "through the means of," the thought can be rendered more concisely and directly.

59. **(A)** (p. 116) *English/Production of Writing/No Change.* The original sentence is correct. (B) is wrong because the comma separates the adjective "several" from the noun it modifies, "centuries." (C) is wrong because "but" suggests a contrast that is not intended by the author. Finally, (D) is wrong because the use of "and" suggests that what follows is similar to what comes before. However, "water lift" is not like "centuries."

60. **(F)** (p. 116) *English/Production of Writing/No Change.* The original sentence is correct as written. It uses the active voice and is more direct than the alternatives, which use the passive voice.

61. **(A)** (p. 116) *English/Production of Writing/No Change.* The original sentence is correct. The author takes up a new topic at this point, so a new paragraph is appropriate and (B) is wrong. (C) is wrong because it creates a sentence fragment from what is otherwise a complete sentence. (D) is wrong because it is needlessly wordy.

62. **(J)** (p. 117) *English/Conventions of Standard English/Grammar and Usage/Faulty or Illogical Comparisons.* The original sentence is incorrect because it implies a comparison of two machines. In fact, the author means to compare one machine with all other such machines; therefore, the superlative "most" should be used. (G) does use the superlative, but "most

simplest" is redundant. Use one or the other, but not both. (H) fails to correct the problem of the original sentence.

63. **(B)** (p. 117) *English/Conventions of Standard English/Sentence Structure/Faulty Parallelism.* The original sentence suffers from a lack of parallelism. The second in the series of two verbs should have the same form as the first: "flourished" and "came." Only (B) makes the needed correction.

64. **(J)** (p. 117) *English/Knowledge of Language/Style/Idiomatic Expression.* The phrase "real iffy" is an example of informal usage that should not be included in formal writing. (G) and (H) are needlessly wordy. "Capricious" solves both of these problems.

65. **(C)** (p. 117) *English/Production of Writing/Strategy/Appropriate Supporting Material.* The phrase "rage into a gale" has an appropriate meaning for the sentence and helps to maximize the importance of the weather by creating vivid imagery.

66. **(G)** (p. 117) *English/Conventions of Standard English/Grammar and Usage/Pronoun Usage.* The original sentence contains an error of pronoun usage. It refers to both "television" and "products," so a plural pronoun is required. (J) fails to make the needed correction. Both (G) and (H) make the correction, but (H) introduces a new error. The use of the subjunctive "would be" implies that an event is contingent upon the occurrence of some other event. However, there is no such other event mentioned in the selection.

67. **(B)** (p. 118) *English/Conventions of Standard English/Grammar and Usage/Subject-Verb Agreement.* The original sentence contains an error of subject-verb agreement. The subject of the sentence is "industry," so the verb should be singular: "industry is." The relative clause introduced by "which" is not part of the simple subject. (C) fails to make the needed correction. (D) corrects the original sentence but is incorrectly punctuated. The relative clause should be marked with two commas, not one comma and a dash.

68. **(F)** (p. 118) *English/Conventions of Standard English/No Change.* The original sentence is correctly punctuated. (G) is incorrect because a comma must be used to separate the first two elements in a series of three or more elements. (H) is wrong because the comma separates an adjective from the noun that it modifies. Finally, (J) is wrong because it separates the definite article "the" from the noun that it modifies.

69. **(A)** (p. 118) *English/Conventions of Standard English/No Change.* The original sentence is correct. The subject of the verb is "the episodic series," a singular noun. Since three items are being compared, "most" is the correct choice.

70. **(F)** (p. 118) *English/Production of Writing/No Change.* The original sentence is correct as written. "With the advent of" is an idiom that identifies a certain point in time. The remaining choices are simply not idiomatic.

71. **(B)** (p. 118) *English/Conventions of Standard English/Grammar and Usage/Sequence and Verb Tense.* The original sentence uses the wrong verb tense. The phrase "with the advent of" pegs the time as belonging to the past. Some form of the past tense is needed. Only (B) supplies a verb that refers to a past event.

72. **(F)** (p. 118) *English/Conventions of Standard English/No Change.* The original sentence is correct as written. The verb "have" correctly agrees with its plural subject. Also, some form of the past tense is required here since the sentence obviously refers to events that belong to the past. Thus, the other choices are incorrect.

73. **(B)** (p. 118) *English/Conventions of Standard English/Grammar and Usage/Verb Tense.* The past participle of "to grow" is "grown." (B) makes the needed change. (C) and (D) are incorrect because their forms are not parallel to the other verb form, "has lost."

Use the Process of Elimination

If you're unable to determine the correct answer from the given choices, eliminate any obviously wrong choices and make an educated guess. For example, in item #64, you may not know what "capricious" means. However, you can determine that (F), (G), and (H) are wrong because they are informal and needlessly wordy. So, you are left with (J) as the most likely correct answer.

74. **(J)** (p. 118) *English/Conventions of Standard English/Sentence Structure/Fragments*. In the original underlined portion, everything following the period is a sentence fragment—there is no main verb. (J) uses a colon to introduce the list. (G) is wrong because the comma incorrectly suggests that the elements of the list will be verbs. (H) is wrong because it fails to mark the transition from the main part of the sentence to the list.

75. **(B)** (p. 118) *English/Conventions of Standard English/Grammar and Usage/Adjectives versus Adverbs*. The original sentence is incorrect because "controversy" is intended to be an adjective that modifies "topics." However, "controversy" is a noun—not an adjective. (B) makes the needed correction.

Section 2: *Mathematics*

1. **(D)** (p. 120) *Mathematics/Number and Quantity/Scientific Notation*. Perform the indicated operations: $2 \times 10^4 = 20,000$, and $121,212 + 20,000 = 141,212$.

2. **(K)** (p. 120) *Mathematics/Algebra and Functions/Manipulating Algebraic Expressions/ Factoring Expressions*. Recognize that $6x + 3$ can be factored and rewrite the equation: $3(2x + 1) = 21 \Rightarrow 2x + 1 = 7$.

   Alternatively, if you failed to see the shortcut, solve the given equation for x: $6x + 3 = 21 \Rightarrow 6x = 18 \Rightarrow x = 3$. Therefore, $2x + 1 = 2(3) + 1 = 7$.

3. **(C)** (p. 120) *Mathematics/Number and Quantity/Rates and Proportions*. The cost of renting a bowling lane for 2 hours is $2 \cdot \$12 = \$24$. For $24, a ping pong table can be rented for $\$24 \div \$3 = 8$ hours.

4. **(K)** (p. 121) *Mathematics/Number and Quantity/Properties of Numbers*. (F) is incorrect since a natural number cannot equal the sum of itself and a number greater than itself. Similar reasoning applies to (G), (H), and (J). (K) is the only choice that could be true: for example, if q is 5 and r is 10, and if s is 15 and t is 20, then $5 + 20 = 10 + 15$.

5. **(A)** (p. 121) *Mathematics/Number and Quantity/Properties of Numbers*. Use $\dfrac{1}{2}$ as a benchmark. Reason in this way: eliminate (C)—since $\dfrac{7}{14}$ is $\dfrac{1}{2}$, $\dfrac{7}{15}$ is less than $\dfrac{1}{2}$. Continue eliminating choices until only the correct answer, (A), is left.

   Alternatively, you can use a calculator to determine which answer choice has a decimal equivalent that is greater than the decimal equivalent of $\dfrac{1}{2}$, or 0.5.

6. **(F)** (p. 121) *Mathematics/Number and Quantity/Percentages*. Use the "is-over-of" strategy: $\dfrac{\text{is}}{\text{of}} = \dfrac{\text{students on track team}}{\text{total students}} = \dfrac{18}{360} = \dfrac{1}{20} = 0.05 = 5\%$.

7. **(C)** (p. 121) *Mathematics/Geometry/Lines and Angles*. (I) must be true because a and x are vertically opposite each other. Similarly, (II) must be true because y and b are equal and z and c are equal. (III), however, is not necessarily true. While x and a are equal and y and b are equal, there is no information on which to base a conclusion about the relationship between x and y or the relationship between a and b.

8. **(G)** (p. 122) *Mathematics/Geometry/Lines and Angles*. Vertical angles have equal measures, so $x + 30 = 2x \Rightarrow x = 30$.

9. **(C)** (p. 122) *Mathematics/Number and Quantity/Properties of Numbers.* Eliminate choices (A), (B), and (D) since they contain numbers that are not prime. Then, calculate the remaining choices:

   C. $2 \cdot 2 \cdot 3 \cdot 5 = 60$ ✓
   E. $3 \cdot 3 \cdot 3 \cdot 5 = 135$ ✗

10. **(F)** (p. 122) *Mathematics/Statistics and Probability/Measures of Center.* Use the method for finding the missing element of an average. Since the average height of all four buildings is 20, the sum of the heights of all four is $4 \cdot 20 = 80$. The three known heights total $3 \cdot 16 = 48$. Therefore, the missing value is $80 - 48 = 32$.

11. **(E)** (p. 122) *Mathematics/Geometry/Lines and Angles.* The angles labeled $4y$ and $5y$ form a straight line, so $5y + 4y = 180 \Rightarrow 9y = 180 \Rightarrow y = 20$. Next, the angles of a triangle total $180°$, so $4y + 2y + x = 180 \Rightarrow 6y + x = 180 \Rightarrow 6(20) + x = 180 \Rightarrow 120 + x = 180 \Rightarrow x = 60$.

12. **(K)** (p. 123) *Mathematics/Number and Quantity/Properties of Numbers.* Each of the marks between the numbered marks is $\frac{1}{5}$ of the distance between the numbered marks. The distance between each numbered mark is 0.1, so each of the others is worth $0.1 \div 5 = 0.02$. Thus, $\overline{PQ} = 0.02 + 0.1 + 2(0.02) = 0.16$.

13. **(A)** (p. 123) *Mathematics/Geometry/Rectangles and Squares.* The perimeter is $2(3a - 2) + 2(2a - 1) = 6a - 4 + 4a - 2 = 10a - 6$.

   Alternatively, assume a value for a. For example, if $a = 1$, then the length of the figure is $3(1) - 2 = 1$, and the width of the figure is $2(1) - 1 = 1$. The perimeter would be $4 \cdot 1 = 4$. Substituting 1 for a into the correct formula yields the value 4.

14. **(G)** (p. 123) *Mathematics/Statistics and Probability/Measures of Center.* The average of the five numbers is 51, so their sum is $5 \cdot 51 = 255$. The two known values total 114. Therefore, the remaining three numbers total $255 - 114 = 141$. And $\frac{141}{3} = 47$.

15. **(C)** (p. 123) *Mathematics/Algebra and Functions/Solving Algebraic Equations or Inequalities with One Variable.* Since $-2 \leq 2x \leq 2 = -1 \leq x \leq 1$, x could be $-1, 0$, or 1.

16. **(K)** (p. 124) *Mathematics/Algebra and Functions/Manipulating Algebraic Expressions/ Manipulating Expressions Involving Exponents.* Since $8 = 2^3$, $8^x = (2^3)^x = 2^{3x}$.

17. **(C)** (p. 124) *Mathematics/Geometry/Rectangles and Squares.* One square has an area of $2 \cdot 2 = 4$, the other an area of $3 \cdot 3 = 9$, and the sum of their areas is $4 + 9 = 13$.

18. **(G)** (p. 124) *Mathematics/Geometry/Solids.* Set up an equation for the volume of the solid: $x(2x)(3) = 54 \Rightarrow 2x^2 = 18 \Rightarrow x^2 = 9 \Rightarrow x = \sqrt{9} = \pm 3 = 3$. (Remember that distances are always positive.)

   Alternatively, "test-the-test" by trying each answer choice until one generates a volume of 54.

19. **(B)** (p. 124) *Mathematics/Number and Quantity/Percentages* and *Algebra and Functions/ Manipulating Algebraic Expressions/Basic Algebraic Manipulations.* Since x is 80% of y, $x = 0.8y$, and $y = \frac{x}{0.8} = 1.25x$. So, y is 125% of x.

20. **(J)** (p. 125) *Mathematics/Algebra and Functions/Manipulating Algebraic Expressions/ Evaluating Expressions.* Consider each answer choice. As for (F), it proves that $m < n$. As for (G), it proves nothing about m and n since m and n might be either negative or positive. The same is true of (H), which is equivalent to $m > -n$. As for (K), it proves nothing because it provides neither relative values for m and n nor their signs. Only (J) works. Rewrite $m - n > 0$ by adding n to both sides: $m > n$.

21. **(A)** (p. 125) *Mathematics/Algebra and Functions/Evaluating, Interpreting, and Creating Algebraic Functions.* First, find $f(2)$: $f(2) = (2)^2 + 2 = 4 + 2 = 6$. Next, find $f(6)$: $f(6) = (6)^2 + 6 = 36 + 6 = 42$. Thus, $f(f(2)) = 42$.

22. **(K)** (p. 125) *Mathematics/Geometry/Complex Figures* and *Lines and Angles* and *Circles.* First, find the area of the circle: $\pi r^2 = \pi(2)^2 = 4\pi$. Since the shaded area is equal to 3π, it accounts for $\frac{3\pi}{4\pi} = \frac{3}{4}$ of the circle. Thus, the unshaded area is $\frac{1}{4}$ of the circle. The degree measure of an arc is equal to the measure of the central angle that intercepts the arc. Therefore, $\angle x$ plus the angle vertically opposite x are equal to $\frac{1}{4}(360°) = 90°$. Thus, $2x = 90$ and $x = 45$.

23. **(D)** (p. 125) *Mathematics/Number and Quantity/Percentages.* Use the "is-over-of" strategy:
$$\frac{\text{is}}{\text{of}} = \frac{\text{tin}}{\text{entire bar}} = \frac{100}{100 + 150} = \frac{100}{250} = \frac{2}{5} = 40\%.$$

24. **(J)** (p. 126) *Mathematics/Algebra and Functions/Manipulating Algebraic Expressions/Basic Algebraic Manipulations.* Solve the given equation for x:
$$\frac{1}{x} + \frac{1}{y} = \frac{1}{z} \Rightarrow \frac{y + x}{xy} = \frac{1}{z} \Rightarrow \frac{z(y + x)}{xy} = 1 \Rightarrow z = \frac{xy}{y + x} = \frac{xy}{x + y}.$$

Alternatively, assume some values. Assume that $x = 1$ and $y = 1$. On that assumption, $z = \frac{1}{2}$. Substitute 1 for x and 1 for y into the choices. Only (J) generates the value $\frac{1}{2}$.

25. **(D)** (p. 126) *Mathematics/Number and Quantity/Basic Arithmetic Manipulations.* Since $|-5| = 5$, $|-12| = 12$, and $|-2| = 2$, the expression is equal to $5 + 12 - 2 + (-6) = 15 - 6 = 9$.

26. **(G)** (p. 126) *Mathematics/Statistics and Probability/Measures of Center* and *Algebra and Functions/Manipulating Algebraic Expressions/Basic Algebraic Manipulations.* Create an equation for the average of the three terms and solve for x:
$$\frac{2x + 2x + 1 + 2x + 2}{3} = x - 1 \Rightarrow \frac{6x + 3}{3} = x - 1 \Rightarrow 6x + 3 = 3(x - 1).$$

27. **(B)** (p. 126) *Mathematics/Number and Quantity/Rates and Proportions.* The profit on each box of candy is $\$2 - \$1 = \$1$. To earn a total profit of $\$500$, it will be necessary to sell $\frac{\$500}{\$1} = 500$ boxes.

28. **(G)** (p. 126) *Mathematics/Number and Quantity/Basic Arithmetic Manipulations.* Perform the indicated operations: $(-2)^2 - (-2)^3 = 4 - (-8) = 12$.

29. **(D)** (p. 127) *Mathematics/Number and Quantity/Properties of Numbers.* If the sum and average of three different integers are equal, one of the integers must be 0:

$$x - x + y = \frac{x - x + y}{3} \Rightarrow y = \frac{y}{3} \text{ can only be true if } y = 0.$$

30. **(F)** (p. 127) *Mathematics/Number and Quantity/Percentages.* Use the "is-over-of" strategy:

$$\frac{\text{is}}{\text{of}} = \frac{\text{seniors}}{\text{total}} = \frac{90}{360} = \frac{1}{4} = 25\%.$$

31. **(C)** (p. 127) *Mathematics/Geometry/Complex Figures* and *Rectangles and Squares* and *Triangles/45°-45°-90° Triangles.* The diagonal of a square creates an isosceles right triangle.

    Since this is a 45°-45°-90° right triangle, each side of the square is equal to $\frac{\sqrt{2}}{\sqrt{2}} = 1$.

    Alternatively, designate the length of a side of the square as x. From the Pythagorean theorem, $x^2 + x^2 = (\sqrt{2})^2 \Rightarrow 2x^2 = 2 \Rightarrow x^2 = 1 \Rightarrow x = \pm 1 = 1$ (since length is positive). Therefore, the perimeter of the square is $4(1) = 4$.

32. **(G)** (p. 127) *Mathematics/Geometry/Lines and Angles.* The angles labeled $3w$ and $(5w + 20)$ form a straight line segment, so $3w + (5w + 20) = 180 \Rightarrow 8w + 20 = 180 \Rightarrow 8w = 160 \Rightarrow w = 20$. The angles labeled $3w$ and $4x$ also form a straight line segment: $3w + 4x = 180 \Rightarrow 3(20) + 4x = 180 \Rightarrow 60 + 4x = 180 \Rightarrow 4x = 120 \Rightarrow x = 30$.

33. **(C)** (p. 128) *Mathematics/Geometry/Rectangles and Squares* and *Number and Quantity/Rates and Proportions.* If the floor were a complete rectangle, it would have a width of $4 \cdot 5 = 20$ meters, a length of $8 \cdot 5 = 40$ meters, and a total area of $20 \cdot 40 = 800$ square meters. However, the floor is not a rectangle—its actual area is smaller. Subtract the area of the missing corner, which is a square since its sides are the same length. Each side is $0.8 \cdot 5 = 4$ meters. Therefore, the corner's area is $4 \cdot 4 = 16$ square meters, and the area of the floor is $800 - 16 = 784$ square meters.

34. **(H)** (p. 128) *Mathematics/Geometry/Triangles/Properties of Triangles* and *Number and Quantity/Properties of Numbers.* The sum of the lengths of any two sides of a triangle must be greater than the length of the third side. If x is the length of the third side, then $x + 4 > 11 \Rightarrow x > 7$, and the smallest integer value for x is 8. Also, $4 + 11 > x \Rightarrow 15 > x$, and the largest integer value for x is 14.

35. **(C)** (p. 128) *Mathematics/Algebra and Functions/Solving Quadratic Equations and Relations.* Put the equation in standard form and factor: $-x^2 = 3 - 4x \Rightarrow 0 = 3 - 4x + x^2 \Rightarrow x^2 - 4x + 3 = 0 \Rightarrow (x - 3)(x - 1) = 0$. Therefore, either $x - 3 = 0 \Rightarrow x = 3$ or $x - 1 = 0 \Rightarrow x = 1$. The solution set is $\{1, 3\}$.

36. **(H)** (p. 129) *Mathematics/Number and Quantity/Basic Arithmetic Manipulations.* The club spent $\frac{2}{5}$ of the budget on the first project and was left with $\frac{3}{5}$ of $300, which is $\frac{3}{5}(\$300) = \$180$. Then, $\frac{1}{3}$ of $180 was spent, leaving $\frac{2}{3}$ of $180, which is $\frac{2}{3}(\$180) = \$120$.

37. (E) (p. 129) *Mathematics/Algebra and Functions/Evaluating, Interpreting, and Creating Algebraic Functions/Functions as Models.* Since n nails cost c cents, each nail will cost $\dfrac{c}{n}$ cents. Then, x nails will cost $x\left(\dfrac{c}{n}\right) = \dfrac{cx}{n}$ cents. A dollar contains 100 cents, so the cost of x nails is $d = \dfrac{cx}{100n}$ dollars.

Alternatively, use the technique of assuming some values for the variables. For example, assume that nails cost 5 cents each and 20 are to be purchased. On that assumption, the cost is \$1. If $n = 1$, $c = 5$, and $x = 20$, then $d = 1$:

A. $1 = 100(5)(1)(20)$ ✘

B. $1 = \dfrac{100(5)(20)}{1}$ ✘

C. $1 = \dfrac{100(1)(20)}{5}$ ✘

D. $1 = \dfrac{(1)(20)}{100(5)}$ ✘

E. $1 = \dfrac{(5)(20)}{100(1)}$ ✓

38. (K) (p. 129) *Mathematics/Number and Quantity/Properties of Numbers and Algebra and Functions/Manipulating Algebraic Expressions/Basic Algebraic Manipulations.* For the given inequality to be true, a, b, and c must all be non-zero. For all real numbers except 0, a^2 is greater than 0, so b^3c must be less than 0. However, $b^3c = b^2bc$, and b^2 is greater than 0. Therefore, bc must be less than 0, and the answer is (K). (Note that either b or c is less than 0, but not both.)

39. (C) (p. 129) *Mathematics/Geometry/Triangles/Properties of Triangles.* Since this is an equilateral triangle, the sides are equal. Set up two of the sides as equal: $2x + 1 = 2x + y$, so $y = 1$. Therefore, the length of one side of the triangle is $y + 2 = 1 + 2 = 3$. The perimeter of the triangle is $3(3) = 9$.

40. (J) (p. 130) *Mathematics/Algebra and Functions/Coordinate Geometry/Distance and Midpoint Formulas.* Sketch a figure of the given information:

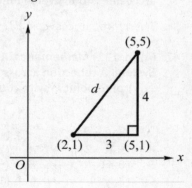

Use the distance formula or the Pythagorean theorem to determine d. Using the distance formula: $d = \sqrt{(5-2)^2 + (5-1)^2} = \sqrt{3^2 + 4^2} = \sqrt{9 + 16} = \sqrt{25} = 5$. Or, using the Pythagorean theorem: $d^2 = 3^2 + 4^2 = 25 \Rightarrow d = 5$.

41. (D) (p. 130) *Mathematics/Number and Quantity/Basic Arithmetic Manipulations.* The key to combining the expressions is recognizing that 45 and 20 are both multiples of 5:

$$\sqrt{9 \cdot 5} - \sqrt{4 \cdot 5} + \sqrt{5} = 3\sqrt{5} - 2\sqrt{5} + \sqrt{5} = 2\sqrt{5}.$$

42. (K) (p. 130) *Mathematics/Number and Quantity/Properties of Numbers.* This is a good item for testing the answer choices:

F. $12 - 3 = 9$ and $15 - 3 = 12$ ✗
G. $12 - 4 = 8$ and $15 - 4 = 11$ ✗
H. $12 - 11 = 1$ and $15 - 11 = 4$ ✗
J. $12 - 12 = 0$ and $15 - 12 = 3$ ✗
K. $12 - 13 = -1$ and $15 - 13 = 2$ ✓

43. (B) (p. 130) *Mathematics/Algebra and Functions/Solving Simultaneous Equations.* First, substitute the values for x and y into the equations. Then, solve the simultaneous equations $3m + n = 15$ and $3n + m = 13$. Use the first equation to solve for n: $n = 15 - 3m$. Substitute this expression for n in the second equation: $3(15 - 3m) + m = 13 \Rightarrow 45 - 9m + m = 13 \Rightarrow 8m = 32 \Rightarrow m = 4$. Only (B) has $m = 4$. You can double-check (B) by substituting $m = 4$ and $n = 3$ into one of the original equations.

44. (G) (p. 131) *Mathematics/Geometry/Rectangles and Squares.* The total length of all 12 of the small line segments is 24. Thus, the length of each small line segment is $24 \div 12 = 2$. So, the area of the square is $2^2 = 4$.

Alternatively, the four large segments total 24, so each large segment is 6 units long. Each of these segments is divided into 3 equal parts, so each part is 2 units long. The shaded area is bounded by a square with sides of 2. Therefore, the area of the shaded part is $2^2 = 4$.

45. (A) (p. 131) *Mathematics/Number and Quantity/Basic Arithmetic Manipulations.* Only (A) is not necessarily true: $|a - b| = -|b - a|$ only when $a - b = 0$.

Alternatively, substitute numbers for a and b. Only (A) does not hold true: $|3 - 2| = -|2 - 3| \Rightarrow |1| = -|-1| \Rightarrow 1 \neq -1$.

46. (H) (p. 131) *Mathematics/Geometry/Trigonometry/Trigonometric Relationships.* The arccosine is the inverse function of the cosine. For all inverse functions f and f', $f'(f(x)) = x$. Therefore, $\arccos\left(\cos\dfrac{\pi}{2}\right) = \dfrac{\pi}{2}$.

47. (A) (p. 132) *Mathematics/Algebra and Functions/Coordinate Geometry/The Coordinate System.* A reflection across the line representing $y = -x$ maps a point P with coordinates (x, y) onto point P' with coordinates $(-y, -x)$:

	(x, y)			$(-y, -x)$
A	$(-1, -2)$	$\rightarrow$	A'	$(2, 1)$
B	$(0, 4)$	$\rightarrow$	B'	$(-4, 0)$
C	$(3, -1)$	$\rightarrow$	C'	$(1, -3)$

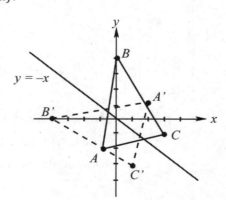

48. (G) (p. 132) *Mathematics/Geometry/Trigonometry/Determining Trigonometric Values.*
Visualize the graphs of the sine and cosine functions:

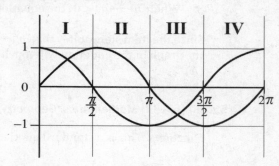

The two functions are equal only in the first and third quadrants, so the angle x can terminate only in those two quadrants.

Alternatively, recall that in quadrant I, at the coordinate $\frac{\pi}{4}$, both sine and cosine values are the same: $\frac{\sqrt{2}}{2}$. Now, look at the same relative coordinates in the other quadrants. In quadrant II, sine values are positive, but cosine values are negative. In quadrant IV, sine values are negative, while cosine values are positive. And in quadrant III, both sine and cosine values are negative and they are the same at the coordinate $\frac{3\pi}{4}$. Therefore, $\sin x = \cos x$ in quadrants I and III.

49. (C) (p. 132) *Mathematics/Algebra and Functions/Coordinate Geometry/Graphs of Quadratic Equations and Relations* **and** *Geometry/Properties of Tangent Lines* **and** *Circles.* The general form of the equation of a circle is $(x-h)^2 + (y-k)^2 = r^2$, where (h,k) is the center of the circle and r is its radius. The circle described in the question stem has a radius of 2 and has its center at $(2,-1)$:

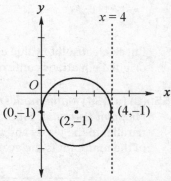

If a line of the form $x = k$ (a vertical line) is tangent to this circle, it passes through points $(0,-1)$ or $(4,-1)$.

50. (J) (p. 132) *Mathematics/Algebra and Functions/Manipulating Algebraic Expressions/Basic Algebraic Manipulations.* According to the binomial theorem, the last term in the expansion of a binomial having the form $(a+b)^n$ is b^n. Therefore, the last term of the expansion will be $(3y)^4 = 81y^4$.

51. (A) (p. 133) *Mathematics/Algebra and Functions/Coordinate Geometry/Graphs of Quadratic Equations and Relations.* The quadratic formula, $x = \dfrac{-b \pm \sqrt{b^2 - 4ac}}{2a}$, is used to find the roots of a quadratic equation having the form $ax^2 + bx + c$. The term $b^2 - 4ac$ is called the discriminant because it discriminates among three possibilities:

1. When $b^2 - 4ac = 0$, the equation has one root.
2. When $b^2 - 4ac > 0$, the equation has two unequal real roots.
3. When $b^2 - 4ac < 0$, the equation has no real roots.

Since the item stem states that $b^2 - 4ac = 0$, $ax^2 + bx + c = 0$ has only one root, which means the graph of the equation will touch the x-axis once at $y = 0$. This is true only for the graph in (A).

52. **(F) (p. 133) *Mathematics/Geometry/Trigonometry/Definitions of the Six Trigonometric***
Functions. This is a standard quotient identity: $\dfrac{\sin \theta}{\cos \theta} = \tan \theta$. This fact can be easily

derived. Given a right triangle with sides a and b and hypotenuse c, let θ be the angle

opposite side b. Since $\sin \theta = \dfrac{\text{side opposite } \theta}{\text{hypotenuse}} = \dfrac{b}{c}$ and $\cos \theta = \dfrac{\text{side adjacent to } \theta}{\text{hypotenuse}} = \dfrac{a}{c}$,

$\dfrac{\sin \theta}{\cos \theta} = \dfrac{b}{c} \div \dfrac{a}{c} = \dfrac{b}{c} \cdot \dfrac{c}{a} = \dfrac{b}{a}$. For θ: $\dfrac{b}{a} = \dfrac{\text{side opposite } \theta}{\text{side adjacent to } \theta} = \tan \theta$.

53. **(E) (p. 133) *Mathematics/Number and Quantity/Rates and Proportions* and *Geometry/Lines***
and Angles. Since 2π radians equals $360°$, use a simple proportion, putting the unknown in

the numerator: $\dfrac{x°}{360°} = \dfrac{\frac{3}{2}\pi}{2\pi} \Rightarrow x = \dfrac{\frac{3}{2}\pi}{2\pi}(360) = \dfrac{3}{4}(360) = 270$.

54. **(K) (p. 134) *Mathematics/Algebra and Functions/Solving Algebraic Equations or Inequalities***
with One Variable/Equations Involving Absolute Value. Since $|n| = n$ or $|n| = -n$,
$|2x - 1| = 2x - 1$ or $|2x - 1| = -(2x - 1) = -2x + 1$, whichever possibility is greater. Thus:

$$
\begin{array}{ccc}
2x - 1 = 3 & & -(2x - 1) = 3 \\
2x = 4 & \text{or} & -2x + 1 = 3 \\
x = 2 & & -2x = 2 \\
& & x = -1
\end{array}
$$

Check all absolute value equations or inequalities. Substituting the two solutions into the original equations confirms that both are actual solutions.

55. **(B) (p. 134) *Mathematics/Algebra and Functions/Coordinate Geometry/Distance and***
Midpoint Formulas. Since the two points have the same x-coordinate, the line segment is parallel to the y-axis and the midpoint will have an x-coordinate of 2. The y-coordinate of the midpoint is the average of the two y-coordinates. The midpoint formula is

$$(x_m, y_m) = \left(\dfrac{x_1 + x_2}{2}, \dfrac{y_1 + y_2}{2}\right), \text{ so } (x_m, y_m) = \left(2, \dfrac{5 + (-4)}{2}\right) = \left(2, \dfrac{1}{2}\right).$$

Alternatively, the line segment length is $5 - (-4) = 9$, half of which is $4\frac{1}{2}$. The y-coordinate of the midpoint is $5 - 4\frac{1}{2} = \frac{1}{2}$, which means the answer must be (B).

56. **(G) (p. 134) *Mathematics/Algebra and Functions/Coordinate Geometry/Slope of a Line.*** To find the slope, rewrite the equation in the form $y = mx + b$, where m is the slope and b is the

y-intercept: $2x + 3y - 2 = 0 \Rightarrow 3y = -2x + 2 \Rightarrow y = \dfrac{-2x + 2}{3} = -\dfrac{2}{3}x + \dfrac{2}{3}$, so $m = -\dfrac{2}{3}$.

PRACTICE TEST II ANSWERS AND EXPLANATIONS • 301

57. **(D)** (p. 134) *Mathematics/Number and Quantity/Basic Arithmetic Manipulations.*
Rationalize the fraction by using the conjugate to remove the radical from the denominator:

$$\frac{1}{\sqrt{3}-1}\left(\frac{\sqrt{3}+1}{\sqrt{3}+1}\right) = \frac{\sqrt{3}+1}{(\sqrt{3}-1)(\sqrt{3}+1)} = \frac{\sqrt{3}+1}{3+\sqrt{3}-\sqrt{3}-1} = \frac{\sqrt{3}+1}{2}.$$

58. **(J)** (p. 135) *Mathematics/Number and Quantity/Basic Arithmetic Manipulations.* Perform the
indicated operations: $(-2)^2 - 2^{-2} = 4 - \dfrac{1}{2^2} = 4 - \dfrac{1}{4} = 3\dfrac{3}{4}$.

59. **(A)** (p. 135) *Mathematics/Algebra and Functions/Solving Quadratic Equations and Relations.*
One way to find the roots or solutions of a quadratic equation of the form $ax^2 + bx + c = 0$

is to use the quadratic formula: $x = \dfrac{-b \pm \sqrt{b^2 - 4ac}}{2a}$. For $x^2 + 3x + 1 = 0$, the roots are

$\dfrac{-3 \pm \sqrt{5}}{2}$. The root given in the question stem has the "plus" form of the "plus or minus"

formula. Therefore, the other root will have the "minus" form.

60. **(H)** (p. 135) *Mathematics/Algebra and Functions/Coordinate Geometry/Graphs of Linear
Equations.* When a graph appears to be a "V" or a rotated "V," you should suspect that the
graph is an absolute value graph. One way to solve this problem is to examine each answer
choice to determine what the graph would look like. The graph of $y = x$ is a straight line
passing through the origin with a slope of $+1$. The graph of $y = -x$ is a straight line passing
through the origin with a slope of -1. The graph of $y = |x|$ will look like the graph of $y = x$
for all $x \geq 0$ and will look like the graph of $y = -x$ for all $x \leq 0$. That is the correct answer.

The graph of the equation $y = 2x$ is a straight line passing through the origin with a slope of
$+2$. The graph of $y = x^2$ is a parabola.

Alternatively, plug x-coordinates of points in the graph, such as $x = 4$ and $x = -3$, into the
equations in the answer choices. Only the equation $y = |x|$ will return values for y that
correspond to the graphed points $(4,4)$ and $(-3,3)$.

Section 3: *Reading*

1. **(D)** (p. 137) *Reading/Key Ideas and Details/Implied Idea.* The passage never specifically
describes the relationship between Turkey and the narrator, but it does suggest that it is an
employee/employer relationship. The narrator is judging Turkey in his professional capacity
and apparently has the authority to discharge him (if necessary), as shown in lines 83–84.

2. **(F)** (p. 137) *Reading/Key Ideas and Details/Implied Idea.* Turkey uses pen and ink and has a
bad habit of spilling ink during the afternoons. That is indicative of a copyist.

3. **(C)** (p. 137) *Reading/Key Ideas and Details/Implied Idea.* The explanation that Turkey
gives to the narrator for his eccentric behavior is age, (B), but the behavior is more than
coincidental. After his lunch, Turkey's face becomes a brilliant red, he becomes careless in
his work, and his behavior becomes erratic. All of these facts suggest the conclusion that
Turkey consumes alcohol at lunchtime, (C).

4. **(G)** (p. 137) *Reading/Key Ideas and Details/Implied Idea.* In the preceding paragraph,
Turkey asks the narrator to excuse his behavior on account of his age and reminds the
narrator that he too is growing older. (The narrator has said that he and Turkey are the same
age.) Thus, the "fellow-feeling" refers to the similarity of their ages.

5. **(D)** (p. 137) *Reading/Key Ideas and Details/Explicit Detail.* In the final paragraph, the
narrator decides to continue to employ Turkey, but resolves that he will deal with the
narrator's "less important papers."

6. **(G) (p. 137)** *Reading/Key Ideas and Details/Explicit Detail.* In the first paragraph, the narrator says Turkey's face veritably blazes "after twelve o'clock, meridian" during his lunch hour.

7. **(A) (p. 137)** *Reading/Key Ideas and Details/Implied Idea.* The narrator compares the increased redness of Turkey's face to dropping cannel coal on anthracite. Thus, the result is a more intense fire.

8. **(G) (p. 137)** *Reading/Key Ideas and Details/Implied Idea.* The narrator implies that although Turkey works well in the morning, his afternoon antics cause the narrator to feel uncomfortable. (H) and (J) are wrong because they are too weak and too strong, respectively. (F) is wrong because the narrator is not amused at all; indeed, he finds nothing funny about Turkey's behavior or his quality of work.

9. **(A) (p. 137)** *Reading/Key Ideas and Details/Implied Idea.* The narrator refers to Turkey of the morning as quick and steady and a valuable asset.

10. **(H) (p. 137)** *Reading/Key Ideas and Details/Explicit Detail.* This item contains a thought-reverser. (F), (G), and (J) are all mentioned as characteristics of Turkey's afternoon behavior. However, the narrator does not say that Turkey becomes lethargic in the afternoon, (H). Rather, he seems to become overly active.

11. **(B) (p. 138)** *Reading/Key Ideas and Details/Main Idea.* (B) is the best title for this selection: it discusses two different approaches to punishment—retributive and corrective. (A) is incorrect because it is basically concerned with the retributive punishment and not with corrective punishment. The answers represented by (C) and (D) are not at all appropriate to the subject of the selection.

12. **(J) (p. 138)** *Reading/Key Ideas and Details/Explicit Detail.* The last two sentences of the third paragraph clearly illustrate that the death penalty is a right of the murderer. The author's discussion of Hegel's views further substantiates this argument. (F) and (G) are in opposition to Hegel's views. (H), although a good answer and acceptable to Hegel, does not indicate the death penalty as a murderer's right and is therefore insufficient.

13. **(B) (p. 139)** *Reading/Key Ideas and Details/Implied Idea.* The author might have chosen to cite just the most frequently quoted version "an eye for an eye, and a tooth for a tooth" but instead goes further to refer to two other formulations of the concept. In doing so, the author makes it clear that the moral intuition underlying the doctrine is not restricted in time and place.

14. **(J) (p. 139)** *Reading/Key Ideas and Details/Application.* The philosophy behind corrective justice is one of treatment and rehabilitation, not death. (F), (G), and (H), although forms of varying degrees of punishment, do not result in death, so they would be consistent with the philosophy of corrective justice; therefore, they are wrong. (J) is the answer that should be selected, as the electric chair results in death and is therefore inconsistent with the philosophy of corrective justice.

15. **(C) (p. 139)** *Reading/Craft and Structure/Development.* In line 14, the author uses the Biblical expression "an eye for an eye" to show that the idea of justice as "a form of equality" (line 2) is expressed as early as in Biblical times.

16. **(J) (p. 139)** *Reading/Key Ideas and Details/Explicit Detail.* The answer to this item is clear from the last sentence of the first paragraph: "The punishment must fit the crime." A fair trial, (F), rehabilitation, (G), and separation, (H) are concepts associated with corrective justice rather than retributive justice.

17. **(B) (p. 139)** *Reading/Key Ideas and Details/Implied Idea.* The key is in the fourth paragraph (lines 48–51). None of the other answers are inferable from the passage.

Master Moves

Be on the lookout for "distractors." In item #22, (B) is an enticing answer because Vienna is mentioned in the passage. But this item is asking in which city the assassination which precipitated WWI took place, and the correct answer is (A), Sarajevo in Bosnia.

18. **(F) (p. 139)** *Reading/Craft and Structure/Implied Idea.* Denying the true self, (G), and accepting punishment, (J), are parts of the retributive justice code. Curing antisocial behavior, (H), is a means of enabling the criminal to act in his own best interests, so while (H) is true, (F) is the correct answer because it best embodies the notion of "normal" in corrective justice systems.

19. **(C) (p. 139)** *Reading/Craft and Structure/Voice.* The author aims to explain the differences between ancient and modern systems of justice.

20. **(J) (p. 139)** *Reading/Key Ideas and Details/Explicit Detail.* Lines 55–57 state the answer explicitly; the cause must be found before the treatment is administered, (J). A fair trial, (G), and a legal code, (H), do not apply to treating the criminal. Punishment, (F), is a last resort of the corrective justice system.

21. **(A) (p. 141)** *Reading/Key Ideas and Details/Explicit Detail.* The precipitating cause of World War I was the assassination of Archduke Francis Ferdinand, the heir to the Austro-Hungarian Empire throne, by a Serbian nationalist on June 28, 1914, as stated in the first paragraph of the passage.

22. **(F) (p. 141)** *Reading/Key Ideas and Details/Explicit Detail.* The assassination occurred in the city of Sarajevo in Bosnia.

23. **(C) (p. 141)** *Reading/Key Ideas and Details/Explicit Detail.* Before the outbreak of WWI, a balance of power had existed for almost a century, or 100 years. As stated in the first sentence of the second paragraph of the passage, WWI shattered the balance of power that had been established by the Congress of Vienna in 1815.

24. **(F) (p. 141)** *Reading/Key Ideas and Details/Explicit Detail.* Russia, the protector of Serbia, and Austria were members of competing alliance systems. When war broke out between them, the member states of their alliances were drawn into the conflict. Germany intervened on the side of Austria, its alliance member, and Great Britain and France joined forces with Russia, with which both countries were allied.

25. **(B) (p. 141)** *Reading/Key Ideas and Details/Explicit Detail.* The second paragraph describes how suspicions enkindled by the failure of diplomacy sparked the order to mobilize the Russian armed forces. German mobilization was ordered after the Russian order was issued.

26. **(F) (p. 141)** *Reading/Key Ideas and Details/Implied Idea.* A spirit of nationalism, not class solidarity, animated the people of the individual nation states that fought against one another in World War I. No longer did the upper classes of Europe act as a unified class. Instead, they joined with their compatriots of the middle and lower classes to wage war against people in other countries with whom they had once shared values, beliefs, and a way of life.

27. **(B) (p. 141)** *Reading/Key Ideas and Details/Explicit Detail.* The Nazi regime that came to power in Germany in 1933 and the regime of Stalin that tyrannized the Soviet people from 1927 to 1953 were ruthless dictatorships dedicated to world conquest.

28. **(J) (p. 141)** *Reading/Key Ideas and Details/Application.* The sense of futility felt throughout Europe during and after World War I would be evident in European literature of the 1920s, 1930s, and 1940s. It is a fair assumption that the literature of a particular period mirrors, as well as illuminates, the spirit of the age.

29. **(B) (p. 141)** *Reading/Key Ideas and Details/Implied Idea.* World War I and its aftermath suggest the idea that war feeds on nationalist sympathies. The sense of affront felt by the Austrian people when the heir to the throne of their empire was assassinated did not allow the Austrian leaders to adopt a moderate stance in their dealings with the government of Serbia (lines 10–12). The passage states that in the aftermath of the war, "national boundaries defined social consciousness" (lines 61–62).

30. **(H)** (p. 141) *Reading/Key Ideas and Details/Explicit Detail.* As noted in lines 4–5, Archduke Francis Ferdinand, as the heir to the Austro-Hungarian Empire, was a member of the Hapsburg family.

31. **(D)** (p. 142) *Reading/Key Ideas and Details/Explicit Detail.* Since Uranus "rolls like a ball along the path of its orbit" with the geographic poles located like axles on either side, one pole is always in direct sunlight and the other is always in darkness.

32. **(G)** (p. 143) *Reading/Key Ideas and Details/Explicit Detail.* According to the second paragraph, Uranus is warmer at its equator than the poles, even though the poles receive direct sunlight.

33. **(B)** (p. 143) *Reading/Key Ideas and Details/Implied Idea.* Because of the way Uranus rotates, one side is always in daylight and the other is always in darkness. A location on the daylight side is not necessarily near the magnetic poles, which lie in indirect sunlight near the planet's equator.

34. **(H)** (p. 143) *Reading/Key Ideas and Details/Explicit Detail.* A planet's equator is by definition located midway between the geographic poles. Since on Uranus these are on the sides of the planet, the equator must ring the planet from top to bottom.

35. **(B)** (p. 143) *Reading/Key Ideas and Details/Application.* The Uranian equator, ringing the planet from top to bottom, is located at the juncture of the planet's daylight and dark sides. An observer at the equator would most likely experience constant indirect sunlight.

36. **(H)** (p. 143) *Reading/Key Ideas and Details/Application.* Auroras appear near a planet's magnetic poles. On Uranus, these are near the equator and nowhere near the geographic poles, so the equator would be the most likely place to see auroras.

37. **(D)** (p. 143) *Reading/Key Ideas and Details/Implied Idea.* On Uranus, the daylight side receives varying amounts of sunlight at different latitudes. However, this appears to have no effect on atmospheric circulation, which instead flows along the equator around the top and bottom of the planet. Clearly, some other factor besides sunlight is in operation.

38. **(F)** (p. 143) *Reading/Key Ideas and Details/Explicit Detail.* The answer to this detail question is found in lines 55 through 79. The passage specifically states that Miranda's terrain has been shaped by geologic activity and that the planet may be geologically active even today, so (H) must be wrong. Then, the passage says specifically that there is no evidence of geologic activity on Ariel, so (G) and (J) must be wrong, making (A) correct. Indeed, the passage does not mention geologic activity on Umbriel.

39. **(C)** (p. 143) *Reading/Key Ideas and Details/Application.* (C) is the only possibility since the passage states that there is no evidence of geological activity on Ariel.

40. **(J)** (p. 143) *Reading/Key Ideas and Details/Explicit Detail.* The final paragraph states that the total number of moons is 27.

Section 4: Science

1. **(D)** (p. 145) *Science/Interpretation of Data/Analysis.* Consider the first column: the radii increase (0.37 Å, 1.52 Å, 1.86 Å, etc.) and the electronegativities decrease or stay the same (2.20, 0.98, 0.93, etc.) as one moves down the column.

2. **(F)** (p. 145) *Science/Interpretation of Data/Comprehension.* Remember that the second number means electronegativity. The greatest value shown is for fluorine (F): 3.98.

3. **(C)** (p. 145) *Science/Interpretation of Data/Comprehension.* According to the passage, bond length is the sum of the bonded atoms' radii. So for P-P, the bond length is $1.10 + 1.10 = 2.20$ Å.

4. **(J)** (p. 145) *Science/Interpretation of Data/Comprehension.* Carbon and nitrogen have the smallest electronegativity difference, 0.49.

5. **(D)** (p. 145) *Science/Interpretation of Data/Analysis.* According to the passage, ionic character increases as the difference in electronegativity increases. In the table, the difference in electronegativity between fluorine and the other elements in the table generally increases the farther the second element is from fluorine in both a different row and a different column.

6. **(F)** (p. 145) *Science/Interpretation of Data/Analysis.* Several choices include the value 0.46, which is the electronegativity difference in HI. Since At is below I, it may be expected to have an electronegativity below the value of 2.66, which is found for I, a prediction that leads to an electronegativity difference for HAt that is less than 0.46.

7. **(A)** (p. 146) *Science/Interpretation of Data/Comprehension.* Venus is only 0.05 units smaller in diameter than Earth (0.95 Earth diameters).

8. **(H)** (p. 146) *Science/Interpretation of Data/Comprehension.* One astronomical unit equals 1 inch in the scale used in Experiment 2. The poster board is only 28 inches long. Neptune's distance is 30 A.U. (30 inches) and would not fit on the paper.

9. **(D)** (p. 146) *Science/Evaluation of Models/Analysis.* As planets get farther from the sun (A.U. column), some are larger than Earth (Jupiter and Saturn have larger diameters), while others are smaller than Earth (Mars has a smaller diameter).

10. **(H)** (p. 146) *Science/Interpretation of Data/Application.* If the asteroids are 2.8 A.U. away from the sun, they would be found between Mars and Jupiter. Thus, an asteroid year is longer than that on Mars but shorter than that on Jupiter.

11. **(A)** (p. 147) *Science/Interpretation of Data/Analysis.* If the sun's diameter is 110 times greater than that of the Earth, its diameter would be $110\,(1\text{ inch}) = 110$ inches (Experiment 1 uses a scale where 1 Earth diameter = 1 inch). Therefore, its radius would be 55 inches.

12. **(H)** (p. 147) *Science/Scientific Investigation/Application.* The relative mass information given in the question is very similar to the order of planets based on their relative diameters (Table 1, Earth diameters column).

13. **(B)** (p. 149) *Science/Scientific Investigation/Analysis.* If carbon dioxide is the variable in question, all factors except carbon dioxide should remain fixed. Only then can the effects of various carbon dioxide levels be evaluated.

14. **(J)** (p. 149) *Science/Evaluation of Models/Analysis.* The only difference between Experiments 1 and 2 is that the concentration of leaf extract (containing a mixture of pigments) was reduced in Experiment 2. Using the lower concentration of pigments, the rate of photosynthesis leveled off, suggesting that the amount was inadequate to maintain the previously observed continued increase in rate.

15. **(A)** (p. 149) *Science/Evaluation of Models/Analysis.* The description of Experiment 3 states that certain wavelengths must be absorbed to maintain photosynthesis (which is measured by counting oxygen bubbles). The bubble counts (and therefore peak absorption) for Pigment A are at approximately 450 and 650 nanometers. For Pigment B, peak count is between 500 and 575 nanometers.

16. **(G)** (p. 149) *Science/Scientific Investigation/Analysis.* Since the reduced concentration of pigments in Experiment 2 led to a leveling off in bubble count, an increase in pigment

concentration should lead to an increase in the rate of photosynthesis and an associated increase in bubble count.

17. **(C) (p. 149)** *Science/Interpretation of Data/Comprehension.* In Figures 1 and 2, use a straight edge, such as the edge of your paper, and follow the graphs up from a light intensity of 4—the graphs indicate an oxygen bubble count of approximately 40 bubbles per minute.

18. **(J) (p. 149)** *Science/Scientific Investigation/Analysis.* Figure 3 shows that at 600 nm (orange light), both Pigments A and B show very little absorption/photosynthetic activity, as measured by the low oxygen bubble count. Since light must be absorbed to provide energy for photosynthesis, orange light would be least effective.

19. **(C) (p. 150)** *Science/Interpretation of Data/Comprehension.* The meters per minute scale increases from bottom to top. The highest point on the chart shows the fastest speed to be approximately 590–600 meters per minute for the 100 yard dash in 1962.

20. **(F) (p. 150)** *Science/Interpretation of Data/Analysis.* The lines represent the best-fitting slopes of points, which show how running speed has increased.

21. **(D) (p. 150)** *Science/Interpretation of Data/Comprehension.* In 1960, the speed for the 1 mile run was approximately 4 minutes/mile, while the speed for the 440 yard dash was approximately 3 minutes/mile. Therefore, the ratio is $\frac{4}{3}$.

22. **(H) (p. 150)** *Science/Interpretation of Data/Comprehension.* The speeds for the 2 mile run are all between 345 and 375 meters per minute. Since $375 - 345 = 30$, the gain in speed must be closest to the "30 meters per minute" choice.

23. **(A) (p. 150)** *Science/Scientific Investigation/Analysis.* This problem, requiring the right-hand scale, asks for an extrapolation beyond the given data. The 880 yard line, when extrapolated in the graph, crosses the 1980 axis at approximately 3.5 minutes per mile.

24. **(G) (p. 151)** *Science/Evaluation of Models/Analysis.* The results from Experiment 1 show temperature rising at an even rate during the time that the sample is heated.

25. **(C) (p. 151)** *Science/Evaluation of Models/Comprehension.* Experiment 1 starts above 0°C, whereas Experiment 2 starts below 0°C. In addition, the temperature in Experiment 2 stabilizes along the "x-axis" for a while.

26. **(H) (p. 151)** *Science/Evaluation of Models/Analysis.* The passage states that constant amounts of heat were added continuously to samples over a defined period of time. Assuming that all of these given conditions remain unchanged, (F), (G), and (J) can be eliminated. Therefore, another process is the best explanation for the flat part of the graph, since it is not a given condition. Also, the passage makes no mention of stopping time.

27. **(A) (p. 151)** *Science/Evaluation of Models/Application.* Ice melts at 0°C. This is the temperature at which the graph temporarily levels off.

28. **(G) (p. 152)** *Science/Evaluation of Models/Analysis.* The experiment utilized constant heating. Yet, temperature change was not constant. Therefore, heat and temperature are not the same thing.

29. **(B) (p. 152)** *Science/Scientific Investigation/Analysis.* At the two phase changes (0°C and 100°C), the graph should be flat, corresponding to the heat absorbed by the solid or liquid.

30. **(H) (p. 153)** *Science/Interpretation of Data/Comprehension.* An examination of the diagram reveals that primary tissue layers and primary germ layers are names for the same developing parts. This information is part of the description of the gastrulation stage.

31. (D) (p. 153) *Science/Interpretation of Data/Application.* The diagram arrows show the changes that occur as each developmental stage follows the previous one. The greatest amount of differentiation in structure and function occurs during organogenesis as the primary germ layers formed in gastrulation become the many specialized systems, organs, and related structures of the organism.

32. (F) (p. 153) *Science/Evaluation of Models/Analysis.* (G), (H), and (J) can be verified from the given chart. As for (F), under the organogenesis stage, arrows show that the body's bones develop from the middle primary germ layer (mesoderm), not the innermost layer (endoderm).

33. (C) (p. 154) *Science/Scientific Investigation/Application.* Structures (receptor cells) that contribute to visual abilities in the monkey would develop as parts of the eye, "a special sensory organ." The arrows show that parts of the special sensory organs arise from the ectoderm.

34. (G) (p. 154) *Science/Evaluation of Models/Comprehension.* The chart indicates that during the cleavage stage, the many new cells that form from the zygote and its materials do not grow. Thus, as the zygote's material is simply subdivided, the resulting cells must be extremely small.

35. (D) (p. 155) *Science/Scientific Investigation/Comprehension.* Hypothesis 1 states that, "[t]he reaction will adjust to the proportions given." Therefore, all proportions of reactants will be used. (D) does not follow this guideline.

36. (J) (p. 155) *Science/Evaluation of Models/Comprehension.* Hypothesis 1 simply states that any proportion of reactants may mix. It does not explain the relation of the amounts of reactants to the amounts of product produced by the reaction.

37. (B) (p. 155) *Science/Evaluation of Models/Analysis.* Hypothesis 2 states that a certain proportion of reactants will react; otherwise, one or another reactant will fail to react completely.

38. (F) (p. 155) *Science/Scientific Investigation/Analysis.* Hypothesis 2 states that both reactants must be in the appropriate proportions to be used in the process of forming more product, so adding more NaCl is the only way to use up the leftover $AgNO_3$.

39. (B) (p. 156) *Science/Scientific Investigation/Analysis.* Adding 2 moles of iron to 4 moles of oxygen is the only response that provides a ratio of iron to oxygen that is different from the two ratios that proved successful in the experiment.

40. (H) (p. 156) *Science/Evaluation of Models/Comprehension.* Hypothesis 1 only states that products contain the original elements.

SAMPLE ESSAY RESPONSES AND ANALYSES

Section 5: *Writing (p. 158)*

Above Average Response

Online activism can be a helpful way to engage with a social issue, depending on the situation, but supporting an issue online does not necessarily lead to change. Online support is truly activism when people's words have direct consequences, such as a journalist who can influence his or her readers or an organization that uses social media to fundraise. However, people who merely express support for a cause online without risking anything or devoting time to the cause cannot call themselves activists.

Expressing one's opinion online can be an effective way to generate support for a cause and can sometimes even put you at risk. It is hard to generalize about online activism because its use around the world varies so greatly. In repressive regimes that prohibit freedom of speech or of the press, online activism may be a courageous way to express or gain support for a cause. For example, during the Arab Spring, social media was crucial for generating support among youth. Recently, a blogger in Saudi Arabia was arrested and condemned to receive 1,000 lashes for promoting religious tolerance online. Even in countries like the United States where freedom of speech is promoted, expressing one's opinion online can still be a brave act for some. Someone might be ostracized for supporting gay rights in a homophobic community or for posting something about his or her faith in an anti-religious community. If one's words or actions online are intended to have consequences, that person is engaging in activism.

Online activism is also a useful tool for journalists or charity organizations to gain support for a cause. In the case of the blogger in Saudi Arabia, journalists worldwide published articles protesting the injustice of his punishment, and their readers spread information on social media. Because of international attention and pressure from foreign governments, the Saudi Arabian government said it would review the case. This is an example of how the viral nature of online information can influence important causes. Online activism can also raise money for charities. For example, in 2014, the ALS Association raised millions of dollars to fund research on the disease because of the "Ice Bucket Challenge" fundraiser on social media. Participants posted a video in which they dumped a bucket of ice on their head, and each participant nominated three other people to post their own video and/or donate to the ALS Association. This example shows how online activism can generate popularity in an entertaining way, yet support a serious cause.

Despite these cases of effective online activism, millions of people engage in "slacktivism," in which they express their support for an issue without causing change or risking any consequences for themselves. After a natural disaster, for example, someone may post an article about the tragedy on social media, but never donate or volunteer his or her own time to help the victims. One could argue that the "slacktivist" is raising awareness about an issue, but if the issue has already received media attention, posting an article about it does not make a difference. Internet users who post such articles might feel like better citizens by doing so, but if nothing is at stake in their actions, they cannot call themselves activists.

It is not easy to generalize about online activism because of the many forms it can take. However, internet users are truly activists if their words put them at risk or lead to direct action. People who merely repost information online have the right to express their opinions in this way, but they are not engaging in activism.

Ideas and Analysis: The writer develops a nuanced perspective on online activism, acknowledging that it is difficult to generalize about the subject because it comes in many different forms. The writer develops criteria to determine whether online "activists" are truly engaged in a cause: Are they taking a risk, or do they intend for their online actions to have consequences? The essay considers multiple points of view, but the writer's own viewpoint is consistent.

Although the writer does not adopt one of the three perspectives, he or she addresses them throughout the essay. For example, the first and second body paragraphs argue that online activism can cause change (Perspective 3), but only in certain situations (Perspective 2). The third paragraph acknowledges that there are many cases in which online "activists" make no difference and are not truly involved in a cause (Perspective 1).

Development and Support: The introduction states the thesis and previews the arguments that will support it. The writer presents these arguments in a thorough and logical manner with many supporting examples:

- The writer states his or her thesis in the first sentence of the introduction: Online activism can be a helpful way to engage with a social issue, depending on the situation, but supporting an issue online does not always make someone an activist. The essay could be stronger, however, if the writer began with a "hook" to grab the reader's attention and stated the thesis in the second sentence.

- The writer previews the main arguments of the essay throughout the remainder of the introduction.
- Each body paragraph begins with a clear topic sentence.
- The writer uses concrete examples to support each argument:
  - Body paragraph 1: The examples show how online activism can be just as risky as more traditional forms of activism, and the writer draws from current events, rather than only providing hypothetical examples. The paragraph could be stronger, though, if the writer elaborated on one or two examples rather than mentioning several examples.
  - Body paragraph 2: The writer chooses two very different examples, which is an effective way to show how online activism can work in a variety of situations.
  - Body paragraph 3: The writer uses a hypothetical example to show how online activism is not always effective. This paragraph would be stronger with a concrete, real-life example.

Organization:

- The writer previews the main ideas in the introduction and begins each body paragraph with a topic sentence.
- The writer uses transitions to begin new paragraphs. For example, the third paragraph begins with "despite" because it introduces an opposing idea.
- The writer organizes the main ideas in a logical order, in order to defend online activism in certain situations. The first two body paragraphs describe legitimate cases of online activism, while the last body paragraph acknowledges that not all online activists are truly engaged in the causes that they claim to support.

Language Use and Conventions:

- The essay does not have any mechanics/usage errors. As a result, the reader's attention is not distracted from the substance of the essay.
- The essay does not have any informal language.
- In the first body paragraph, however, the writer inconsistently uses "one" and "you": "Expressing **one's** opinion online can be an effective way to generate support for a cause and can sometimes even put **you** at risk."

Summary and Conclusions: The writer develops a nuanced viewpoint on the issue and incorporates all three perspectives into his or her argument. Even though the author examines multiple opinions, he or she maintains a consistent argument throughout the essay. The essay would likely receive a score of 10.

Below Average Response

Online activism is a useful tool because it raises awareness and gaining support for important causes. It is unfair to call this "slacktivism" because even though it is different than traditional forms of activism, it is still an important activity.

Sharing information online can make more people care about an issue. Information gets spread so quickly online, which makes it easier to gain the attention of thousands and even millions of people. By sharing an article about an event that happened in another country, you can make your friends aware of the issue. Then if they share the article, their friends can also read about the issue. This seems like the most efficient way to spread information.

Online activism is also useful because it shows when large amounts of people care about an issue. For example, when I signed an online petition for Congress, I saw that over 100,000 people had also signed it. When Congress sees that so many people care about that issue, will be more likely to listen to us. This would not be possible without a website where you could see how many people in your country or worldwide support a cause.

Online activism is also practical because you can become involved with many causes at once. If you are volunteering for a local cause, it takes up all of your time and you don't have time to learn about anything else. However, when I use the internet to learn about social causes, I can learn about what's happening in many places that are thousands of miles away from me. I feel more involved in the world this way.

As these situations show, online activism is a useful tool for raising awareness of issues and getting many people involved. With the internet, people care about a lot more issues than they used to.

Ideas and Analysis: The writer clearly states his or her opinion, and the body paragraphs all support this opinion. However, the writer does not take any opposing arguments into account. Students should know that it is possible to write an essay that firmly supports one side instead of developing a "compromise" position, but such an essay should mention the opposing viewpoint and argue against it.

Furthermore, the writer's analysis contains few concrete examples and is often weak. The main point of the third paragraph, in particular, is not logical. The writer seems to misunderstand the prompt and argues that learning about an issue while not taking any action is a form of activism.

Development and Support:

- The writer states his or her thesis in the introduction. However, the introduction does not preview the essay's main arguments.
- The writer should use more examples in the body paragraphs. The second body paragraph is the most effective, with the example of petitioning Congress. However, the first and third body paragraphs only use hypothetical examples or generalizations.
- The argument in the third body paragraph does not develop the essay or show, concretely, how online activism makes a difference. In fact, the writer's description in this paragraph is a perfect example of the "slacktivism" that Perspective 1 criticizes.

Organization:

- The writer should preview his or her main arguments in the introduction.
- Sometimes, the writer uses repetitive transitions. For example, both the second and third body paragraphs begin with "Online activism is also."
- The wording in the conclusion is too similar to the wording in the introduction. The writer should restate his or her thesis in the conclusion, but the wording should not be exactly the same.

Language Use and Conventions: The essay contains several weaknesses in this area:

- The essay contains some usage and mechanics errors.
  - Introduction: The first sentence does not use parallel verb structure: "Online activism is a useful tool because it **raises** awareness **and gaining** support for important causes." The sentence should either say, "Online activism is a useful tool because it **raises** awareness **and gains** support for important causes" or "Online activism is a useful tool for **raising** awareness and **gaining** support for important causes."
  - Body paragraph 2: "When Congress sees that so many people care about that issue, will be more likely to listen to us." This is not a complete sentence because it is missing a subject. The writer could say, for example, "When Congress sees that so many people care about that issue, **lawmakers** will be more likely to listen to us."
- The essay contains many examples of informal language. For example, in the third body paragraph, the writer says that he or she can learn about "what's happening" in many places. Instead, the writer should use a formal, more concrete word, such as "current events."

Summary and Conclusions: The essay has a clear thesis and three main arguments. However, the writer does not consider the opposing viewpoints in Perspectives 1 and 2, and the essay contains faulty reasoning and weak examples. This essay would likely receive a score of 5.

PRACTICE TEST III

MULTIPLE-CHOICE ANSWER KEYS

DIRECTIONS: For each <u>correct</u> answer, check the corresponding box. Then, total the number of checkmarks to determine the raw score for that test.

Section 1: English (Student Text, p. 161)

	Correct		Correct		Correct		Correct		Correct
1. C		16. J		31. B		46. H		61. D	
2. F		17. A		32. G		47. D		62. F	
3. C		18. H		33. B		48. G		63. B	
4. G		19. D		34. J		49. B		64. J	
5. B		20. H		35. B		50. F		65. C	
6. F		21. A		36. J		51. A		66. H	
7. C		22. G		37. D		52. G		67. A	
8. F		23. D		38. G		53. D		68. G	
9. C		24. H		39. A		54. G		69. D	
10. H		25. D		40. J		55. B		70. H	
11. B		26. F		41. B		56. H		71. C	
12. F		27. B		42. F		57. A		72. G	
13. D		28. F		43. A		58. H		73. D	
14. H		29. D		44. G		59. A		74. H	
15. B		30. J		45. A		60. J		75. D	

Raw Score: _____ /75

Section 2: Mathematics (Student Text, p. 175)

	Correct		Correct		Correct		Correct
1. D		16. G		31. A		46. K	
2. K		17. D		32. H		47. A	
3. C		18. F		33. D		48. H	
4. J		19. B		34. K		49. D	
5. E		20. F		35. E		50. G	
6. K		21. E		36. F		51. C	
7. B		22. F		37. B		52. G	
8. G		23. C		38. K		53. D	
9. D		24. G		39. B		54. K	
10. G		25. A		40. K		55. C	
11. B		26. H		41. C		56. G	
12. G		27. A		42. J		57. A	
13. E		28. H		43. D		58. F	
14. H		29. C		44. J		59. E	
15. C		30. K		45. C		60. F	

Raw Score: _____ /60

Section 3: Reading (Student Text, p. 194)

		Correct			Correct			Correct			Correct
1.	B		11.	B		21.	A		31.	C	
2.	J		12.	G		22.	J		32.	J	
3.	A		13.	C		23.	D		33.	A	
4.	H		14.	F		24.	G		34.	H	
5.	A		15.	D		25.	D		35.	A	
6.	J		16.	G		26.	G		36.	J	
7.	B		17.	D		27.	A		37.	B	
8.	F		18.	H		28.	H		38.	J	
9.	A		19.	B		29.	A		39.	D	
10.	F		20.	F		30.	H		40.	H	

Raw Score: _____ /40

Section 4: Science (Student Text, p. 205)

		Correct			Correct			Correct
1.	B		12.	G		25.	A	
2.	H		13.	D		26.	J	
3.	A		14.	H		27.	D	
4.	H		15.	A		28.	J	
5.	B		16.	F		29.	C	
			17.	C		30.	J	
6.	J		18.	G				
7.	A					31.	C	
8.	F		19.	D		32.	J	
9.	C		20.	G		33.	A	
10.	G		21.	C		34.	H	
11.	A		22.	J		35.	C	
			23.	A				
			24.	F		36.	H	
						37.	D	
						38.	G	
						39.	B	
						40.	G	

Raw Score: _____ /40

MULTIPLE-CHOICE EXPLANATIONS

Section 1: English

1. **(C)** (p. 161) *English/Conventions of Standard English/Grammar and Usage/Diction.* The original sentence is not idiomatic. "On account of" cannot be used as a substitute for "because of." (C) is the correct answer because it makes the needed correction. As for the other answer choices, (B) is wrong because "since" is a conjunction that can only be used to introduce a dependent clause; however, the material that follows is not a clause since it does not include a verb. As for (D), "for" can be a preposition; however, its meaning is not appropriate in this context.

2. **(F)** (p. 161) *English/Production of Writing/No Change.* The original sentence is correct. "Nonetheless" provides the meaning required in this context since it means "in spite of this." As for the other answer choices, (G) and (H) are wrong because the author means to say that smuggling grew in spite of government efforts (not because of government efforts). As for (J), "on the contrary" generally means "in opposition to what has been stated"; however, it does not provide the precise meaning ("in spite of this") that is required here.

3. **(C)** (p. 161) *English/Conventions of Standard English/Grammar and Usage/Adjectives versus Adverbs and Punctuation/Commas.* The original sentence contains two errors. First, an adjective cannot modify an adjective ("heavy timbered islands"). Only an adverb can modify an adjective ("heavily timbered islands"). Second, a comma is needed after "countless" ("countless, heavily timbered islands") to make it clear that "countless" modifies "islands" (and not "heavily timbered"). (C) is the correct answer choice because it makes both of these corrections.

4. **(G)** (p. 162) *English/Conventions of Standard English/Grammar and Usage/Diction.* The original sentence, (H), and (J) are all incorrect because they are not idiomatic. The correct idiomatic phrase is "well founded."

5. **(B)** (p. 162) *English/Conventions of Standard English/Grammar and Usage/Sequence and Verb Tense.* The original sentence is incorrect because "seize" (a present tense verb) is inconsistent with the past tense verbs used throughout the rest of the paragraph. Past events are being described here, so "seized" (a past tense verb) is the correct answer choice. As for the other answer choices, (C) and (D) refer to past events; however, they provide meanings that are inappropriate in this context. First, "were seizing" (a progressive past tense verb) implies an action that occurred over and over again in the past (e.g., "during this period, customs officials were seizing tons of wool each month"). Second, "have seized" (a present perfect tense verb) implies an action that began in the past but that also continues into the present (e.g., "the British have repeatedly seized our ships and continue to do so"). Neither of these meanings is appropriate here, so both (C) and (D) are incorrect.

6. **(F)** (p. 162) *English/Production of Writing/No Change.* The original sentence is correct. As for the other answer choices, both (G) and (J) are awkward and needlessly wordy compared to the original sentence. (H) is incorrect because it misconstrues the meaning of the original sentence. Specifically, the original states that the *Beaver* was seized because of a "technical violation"; in contrast, (H) says the *Beaver* was seized "for technically being in violation" of the law, which incorrectly suggests that the author believes the violation was minor or perhaps even non-existent.

7. **(C)** (p. 162) *English/Conventions of Standard English/Grammar and Usage/Diction.* The original sentence is incorrect because it includes an incorrect word choice. "Principle" is a noun which means "rule" or "belief," and it cannot modify the plural noun "articles." The word required here is the adjective "principal," which means "main" or "important." Therefore, (C) is the correct answer choice. As for the other answer choices, (B) is wrong for two reasons. First, it does not fix the original, incorrect word choice. Second, it introduces a

singular verb ("was"), which does not agree with the plural subject ("British wool, blankets, and liquor") of the sentence. (D) is also incorrect because it introduces a singular verb, "was," which does not agree with the plural subject of the sentence.

8. **(F) (p. 162) *English/Production of Writing/No Change*.** The original sentence is correct. "In fact" is used to introduce a sentence that illustrates or emphasizes a point made in the previous sentence. In this paragraph, the sentence about British wool being smuggled into the San Juan Islands illustrates the point made in the previous sentence—namely, that British wool was a principal article of illicit trade. So, "in fact" is correctly used here. As for the other answer choices, (G) and (H) are wrong for the same reason. "Furthermore" and "moreover" are used to introduce a sentence that includes an idea similar to (but that is not an illustration of) an idea from the previous sentence. In this paragraph, though, the sentence about British wool being smuggled into the San Juan Islands is an illustration of an idea in the previous sentence; so, both "furthermore" and "moreover" are incorrect answer choices. Finally, (J) is incorrect because "on the contrary" is used to signal that a contrasting idea will be introduced; however, the author does not introduce a contrasting idea.

9. **(C) (p. 162) *English/Conventions of Standard English/Grammar and Usage/Verb Tense*.** The original sentence is incorrect because it includes an incorrect verb form. A passive past tense verb ("was smuggled") is used earlier in the sentence, and another passive past tense verb ("and sold") is needed to agree with it. So, (C) is the correct answer choice. As for the other answer choices, they are all incorrect because they do not provide the required passive past tense verb.

10. **(H) (p. 162) *English/Conventions of Standard English/Grammar and Usage/Diction*.** The original sentence is incorrect because it sets up an idiom ("so much...that") but does not successfully complete it. (H) is the correct answer choice because it successfully completes the idiomatic phrase. As for the other answer choices, they are all incorrect because they do not complete the idiomatic phrase.

11. **(B) (p. 163) *English/Production of Writing/No Change*.** The original sentence is correct. In the sentence, there is a contrast between how settlers welcomed national control and how they resented the accompanying restrictions on trade. "Although" is the right word for introducing this type of contrast. As for the other answer choices, none of them would be appropriate for introducing the type of contrast discussed in this sentence.

12. **(F) (p. 163) *English/Conventions of Standard English/No Change*.** The original sentence is correct. The simple past tense verb ("welcomed") is consistent with the other verb in this sentence ("they were less amenable") as well as the other past tense verbs in the passage. As for the other answer choices, (G) is incorrect because it eliminates the only conjugated verb ("welcomed") in the clause; as a result, the sentence becomes a sentence fragment. (H) is wrong because "would welcome" is inconsistent with the past tense verbs in the paragraph. (J) is incorrect because it creates a completely illogical sentence; in short, an "assertion of national control" cannot welcome people.

13. **(D) (p. 163) *English/Conventions of Standard English/Grammar and Usage/Diction*.** The original sentence is incorrect because it includes an incorrect verb form. An active past tense verb ("They wanted") is used earlier in the sentence, and another active past tense verb ("but feared") is needed here to agree with it. So, (D) is the correct answer choice. As for the other answer choices, (A) and (B) are incorrect because "were fearing" is not an idiomatic expression; the correct idiomatic expression is "were fearful." (C) is incorrect because, although it uses the correct idiomatic phrase ("was fearful"), the singular verb ("was") does not agree with the plural subject ("they") of the sentence.

14. **(H) (p. 163) *English/Conventions of Standard English/Grammar and Usage/Sequence and Verb Tense and Diction*.** The original sentence includes two errors. First, the underlined portion includes a verb phrase ("might be resulting") that is awkward and needlessly wordy; it should be replaced by the more accurate and succinct verb phrase "might result." Second, the underlined portion includes a prepositional phrase ("in the losing of") that is non-

idiomatic; the correct idiomatic phrase is "in the loss of." (H) is the correct answer choice because it makes both of these corrections. As for the other answer choices, (G) is incorrect because it only makes one of these corrections. (J) is incorrect because a present tense verb ("results") does not suggest the element of uncertainty or contingency required here. Verb phrases such as "might result" or "would result" accomplish this task. However, a present tense verb ("results") does not.

15. **(B) (p. 163)** *English/Production of Writing/Organization/Passage-Level Structure.* The paragraphs need to be in chronological order. Therefore, (B) is the correct answer choice here. Paragraph 1 is first because it describes the earliest event (the opening of the customs office). Paragraph 3 is next because it describes events that followed (the settlers' concerns about the new office). Paragraph 2 is last because it describes events that occurred last (the Americans' concerns turned out to be true).

16. **(J) (p. 163)** *English/Production of Writing/Organization/Passage-Level Structure.* The author does not provide any quotations in the essay. So, (J) is correct. (F) is incorrect because the author describes or provides a narrative of several events. (G) is incorrect because the author gives specific examples in the essay. (H) is incorrect because the author provides statistics related to the production of wool.

17. **(A) (p. 164)** *English/Production of Writing/No Change.* The original sentence is the best choice. In comparison, the other answer choices are awkward and needlessly wordy.

18. **(H) (p. 164)** *English/Conventions of Standard English/Sentence Structure/Faulty Parallelism.* The original sentence is incorrect due to a lack of parallelism. All three verbs in the sentence ("step," "gaze," and "become") are governed by the first instance of "can," which establishes the present tense. It is unnecessary for another instance of "can" to appear in the sentence. However, the original sentence has an instance of "can" before "become." As a result, a series is created in which the elements are not parallel or do not have exactly the same form. (H) is the correct answer choice because it eliminates the problem and brings the third verb into line with the other two. As for the other answer choices, (G) is incorrect because a past tense verb ("became") destroys the parallelism needed here. (J) is incorrect because the verb ("becomes") does not agree in number with the subject ("anyone") of the sentence.

19. **(D) (p. 164)** *English/Conventions of Standard English/Sentence Structure/Comma Splices.* The original sentence is incorrect because it is a run-on sentence. A run-on sentence is two or more complete sentences joined together without the necessary punctuation or conjunctions. For example, the first clause in the sentence ("The same questions come to mind time and again") is a complete sentence by itself. For the sake of correctness and clarity, it would be best to put a piece of end-stop punctuation at the end of this clause and then start an entirely new sentence. (D) is the correct answer choice because it accomplishes this task. As for the other answer choices, (B) and (C) are incorrect because they also result in run-on sentences.

20. **(H) (p. 164)** *English/Conventions of Standard English/Sentence Structure/Misplaced Modifiers.* The original sentence is incorrect because it is too ambiguous. Specifically, "ending" seems to modify "suns"; however, the author intends for it to modify "island universe." The ambiguity is eliminated by replacing the ambiguous "ending" with the relative clause "that ends...." It is now clear that the relative clause modifies "island universe." So, (H) is correct. (G) creates the appropriate relative clause to modify "island universe"; however, the plural verb "end" does not agree in number with the singular noun antecedent of the relative clause ("island universe"). Finally, (J) is incorrect because it suffers from the same defect as the original; "ended" seems to modify "suns" rather than "island universe."

21. **(A) (p. 164)** *English/Conventions of Standard English/No Change.* The original sentence is correct. Standard written English requires the infinitive "to chart" in this context. (B) and (C) are incorrect because standard written English does not allow for participles ("charting" or "having charted") in this context. (D) is incorrect because it creates a sentence that is illogical and impossible to understand.

22. (G) (p. 164) *English/Conventions of Standard English/Grammar and Usage/Verb Tense.* The original sentence is incorrect because it includes an incorrect verb tense. The past perfect tense ("progress had been made") implies that progress was actually made *before* the twentieth century. Of course, the author intends to say that progress was made "in the twentieth century," so a simple past tense verb ("was made") is needed. Therefore, (G) is the correct answer choice. (H) is incorrect because a present tense verb form ("is made") fails to communicate that progress has already been made during the twentieth century. (J) is incorrect because a future tense verb form ("will be made") incorrectly suggests that progress has not yet been made at all.

23. (D) (p. 164) *English/Production of Writing/Strategy/Effective Transitional Sentence.* The original sentence is incorrect because it begins with a misleading introductory phrase. "As such" is a phrase which suggests a connection between two events or ideas. For example, "He is the head of security. As such, he helped develop the emergency response procedures." So, because he is head of security he helped develop the procedures. As for this particular sentence, though, it is certainly not the case that the Milky Way was so named because our solar system was discovered to be part of it. In fact, there is not a cause-and-effect relationship between the name of the Milky Way and our solar system's relationship to it. (D) is the correct answer choice here because it eliminates any suggestion that there is any relationship of this type. As for the other answer choices, (B) and (C) are both incorrect because it is not clear why the statement made is obvious or beyond doubt.

24. (H) (p. 165) *English/Production of Writing/Organization/Paragraph-Level Structure.* The original sentence is incorrect because the material in it belongs in the next paragraph. Therefore, the original sentence should actually be the first sentence of the following paragraph. It should then be immediately followed (i.e., without a break for a new paragraph) by the sentence that used to begin that paragraph ("Since they are so near..."). Both (H) and (J) make the required changes. However, (J) is incorrect because "As" would turn the sentence into a dependent clause that did not have a supporting independent clause. (H) does not introduce this error. So, (H) is the correct answer choice.

25. (D) (p. 165) *English/Conventions of Standard English/Punctuation/Commas.* The original sentence is incorrect because only a comma or a dash (and not a semicolon) should be used to separate an appositive phrase ("the 'crown jewels' of the southern skies") from the main part of the sentence. (D) is the correct answer choice because it provides the appropriate punctuation. As for the other answer choices, (B) also provides the appropriate punctuation. However, it improperly removes the quotation marks from "crown jewels." The phrase is an example of words that are used in an uncommon, unusual, or unfamiliar way (i.e., the galaxies are not literally jewels); as a result, the phrase needs to appear inside quotation marks. (C) is incorrect because a singular verb ("is") does not agree with a plural noun ("Magellanic Clouds").

26. (F) (p. 165) *English/Conventions of Standard English/No Change.* The original sentence is correct. As for the other answer choices, they are either not idiomatic or not grammatically correct.

27. (B) (p. 165) *English/Knowledge of Language/Style/Conciseness.* The original sentence is incorrect because the "to" in the underlined portion is unnecessary and makes the phrasing stilted. Both (B) and (C) make the needed correction. However, (C) is incorrect because a plural verb ("provide") does not agree with the singular subject ("galaxy") of the sentence.

28. (F) (p. 165) *English/Production of Writing/No Change.* The original sentence is the best choice. In comparison, the other answer choices are awkward and needlessly wordy.

29. (D) (p. 166) *English/Production of Writing/Organization/Paragraph-Level Structure.* (A), (B), and (C) are incorrect because the author does pose questions for these very reasons in the essay. (D) is the correct answer choice because the author does not promise that answers will be provided later in the essay to what are, simply, many unanswerable questions (i.e., How many stars are there? Where and how does the universe end?).

30. **(J)** (p. 166) *English/Conventions of Standard English/Grammar and Usage/Diction*. The original sentence is incorrect because it includes an improperly formed appositive. The final phrase in the sentence ("graduated of test pilot schools") is meant to be an appositive for "volunteer, military pilots." To properly form the appositive, simply rewrite the final phrase as "graduates of test pilot schools." (J) is the correct answer choice because it makes this revision. As for the other answer choices, both (G) and (H) are wrong because an appositive can be set off only by a comma or a dash.

31. **(B)** (p. 166) *English/Conventions of Standard English/Grammar and Usage/Subject-Verb Agreement* **and Diction.** The original sentence is incorrect for two reasons. First, a plural verb ("were") does not agree with the singular subject ("each") of the sentence. Second, the use of a present participle ("having") here is not idiomatic. (B) is the correct answer choice because it corrects both of these errors. As for the other answer choices, (C) does not correct the second error. (D) corrects both errors, but the past perfect "had been required" is inconsistent with the past tense verbs in the rest of the paragraph.

32. **(G)** (p. 166) *English/Knowledge of Language/Style/Idiomatic Expression*. The original sentence is incorrect because it includes informal usage. Specifically, it is not acceptable standard written English to use "got" when forming a passive verb form. Instead, use a form of the verb "to be" (e.g., "was," "were," etc.). (G) is the correct answer choice because it makes the needed correction. As for the other answer choices, (H) is a form of the passive voice; however, the past perfect "had been chosen" is inconsistent with the past tense verbs in the rest of the paragraph. (J) is incorrect for two reasons. First, the present perfect "has been" is not consistent with the past tense verbs in the rest of the paragraph. Second, a singular verb ("has") does not agree with the plural subject ("seven") of the sentence.

33. **(B)** (p. 167) *English/Production of Writing/Strategy/Appropriate Supporting Material*. The information contained in the parentheses explains why only seven astronauts were chosen. However, this information is not vital to the development of the passage. By placing the explanation in parentheses, the author signals to the reader that the information is not vital.

34. **(J)** (p. 167) *English/Conventions of Standard English/Sentence Structure/Comma Splices*. The original sentence is incorrect because it is a run-on sentence. A run-on sentence is two or more complete sentences joined together without the necessary punctuation or conjunctions. For example, the first clause in the sentence ("These men were true pioneers") is a complete sentence by itself. For the sake of correctness and clarity, it would be best to put a piece of end-stop punctuation at the end of this clause and then start an entirely new sentence. (J) is the correct answer choice because it accomplishes this task. As for the other answer choices, (G) and (H) are incorrect because they also result in run-on sentences.

35. **(B)** (p. 167) *English/Production of Writing/Strategy/Effective Transitional Sentence*. The topic of the second paragraph is the failures experienced during the early days of the Mercury space program. (B) is the correct answer choice because it provides the best signal to the reader that this will be the topic of the paragraph.

36. **(J)** (p. 167) *English/Conventions of Standard English/Grammar and Usage/Pronoun Usage*. The original sentence is incorrect for two reasons. First, the subject ("they") of the original sentence is too ambiguous. Who were "they"? The scientists? The pilots? The full scientific staff? It is not clear. Second, "fortunately" should be set off from the rest of the sentence by a comma. (J) is the correct answer choice because it eliminates both of these errors. As for the other answer choices, (G) is incorrect because it does not correct the first error. (H) is incorrect because "fortunately" is improperly placed in the sentence; as a result, it almost sounds as if "fortunately" were intended to modify "early."

37. **(D)** (p. 167) *English/Knowledge of Language/Style/Conciseness*. (A), (B), and (C) are all incorrect because they are needlessly wordy. (D) is the correct answer choice because it is succinct and to the point.

38. (G) (p. 168) *English/Production of Writing/Strategy/Appropriate Supporting Material.* When the author uses the word "spectacular" to describe a failure during a rocket flight, the reader is led to expect sensational, extraordinary, and quite likely terrifying details. However, as the author quickly points out, the details of this "spectacular" failure were instead quite mundane and pathetic. In short, after all the preparation leading up to the launch, the rocket only traveled two inches due to a circuit error. This is a classic case of irony, where there is a great incongruity or difference between anticipated and actual results.

39. (A) (p. 168) *English/Conventions of Standard English/No Change.* The original sentence is correct. Only an adverb ("relatively") can modify an adjective ("simple"). As for the other answer choices, (B) is incorrect because "relative" is intended to modify "simple" in this context; and, as stated above, only an adverb can modify an adjective. (D) is incorrect because an adjective cannot modify an adverb.

40. (J) (p. 168) *English/Conventions of Standard English/Sentence Structure/Faulty Parallelism.* The original sentence is incorrect because the underlined verb ("shutting") is not parallel with the other verb ("to ignite") in the sentence. (J) is the correct answer choice because it makes the needed correction ("to ignite and then to shut down"). As for the other answer choices, neither (G) nor (H) solves the original problem. In addition, (H) suffers from the further defect that "they" does not have a referent; in other words, it is not at all clear who or what "they" are.

41. (B) (p. 168) *English/Conventions of Standard English/Punctuation/Quotation Marks.* This is another example of irony. The rocket never really launched, and it never achieved true flight. In fact, as the passage tells us, the rocket only moved two inches. So, the quotation marks signal that the word "flight" is being used in a non-standard way.

42. (F) (p. 168) *English/Production of Writing/No Change.* The original sentence is correct. A new topic is being introduced (i.e., the role of animals in the Mercury space program), so a new paragraph should be started. As for the other answer choices, they are all incorrect because they do not introduce a change in paragraphs to signal the change in topics.

43. (A) (p. 168) *English/Production of Writing/No Change.* The original sentence is correct. In comparison with the other answer choices, it is the most concise and least awkward.

44. (G) (p. 169) *English/Conventions of Standard English/Grammar and Usage/Sequence and Verb Tense.* The original sentence is incorrect because it includes a verb tense error. The "delay" in picking up the spacecraft and the "leak" of water into the capsule belong to the same time frame. So, they should be expressed in the same verb tense. The "delay" is expressed in the past tense ("The pickup...was delayed"), so the "leak" should also be expressed in the past tense ("water leaked into the capsule"). For this reason, (G) is the correct answer choice.

45. (A) (p. 169) *English/Conventions of Standard English/No Change.* The original sentence is correct. As for the other answer choices, none of the other suggested positions for "unharmed" are idiomatic.

46. (H) (p. 169) *English/Conventions of Standard English/Sentence Structure/Fragments.* The original sentence is incorrect because "returning" is not a conjugated verb and, thus, cannot be the main verb of a sentence. (H) is the correct answer choice because it provides a conjugated verb that is consistent with the other past tense verbs in the paragraph. As for the other answer choices, (G) and (J) are incorrect because neither a present tense verb ("return") nor a future tense verb ("will return") are consistent with the past tense verbs in the paragraph.

47. (D) (p. 169) *English/Conventions of Standard English/Grammar and Usage/Sequence and Verb Tense.* The original sentence is incorrect because it includes a verb tense error. The question of how long an astronaut could tolerate weightlessness was unanswered at the time. So, a verb is required here that reflects that uncertainty. (D) is the correct answer choice because it provides the appropriate verb ("could tolerate"). As for the other answer choices, they are all incorrect because they do not supply a verb which suggests the degree of uncertainty required here.

48. **(G)** (p. 169) *English/Conventions of Standard English/Grammar and Usage/Diction.* The original sentence is incorrect because it includes language that is both superfluous and not idiomatic. Specifically, in the underlined portion, "like" is not grammatically required and also makes the sentence sound stilted. (G) is the correct answer choice because it eliminates this unnecessary word. As for the other answer choices, (H) and (J) are both incorrect because they introduce new language that is similarly superfluous and not idiomatic.

49. **(B)** (p. 169) *English/Conventions of Standard English/Grammar and Usage/Verb Tense.* The original sentence is incorrect because it includes a grammar error. Specifically, the underlined portion is an infinitive verb ("to have"). However, an infinitive verb cannot serve as the main verb for a clause. (B) is the correct answer choice because it supplies a main verb for the clause ("astronauts have…methods…") that is consistent with the verb tenses in the rest of the paragraph. As for the other answer choices, (C) is incorrect because the past perfect tense ("had had") suggests a sequence of events not supported by the meaning of the sentence. (D) is incorrect because the phrase "are sure to" is unnecessary before "have," and it creates a sentence that is not idiomatic.

50. **(F)** (p. 169) *English/Production of Writing/Strategy/Effective Concluding Sentence.* Over the course of the passage, the author emphasizes the successes of the Mercury space program and downplays its failures. (F) is the correct answer choice because it best reflects the general theme and argument of the essay.

51. **(A)** (p. 170) *English/Conventions of Standard English/No Change.* The original sentence is correct. As for the other answer choices, (B) is incorrect for two reasons. First, it omits a required comma; specifically, both the beginning and the end of an aside ("in any broad and real way") must be marked with a comma. Second, the phrase "of help" is simply not idiomatic or grammatically correct. (C) is incorrect because it too omits the required comma that is mentioned above. Finally, (D) is incorrect because the phrase "of helping" is not idiomatic or grammatically correct.

52. **(G)** (p. 170) *English/Knowledge of Language/Style/Conciseness.* The original sentence is incorrect because it is needlessly wordy. "And" and "also" mean the same thing, so it is redundant to include both. (G) is the correct answer choice because it replaces the redundant phrase ("and also") with "as well as," a phrase which means "and." As for the other answer choices, (H) is incorrect because "with" does not provide the meaning required in this context. (J) is incorrect because "as opposed to" signals a contrast between two ideas; however, the author does not intend to contrast two ideas.

53. **(D)** (p. 170) *English/Conventions of Standard English/Grammar and Usage/Sequence and Verb Tense.* The original sentence is incorrect because it includes a verb tense error. Earlier in the sentence, a simple past tense verb ("aided") is used. For the sake of consistency, another simple past tense verb ("emerged") should be used here. (D) is the correct answer choice because it is the only option that provides the appropriate verb form.

54. **(G)** (p. 170) *English/Conventions of Standard English/Grammar and Usage/Subject-Verb Agreement.* The original sentence is incorrect because it includes an error of subject-verb agreement. The plural subject of the sentence ("All aspects of medicine") requires a plural verb ("were enjoying"). (G) is the correct answer choice because it supplies the appropriate verb form. As for the other answer choices, (H) and (J) are incorrect because they do not supply plural verbs.

55. **(B)** (p. 170) *English/Conventions of Standard English/Grammar and Usage/Diction.* The original sentence is incorrect because it includes an expression that is not idiomatic. The correct idiom is "not only this but also that." (B) is the correct answer choice because it

provides the language needed to complete the idiom correctly. As for the other answer choices, (C) is incorrect because "not only this consequently that" is not a correct idiom. (D) supplies the correct idiom ("not only this but also that"), but it includes a new error. Specifically, the comma after "also" is illogical and grammatically incorrect.

56. **(H)** (p. 170) *English/Conventions of Standard English/Sentence Structure/Run-On Sentences.* The original sentence is incorrect because it is a run-on sentence. A run-on sentence is two or more complete sentences joined together without the necessary punctuation or conjunctions. For example, the first clause ("With somewhat more luck, the doctor could select the proper treatment") is a complete sentence by itself. Similarly, the following clause ("he could also mitigate the symptoms...") is also a complete sentence by itself. Usually, there are two ways to fix a run-on sentence. First, it could be divided into two separate and correctly punctuated sentences. Second, it could be fixed by supplying the punctuation and conjunction needed between the two clauses. Since neither option is offered here, review the answer choices for the best solution possible. (H) is the correct answer choice because it rewrites the underlined portion so there is only one subject in the sentence ("the doctor"); as a result, the sentence is no longer a run-on sentence. As for the other answer choices, (G) is incorrect because "but" signals a contrast; however, a contrast is not then introduced. (J) is incorrect because it creates a sentence where the verbs are not parallel ("the doctor could select...and can mitigate...").

57. **(A)** (p. 171) *English/Conventions of Standard English/No Change.* The original sentence is correct. The subjunctive verb form ("be available") is the appropriate verb form in this context. As for the other answer choices, (B) is incorrect because the past tense ("was available") is not required here. (C) is incorrect for two reasons. First, a present tense verb ("is available") is inconsistent with the past tense verbs in the rest of the paragraph. Second, "for" does not have the same meaning as "to"; as a result, the sentence becomes grammatically incorrect. Finally, (D) is wrong because "as" does not have the same meaning as "to"; as a result, the sentence again becomes grammatically incorrect.

58. **(H)** (p. 171) *English/Conventions of Standard English/Grammar and Usage/Sequence and Verb Tense.* The original sentence is incorrect because a present tense verb ("presupposes") is not consistent with the past tense verbs in the rest of the paragraph. (H) is the correct answer choice because it provides the past tense verb required here. As for the other answer choices, (G) is incorrect because the passive verb form ("it is presupposed") is inconsistent with the past tense verbs in the rest of the paragraph and also creates a sentence that is grammatically incorrect. (J) is incorrect for two reasons. First, a present tense verb ("presuppose") is not consistent with the past tense verbs in the rest of the paragraph. Second, a plural subject ("they") is not consistent with the singular subject ("it") used in the rest of the paragraph.

59. **(A)** (p. 171) *English/Production of Writing/No Change.* The original sentence is correct. A new topic is being introduced, so a new paragraph should be started. As for the other answer choices, (B) and (D) are incorrect because they do not introduce a change in paragraphs to signal the change in topics. (C) is incorrect because it results in a subordinate or dependent clause that does not have a supporting independent clause.

60. **(J)** (p. 171) *English/Production of Writing/Organization/Sentence-Level Structure.* The first three paragraphs are a general discussion of medical advances during the nineteenth century. The last two paragraphs are about a specific example of this progress. As for the first sentence of the fourth paragraph, it serves as a transition from the general discussion to a more detailed look at the specific example. So, (J) is the correct answer choice.

61. **(D)** (p. 171) *English/Knowledge of Language/Style/Conciseness.* The original sentence, (B), and (C) are all awkward and needlessly wordy. (B) and (C) also introduce grammatical errors into the sentence. (D) is the correct answer choice here because it concisely and clearly conveys the idea; in addition, it also does not introduce any new errors.

62. **(F)** (p. 171) *English/Production of Writing/No Change*. The original sentence is correct. The underlined portion is clear, concise, and contains no errors. As for the other answer choices, (H) is incorrect because it is awkward and needlessly wordy. (G) and (J) are both wrong because they incorrectly start a new paragraph—a new paragraph should not be started because this portion of the essay continues to be about Dr. Beaumont. (J) is also incorrect for the same reason as (H).

63. **(B)** (p. 172) *English/Conventions of Standard English/Sentence Structure/Problems of Coordination and Subordination*. The original sentence is incorrect because it includes a logical error. The conjunction "but" should only be used to introduce an idea that modifies or contrasts with another idea. For example, "It was sunny, but clouds were approaching." In this sentence, though, "but" introduces a clause ("for the next 10 years he conducted hundreds of experiments...") that in no way modifies or contrasts with the earlier part of the sentence. So, it is a logical error to use "but" here. (B) is the correct answer because "and" correctly signals that the following clause continues and elaborates upon information from the earlier part of the sentence. As for the other answer choices, (C) is incorrect because it creates a run-on sentence. (D) is incorrect for the same reason as (A).

64. **(J)** (p. 172) *English/Conventions of Standard English/Sentence Structure/Faulty Parallelism*. The original sentence is incorrect because it includes an example of faulty parallelism. The forms of "demonstrate" and "describe" have the same function in this sentence, and they should be expressed in the same or parallel verb forms. "Demonstrating" is a present participle, so the present participle of "describe" must also be used. Therefore, (J) is the correct answer choice. As for the other answer choices, (G) and (H) are both wrong because they do not create the required parallelism.

65. **(C)** (p. 172) *English/Conventions of Standard English/Grammar and Usage/Pronoun Usage*. The original sentence is incorrect because it includes an error of pronoun usage. The subject of the sentence ("Newborn babies") is a plural noun. So, any pronoun used in its place must also be plural. (C) is the correct answer choice because it provides the appropriate plural pronoun. As for the other answer choices, (B) and (D) are incorrect for the same reason as the original. (B) and (D) are also incorrect because they introduce singular verbs ("was" and "is") that do not agree with the plural subject of the sentence.

66. **(H)** (p. 172) *English/Conventions of Standard English/Grammar and Usage/Diction*. The original sentence is incorrect because it is not idiomatic. The correct idiom is "endowed with." As for the other answer choices, (G) is incorrect because it is not idiomatic in any context. (J) is incorrect because, although the phrase "endowed by" is idiomatic, it is not appropriate in this context. It would be appropriate in other contexts (i.e., "...endowed by their Creator with certain inalienable rights"), but it is not correct here.

67. **(A)** (p. 173) *English/Conventions of Standard English/No Change*. The original sentence is correct. As for the other answer choices, (B) and (C) both create run-on sentences. (D) is incorrect because it removes the subject ("This") of the second clause; as a result, the reader is left with a hybrid of the two sentences that is illogical, grammatically incorrect, and nearly impossible to understand.

68. **(G)** (p. 173) *English/Conventions of Standard English/Sentence Structure/Problems of Coordination and Subordination*. The original sentence is incorrect because it includes an error related to word choice. The author intends to say that an infant's cry causes two parallel reactions—a biological reaction as well as an emotional reaction. As the sentence is currently written, though, "including" illogically implies that the emotional reaction is a part or a component of the biological reaction. (G) is the correct answer choice because "and" is a conjunction that allows the reader to understand that the author is talking about two distinct and parallel reactions. Neither (H) nor (J) accomplishes the same task.

69. **(D)** (p. 173) *English/Production of Writing/Strategy/Effective Transitional Sentence*. The original sentence is incorrect because "unfortunately" has a meaning that is not appropriate here. In the last sentence of this paragraph, the author intends to make a statement that

summarizes the details provided earlier in the paragraph. The word "unfortunately" is only used when introducing information that contradicts or contrasts with earlier information. For example, "He is very handsome; unfortunately, he is also unfriendly." (D) is the correct answer choice here because the phrase "in fact" can be used to introduce an idea that complements or is related to earlier ideas. As for the other answer choices, (B) and (C) are incorrect for the same reason as the original.

70. **(H)** (p. 173) *English/Knowledge of Language/Style/Conciseness.* The original sentence is incorrect because the underlined portion is needlessly wordy. (H) is the correct answer choice because it clearly and concisely summarizes the underlined portion in one word. As for the other answer choices, (G) is incorrect because a past tense verb ("possessed") is inconsistent with the present tense verbs in the paragraph. (J) is incorrect for the same reason as the original; in addition, a plural verb ("are") does not agree with the singular subject ("the human infant") of the sentence.

71. **(C)** (p. 173) *English/Conventions of Standard English/Grammar and Usage/Verb Tense.* The original sentence is incorrect because it includes a verb tense error. A present progressive verb ("are guaranteeing") is used to describe and emphasize activity happening at this very moment. However, the author is speaking in broad terms about babies in general; the author is not talking about a specific baby and what that particular baby is doing at this very moment. (C) is the correct answer choice here because a simple present tense verb ("guarantee") is consistent with the other simple present tense verbs in the rest of the paragraph. As for the other answer choices, (B) is incorrect because a past tense verb is not consistent with the present tense verbs in the rest of the paragraph. (D) is incorrect because a singular verb ("guarantees") does not agree with its plural subject ("attributes").

72. **(G)** (p. 173) *English/Conventions of Standard English/Grammar and Usage/Diction.* The original sentence is incorrect because it is not idiomatic. The correct idiom required here is "whether *this*... or whether *that*..." The phrase "whether or not" is another English idiom, but its use here is not appropriate. As for the other answer choices, (H) and (J) are both incorrect because "whether if" is not idiomatic in any context.

73. **(D)** (p. 173) *English/Conventions of Standard English/Sentence Structure/Fragments.* The original sentence is incorrect because the period after "infant" turns the first clause into a dependent clause without a supporting independent clause; in other words, it turns the dependent clause into a sentence fragment. (D) is the correct answer choice because it connects the initial dependent clause to a supporting independent clause, combines them in one sentence, and does so without introducing any grammatical or punctuation errors. As for the other answer choices, (B) and (C) are incorrect for the same reason as the original.

74. **(H)** (p. 174) *English/Production of Writing/Organization/Sentence-Level Structure.* The final sentence summarizes the author's main point in an emphatic way. So, (H) is the correct answer choice. As for the other answer choices, they are all incorrect because they are simply not true.

75. **(D)** (p. 174) *English/Production of Writing/Organization/Passage-Level Structure.* The passage is an argument. The author makes a claim (i.e., newborn infants are not passive creatures) and then supports the claim with several examples of how newborn infants actively engage with their worlds and their caregivers. So, (D) is the correct answer choice. As for the other answer choices, (A) is incorrect for two reasons: first, the author does not provide contrasting information in an attempt to disprove the main argument; second, the author does not supply any anecdotes or specific stories. (B) is incorrect because this essay is not a narrative or story filled with examples or anecdotes about specific newborn infants. Finally, (C) is incorrect because the author never uses statistics.

Section 2: Mathematics

1. **(D)** (p. 175) *Mathematics/Statistics and Probability/Counting Methods.* Since there is a restriction on the placement of the circle, the counting principal must be modified. Four shapes can be placed as normal, so the total number of arrangements including only these four shapes is $4! = 4 \cdot 3 \cdot 2 \cdot 1 = 24$. The restriction on the circle limits it to the three center places, so there are a total of $24 \cdot 3 = 72$ different arrangements of the five shapes that meet the stated condition.

2. **(K)** (p. 175) *Mathematics/Algebra and Functions/Evaluating, Interpreting, and Creating Algebraic Functions/Functions as Models.* Let J be John's age and P be Pat's age. John is three times as old as Pat: $J = 3P$. In four years, John's age will be $x = J + 4$. Substitute $3P$ for J and solve for P: $x = 3P + 4 \Rightarrow x - 4 = 3P \Rightarrow \dfrac{x - 4}{3} = P$.

   Alternatively, plug in numbers: if Pat is 9 years old, then John is 27 years old; in 4 years, John will be 31. "Test-the-test" by plugging 31 into the given formulas to produce an answer of 9—only (K) works.

3. **(C)** (p. 176) *Mathematics/Algebra and Functions/Manipulating Algebraic Expressions/Evaluating Expressions.* If $\dfrac{3}{4}$ of x equals 36, then $\dfrac{3}{4}x = 36 \Rightarrow x = 36 \cdot \dfrac{4}{3} = 48$ and $\dfrac{1}{3}x = \dfrac{1}{3}(48) = 16$.

4. **(J)** (p. 176) *Mathematics/Geometry/Lines and Angles.* The measure of the unlabeled angle in the top triangle is 90°. The angle vertically opposite it in the bottom triangle is also equal to 90°. Since the angles of a triangle sum to 180°, $x + y + 90 = 180$ and $x + y = 90$.

5. **(E)** (p. 176) *Mathematics/Number and Quantity/Properties of Numbers.* There are two ways to attack this question. One is to reason as follows:

   A. $2 + n$ cannot be a multiple of 3: since n is a multiple of 3, when $2 + n$ is divided by 3 there will be a remainder of 2.
   B. $2 - n$ cannot be a multiple of 3: since n is a multiple of 3, when $2 - n$ is divided by 3 there will be a remainder of 1.
   C. $2n - 1$ cannot be a multiple of 3: since n is a multiple of 3, $2n$ will also be a multiple of 3, and $2n - 1$ cannot be a multiple of 3.
   D. $2n + 1$ cannot be a multiple for the same reason that $2n - 1$ cannot be a multiple of 3.
   E. $2n + 3$ is a multiple of 3: $2n$ is a multiple of 3; 3 is a multiple of 3; thus, $2n + 3$ is a multiple of 3.

   Alternatively, substitute an assumed value into the choices. For example, let $n = 3$:

   A. $2 + n = 2 + 3 = 5$ ✘ (not a multiple of 3)
   B. $2 - n = 2 - 3 = -1$ ✘ (not a multiple of 3)
   C. $2n - 1 = 2(3) - 1 = 6 - 1 = 5$ ✘ (not a multiple of 3)
   D. $2n + 1 = 2(3) + 1 = 6 + 1 = 7$ ✘ (not a multiple of 3)
   E. $2n + 3 = 2(3) + 3 = 6 + 3 = 9$ ✓ (a multiple of 3)

6. **(K)** (p. 176) *Mathematics/Number and Quantity/Rates and Proportions.* A ratio is just another way of writing a fraction. Simply inspect each of the answer choices. As for (F), $\left(\dfrac{1}{5}\right)^2$ is equal to $\dfrac{1}{25}$, and both 1 and 25 are whole numbers. Choice (G) is not the correct because

5% can be written as $\dfrac{5}{100}$, or $\dfrac{1}{20}$, which is a ratio of two whole numbers. As for (H), $\dfrac{1}{5}$ is the ratio of 1 to 5, so (H) is a ratio of two whole numbers. As for (J), 0.25 is equal to $\dfrac{1}{4}$, the ratio of two whole numbers. Only (K) is not a ratio of two whole numbers.

7. **(B) (p. 177) *Mathematics/Geometry/Rectangles and Squares.*** Let L equal the length and W equal the width of each playing card. The area of the large rectangle is equal to the sum of the areas of the nine playing cards: $\text{area}_{\text{rectangle}} = 9(\text{area}_{\text{card}}) \Rightarrow 180 = 9(LW) \Rightarrow LW = 20$. Both $5W$ and $4L$ are equal to the length of the large rectangle, and $L + W$ is equal to its width: $\text{area}_{\text{rectangle}} = (\text{length}_{\text{rectangle}})(\text{width}_{\text{rectangle}}) \Rightarrow 180 = (5W)(L+W) = 5LW + 5W^2 \Rightarrow LW + W^2 = 36 \Rightarrow W^2 = 36 - 20 \Rightarrow W = \sqrt{16} = 4$.

    Since $5W = 4L$, $L = 5$. Therefore, the perimeter of the large rectangle is
    $2[5W + (L+W)] = 2(20 + 9) = 58$.

8. **(G) (p. 177) *Mathematics/Number and Quantity/Rates and Proportions* and *Algebra and Functions/Evaluating, Interpreting, and Creating Algebraic Functions* and *Solving Simultaneous Equations.*** Let t be the train's scheduled arrival time. If the train travels at 40 mph (and arrives 10 minutes late), the journey takes $t + \dfrac{10}{60} = t + \dfrac{1}{6}$ hours; if it travels at 30 mph (and arrives 16 minutes late), the journey takes $t + \dfrac{16}{60} = t + \dfrac{4}{15}$ hours. Since the distance traveled is the same in each case, write an equation

    equating the two distances, where the distances are written in terms of the travel time and the train speed. When formulating the equation, make sure that the units on each side of the equality are equivalent and that the final answer will be in miles:

    $$\left(\frac{40 \text{ miles}}{\text{hour}}\right)\left(t + \frac{1}{6} \text{ hours}\right) = \left(\frac{30 \text{ miles}}{\text{hour}}\right)\left(t + \frac{4}{15} \text{ hours}\right) \Rightarrow 40t + \frac{40}{6} = 30t + \frac{30 \cdot 4}{15} \Rightarrow$$

    $10t = \dfrac{120}{15} - \dfrac{40}{6} = 1\dfrac{1}{3}$ hours $= 80$ minutes $\Rightarrow t = 8$ minutes. Distance is equal to the product

    of speed and time, so use either train's speed and the total time that train traveled: $d = \left(\dfrac{40 \text{ miles}}{\text{hour}}\right)\left(\dfrac{8}{60} + \dfrac{10}{60} \text{ hour}\right) = (40 \text{ miles})\left(\dfrac{18}{60}\right) = 12 \text{ miles}$.

9. **(D) (p. 177) *Mathematics/Algebra and Functions/Manipulating Algebraic Expressions/ Factoring Expressions.*** The coefficients are 3, 6, and 2: 1 is the only common factor of those numbers. The smallest term containing the variable x is simply x. The same is true for the terms containing y and z. Therefore, the greatest common factor is xyz.

10. **(G) (p. 177) *Mathematics/Number and Quantity/Properties of Numbers.*** The sum of $3k$, $4k$, $5k$, $6k$, and $7k$ is $25k$, which is divisible by 7 if the value of k is divisible by 7. If, however, the coefficient of k were divisible by 7, then that number would be divisible by 7 regardless of the value of k. Dropping the term $4k$ from the group, the sum of the remaining terms is $21k$. Since 21 is divisible by 7, $21k$ will be divisible by 7, regardless of the value of k.

11. **(B) (p. 178) *Mathematics/Number and Quantity/Properties of Numbers.*** Rewrite $\dfrac{1}{3}$ and $\dfrac{3}{8}$ with a common denominator of 24: $\dfrac{3}{24} < x < \dfrac{9}{24}$. This eliminates (C), (D), and (E) because the answer choices are arranged in increasing order. To decide between (A) and (B), notice that $\dfrac{17}{48} = \dfrac{8.5}{24}$. Therefore, (B) is between $\dfrac{1}{3}$ and $\dfrac{3}{8}$.

Alternatively, use a benchmark or approximate to eliminate the wrong answer choices. First, eliminate (E): $\frac{1}{2}$ is more than $\frac{3}{8}$. Next, eliminate (A): $\frac{3}{15}$ is equal to $\frac{1}{3}$, so $\frac{3}{16}$ is smaller than $\frac{1}{3}$. As for (C), $\frac{9}{24}$ is equal to $\frac{3}{8}$, not less than $\frac{3}{8}$. As for (D), $\frac{5}{12}$ is equal to $\frac{10}{24}$, and $\frac{3}{8}$ is equal to $\frac{9}{24}$. Only (B) is a possible value for x: $\frac{17}{48}$ is close to and slightly less than $\frac{18}{48} = \frac{3}{8}$. You can also use your calculator to evaluate and compare the fractions.

12. **(G) (p. 178)** *Mathematics/Algebra and Functions/Manipulating Algebraic Expressions/ Factoring Expressions.* Simply factor the expression as the difference of two squares: $x^2 - y^2 = (x+y)(x-y) = 3$. Since $x - y = 3$, then $(x+y)(3) = 3 \Rightarrow x+y = 1$.

13. **(E) (p. 178)** *Mathematics/Number and Quantity/Properties of Numbers.* As for (A), whether $n+1$ is odd or even will depend on whether n is odd or even. The same is true for (B) and (C) since whether $3n$ is odd or even will depend on whether n is odd or even. As for (D), n^2 will be odd or even depending on whether n is odd or even. However, (E) is even regardless of whether n is odd or even: $n^2 + n$ can be factored as $n(n+1)$, and since either n or $n+1$ is even, the product must be even.

14. **(H) (p. 178)** *Mathematics/Geometry/Complex Figures* and *Rectangles and Squares* and *Circles.* For any square with a side of x, the diagonal of that square is equal to $x\sqrt{2}$. Since the square has an area of 16, it has a side of 4 and a diagonal of $4\sqrt{2}$. The diagonal of the square is also the diameter of the circle. Therefore, the circle has a diameter of $4\sqrt{2}$ and a radius of $2\sqrt{2}$. Finally, a circle with a radius of length $2\sqrt{2}$ has an area of $\pi r^2 = \pi(2\sqrt{2})^2 = 8\pi$.

15. **(C) (p. 178)** *Mathematics/Number and Quantity/Percentages.* First, calculate the sale price of the CD player that Ellen bought: $\$120 - (25\% \text{ of } \$120) = \$120 - (0.25 \cdot \$120) = \$120 - \$30 = \$90$. Next, calculate the sales tax: 8% of $90 is $0.08 \cdot \$90 = \$7.20$. Therefore, the total price was $\$90 + \$7.20 = \$97.20$.

16. **(G) (p. 179)** *Mathematics/Number and Quantity/Percentages.* Use the "is-over-of" equation. The "of," which is the denominator of the fraction, is the mixture. There is a total of $2.5 + 12.5 = 15$ kilograms of mixture. The word "is," which is the numerator of the fraction, is the 2.5 kilograms of gravel. Thus, $\frac{\text{is}}{\text{of}} = \frac{\%}{100} \Rightarrow \frac{2.5}{15} = \frac{\%}{100} \Rightarrow \frac{250}{15} = 16\frac{2}{3}\%$.

17. **(D) (p. 179)** *Mathematics/Geometry/Triangles/Properties of Triangles.* The resulting triangle has sides of 6, 8, and 10 (multiples of 3, 4, and 5), so it's a right triangle. The sides of 6 and 8 form the right angle, so they can be used as altitude and base for finding the area: $\text{area}_{\text{triangle}} = \frac{1}{2} \cdot \text{altitude} \cdot \text{base} = \frac{1}{2} \cdot 6 \cdot 8 = 24$.

18. **(F) (p. 179)** *Mathematics/Number and Quantity/Rates and Proportions.* First, determine the amount of fuel used by Motorcycle A using a direct proportion: $\frac{\text{Fuel Used } X}{\text{Fuel Used } Y} = \frac{\text{Kilometers Driven } X}{\text{Kilometers Driven } Y} \Rightarrow \frac{1}{x} = \frac{40}{300} \Rightarrow 40x = 300 \Rightarrow x = 7.5$. Thus, Motorcycle A uses 7.5 liters of fuel for the 300-kilometer trip. Now, do the same for Motorcycle B: $\frac{1}{x} = \frac{50}{300} \Rightarrow 50x = 300 \Rightarrow x = 6$. Therefore, Motorcycle B uses 6 liters. Since Motorcycle

A uses $7.5 - 6 = 1.5$ liters more than Motorcycle B, the fuel for Motorcycle A costs an additional $1.5 \text{ liters} \cdot \dfrac{\$2}{\text{liter}} = \$3$.

19. **(B) (p. 180)** *Mathematics/Algebra and Functions/Evaluating, Interpreting, and Creating Algebraic Functions/Function Notation.* First, substitute 3 for x in $f(x)$: $f(3) = 3^2 - 2(3) + 1 = 9 - 6 + 1 = 4$. Now, substitute 4 for x in $f(x)$: $f(4) = 4^2 - 2(4) + 1 = 16 - 8 + 1 = 9$. Therefore, $f(f(3)) = 9$.

20. **(F) (p. 180)** *Mathematics/Algebra and Functions/Manipulating Algebraic Expressions/Factoring Expressions.* Apply the given definition for the factorial, !, to both the numerator and the denominator: $\dfrac{N!}{(N-2)!} = \dfrac{N(N-1)(N-2)(N-3)(N-4)\ldots[N-(N-1)]}{(N-2)(N-3)(N-4)\ldots[N-(N-1)]}$.

Canceling like factors in the numerator and the denominator leaves only $\dfrac{N(N-1)}{1} = N(N-1) = N^2 - N$.

21. **(E) (p. 180)** *Mathematics/Algebra and Functions/Evaluating, Interpreting, and Creating Algebraic Functions/Functions as Models.* The formula will be x, the cost for the first ounce, plus an expression to represent the additional postage for each additional ounce over the first ounce. The postage for the additional weight is y cents per ounce, and the additional weight is w minus the first ounce, or $w - 1$. Therefore, the additional postage is $y(w-1)$, and the total postage is $x + y(w-1)$.

Alternatively, assume some numbers. For ease of calculations, assume that the first ounce costs 1 cent and every additional ounce is 2 cents. If $x = 1$ and $y = 2$, then a letter of, for example, 3 ounces ($w = 3$) will cost $1 + 2(2) = 5$ cents. Substitute these values for x, y, and w into the answer choices and the correct choice will return the value 5:

A. $w(x+y) = 3(1+2) = 3(3) = 9$ ✗
B. $x(w-y) = 1(3-2) = 1(1) = 1$ ✗
C. $x(x-1) + y(w-1) = 1(1-1) + 2(3-1) = 1(0) + 2(2) = 4$ ✗
D. $x + wy = 1 + 3(2) = 7$ ✗
E. $x + y(w-1) = 1 + 2(3-1) = 1 + 2(2) = 5$ ✓

22. **(F) (p. 180)** *Mathematics/Number and Quantity/Basic Arithmetic Manipulations.* Apply the absolute value function: $|-3| = 3$, $|2| = 2$, and $\left|-\dfrac{1}{2}\right| = \dfrac{1}{2}$. Therefore, $|-3| \cdot |2| \cdot \left|-\dfrac{1}{2}\right| + (-4) = 3 \cdot 2 \cdot \dfrac{1}{2} - 4 = 3 - 4 = -1$.

23. **(C) (p. 181)** *Mathematics/Geometry/Complex Figures* and *Rectangles and Squares* and *Circles.* The side of the square is also the radius of the circle. Since the square has an area of 2, $s^2 = 2 \Rightarrow s = \sqrt{2}$ (distances are positive), and $\sqrt{2}$ is the radius of the circle. Therefore, the area of the circle is $\pi r^2 = \pi\left(\sqrt{2}\right)^2 = 2\pi$.

24. **(G) (p. 181)** *Mathematics/Number and Quantity/Properties of Numbers.* Test each statement. As for statement (I), the product of 2 (the first prime number) and any other number must be even. Thus, (I) is not part of the correct answer. As for (II), the sum of two prime numbers might be odd (e.g., $2 + 3 = 5$), but the sum of two prime numbers might also be even (e.g., $3 + 5 = 8$). As for (III), however, the product of two odd numbers is necessarily odd.

25. **(A)** (p. 181) *Mathematics/Algebra and Functions/Evaluating, Interpreting, and Creating Algebraic Functions/Functions as Models* and *Coordinate Geometry/The Coordinate System* and *Geometry/Rectangles and Squares*. The coordinates establish that the shaded part of the figure is a rectangle. The width of the rectangle is a, and the length is $b - a$. Therefore, the area is $a(b - a)$.

Alternatively, "test-the-test," assuming that $a = 2$ and $b = 4$. The rectangle has a width of 2, a length of $4 - 2 = 2$, and an area of $2 \cdot 2 = 4$. Substitute 2 for a and 4 for b into the answer choices and the correct formula will yield 4.

26. **(H)** (p. 182) *Mathematics/Number and Quantity/Basic Arithmetic Manipulations*. Perform the indicated operations: $\sqrt{(43 - 7)(29 + 7)} = \sqrt{(36)(36)} = 36$.

27. **(A)** (p. 182) *Mathematics/Number and Quantity/Rates and Proportions*. Set up a direct proportion and solve for the unknown value:

$$\frac{\text{Cement } X}{\text{Cement } Y} = \frac{\text{Grit } X}{\text{Grit } Y} \Rightarrow \frac{4}{50} = \frac{20}{x} \Rightarrow 4x = (20)(50) \Rightarrow x = \frac{(20)(50)}{4} = 250.$$

28. **(H)** (p. 182) *Mathematics/Geometry/Lines and Angles*. Label the other two angles in the triangle:

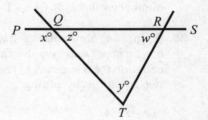

Therefore, $x + z = 180 \Rightarrow 150 + z = 180 \Rightarrow z = 30$. Furthermore, since $\overline{QT} = \overline{QR}$, $y = w$, and $w + y + z = 180 \Rightarrow 30 + y + y = 180 \Rightarrow 2y = 150 \Rightarrow y = 75$.

29. **(C)** (p. 182) *Mathematics/Algebra and Functions/Manipulating Algebraic Expressions/Basic Algebraic Manipulations*. There is only one equation but two variables, so x and y cannot be solved for individually. Instead, look for a way to rewrite the first equation to give the information needed: $\frac{x}{y} = -1 \Rightarrow x = -y \Rightarrow x + y = 0$.

30. **(K)** (p. 183) *Mathematics/Statistics and Probability/Data Representation/Tables* and *Number and Quantity/Rates and Proportions*. Set up the cost per yard of each fabric as a decimal and compare the decimals directly:

F. $\dfrac{\$8}{3 \text{ yd.}} \approx \$2.67/\text{yd.}$

G. $\dfrac{\$6}{2 \text{ yd.}} = \$3/\text{yd.}$

H. $\dfrac{\$9}{4 \text{ yd.}} = \$2.25/\text{yd.}$

J. $\dfrac{\$7}{5 \text{ yd.}} = \$1.4/\text{yd.}$

K. $\dfrac{\$10}{8 \text{ yd.}} = \$1.25/\text{yd.}$

Therefore, the (K) fabric costs the least per yard.

31. (A) (p. 183) _Mathematics/Geometry/Lines and Angles._ Since $\overline{PQ} \parallel \overline{ST}$, we know that $x = y$ because the alternate interior angles of parallel lines are equal. Furthermore, since the sum of angles in $\triangle PRQ$ is 180°, $75 + 65 + x + x = 180 \Rightarrow 2x + 140 = 180 \Rightarrow 2x = 40 \Rightarrow x = 20$. Therefore, $y = 20$.

32. (H) (p. 183) _Mathematics/Number and Quantity/Basic Arithmetic Manipulations._ Perform the indicated operations: $\dfrac{10^3(10^5 + 10^5)}{10^4} = \dfrac{10^5 + 10^5}{10} = 10^4 + 10^4 = 2(10^4)$.

33. (D) (p. 183) _Mathematics/Algebra and Functions/Solving Quadratic Equations and Relations._ Factor the quadratic equation: $x^2 - 5x + 4 = 0 \Rightarrow (x - 4)(x - 1) = 0$. So, either $x - 4 = 0 \Rightarrow x = 4$ or $x - 1 = 0 \Rightarrow x = 1$.

Alternatively, substitute the values in the choices back into the equation to find the set that works.

34. (K) (p. 184) _Mathematics/Statistics and Probability/Measures of Center._ Use the method for finding the missing elements of an average. The smallest possible sum for 6 different positive integers is $1 + 2 + 3 + 4 + 5 + 6 = 21$. The sum of all 7 integers is $7 \cdot 12 = 84$. Therefore, the largest that the seventh number could be (with the average of the seven numbers still 12) is $84 - 21 = 63$.

35. (E) (p. 184) _Mathematics/Algebra and Functions/Solving Simultaneous Equations._ To find b in terms of x and y, solve the first equation or b in terms of x and then solve the second equation for b in terms of y: $x = b + 4 \Rightarrow b = x - 4$ and $y = b - 3 \Rightarrow b = y + 3$. Combine the two equations by adding:

$$b = x - 4$$
$$\underline{+b = y + 3}$$
$$2b = x + y - 1 \Rightarrow b = \frac{x + y - 1}{2}$$

Alternatively, substitute some numbers. If $b = 1$, then $x = 1 + 4 = 5$ and $y = 1 - 3 = -2$. Substitute 5 for x and -2 for y in the answer choices. The correct choice will yield the value 1.

36. (F) (p. 184) _Mathematics/Number and Quantity/Properties of Numbers._ Since $z = 5x = 3y$, and x, y, and z are integers, z is a multiple of both 3 and 5, so z is evenly divisible by 5, (G), 3, (H), and 15, (J). And since $5x = 3y$, and x and y are integers, x is a multiple of 3 (and evenly divisible by 3), (K). However, while z is divisible by both x and y individually, z is not necessarily divisible by the product of x and y, (F).

Alternatively, substitute some numbers. The most natural assumption is to let z equal 15, so $x = 3$ and $y = 5$. However, on that assumption, every answer choice is an integer. Try the next multiple of 15. Let z equal 30, so $x = 6$ and $y = 10$. Only (F) is no longer an integer:

$$30 \div (6 \cdot 10) = \frac{1}{2}.$$

37. (B) (p. 184) _Mathematics/Geometry/Rectangles and Squares._ Use the equation for the area of a rectangle: $\text{area}_{\text{rectangle}} = \text{width} \cdot \text{length} \Rightarrow 48x^2 = w(24x) \Rightarrow w = \dfrac{48x^2}{24x} = 2x$.

Alternatively, substitute a number, such as $x = 2$. The area of the rectangle is $48(2^2) = 48(4) = 192$, and the length is 48. And 48 times the width is equal to 192, so the width is $192 \div 48 = 4$. Therefore, if $x = 2$, the correct choice yields the value 4. Only (B) works.

38. (K) (p. 185) *Mathematics/Algebra and Functions/Manipulating Algebraic Expressions/Basic Algebraic Manipulations*. Rewrite the equation:

$$x = \frac{1}{y+1} \Rightarrow x(y+1) = 1 \Rightarrow y+1 = \frac{1}{x} \Rightarrow y = \frac{1}{x} - 1 \Rightarrow y = \frac{1-x}{x}.$$

39. (B) (p. 185) *Mathematics/Algebra and Functions/Coordinate Geometry/ The Coordinate System* and *Geometry/Triangles/Properties of Triangles*. The length of the base of the triangle is $4x - x = 3x$, and the length of the altitude is $3x - 0 = 3x$. Use the formula for finding the area of a triangle to determine x:

$$\frac{1}{2}(3x)(3x) = 54 \Rightarrow (3x)(3x) = 108 \Rightarrow 9x^2 = 108 \Rightarrow x^2 = 12 \Rightarrow x = \pm\sqrt{12} = 2\sqrt{3} \quad \text{(distances}$$
are positive).

40. (K) (p. 185) *Mathematics/Statistics and Probability/Probability*. This question is a little tricky, but it does not require advanced mathematics. If the room were completely dark, what is the worst thing that might happen? You might happen to pull all the blue and white socks first (the two colors with the largest number of socks). So you might have pulled 16 socks. Now, the only color left is the color (green) with the smallest number of socks. Then you would need to pull 2 of the only 4 socks left. So, on the worst assumption, $16 + 2 = 18$ picks will *guarantee* you a pair of each color.

41. (C) (p. 186) *Mathematics/Geometry/Complex Figures* and *Circles* and *Lines and Angles* and *Triangles/Properties of Triangles*. The question supplies the area of the shaded part of the figure, which is a portion of the circle. First, find what fraction of the circle is shaded. Then, use that value to determine the value of the unshaded angle at the center of the circle. The area of the entire circle is $\pi r^2 = \pi(4^2) = 16\pi$. Since $\frac{14\pi}{16\pi} = \frac{7}{8}$ of the circle is shaded, $\frac{1}{8}$ of the circle is unshaded. Therefore, the unshaded angle at the center of the circle is $\frac{1}{8}$ of $360° = 45°$. Now, find x: $x + 45 + 90 = 180 \Rightarrow x + 135 = 180 \Rightarrow x = 45$.

42. (J) (p. 186) *Mathematics/Geometry/Complex Figures* and *Circles* and *Triangles/45°-45°-90° Triangles*. This is a composite figure, so redefine one figure in terms of another. The diameter of the smaller circle is equal to the side of the square. The diagonal of the square is the diameter of the larger circle. First, let r be the radius of the smaller circle, so the smaller circle has an area of πr^2. The diameter of the smaller circle is $2r$, which is also the side of the square:

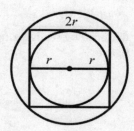

The diagonal of the square creates a 45°-45°-90° triangle with the sides of the square, so the hypotenuse of that triangle is equal to $\frac{2\sqrt{2}r}{2} = \sqrt{2}r$. Thus, the larger circle has a radius of $2\sqrt{2}r \div 2 = \sqrt{2}r$, and an area of $\pi(\sqrt{2}r)^2 = 2\pi r^2$. Therefore, the ratio of the area of the larger circle to the area of the smaller circle is $2\pi r^2 : \pi r^2 = 2:1$.

43. (D) (p. 186) *Mathematics/Number and Quantity/Basic Arithmetic Manipulations.* Just perform the indicated operations:

$$2^0 = 1$$
$$2^3 = 8$$
$$2^{-2} = \frac{1}{2^2} = \frac{1}{4}$$

$$1 + 8 - \frac{1}{4} = 8\frac{3}{4}$$

44. (J) (p. 187) *Mathematics/Algebra and Functions/Coordinate Geometry/Graphs of Quadratic Equations and Relations.* Since the axis of symmetry of the parabola is given by the equation $x = 0$, the parabola is symmetric about the y-axis. The point symmetric to the point with coordinates $(-1,-2)$ will have the same y-coordinate, and the x-coordinate of the point will be the same distance from the y-axis but in a positive direction: $(1, -2)$. It might be easier to find the solution using your calculator to graph of the equation:

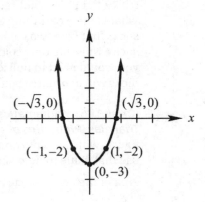

45. (C) (p. 187) *Mathematics/Algebra and Functions/Coordinate Geometry/Slope-Intercept Form of a Linear Equation.* Each equation is written in slope-intercept form, so the slope of the first line is m_1, and the slope of the second line is m_2. If two lines in the coordinate plane are perpendicular to each other, then the product of their slopes is -1. Thus, $m_1 m_2 = -1$.

46. (K) (p. 187) *Mathematics/Geometry/Complex Figures and Triangles/Pythagorean Theorem and Properties of Triangles and Rectangles and Squares.* Draw some additional lines to carve the figure into more familiar shapes, and use the Pythagorean theorem to determine the length of the shared third side of the two small triangles: $a^2 + 8^2 = 10^2 \Rightarrow a^2 + 64 = 100 \Rightarrow a^2 = 36 \Rightarrow a = 6$. Note that this can also be immediately deduced by recognizing the triangles as Pythagorean triples. Add the information to the figure:

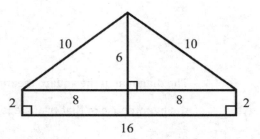

The area of the large rectangle is $16 \cdot 2 = 32$. The total area of the large triangle is $\frac{1}{2} \cdot 6 \cdot 16 = 48$. Therefore, the area of the composite figure is $32 + 48 = 80$.

47. (A) (p. 188) *Mathematics/Algebra and Functions/Manipulating Algebraic Expressions/Basic Algebraic Manipulations.* Rationalize the denominator by multiplying the numerator and denominator by the conjugate of the denominator:

$$\frac{\sqrt{x}}{2\sqrt{x}-\sqrt{y}}\cdot\frac{2\sqrt{x}+\sqrt{y}}{2\sqrt{x}+\sqrt{y}}=\frac{2x+\sqrt{xy}}{4x+2\sqrt{xy}-2\sqrt{xy}-y}=\frac{2x+\sqrt{xy}}{4x-y}.$$

Alternatively, assume some values for x and y. Since the problem involves square roots, pick a couple of perfect squares, e.g., $x=9$ and $y=4$. The expression in the question stem becomes $\frac{\sqrt{9}}{2\sqrt{9}-\sqrt{4}}=\frac{3}{2(3)-2}=\frac{3}{4}$. Now, substitute 9 for x and 4 for y into the answer choices. The correct choice will generate the value $\frac{3}{4}$:

A. $\dfrac{2x+\sqrt{xy}}{4x-y}=\dfrac{2(9)+\sqrt{(9)(4)}}{4(9)-4}=\dfrac{18+6}{32}=\dfrac{24}{32}=\dfrac{3}{4}$ ✓

B. $\dfrac{4x+\sqrt{xy}}{4x-y}=\dfrac{4(9)+\sqrt{(9)(4)}}{4(9)-4}=\dfrac{36+6}{36-4}=\dfrac{42}{32}$ ✗

C. $\dfrac{2\sqrt{x}+\sqrt{y}}{4xy}=\dfrac{2\sqrt{9}+\sqrt{4}}{4(9)(4)}=\dfrac{2(3)+2}{144}=\dfrac{8}{144}$ ✗

D. $\dfrac{2\sqrt{x}+\sqrt{xy}}{2x-y}=\dfrac{2\sqrt{9}+\sqrt{(9)(4)}}{2(9)-4}=\dfrac{6+6}{14}=\dfrac{12}{14}$ ✗

E. $\dfrac{2\sqrt{x}-\sqrt{y}}{2}=\dfrac{2\sqrt{9}-\sqrt{4}}{2}=\dfrac{2(3)-2}{2}=\dfrac{4}{2}=2$ ✗

48. (H) (p. 188) *Mathematics/Geometry/Lines and Angles* **and** *Triangles/Properties of Triangles.* Since vertical angles are equal, the figure becomes:

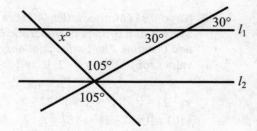

And the interior angles of a triangle total 180°, so $30+105+x=180\Rightarrow x=45$.

49. (D) (p. 188) *Mathematics/Geometry/Trigonometry/Graphs of Trigonometric Functions.* The graph intersects the y-axis where $x=0$: $y=2\cos(2\cdot0)+2=2\cos0+2$. Since $\cos0=1$, $y=2(1)+2=4$.

50. (G) (p. 189) *Mathematics/Geometry/Complex Figures* **and** *Rectangles and Squares* **and** *Circles.* The shaded area is equal to the whole square minus the four circles. On the assumption that each circle has a radius of r, the side of the square must be $4r$, and the area of the square is $4r\cdot4r=16r^2$. Furthermore, each circle with radius r has an area of πr^2, so the shaded area is $16r^2-4\pi r^2$. And the ratio of the shaded area to the area of the square is

$$\frac{16r^2-4\pi r^2}{16r^2}=\frac{4r^2(4-\pi)}{16r^2}=\frac{4-\pi}{4}.$$

Note that a little common sense goes a long way when applied to the answer choices. Since π is less than 4, (F) is a negative number and is therefore impossible. Both (J) and (K) are greater than 1, asserting that the shaded area is larger than the square, an equally absurd conclusion. Now, there are only two answer choices remaining: (G) asserts that the shaded area is a little less than one-quarter of the square, and (H) asserts that the shaded area is about three-quarters of the square. After careful inspection of the figure, it is safe to assume that (G) is correct.

51. **(C)** (p. 189) *Mathematics/Geometry/Trigonometry/Trigonometric Relationships.*

The Pythagorean trigonometric identity is $\sin^2 \theta + \cos^2 \theta = 1$. Therefore, $\dfrac{\sin^2 \theta + \cos^2 \theta}{\sin \theta} = \dfrac{1}{\sin \theta}$. And the reciprocal identity for the sine function is the cosecant function: $\dfrac{1}{\sin \theta} = \csc \theta$.

52. **(G)** (p. 189) *Mathematics/Geometry/Trigonometry/Definitions of the Six Trigonometric Functions.* Since $\tan \theta = \dfrac{\text{side opposite } \theta}{\text{side adjacent } \theta}$, $\tan 55° = \dfrac{6}{AC} \Rightarrow 1.4 \approx \dfrac{6}{AC} \Rightarrow \overline{AC} \approx \dfrac{6}{1.4} \approx 4.28$.

53. **(D)** (p. 190) *Mathematics/Algebra and Functions/Evaluating, Interpreting, and Creating Algebraic Functions/Concepts of Domain and Range.* The expression is undefined for every value of x that makes the denominator equal to zero. The denominator is zero if either $x - 1$ or $x + 2$ equals zero. Therefore, the expression is undefined for $x = 1$ or $x = -2$.

54. **(K)** (p. 190) *Mathematics/Algebra and Functions/Solving Simultaneous Equations.* Since $x + y \le 6$, y will have its maximum value when x has its minimum value. The minimum value of x is 0; the maximum value of y is 6. Therefore, the minimum value for $3y$ is $3(6) = 18$.

Alternatively, test the answer choices. Since the question asks for the maximum value of y, start with the largest choice: 18. If $3y = 18$, then $y = 6$. And $x + y \le 6 \Rightarrow x + 6 \le 6 \Rightarrow x \le 0$. Since x can be 0, $y = 6$ satisfies the system of inequalities.

55. **(C)** (p. 191) *Mathematics/Algebra and Functions/Coordinate Geometry/The Coordinate System* and *Graphs of Quadratic Equations and Relations* and *Evaluating, Interpreting, and Creating Algebraic Functions/Concepts of Domain and Range.* Find the corresponding values for y when $x = -1$, 0, and 1:

$$y(-1) = \left|(-1)^2 - 3\right| = |-2| = 2$$
$$y(0) = \left|(0)^2 - 3\right| = |-3| = 3$$
$$y(1) = \left|(1)^2 - 3\right| = |1 - 3| = |-2| = 2$$

Only (C) shows the correct plotting of the points $(-1,2)$, $(0,3)$, and $(1,2)$.

56. **(G)** (p. 192) *Mathematics/Algebra and Functions/Coordinate Geometry/Graphs of Linear Equations* and *Slope-Intercept Form of a Linear Equation.* Each answer choice is an equation of a line in slope-intercept form ($y = mx + b$), and each has a different slope. Calculate the slope of the line shown in the graph: $m = \dfrac{(-2) - (4)}{(2) - (-1)} = \dfrac{-6}{3} = -2$. Only (G) has the correct slope.

57. **(A)** (p. 192) *Mathematics/Algebra and Functions/Solving Quadratic Equations and Relations.* The best approach to solving this item is to see that the roots are expressed in a form suggestive of the quadratic formula, the solution to the quadratic equation $ax^2 + bx + c = 0$:

$x = \dfrac{-b \pm \sqrt{b^2 - 4ac}}{2a}$. Thus, $-b = -3$, so $b = 3$, which eliminates (B) and (D). Next, $2a = 2$, so

$a = 1$, which eliminates (E). Finally, $b^2 - 4ac = 5$. Since $b = 3$ and $a = 1$, $b^2 - 4ac = 5 \Rightarrow (3)^2 - 4(1)(c) = 5 \Rightarrow 9 - 4c = 5 \Rightarrow 4c = 4 \Rightarrow c = 1$. Thus, the equation is $x^2 + 3x + 1 = 0$.

58. **(F) (p. 192) *Mathematics/Algebra and Functions/Expressing and Evaluating Algebraic Functions/Concepts of Domain and Range*.** A function is a relationship such that each element of the domain is paired with one and only one element in the range. The domain is the set of all possibilities for the first coordinate. In the relationship given in the question stem, two pairs—(0,3) and (0,5)—have the same first coordinate. So, one element of the domain, 0, is paired with two different elements in the range: 3 and 5. We need to eliminate either (0,3) or (0,5). By dropping (0,3), the element 0 is paired only with 5, and the set becomes a function.

59. **(E) (p. 193) *Mathematics/Geometry/Complex Figures* and *30°–60°–90° Triangles* and *Rectangles and Squares*.** Consider the trapezoid as a composite figure. Draw a line from point B perpendicular to $\overline{CD}$: the trapezoid is a combination of a right triangle and a rectangle. Since the triangle has angle measures of 30°, 60°, and 90°, the side opposite the 30° angle has a length half that of the hypotenuse, or 4. Thus, the rectangle has sides of 4 and

9 and an area of 36. Then, the side of the triangle opposite the 60° angle has a length equal to $\dfrac{\sqrt{3}}{2}$ times the hypotenuse, or $4\sqrt{3}$. The area of the triangle is $\dfrac{ab}{2} = \dfrac{(4)(4\sqrt{3})}{2} = 8\sqrt{3}$. So, the area of the trapezoid is $36 + 8\sqrt{3}$.

60. **(F) (p. 193) *Mathematics/Geometry/Trigonometry/Definitions of the Six Trigonometric Functions*.** The cotangent and tangent are reciprocal functions, so if $\cot \theta = \dfrac{4}{3}$, then $\tan \theta = \dfrac{3}{4}$.

Section 3: Reading

1. **(B)** (p. 195) *Reading/Craft and Structure/Development.* The author is arguing that most of the stories in the newspaper are not really worth reading. He includes this report as an example to show how silly some news coverage is. It is an odd occurrence that does not really affect the person who reads about it—except as idle gossip. The other choices must be wrong because the event is not significant.

2. **(J)** (p. 195) *Reading/Craft and Structure/Development.* In the second paragraph, the author of Passage A is making the point that the foreign news is not really news and mentions the examples of Spain, England, and France. He writes that it is possible just to toss in some generic information about Spain, and the resulting report will be accurate. (J) best summarizes how the author uses this example. The other choices are wrong because the author is not offering real news, only a parody of the news.

3. **(A)** (p. 195) *Reading/Key Ideas and Details/Voice.* The point of Passage A is that the reports contained in the newspaper are really worthless, covering all kinds of events that ultimately have no significance. At key points in the passage, the author pokes fun at the news: people would come running in response to a fire alarm in the hope of seeing a good fire, even if it were the church that was burning. Since the author's attitude is negative, you can eliminate (B), (C), and (D).

4. **(H)** (p. 195) *Reading/Craft and Structure/Vocabulary.* Because this is a Vocabulary item, you can be pretty sure that the correct answer is not going to be the most common meaning of "attend." As a result, (F) is wrong. In this context, "attend" means to "pay attention to," and (H) is a good match. The other choices do not fit the meaning of the sentence; in fact, (G) and (J) are never synonymous with "attend."

5. **(A)** (p. 195) *Reading/Craft and Structure/Development.* The author says that people would respond to the fire alarm not because they want to help save property from destruction but because they want to watch a fire. The author adds that this is particularly true if the church itself is on fire. The author is adding emphasis to the point by saying that people would show up to watch their own church burn. As for (B), while it seems that these people might not care enough about property to put out the fire, this is not the point that the author wants to prove. He wants to prove that they would enjoy watching the church burn. (C) is wrong because the point is not that people are legitimately interested in local affairs but that in this case they are fascinated by something unusual. (D) has to be wrong because the point is that people are less interested in the church than in watching a fire.

6. **(J)** (p. 195) *Reading/Key Ideas and Details/Explicit Detail.* The author states that the people on the island had continued to act as friends even though they were enemies (meaning that the countries from which they originally came were at war). (F) and (G) are ideas mentioned in the selection but do not respond to the question asked. (H) is not discussed in that paragraph.

7. **(B)** (p. 195) *Reading/Craft and Structure/Explicit Detail.* The "plight" that both the islanders and the residents of Europe shared was the delay in the news reporting. Though the delay may have been longer (in the case of the islanders) or shorter (in the case of Europeans nearer to the events), there was still a delay during which people were in the position of acting on outdated and wrong information. As for (A), the reporting was not wrong; it was merely delayed. As for (C), even regular reports can be outdated. As for (D), the problem was not biased news but late news.

8. **(F)** (p. 196) *Reading/Key Ideas and Details/Implied Idea.* In the final paragraph, the author states that from our perspective we can see that results were achieved even though people were working with outdated or wrong information. The author offers overseas exploration as an example; with the backing of the Spanish government, Columbus set sail for India only to land in what is now the Americas, and was credited with a significant achievement. As for (G), while the Spanish government and Columbus worked with wrong information, this

is not the author's point—the results are what matters. As for (H), the author talks about hindsight and does not fault those who made errors because their information was limited. (J) represents a misunderstanding of the final paragraph.

9. **(A)** (p. 196) *Reading/Integration of Knowledge and Ideas/Application.* The author of Passage A thinks that the news is only gossip. The author of Passage B thinks that news is important, even if it arrives a little late. As for (B), the author of Passage A does not really care whether news is accurate or not; it's just gossip. As for (C), again, the author of Passage A insists that the news has no value at all. As for (D), the author of Passage B really does not hold out much hope for the news, though he or she might allow that faster reporting is better than slower reporting.

10. **(F)** (p. 196) *Reading/Integration of Knowledge and Ideas/Implied Idea.* We do not know what the authors would have said about the web because they obviously died before it was invented, but we can make a good guess. The author of Passage A would probably say, "See I told you so, more and faster junk." Figuring out author two is a little harder. The point of the second passage is that no matter how fast the news comes, there is always some delay between the event and the report, and during that time, we are operating on wrong information. That point is nicely summarized by the first sentence of the third paragraph in passage B: how indirectly we know the environment. Thus, the second author would probably say that while the web closes the gap somewhat, it does not eliminate it. As for (G), there is no way that author one is going to buy into this point. As for (H), surely author two would allow that the web is faster and therefore at least a little better. In any event, author one is going to say that both sources are terrible. The same reasoning applies to (J).

11. **(B)** (p. 198) *Reading/Key Ideas and Details/Main Idea.* The passage covers a number of different takeover strategies including opportunistic, strategic, friendly, private, and hostile. And though the author does spend quite a bit of space discussing the hostile takeover in particular, this topic is not the focus of the entire passage. Instead, the best description of the main idea is provided by (B), which refers to the availability of a number of takeover options.

12. **(G)** (p. 198) *Reading/Key Ideas and Details/Application.* (G) is the correct answer choice. In lines 80–84, the author outlines the basic details of how a "golden parachute clause" works. The description in this item stem matches what is described in the passage.

13. **(C)** (p. 198) *Reading/Key Ideas and Details/Implied Idea.* (C) is the correct answer choice. In lines 45–54, the author gives the defining characteristic of a hostile takeover; specifically, the current management is opposed to it.

14. **(F)** (p. 198) *Reading/Craft and Structure/Explicit Detail.* (F) is the correct answer choice. In the fifth paragraph, the author explains how raiders must raise substantial capital to buy large quantities of a targeted company's stock (usually at above market price). According to the author, the raiders acquire "debt" (line 70) that they then attempt to liquidate by selling parts of the targeted company or by running the targeted company more efficiently.

15. **(D)** (p. 198) *Reading/Key Ideas and Details/Explicit Detail.* (D) is the correct answer choice. In lines 84–86, the author outlines the basic details of a "poison pill" strategy. The description in (D) matches what is outlined. As for the other answer choices, (A) is incorrect because it describes the "greenmail" strategy (lines 87–90). (B) is incorrect because it describes the "golden parachute" strategy (lines 80–84). Finally, (C) is incorrect because it is not supported by any material in the passage.

16. **(G)** (p. 198) *Reading/Key Ideas and Details/Explicit Detail.* (G) is the correct answer choice. In the final paragraph, the author explicitly says that supporters of corporate takeovers believe "the threat of a takeover...makes managers more efficient" (lines 94–95). As for the other answer choices, they are all incorrect because there is no evidence in the passage to suggest that supporters of corporate takeovers would hold these beliefs.

17. **(D)** (p. 198) *Reading/Key Ideas and Details/Explicit Detail.* (D) is the correct answer choice. A proxy fight is defined in lines 55–57. The description in (D) matches what is outlined in lines 55–57. As for the other answer choices, they are all incorrect because they are unrelated to proxy fights.

18. **(H)** (p. 199) *Reading/Key Ideas and Details/Application.* (H) is the correct answer choice. In the final paragraph, the author says that supporters of corporate takeovers believe "the threat of a takeover...makes managers more efficient" (lines 94–95). Selling unprofitable subsidiaries to raise cash and cut expenses is an example of being more efficient. As for the other answer choices, see the second to last paragraph of this passage for correct definitions of these terms.

19. **(B)** (p. 199) *Reading/Key Ideas and Details/Explicit Detail.* The passage cites Berkshire Hathaway as a large company that has a history of successfully acquiring companies that are undervalued. Because the companies are undervalued, they are attractive acquisition for the same reason that buying almost anything at a bargain price is attractive.

20. **(F)** (p. 199) *Reading/Key Ideas and Details/Explicit Detail.* The passage explains that a proxy battle involves the gathering of shareholder votes in order to use the larger number of votes to win a voting battle for control of the company.

21. **(A)** (p. 201) *Reading/Key Ideas and Details/Main Idea.* Although the passage includes an abundance of detail, nearly all of these details can be grouped into two main categories: first, a general introduction to Josquin des Prez; and second, an explanation as to why he is relatively unknown. (A) is the correct answer choice because it mentions both of these main points.

22. **(J)** (p. 201) *Reading/Key Ideas and Details/Explicit Detail.* (J) is the correct answer choice because the author never mentions any of Josquin's students. As for the other answer choices, (F) is answered in the second paragraph (*El Grillo, Allegez moy*, etc.). (G) is answered in the final paragraph (sackbuts, krummhorns, etc.). (H) is answered in the second paragraph (Ockeghem).

23. **(D)** (p. 201) *Reading/Key Ideas and Details/Implied Idea.* In the sixth paragraph, the author lists several difficulties associated with reading a musical score from the Renaissance. The author specifically mentions that no tempos are given, flats and sharps are not specified, and no instructions are provided as to which instruments are to play each part. It is logical to assume that, since these are mentioned as difficulties associated with musical scores from the Renaissance, modern musical notation must contain all of these features.

24. **(G)** (p. 201) *Reading/Key Ideas and Details/Implied Idea.* In the fifth paragraph, the author discusses a distinction between concept and performance. The author states that music does not exist in notes printed on a page; instead, the author argues, a musical score is merely a set of instructions for producing music. Therefore, the author would agree with (G).

25. **(D)** (p. 201) *Reading/Key Ideas and Details/Application.* Each answer choice provided here has a certain amount of merit. On the one hand, (A) seems like a good choice because the author mentions that members of *collegia musica* are generally the only ones who attempt to perform Renaissance music; however, the author also lists several shortcomings associated with these organizations. (B) seems like a good choice because study in general is an excellent method for producing positive results; however, the author mentions several deficiencies associated with musical scores from the Renaissance that even a lifetime of dedicated study could never overcome. (C) might seem like a good choice for the same reason as (B) since additional study or attention normally leads to positive results; however, the essay gives no specific evidence that merely adding Renaissance music to a college curriculum would increase public appreciation of this remote and esoteric art form. In the end, (D) is the best answer choice because it is actually supported by evidence from the essay. In lines 105–106, the author explicitly mentions that musicians cannot afford to study the type of music written by Josquin des Prez due to lack of financial support from an

audience. If financial support were available from another source, though, musicians could afford to study and promote the music of Renaissance composers like Josquin des Prez.

26. **(G) (p. 201)** *Reading/Key Ideas and Details/Explicit Detail.* (G) is the correct answer choice because, although the author says that musicians who read modern musical notation have difficulty reading Renaissance notation, the author never says that these musicians cannot play Renaissance instruments. As for the other answer choices, (F) is mentioned in the sixth paragraph. (H) and (J) are mentioned in the final paragraph.

27. **(A) (p. 202)** *Reading/Key Ideas and Details/Implied Idea.* (A) is the correct answer choice because there are at least two reasons to believe that the author admires Galileo. First, in lines 28–31, the author says that both Josquin and Galileo "asserted a new importance for man." The author does not qualify or give any reason to doubt the goodness of this accomplishment. Second, the author has only praise and admiration for Josquin. If the author then says that Josquin and Galileo were comparable figures in their respective fields, we can assume that the author would have similar praise and admiration for Galileo.

28. **(H) (p. 202)** *Reading/Key Ideas and Details/Implied Idea.* In line 6, the author states that the dominant theme of liturgical music "was reverence." So, (H) is the correct answer choice.

29. **(A) (p. 202)** *Reading/Key Ideas and Details/Implied Idea.* (A) is the correct answer choice. In lines 74–75, the author says that "in fine art, concept and performance are one." Specifically, in arts such as painting and poetry, there is a permanent and physical artifact (i.e., a mural or a book of poems) that does not change. In contrast, the author says there is a "separation of concept from performance in music" (lines 73–74). Specifically, a composer writes a musical score that consists of notes on a page. However, the music itself does not exist until musicians perform it; the music then varies from performance to performance based on the quality and the interpretation of the musicians. Similarly, a choreographer creates a ballet and leaves instructions as to its performance. However, the ballet itself does not exist until dancers perform it; and, again, the ballet varies from performance to performance based on the same factors mentioned above.

30. **(H) (p. 202)** *Reading/Key Ideas and Details/Implied Idea.* (H) is the correct answer choice. In lines 1–2, the author says that Western music was only liturgical up until the time of Josquin des Prez. The author then says that, while Josquin des Prez wrote liturgical music, he also "stepped with the other [foot] into the human world" (lines 13–15). In other words, Josquin des Prez also wrote nonreligious music. For example, the author cites the *Deploration d'Ockeghem*, a musical piece written in tribute to a fellow composer, as well as *Allegez moy*, a musical piece about a beautiful woman.

31. **(C) (p. 203)** *Reading/Key Ideas and Details/Explicit Detail.* (C) is the correct answer choice. In the first sentence of the second paragraph, the author says that a supernova occurs about "twice every century" (line 13) or about once every fifty years.

32. **(J) (p. 204)** *Reading/Key Ideas and Details/Explicit Detail.* (J) is the correct answer choice. The passage never mentions or implies that supernovas are caused by the collision of large galaxies. As for the other answer choices, (F) is incorrect because supernovas are described as extremely bright (lines 44–45). (G) is incorrect because supernovas are described as a type of explosion (lines 14–15). Finally, (H) is incorrect because supernovas are said to emit large quantities of X-rays (lines 49–50).

33. **(A) (p. 204)** *Reading/Craft and Structure/Development.* (A) is the correct answer choice. Starting at line 24, the author compares a star to a leaky balloon. An analogy is a comparison.

34. **(H)** (p. 204) *Reading/Key Ideas and Details/Implied Idea.* (H) is the correct answer choice. The key word used to describe these meteorites is "anomalous," which means "uncharacteristic." These meteorites are uncharacteristic because they contain "certain isotopes" (line 64) not found in our solar system. If these isotopes are not found in our solar system, it can be inferred that they came from a supernova that gave birth to our solar system. As the author notes, elements such as these isotopes "are manufactured deep in the interior of stars and would...remain there if it were not for the cataclysmic supernova explosions that blow giant stars apart" (lines 72–75).

35. **(A)** (p. 204) *Reading/Key Ideas and Details/Implied Idea.* (A) is the correct answer choice. In the fourth paragraph, the author explains that the hot gas from a supernova "will emit most of its energy at X-ray wavelengths, so it is not surprising that X-ray observatories have provided some of the most useful insights into the nature of the supernova phenomenon" (lines 49–53). The author also notes that X-ray studies have detected "more than twenty supernova remnants" (line 53–54). In short, the author implies it is easiest to find evidence of a supernova using equipment that detects X-rays (rather than equipment that views visible light).

36. **(J)** (p. 204) *Reading/Key Ideas and Details/Explicit Detail.* (J) is the correct answer choice. In the second paragraph, the author describes how a star becomes a supernova. The sequence of events begins when, within the star, "the nuclear fuel is exhausted...[and] the matter in the center of the star collapses inward" (lines 31–34).

37. **(B)** (p. 204) *Reading/Key Ideas and Details/Explicit Detail.* (B) is the correct answer choice. In the second paragraph, the author begins the process of describing how a star becomes a supernova. According to the author, once a star completes its initial collapse, its "nuclei and electrons are fused into a super-dense lump of matter known as a neutron star" (lines 35–37). In the third paragraph, the author explains what follows this stage—namely, a supernova. Therefore, a neutron star is an intermediate stage between an ordinary star and a supernova.

38. **(J)** (p. 204) *Reading/Key Ideas and Details/Main Idea.* (J) is the correct answer choice for two reasons. First, it accurately summarizes the author's main purpose, which is to describe the sequence of events that precedes and follows a supernova. Second, it is the only statement general enough to cover the full range of information discussed in the passage. As for the other answer choices, they are all incorrect because they focus on only one element of the passage; in other words, (F), (G), and (H) are all too narrow to describe fully the author's main purpose in writing this passage.

39. **(D)** (p. 204) *Reading/Key Ideas and Details/Explicit Detail.* (D) is the correct answer choice. In line 66–67, the author says our galaxy was formed "more than four and a half billion years ago."

40. **(H)** (p. 204) *Reading/Key Ideas and Details/Implied Idea.* (H) is the correct answer choice. In the fifth paragraph, the author says "supernovas produce clouds of high-energy particles... [which] are responsible for many of the genetic mutations that are the driving force of the evolution of species" (lines 75–80).

Section 4: Science

1. **(B)** (p. 205) *Science/Interpretation of Data/Analysis*. Generally, the Wright data show lower lift at a given angle than the Lilienthal data.

2. **(H)** (p. 205) *Science/Interpretation of Data/Comprehension*. The highest point on the graph is at 14 degrees (approximately 5.7 pounds/sq. ft.).

3. **(A)** (p. 205) *Science/Interpretation of Data/Comprehension*. By extending both lines to the 50° mark, the difference between them is clearly less than 1 pound/sq. ft. The two experiments never differed by more than 1 pound/sq. ft.

4. **(H)** (p. 205) *Science/Interpretation of Data/Comprehension*. According to the graph, the greatest difference in lift for the two experiments (corresponding to the greatest distance between the two curves for a given angle of incidence) occurs at approximately 30°.

5. **(B)** (p. 205) *Science/Interpretation of Data/Comprehension*. The widest region is between 18° and 43°: 43° – 18° = 25°.

6. **(J)** (p. 206) *Science/Scientific Investigation/Analysis*. Since plastic beads are not alive, they cannot possibly carry out cellular respiration. This control is designed to detect any atmospheric changes (in the laboratory) that may cause a change in pressure inside the tubes.

7. **(A)** (p. 206) *Science/Scientific Investigation/Comprehension*. Oxygen in the air of the tube is consumed by the peas during cellular respiration (see summary equation).

8. **(F)** (p. 206) *Science/Scientific Investigation/Analysis*. Without KOH to remove the carbon dioxide produced during cellular respiration, the same number of gas molecules ($6CO_2$) would always be added to the tube as gas molecules were being consumed from the tube ($6O_2$) and the pressure would remain constant.

9. **(C)** (p. 206) *Science/Evaluation of Models/Analysis*. Experiment 2 was conducted at a higher temperature than Experiment 1. The greater decrease in pressure in the same time period demonstrates a faster consumption of oxygen.

10. **(G)** (p. 207) *Science/Scientific Investigation/Analysis*. If results are identical in light and dark, then light/dark conditions are irrelevant to cellular respiration rates in the experiment; only temperature conditions are important.

11. **(A)** (p. 207) *Science/Evaluation of Models/Comprehension*. Glucose must be consumed in order for cellular respiration to occur, eliminating (B) and (D). Cellular respiration did not occur at equal rates in Experiments 1 and 2, eliminating (C), so (A) is the only possible answer: peas are seeds containing a supply of glucose.

12. **(G)** (p. 208) *Science/Scientific Investigation/Comprehension*. Scientist 1 believes that processes associated with sudden events in the past shaped Earth, whereas Scientist 2 believes that the processes are continuing in the present.

13. **(D)** (p. 208) *Science/Evaluation of Models/Analysis*. Mountains could not have formed only when land masses were raised at the beginnings of Earth if recent fossils of sea creatures are found at mountain tops. This evidence suggests that the rocks were underwater relatively recently.

14. **(H)** (p. 208) *Science/Evaluation of Models/Analysis*. The two scientists agree that the changes that have shaped the landscape have operated over a long time span, but they disagree as to whether those changes were sudden and violent (catastrophism) or constant and gradual (principle of uniform change). Furthermore, catastrophism holds that the cataclysmic events happened in the distant past, not recently, eliminating (F).

15. (A) (p. 209) *Science/Evaluation of Models/Comprehension.* According to Scientist 1, the worldwide ocean precipitated granite first, so it must be the lowest layer, with other precipitated materials covering it later.

16. (F) (p. 209) *Science/Interpretation of Data/Comprehension.* According to Scientist 1, the three major rock types formed when the worldwide ocean precipitated different materials on three occasions, so no further types can be expected since this ocean no longer exists (possibly due to evaporation).

17. (C) (p. 209) *Science/Evaluation of Models/Analysis.* By arguing that processes that formed the earth at its origin differed from those that maintain and mold Earth as an existing planet, Scientist 1 would be refuting Scientist 2's view that processes are uniform from the beginning.

18. (G) (p. 209) *Science/Evaluation of Models/Analysis.* Scientist 1 refers to three rock types forming during three separate precipitations. Regions of lava (with no present volcanoes), rivers presently continuing to cut their channels, and "related" fossils that could not have immigrated from other geographic areas are factors that support the views of Scientist 2.

19. (D) (p. 210) *Science/Interpretation of Data/Comprehension.* Ten individuals had their heart rates recorded every 10 minutes during a 30-minute experiment (three times each). Therefore, 10(3) = 30 values were used to calculate the average heart rate for each of the experiments.

20. (G) (p. 210) *Science/Evaluation of Models/Analysis.* Since Species B had an increase in heart rate when environmental temperature increased, it is the likely species to be cold-blooded (Species A's heart rate stayed about the same).

21. (C) (p. 210) *Science/Scientific Investigation/Analysis.* Just by chance alone, any one individual might have an extremely high or extremely low heart rate. The larger the sample of individuals tested, the lower the chances of getting extreme average values.

22. (J) (p. 210) *Science/Interpretation of Data/Analysis.* Since Species B (cold-blooded) had an increase in average heart rate when environmental temperature increased, a decrease in average heart rate is likely when temperatures drop. Species A should have approximately the same average heart rate at all three temperatures.

23. (A) (p. 210) *Science/Interpretation of Data/Analysis.* At 22°C, Species A had an average heart rate of 150 beats/minute, while Species B averaged 100 beats/minute.

24. (F) (p. 211) *Science/Scientific Investigation/Analysis.* The cold-blooded Species B should have an increase in body temperature in Experiment 2 (35°C conditions in the incubator compared to 22°C in Experiment 1). The warm-blooded Species A should have no significant change in body temperature during the experiments.

25. (A) (p. 212) *Science/Interpretation of Data/Comprehension.* Each photon can promote an electron from level 1 to level 2 since the difference in energies is 0.60 eV. (Note that the actual value of level 1 alone, which happens to be 0.60 eV also, does not determine the answer. Differences in energy are what matter.)

26. (J) (p. 212) *Science/Evaluation of Models/Comprehension.* There is no way to distinguish between the emission from level 3 to level 4 or from level 5 to level 4 since each releases a photon of 0.32 eV.

27. (D) (p. 212) *Science/Interpretation of Data/Comprehension.* Only the level 3 to level 1 emission has an energy difference of 0.92 eV.

28. **(J)** (p. 212) *Science/Evaluation of Models/Comprehension*. Each electron can go from level 5 to any other level, with each of the four transitions requiring the emission of a photon of a different energy.

29. **(C)** (p. 212) *Science/Interpretation of Data/Analysis*. Since absorption of photons occurs first, then emission, electrons must be promoted (gaining the necessary energy from the absorbed photons), then emitted. Transitions between levels 3 and 4 have the necessary energy: 0.23 eV.

30. **(J)** (p. 212) *Science/Evaluation of Models/Comprehension*. Although 2.07 eV is the absolute energy of level 5, there is no difference of energy levels anywhere on the diagram that equals 2.07 eV; hence, the photons will not be absorbed: no electron transitions will occur between levels 1 and 5.

31. **(C)** (p. 213) *Science/Interpretation of Data/Comprehension*. Note how θ_1 and θ_2 are defined on the original drawing, then imagine how the diagram will change as the angles become smaller approaching zero: they would align along the vertical axis. Note that (B) would be correct if the angles were defined as those between the ray and the horizontal, not vertical, axis.

32. **(J)** (p. 213) *Science/Evaluation of Models/Analysis*. In Experiment 1 the angle in water is equal to the angle in air. In Experiment 2 the angle in water is less than the angle in air. So, only the last choice fits both experiments.

33. **(A)** (p. 213) *Science/Interpretation of Data/Comprehension*. This question simply requires interpretation of the meaning of the diagram: in Experiment 3, the beam is shown hitting the water surface and reflecting back, but not back on the beam itself.

34. **(H)** (p. 214) *Science/Evaluation of Models/Comprehension*. The beam of light only passes into the air for observation in Experiment 2.

35. **(C)** (p. 214) *Science/Evaluation of Models/Analysis*. Only this response covers all elements of the three diagrams.

36. **(H)** (p. 215) *Science/Interpretation of Data/Comprehension*. The number of butterflies captured for marking is found under the heading "Marked." Reading across the table for each size group, the "dark brown" category always has the fewest butterflies marked.

37. **(D)** (p. 215) *Science/Interpretation of Data/Comprehension*. Compare the number of butterflies recaptured to the number marked to derive a proportion that represents how easy it is to recapture each type of butterfly. The proportion for small, white butterflies (30/35) is much higher than that for any of the other choices.

38. **(G)** (p. 215) *Science/Interpretation of Data/Analysis*. An examination of the table shows that for all colors, as size increases, the number of butterflies marked increases.

39. **(B)** (p. 215) *Science/Evaluation of Models/Application*. A poisonous chemical will have adverse effects on the butterfly after marking (perhaps by killing or by preventing flight). The group with the lowest proportion of individuals recaptured in flight (10/40 = 1/4 recaptured) is the group consisting of small, tan butterflies.

40. **(G)** (p. 215) *Science/Evaluation of Models/Analysis*. For medium–sized butterflies, the proportion of individuals recaptured in each color is as follows: white (15/30 = 1/2), tan (20/40 = 1/2), and dark brown (10/20 = 1/2).

SAMPLE ESSAY RESPONSES AND ANALYSES

Section 5: Writing (p. 216)

Above Average Response

With online systems, Americans could easily register and vote without leaving their homes. While this method is a practical solution to increase voter registration, it should not be used for voting on Election Day because of the potential for technical problems and voter fraud. Online voter registration would make the process more convenient and would not necessarily result in less informed voters. However, since errors due to technical problems could skew election results, this system should not be used for voting itself.

Online systems could make voter registration a faster, easier process and, therefore, accessible to more people. As Perspective 3 states, a high voter turnout is crucial for a healthy democracy. The ability to register online would especially encourage younger voters who are used to the convenience of online services and may not take time out of their schedule to travel to a designated place to register. States that have implemented online registration have recorded an increase in youth voter turnout. Moreover, this option would also help people who cannot leave their homes due to illness or disability, and it would make it easier to register for an absentee ballot if you are living out of state. With one obstacle to registration removed, voter turnout could increase.

Online voter registration or voting would not necessarily lead to less informed voters. While the task of going to a designated place to register or to vote demands more effort from voters, this does not prevent people who are uninformed about the candidates from traveling to a polling station. One can accomplish many important tasks online, such as financial or legal transactions, and the online convenience does not make these actions any less important. Onsite registration and voting does, however, stop citizens who do not have the ability to reach a polling place, such as people with illnesses or inflexible work or childcare schedules. Although employers in some states are legally required to give employees time off for voting, employees may not be aware of this right, and in many states, they would lose pay while leaving work to vote.

While the convenience of online voting and registration would make voting accessible to more people, technological problems might lead to unfair elections. For example, an unreliable Internet connection might prevent one's vote from being counted, or it may be possible to tamper with an online system to skew election results. Voting remotely might also allow someone to vote multiple times. It is true that more traditional voting methods are not foolproof; for example, during the Presidential Election of 2000, problems with punch cards called into question the election results in Florida. However, a new method of voting could introduce even more technological problems. Voter registration could be moved online, since one can always verify whether the registration worked. However, voting itself is a time-sensitive issue, and accidental or intentional errors in an online system may go unnoticed until the election is over.

Online registration could make voter registration more accessible and therefore increase voter turnout. However, while the convenience of online voting may also increase turnout, there are too many technological risks involved to rely on it.

Ideas and Analysis: The writer clearly states his or her thesis in the introduction: an online system should be used for voter registration, but realistically, not for voting itself. The body paragraphs consider arguments for and against online registration and/or voting. The first paragraph addresses the accessibility of online voting (Perspective 3), and the second paragraph argues against the correlation between online voters and uninformed voters (Perspective 1). The third paragraph acknowledges the technical problems that could occur (Perspective 2).

Development and Support:

- The introduction states the thesis in its second sentence and previews the arguments that will support it.

- The body paragraphs begin with topic sentences that clearly state the main point or argument to be made in the paragraph.

- The body paragraphs include a mix of arguments and examples to support the author's opinion.

- The writer develops a "compromise" position on the subject by arguing for online registration but recognizing that online voting could cause too many technological problems. The writer is able to acknowledge both sides without contradicting his or her own arguments.

Organization:

- The writer introduces each paragraph with a topic sentence.

- The writer uses transitions to connect ideas between and within paragraphs. For example, the third body paragraph begins with the clause "While the convenience of online voting and registration would make voting accessible to more people" because the paragraph introduces an opposing argument to online voting.

- The second body paragraph could be stronger without the last sentence (about leaving work to vote). The argument of the paragraph is that online voting would not lead to uninformed voters, so this sentence might be seen as off-topic.

- The essay could also be improved with a longer and slightly more developed conclusion.

Language Use and Conventions:

The essay contains at least three principal strengths in this area:

- The essay does not have any mechanics/usage errors. As a result, the reader's attention is not distracted from the substance of the essay.

- The writer does not use any informal language.

- Stylistically, the writer varies sentence structures.

- The writer uses vivid verbs and avoids vague language. The verb choice shows a sophisticated vocabulary.

Summary and Conclusions: This essay demonstrates writing skills that are very well developed and analyzes multiple viewpoints of the issue. The writer incorporates all three perspectives in his or her argument. This essay would likely receive a score of 10.

Below Average Response

Online voting and registration is a great idea because it would allow more people to vote and would make our democracy stronger. It is elitist to assume that more people voting would lead to less informed voters. I also don't think that we should be afraid of using this technology we do so much online and it works really well, so why not vote online?

Online voting is a good idea because it is more convenient than going to a polling place or a government building and waiting in line to vote or to register. Our lives are much busier now since we work so much, so why not make voting easier to do? Young people are also used to doing everything online, and as these people make up more and more of the voting population, it makes sense to adapt to their ways and vote online.

I don't think that online voting would necessarily lead to less informed voters. The purpose of a democracy is to have citizens elect their leaders, not to only allow an elite group to vote. Also, so many people keep up with current events by reading online news. The internet has made people more informed, not less.

Some might worry about the technological problems involved with online voting and what would happen if the system didn't work. However, we do so many important things online, like transfer money and enter important information onto websites. If we can do this, why can't we vote?

Online voting seems like a logical, practical solution that will make voting more accessible to more people.

Ideas and Analysis: The writer clearly expresses his or her point of view in favor of online voting. However, the arguments are superficial because the writer offers little concrete evidence in favor of his or her argument and does not give enough consideration to opposing viewpoints.

Development and Support:

- The introduction clearly states the writer's opinion, but the writer should use more specific language rather than saying that online voting "is a great idea."
- The writer attempts to support the arguments with generalizations, rather than using concrete examples or clear logic.
  - In the first body paragraph, the writer has one relevant argument (that online voting would engage younger, technology-oriented voters). However, the statement that "our lives are much busier" is too general to be used as an argument.
  - In the second body paragraph, the writer claims to argue that online voting will not lead to uninformed voters. However, the writer attempts to support the argument with a generalization: "The purpose of a democracy is to have citizens elect their leaders, not to only allow an elite group to vote." This generalization does not answer the question that the writer needs to address: *Why* wouldn't online voting lead to uninformed voters?
  - In the third body paragraph, the writer acknowledges that there might be technological problems involved with online voting. However, the writer simply dismisses this argument without thoroughly engaging with it. He or she does not reflect on how technological problems could influence elections.
- The conclusion should be more developed and should revisit the writer's three main arguments.

Organization:

- The introduction has three separate sentences that show that the writer agrees with Perspective 3 and argues against Perspectives 1 and 2. However, the introduction would be stronger if the writer combined these opinions into a coherent thesis.
- The topic sentences should have transitions to introduce new ideas in the following paragraph.
- The last two sentences of the second paragraph do not support its main topic. ("Also, so many people keep up with current events by reading online news. The internet has made people more informed, not less.") The prompt does not ask whether the Internet makes people better informed about the news in general; it asks whether online voting could lead to less informed voters.

Language Use and Conventions:
The essay contains several weaknesses in this area:
- The essay contains some usage and mechanics errors.
  - Introduction: "I also don't think that we should be afraid of using this technology we do so much online and it works really well, so why not vote online?" is a run-on sentence. The first sentence should end after "technology."
- The writer uses informal language, such as "so many important things" (Body paragraph 3).
- The writer uses vague language. In the first body paragraph, when the writer says "**Our** lives are much busier now since **we** work so much" it is unclear what "our" and "we" are referring to.

Summary and Conclusions: The writer's opinion is clear, but the essay relies too much on generalizations and does not give enough consideration to opposing arguments. The body paragraphs do not have enough evidence to support their arguments. This essay would likely receive a score of 5.

Cambridge *The Practice Book, 14th Edition*
Error Correction and Suggestion Form

Name/Location: _____ Day Phone: _____ E-mail Address: _____

Part of Materials:
- ☐ *Victory* Student Text, Specify Subject: _____ Page: _____ Item: _____
- ☐ *Victory* Teacher's Guide, Specify Subject: _____ Page: _____ Item: _____
- ☐ *Essential Skills* Student Text, Specify Subject: _____ Page: _____ Item: _____
- ☐ *Essential Skills* Teacher's Guide, Specify Subject: _____ Page: _____ Item: _____
- ☐ *The Practice Book*, Specify Subject: _____ Page: _____ Item: _____

Error/Suggestion: _____
_____
_____

Part of Materials:
- ☐ *Victory* Student Text, Specify Subject: _____ Page: _____ Item: _____
- ☐ *Victory* Teacher's Guide, Specify Subject: _____ Page: _____ Item: _____
- ☐ *Essential Skills* Student Text, Specify Subject: _____ Page: _____ Item: _____
- ☐ *Essential Skills* Teacher's Guide, Specify Subject: _____ Page: _____ Item: _____
- ☐ *The Practice Book*, Specify Subject: _____ Page: _____ Item: _____

Error/Suggestion: _____
_____
_____

Part of Materials:
- ☐ *Victory* Student Text, Specify Subject: _____ Page: _____ Item: _____
- ☐ *Victory* Teacher's Guide, Specify Subject: _____ Page: _____ Item: _____
- ☐ *Essential Skills* Student Text, Specify Subject: _____ Page: _____ Item: _____
- ☐ *Essential Skills* Teacher's Guide, Specify Subject: _____ Page: _____ Item: _____
- ☐ *The Practice Book*, Specify Subject: _____ Page: _____ Item: _____

Error/Suggestion: _____
_____
_____

Part of Materials:
- ☐ *Victory* Student Text, Specify Subject: _____ Page: _____ Item: _____
- ☐ *Victory* Teacher's Guide, Specify Subject: _____ Page: _____ Item: _____
- ☐ *Essential Skills* Student Text, Specify Subject: _____ Page: _____ Item: _____
- ☐ *Essential Skills* Teacher's Guide, Specify Subject: _____ Page: _____ Item: _____
- ☐ *The Practice Book*, Specify Subject: _____ Page: _____ Item: _____

Error/Suggestion: _____
_____
_____

Mail form to Cambridge Educational Services, Inc. or fax form to 1-847-299-2933. For teacher's assistance, call 1-800-444-4373 or email solutions@CambridgeEd.com. Visit our website at www.CambridgeEd.com.